Explorations and Explanations

ESSAYS IN THE SOCIAL HISTORY

OF

VICTORIAN WALES

IEUAN GWYNEDD JONES

Sir John Williams Professor of Welsh History
at the University College of Wales, Aberystwyth

GWASG GOMER
1981

First Impression - April 1981

ISBN 0 85088 644 9

PRINTED BY J. D. LEWIS & SONS,
GWASG GOMER, LLANDYSUL

I MAISIE

CONTENTS

ABBREVIATIONS

Arch. Camb.	*Archaeologia Cambrensis*
B.B.C.S.	*Bulletin of the Board of Celtic Studies*
Baner	*Baner ac Amserau Cymru*
B.M.	British Museum
C. & D.H.	*Carnarvon and Denbigh Herald*
Ceredigion	*Journal of the Cardiganshire Antiquarian Society*
Cronicl	*Y Cronicl Cymraeg*
D.N.B.	*Dictionary of National Biography*
D.W.B.	*Dictionary of Welsh Biography down to* 1940
Herald	*Yr Herald Gymraeg*
J.N.L.W.	*Journal of the National Library of Wales*
L.C.C.	London County Council
N.L.W.	National Library of Wales
J.E.H.	*Journal of Ecclesiastical History*
J.M.H.S.	*Transactions of the Merioneth Historical and Record Society*
T.C.H.S.	*Caernarvonshire Historical Society Transactions*
P.P.	Parliamentary Papers
P.R.O.	Public Record Office
U.C.N.W.	University College of North Wales
W.L.C.R.	Royal Commission on Land in Wales and Monmouthshire

PREFACE

ALTHOUGH the essays brought together in this volume were written over a period of years they have in common one overarching theme, namely, the nature of social change in Wales in the two decades or so after 1850. It has long been my conviction that these two decades are central to the understanding of social developments in the century or so after 1800 in senses other than the merely chronological one, and that they confront the historian with profound and challenging problems of understanding. At first sight, these twenty-odd years would seem to lack the turmoil and excitement, much of the passion and some of the heroic quality that suffuses the momentous social changes and the dramatic events of the fifty years that precede them. Likewise, they do not appear, at least at first glance, to have the kind of solid achievements and astonishing creativity that was so characteristic of the social and political developments of the fifty years that followed. But contemporaries were under no such illusions, and those men who had lived long enough to have experienced something both of the confusion and excitement of the first and of the steady social betterment and profound political advances of the second were convinced that that generation in their history was the most creative of all. The purpose of the essays that follow is to explore this attitude and to explain why such a relatively quiet time should have been so prominent in the developing consciousness of the people.

This is why I have given the title ' Explorations and Explanations ' to the collection. The object of the individual essays is to understand, so far as is possible in terms of the contemporary experience, some of the main religious and political movements and changes characteristic of the time. The first two essays are largely empirical investigations into the nature of some features of organized religion as it had developed in two contrasting regions of the country up to that time. The three essays on politics that follow are likewise largely empirical in approach, and they apply to three widely contrasting constituencies, and in chronological order, a methodology designed to penetrate below the explanation about the nature and course of Welsh politics which contemporaries provided for themselves but which was, of course, an essential ingredient of political change as they experienced it. The problem all these essays have in common is the fundamental one of how a people came to be politicized, and that astonishing transition made from the ' non-political ' attitudes and ingrained conservatism of the past to the self-conscious and mature politics of the elections of 1868 which laid the foundations for that immensely powerful Liberal political culture that survived into our own days. The three final essays range more widely and seek to assess and to explain the extraordinary strength of religious organizations in Wales, and the means by which, in those few years in the middle of the century, Nonconformity came to be the most powerful and most effective force in national politics and to provide the dynamism which was to inform and to direct the aspirations and the achievement of the Welsh people until the end of the century.

I am grateful to the following friends and colleagues in whose journals the essays first appeared for so readily granting me permission to reproduce them here : Dr. A. D. Carr, Hon. Editor of the Caernarfonshire Historical Society (No. 1) : Professor Gwynedd O. Pierce, Chairman of the Glamorgan Historical Society (No. 2) : Dr. E. D. Jones, Hon. Editor of the Merioneth Historical and Record Society (No. 3) : Mr. Dafydd Morris Jones, Hon. Secretary of the Cardiganshire Historical and Antiquarian Society (No. 4) : Professor William H. McNeill, Editor of the *Journal of Modern History* (No. 5) : Dr. K. O. Morgan, Editor of the *Welsh History Review* (No. 7) : Professor T. O. Roberts, Editor of *Efrydiau Athronyddol* (No. 6 translated), and Mr. John Rhys, Director of the University of Wales Press (No. 8).

Gathering these essays together in this way brings home to me the enormous debt of gratitude I owe to my former and present colleagues from whose kind and steady criticism my work has consistently benefited. Only those who have worked in the field will know to what an extent the study of the history of Wales is under-pinned, given structure and purpose and something of the excitement of an enterprise by the sense of community that informs the studies of those engaged in it. To this my post-graduate students both here at Aberystwyth and earlier at

Swansea have contributed largely and it is a pleasure to record my debt to them. Pre-eminent in the field of Welsh historical studies is my friend Professor Glanmor Williams who more than anyone else inspired my own work and, come to that, the work of almost every other Welsh historian of these latter years. The post-war renaissance in Welsh historical studies which is now yielding rich fruit in a number of different fields owes a great deal to his inspiration and leadership.

I would also like to express my appreciation for the help so unstintingly given by the staffs of the many libraries, in particular of the National Library of Wales, and of the County Record Offices in Wales. Miss Siân Jones, retyped some of the essays and I am grateful for her help. Finally, I wish to record my thanks to my wife for her unfailing help and encouragement over the years. It is for this reason that I dedicate this book to her.

THE COUNTY AND REGISTRATION DISTRICTS
OF WALES IN 1851

This is a copy of the map in the 1851 census tables and the spellings there have been maintained. The Registration Districts were :-

No.	Name	Area in acres	Population
Monmouthshire Division			
576	Chepstow	81255	19057
577	Monmouth	101791	27379
578	Abergavenny	88176	59229
579	Pontypool	51429	27993
580	Newport	110255	43472
South Wales Division			
581	Cardiff	117797	46491
582	Merthyr Tydfil	112886	76804
583	Bridgend	109511	23422
584	Neath	162817	46471
585	Swansea	103769	46907
586	Llanelly	73451	23507
587	Llandovery	154572	15055
588	Llandilofawr	97207	17968
589	Carmarthen	172546	30142
590	Narberth	124903	22130
591	Pembroke	70276	22960
592	Haverfordwest	170861	39382
593	Cardigan	85481	20186
594	Newcastle-in-Emlyn	113346	20173
595	Lampeter	75710	9874
596	Aberayron	65704	13224
597	Aberystwyth	132592	23753
598	Tregaron	122050	10404
599	Builth	102953	8345
600	Brecknock	196793	18174
601	Crickhowell	53692	21697
602	Hay	89695	10962
603	Presteigne	104963	15149
604	Knighton	97492	9480
605	Rhayader	105532	6796
North Wales Division			
606	Machynlleth	116647	12116
607	Newtown	189537	25107
608	Montgomery	88902	20381
609	Llanfyllin	173035	19538
610	Holywell	89479	41047
611	Wre.ham	86885	42295
612	Ruthin	92853	16953
613	St. Asaph	93934	25288
614	Llanrwst	100631	12479
615	Corwen	123807	15418
616	Bala	58292	6736
617	Dolgelly	145213	12971
618	Festiniog	138714	16182
619	Pwllheli	93319	21788
620	Carnarvon	97635	30446
621	Bangor	92478	30810
622	Conway	57131	11630
623	Anglesey	138884	43243

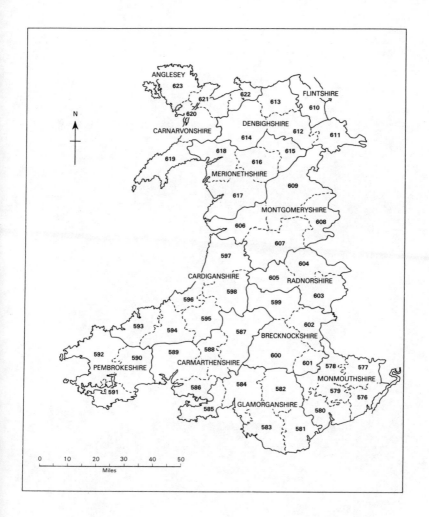

ANGLESEY
623
621
622
613
FLINTSHIRE
620
610
CARNARVONSHIRE
DENBIGHSHIRE
612
611
614
615
619
618
616
MERIONETHSHIRE
609
617
MONTGOMERYSHIRE
606
608
607
597
604
CARDIGANSHIRE
605
RADNORSHIRE
598
603
596
599
595
602
593
594
587
BRECKNOCKSHIRE
589
588
592
590
600
601
578
577
PEMBROKESHIRE
586
584
MONMOUTHSHIRE
591
579
576
585
GLAMORGANSHIRE
580
583
581

N

0   10   20   30   40   50
Miles

Part I
RELIGION

DENOMINATIONALISM IN CAERNARFONSHIRE IN THE MID-NINETEENTH CENTURY AS SHOWN IN THE RELIGIOUS CENSUS OF 1851

RELIGION, religiousness, religiosity—these are terms which it is difficult to define. They are multi-dimensional,[1] and we need always to be on our guard as to exactly what dimension we are thinking of when we use any of these terms. Most sociologists of religion have their ways of ensuring this, and most would agree that religion as a concept would seem to be divisible into at least four different dimensions which can be separately studied. There is the experiential or the devotional—those feelings, perceptions, sensations experienced by individuals or groups or communities—their ' spirituality ', or their experience of a transcendent reality, of God. There is also the ideological dimension, that is, the beliefs of the individual or of the collective, and what needs to be studied here is the social role of belief, of theology. There is also what some students call the ' consequential ' dimension of religion, the actual social consequences of belief and adherence to some form of organised religion. Finally, there is the ' ritualistic ' dimension, that is, the observable external activities of individuals or groups in their religious lives—measureable things like church attendance, worship, contributions and the like, which most religious organisations, whether churches, denominations, or sects, possess as of definition and which constitute a primary category by which they can be differentiated and identified. None of these dimensions is independent of the others, but it does make for clarity if, at least initially, they are kept separate, and this is why this paper is confined to the ritualistic aspects of the religious life of this county in the middle of the last century. This, anyway, is pretty well the only aspect of the religious life of the county which can be studied with a fair degree of accuracy and of objectivity. Facts about church attendance, the number and size of places of worship do exist, and there can be more agreement about this kind of dimension than about any of the others.

The most important aspects of religion probably cannot be measured and he would be rash indeed who attempted to do so. The qualitative aspects of religious life in the past are not amenable to quantitative analysis : here it is criticism that is called for, here is the place for the literary critic, for the social psychologist and anthropologist. And yet it is possible that some of the most important clues to the nature of religion in the past will rise out of a study which does try to confine itself to what is measurable. My object, therefore, is to make some generalisations about certain measurable aspects of religion in Caernarfonshire in the middle of the last century, and to suggest some of the larger questions which will be relevant to a more general study of social and political change.

*   *   *

The questions I wish to ask initially are all concerned with the changing pattern of religious adherence in the county in the first half of the century, and the source of which I ask these questions is the Religious Census of 1851.[2] This must be the source because it is the only official, systematic count of religious worship ever to have been made in modern times.[3] Certain Royal Commissions have subsequently attempted to gather the same kind of information, but the way in which they collected this evidence makes their statistics more suspect than criticism would lead us to suppose are those collected in 1851. The 1851 count was official in that it was made as an essential part of the decennial enumeration of that year, and was carried out both locally and centrally by bureaucrats whose probity was relatively unquestioned.[4] On the Sunday preceding Census Monday, 31 March 1851, a count was made of every person attending religious worship in the morning, afternoon and evening in every place of religious worship of whatever kind in England and Wales. Printed forms,[5] called schedules, were despatched by the Registrar-General through the District Registrars of Births and Deaths to enumerators who delivered them to the incumbents, ministers, or other persons competent to give the necessary information in their assigned localities. Lists of places of religious worship had been prepared earlier, and the District

Registrars were thus enabled to check on the distribution of the schedules. The printed forms themselves asked for certain information, including the name of the place of worship, the date of its erection, its denomination, its capacity—differentiating between free and other kinds of seating—and finally, the actual number of attendants at all services. Incumbents of parish and other churches were asked additionally to state the cost of any rebuilding, and the sources of the income of the benefice. The returns having been made, they were then collected by the enumerators in the course of their perambulations on the following day, and after being checked by the District Registrars were put in order, numbered according to the Census enumeration, and despatched to London. Here they were again checked by the Registrar-General, and any deficiencies were made good by correspondence with the District Registrars or, in many cases, with actual incumbents and ministers. There is no doubt that so far as the central machinery of the operation was concerned it was carried out in Caernarfonshire in a completely satisfactory manner.

Such a method of counting, however, also had serious weaknesses. The actual counting of seats and attendances was in the hands of the ministers themselves, and there was no method of testing their returns objectively, and, in the case of incumbents of benefices, of extracting all the information asked for concerning endowments. Thomas Lloyd, the rector of Bodfean, gave only that information which in *his* opinion was relevant to what *he* considered should have been the main purpose of the questionnaire, so he gave no information concerning attendances.[6] The schedules themselves appear to have been simple enough, but for many ministers and deacons in 1851 it is clear that the questions were far from simple. Did ' space ' mean ' seating capacity ' or ' cubic capacity ' ? Many were in doubt about this and gave not only the number of seats but also the internal measurements of the buildings. Some obviously did not know the meaning of ' average ', and gave instead aggregations. These misunderstandings may have been due to a language difficulty : for people unaccustomed to filling in forms to receive one in English must have been an additional hazard. Daniel Jones, minister of Hermon (CM), Llandygái was deeply resent-

ful of the implied insult to his own language : ' What was the
care that you sent us these papers in English instead of Welsh.
We believe that our Language ought to be loved by any heart
that can talk it. We think it the best Language now in the whole
earth and if you cant talk Welsh there we can talk English here.
We love our dear language and we like to have every paper
belonging to us in Welsh.'[7] In addition, it must be confessed
that for many there must have been a sore temptation to
exaggerate the attendants or the size of the building. A great
deal of publicity and denominational wrangling had preceded
the taking of the Census and a great deal of speculation as to
which would emerge as the largest religious body. It is quite
clear, for instance, that denominational mobility so typical of
many parts of the region, would be reduced to a minimum. The
incumbent of Llangeinwen, in the neighbouring county of
Anglesey, for instance, stated that his attendance figures were
only a half of what they normally were since many of his parishioners who customarily attended both Church and chapel did
not turn up because of the Census.[8] For many it must have
been a case of ' stand up and be counted ', and while this would
clearly distinguish denominational allegiances in the county it
would distort the picture of religious practice and custom. One
suspects that relatively few congregations were actually counted
one by one as they entered or left their places of worship : most
of the figures suggest estimates rather than enumerations ; and
that the totals given are to the nearest 10, or even 50 in one or
two cases. (There are instances in south Wales of attendances
to the nearest 100 !) Sunday School attendances seem to be
more accurate : possibly registers were kept or systematic
counts made much as today. But the most serious weakness of
the Census arises from a total failure to distinguish individual
attendances. Figures are given for all separate services, but
there are absolutely no means of knowing how many individuals
attended particular services. Presumably, a large proportion of
worshippers attended all services, but what proportion did
so it is not possible to tell. Here we must make the best use
of such information as we have, and the method I have
adopted is the simple one of expressing the total of all
attendances in each place of worship in each parish as

a proportion of the total population of each parish. This gives us a statistical device by which to judge the comparative strength or weakness of particular religious bodies in particular places. One final point. The returns for the Caernarfonshire parishes included in the Ffestiniog Union District are missing, and since there are no means of supplying the missing information all my statistics and conclusions must be understood as excluding that particular area extending from Beddgelert to Tremadoc.[9] To sum up : this source enables us to count with complete accuracy the numbers and types of places of worship in the county, to count with rather less accuracy the accommodation provided by them, and with least accuracy the actual number of people who attended religious services on 30 March 1851.

*   *   *

The Census, when the results were published in summary form in 1853, confirmed what many people of all religious persuasions and of none had long suspected, namely, that in the terms used by the Census itself to measure religiosity, Wales was very much more religious than England.[10] In England (excluding Wales) the religious bodies between them provided seating for just over half the total population : there were 8.5 million seats for 16.5 million people, or 51.4 *per cent*. In Wales as a whole slightly over ¾ of the total population could be seated in places of worship : 898,442 out of a population of 1,188,914. This was an extraordinarily high proportion—the highest of any single region in England and Wales together. The best provision in England was in the north Midland counties (Leicestershire, Rutlandshire, Lincolnshire, Nottinghamshire, Derbyshire) where the proportion was 64.8 *per cent*. Indeed, the most startling and alarming fact to emerge from the Census was the extent to which there were these great regional variations. Whether one looked macroscopically at the whole or microscopically at the parts there would seem to have been an iron law in operation by which the parts of the country with the densest population had the least provision, and vice versa. Thus, London could provide for only a little more than 29 *per*

cent of its population, and parts of London, the most densely
populated areas such as Lambeth and Tower Hamlets, even less
than that. The same was true of the largest provincial cities in
the country. Manchester, that metropolis of the dissenting
ideal, provided for only 31.6 *per cent* of its rapidly growing population. Horace Mann, who was responsible under the Registrar General for the Census, estimated that to be minimally
effective the churches between them ought to make provision
for 58.4 *per cent* of the population equally, in all regions,
throughout the country.[11] The actual figure of just over 50 *per
cent* meant that there must have been well over 1.5 million
people for whom no provision was made. He thought that there
was a shortage of over 2,000 places of worship in the country as
a whole, and that this shortage was primarily in the great towns
and growing conurbations.

Looked at with Mann's 58.4 *per cent* optimum in mind, Wales
was sufficiently provided with accommodation for public
worship, but to leave our analysis there would be to ignore the
fact of the operation here in Galilee of that law which we saw to
be operating in Samaria. For in Wales also there was the same
kind of regional variation—of places with relatively high and
places with relatively low religiosity.[12] A glance at the provision rate in the individual counties will illustrate this. Merioneth and Breconshire had more seats available than they had
population. In both these counties if by a miracle every man,
woman and child had wanted to worship on that particular
Sunday there would have been room and to spare. They would
have needed a computer to tell them where to go, but some-
where there would have been room. At the other end of the
scale, Glamorgan and Monmouthshire were both about 30 *per
cent short* of seating. When we examine the provision in the
Unions of parishes into which the administrative counties were
divided, this basic variation becomes even more marked. Some
of them were astonishingly well provided. The Machynlleth
group of parishes had space for 23 *per cent more* than its total population, and it headed the District league for England and
Wales. But Cardigan, Lampeter, Aberystwyth, Builth, Brecon,
Rhayadr, Llanfyllin, Ruthin, Bala, Dolgellau, Ffestiniog, Pwllheli, and Llanrwst could all accommodate more than their total

populations. What of the other end of the District league ? As we have seen, only one of the Welsh Districts fell below Mann's optimum of 58.4 *per cent* but others came very close to it, and some parishes within them much lower. Merthyr Tydfil was the lowest with an accommodation rate of 57.9 *per cent*. Newport (66.3 *per cent*), Chepstow (67.6 *per cent*) and Newtown (67.8 *per cent*) were not very far above. Obviously, the rule applies in Wales as in England. The regions with a high accommodation rate were invariably rural areas, those with low accommodation rates were all industrialized regions usually centred upon towns of relatively substantial size. There was therefore some kind of correlation between religious provision and the size and social complexity of any particular region. I shall look more closely at that in the last essay in this collection, but for the moment we can leave it at that.

Coming nearer to Caernarfonshire, we can therefore expect to find that north Wales was better provided with the means of religious worship than south Wales. And this is so : north Wales had provision for 83 *per cent* of its population, south Wales for 73 *per cent*. The reason for this difference is clear : there were no large towns in north Wales (i.e. towns of over 20,000 inhabitants), and no large towns of an exclusively manufacturing kind such as there were in south Wales, and consequently no great masses of people congregated together in entirely urban centres. In Unions where there were sizeable industrial or manufacturing towns, as in the Wrexham Union, the provision rate sank (79.2 *per cent*). Where the Districts were entirely rural the rates were very high : e.g. Bala with 109.1 *per cent*, Dolgellau with 116.0 *per cent*. Looking at Caernarfonshire as a whole we find the same kind of variation in the provision rates of its particular regions. For the county as a whole—the ancient county rather than the registration or administrative county—we find that provision was made for 88.25 *per cent* of the total population. Looking at the Unions, or Registration Districts we find that there were very considerable variations from region to region. Llanrwst with 108.1 *per cent* and Pwllheli with 104.5 *per cent* were much better provided that Conway with 87.9 *per cent*, Bangor with 81.6 *per cent* and Caernarfon with 77.3 *per cent*.[13] But this is what we should expect to find. Pwllheli, which included almost all the Llŷn parishes, was to all intents and purposes deeply rural, its population consisting primarily of small farmers, fishermen, craftsmen and a relatively small proportion of quarry workers. Llanrwst, which included the large upland parishes of the Betws-y-coed and Ysbyty regions, was likewise mainly rural, the economy being diversified by relatively small and scattered mining villages. Where there were pockets of industry they were never on such a scale as to upset the rural balance in the economy. By contrast, the other Unions contained very large quarry undertakings. New towns had grown up where none had existed before, rural villages had expanded into towns and lost some of their agricultural, peasant characteristics, and ancient boroughs and sea ports had grown significantly as commercial, manufacturing and administrative centres. It should not come as a surprise that the Caernarfon Union of parishes should have an accommodation rate no higher than the significantly industrial unions of south Wales, such as Swansea (78.8 *per cent*), Monmouth (76.8 *per cent*) or Cardiff (75.4 *per cent*), or that it should be rather less well provided than the big industrial complex of Pontypool.

We can pursue this kind of analysis in a much more refined way and observe that it applies at parish level also.[14] For instance, all the parishes with accommodation indexes greater than 100—and one third of the 64 parishes were of this kind—had some things in common. They were all small, with populations averaging only 552 : some, like Ceidio and Betws Garmon, were minute (160 and 97, respectively), and the largest, Aberdaron and Llaniestyn, had populations of only 1000 or 1200. We note also that they were all deeply rural, or were fishing communities, rarely industrial parishes. Last, we notice that all, with the exception of Carnguwch, had more than one place of worship. The multiplication of places of worship in such small parishes would obviously make an incommensurate difference in the accommodation ratio, because most of them were already provided with parish churches spacious enough to accommodate most, if not all, of their populations. But when, as for instance at Botwnnog, there were two chapels in addition to a parish church to serve a population of 163, then clearly that parish is going to be well provided. The Calvinistic Methodist chapel *alone* could accommodate nearly three times the total population. Or take Aberdaron. Here, in a parish of fishermen and small farmers, with a population of 1239 there were 8 places of worship. The parish church could accommodate almost half the population, the three Calvinistic Methodists another half, the Baptist and Independent chapels a good quarter, and the Wesleyans provided seats for 109. In parishes such as these—and most, as we have noted, were in Llŷn—the differences which helps to explain their religious differences stem from the contrasts in their *occupational*[15] structure. Inland, the great majority of heads of households described themselves as farmers : we should call them smallholders since their farms were mostly minute. In Llanfaelrhys (42 households), for instance, there were 23 farming households, the average holding being 51 acres. Only 3 of these farms were over 100 acres, and the majority were under 20 acres. Tradesmen or craftsmen were very few in number : two tailors, a shoemaker, a weaver, a fuller, a carpenter—the rest were labourers, or paupers. Where there were little townships in these inland parishes there would be a greater occupational diversity : more weavers, joiners, shoemakers, masons, shopkeepers : but all more or less rural in their way of life conforming to the agricultural life around them which they existed to serve. Many of the coastal parishes were dominated by industries connected with the sea, and these constituted quite distinct communities in their structural characteristics. Shipbuilding and handicrafts of various kinds brought together men and their families dependent upon their specialised skills and to that extent independent of the land for a livelihood. The accommodation ratios of such maritime parishes were higher generally than those of the inland parishes because the former tended to be multidenominational. The mariner and fisherman and craftsmen tended to express his individuality and, perhaps, his occupational solidarity through his chapel.

What of the parishes with below county average accommodation rates—that is, below 90 *per cent*. There were 19 parishes with rates below 90 *per cent* and above 66 *per cent*. Most were to be found in the Unions of Caernarfon and Bangor, but included also were some of the larger towns in Llŷn, like

Cricieth, Llanystumdwy, and Abererch, as well as Conway in the neighbouring Union. The first thing to note about them is that they were on the whole much larger than our first group, having an average population of 2347 as against 552. Second, we note that they included most if not all of the great quarry regions and the new industrial towns. Llanddeiniolen, for example, had a population of nearly 5000, Llandygái of 3398, and of course, the major county towns, both approaching 10,000, were in this group. Third, we note that these parishes also were well provided with places of worship, some of them quite extraordinarily so. Llanddeiniolen had 14 places of worship for a population of 4894—the same number as Llanbeblig with Caernarfon Borough which had double its population. Llanddeiniolen typifies the large upland parish supporting a number of relatively small quarrying villages scattered over a wide area. It was a parish of small chapels (only 2 of the 13 were over 200 seats in size) designed for a scattered population of quarryworkers and farmers. Where, as in othere quarrying areas where larger urban communities had been formed, the accommodation was higher : at Llanllechid, for instance, it was 98 *per cent* and in Llanberis 99 *per cent*.

Enough has been said to show that a study of the statistics of accommodation raises interesting questions concerning the development of religion at that time, and suggests that it might be profitable to investigate further the correlation between the religiosity of an area and its economic and social structure. The other aspects of the religious state of the county revealed by the Census raise such questions in a more acute and stark form : I mean, the pattern of denominationalism and of the religious adherence revealed in it.

It was well known, of course, that Wales had become predominantly a nonconformist county in the sense that a majority among those who professed some form of the Christian religion gave their adherence to denominations outside the establishment. This was the reverse of the position in England and Wales as a whole where the Church of England remained by far the strongest among the main religious bodies.[16] Judged by the criteria of provision of places and of seating the Church of England provided 52 *per cent* of the accommodation, the

Independents or Congregationalists 11 *per cent*, the Baptists 7 *per cent*, the Wesleyan Methodists 21 *per cent*, and the Calfinistic Methodists 2.5 *per cent*. Of the seats available in Wales the Church provided 30.5 *per cent*, the other bodies the remainder. It was these figures which people had in mind when they stated that Wales was a nonconformist nation, and it was on facts such as these that radical politicians based their strategy for an attack on the parliamentary system in the following decade. But what these simple over-all figures obscure is the relative strength of various religious bodies in different parts of of the country. It is the variations which the historian of religion must be primarily concerned with.

Now, the established church was relatively strongest in south Wales in its provision of places, but it was stronger in north Wales in its provision of actual seating. This difference, of course, probably reflects the difference in relative size of the parishes, there being more small parishes in south Wales than in north Wales. In the latter the church provided 31.27 *per cent* of available seats, in south Wales 29.72 *per cent*. The difference is slight, and need not concern us now. Much more striking are the differences in the distribution of the nonconforming bodies. Generally speaking, south Wales was strongly dissenting : it showed a marked preference for the old historic churches of the Reformation period. The Independents provided 24 *per cent* of the total seating, and were the strongest body next to the Church. The Baptists provided another 17 *per cent*, so that between them these two denominations provided more than 40 *per cent* of the total seating available. The Unitarians and the Friends provided another 2 *per cent*. The various Wesleyan bodies were considerably weaker, contributing only 8.2 *per cent*, with the Calvinistic Methodists providing another 18 *per cent*. The position was quite different in North Wales. Here the Independents and the Baptists could provide only an aggregate of 21 *per cent*, and of this the Baptists contributed only 6 *per cent*. It was the Methodist bodies who dominated the denominational structure in north Wales. Together, the Calvinistic Methodists and the Wesleyans accounted for 46 *per cent* of the total seating with the Calvinistic Methodist contribution to this being nearly 31 *per cent*.

A feature of this denominational pattern in Wales as a whole was its great simplicity as compared with some other comparable regions in the country. It is not only that sects as such were weak or relatively non-existent ; only the Mormons come into this category with 18 congregations in the south and 7 in the north ; but that offshoots of the great historical churches were likewise relatively insignificant. Baptists were invariably Particular Baptists ; the General Baptists, who were Unitarian in their theology, had only 3 congregations in Wales, and Baptists of the New Connexion had 3. Or consider the various radical offshoots of the original Wesleyan body. Historically, these were rarely organized around differences in doctrine ; most had broken away, and more were yet to break away, from the parent body for political reasons. It had not been Bunting's theology which had been called into question but his notions of church government which offended the political ideologies of some and which for others seemed to restrict the free operation within the churches of divine grace. Now such congregations were comparatively rare in Wales : the New Connexion, the Primitive Methodists, the Wesleyan Association, and the Wesleyan Reformers between them provided only 12,072 seats or 2.77 *per cent* of the total. And, as we should expect, these new denominations were stronger in north than in south Wales where, if one had particularly strong views on church government, the obvious thing to do was to join the Independents. We are therefore justified in claiming that Welsh Nonconformity was distinguished by a massive orthodoxy so far as belief was concerned, and that the great historical divisions over questions of church government were so polarized as between dissent and methodism that a relative simplicity was the characteristic of this aspect of the religious life of the country also. ' Confrontation ' would be too strong a word to describe the relationship between dissent and Methodism, but it does look as if by 1851 a division in denominational allegiance, stimulated mainly by considerations of ecclesiastical polity, had developed in the country as a whole corresponding to that other great division in the economic life of the country which likewise had become very evident by that date. The older dissent was the religion of the heavily populated industrial south ; Methodism, especially Calvinistic Methodism, was the religion of the rural centre and north. Obviously, such a statement needs to be examined closely, but I would assert that Independency in particular seems to have been able to adapt itself more readily than the other denominations to the new urban civilization of the coal-fields. In doing so it was in general conforming to the spirit of its seventeenth century origins, and thus moving away from, rather than closer to, the Methodism of the rest of the county.

What then was the pattern in Caernarfonshire ?[17] The strongest individual denomination were the Calvinistic Meth-odists. They had 104 places out of a total of 296 in the country (slightly under one third—31.13 *per cent*) and provided seating for 30,208 (or 42.08 *per cent* of the total made available by all religious bodies). Next came the Established Church, with 70 places (23.64 *per cent*) and accommodation for 18,657 (or 25.99 *per cent*). Then came the Independents with 58 places and seats for 12,067 (16.81 *per cent*). The Wesleyans were fourth, with 35 places and 6,979 seats (9.72 *per cent*), and finally, the Baptists with 27 places and 3,462 seats (4.82 *per cent*). This, as we have seen, almost exactly reverses the pattern which was dominant in the south. The Calvinistic Methodists were almost doubly more effective than the Church, and almost three times more effective than the Independents. Notice the weakness of the Baptists, and above all, mark that, with the exception of one congregation of Independent Methodists (and there is doubt about these) there are no minor denominations to be found in the county, only one Roman Catholic church, and only two sectarian congregations—namely, the two Mormon churches, one in Bethesda and the other at the Bank Quay in Caernarfon.

This kind of pattern was fairly faithfully reproduced in the four Unions in the county. The Calvinistic Methodist were strongest in all Unions except Conway, where they took second place to the church. The Church itself was the second largest body in all Unions except Conway where it was first. The Independents came third in all unions, the Wesleyans fourth, except in Pwllheli where they were fifth, and the Baptists were the weakest denomination of all everywhere : there were no Baptists in Llanrwst. But no solid conclusion can be drawn from this remarkable degree of uniformity or consistency of pattern :

what we require to know is to what denominations people
adhered in their actual worshipping habits. It is here that our
statistics fail us, or become less reliable. As I have already
explained, the figures for attendances do not distinguish individual worshippers, and because it is quite clear, from other
sources, that worshipping habits varied greatly from district to
district and from parish to parish, it is not possible to generalize
about the whole. However, some consistent yard-stick must be
adopted, and I have worked out an attendance rate for each
parish and denomination by adding together the total of
attendances and expressing them as a proportion of the total
population. This will give us as reliable a guide to the popularity of the various bodies as we can hope to get in the Census
itself.

Using this device, a more realistic picture of denominational
adherence emerges.[18] Thus, Calvinistic Methodists retain their
overwhelming superiority in all five Union districts. Of each
100 attendances in Pwllheli, 62 were to Calvinistic Methodist
chapels, in Bangor 44, in Conway 37, and in Llanrwst 65. But
the church, which was second to ' yr Hen Gorff ' in its provision
record, comes out very weakly in its attendance index. In
Pwllheli (despite the large new church) only 6 in each 100
worshippers went to church ; 7 in Caernarvon, 13 in Bangor,
16 in Conway, and 3 in Llanrwst. It is the Independents who
take second place to the Calvinistic Methodists. In Pwllheli 15
out of each 100 went to their chapels, 21 in Caernarvon, 22 in
Bangor, 22 in Conway, and 14 in Llanrwst. The Wesleyans
were moderately strong in Bangor (16) Conway (14) and Llanrwst (16), but weak in Pwllheli (7) and Caernarvon (6). The
Baptists were moderately weak in Pwllheli (9) and Conway (9)
and very weak in Caernarfon (3) and Bangor (3).

When one looks microscopically at this pattern one is faced
with questions of enormous complexity, and it is at this kind of
level that one sees the need for sustained and systematic study
of the differing societies which produced this pattern. Take that
overwhelming power of Calvinistic Methodism, for instance ;
present in 52 of the 64 parishes, contributing in all but 14
parishes more than half the total attendants on Census Sunday.
How had this come about ? What makes the Baptists so weak,

even in the industrial parishes where one would expect their brand of unyielding dissent, their grim determination to cling to those vestiges of sectarianism, to find a ready acceptance ? Why was not Independency *more* attractive to the inhabitants of the small towns ? They certainly find a readier response in the industrial towns, but why not more ? On a more general level, should one think in terms of an optimum degree of urbanization before the primeval unities of the rural communities begin to break down ? It is questions such as these which arise as one contemplates these patterns, and it is quite certain that an enormous amount of research into the quality of men's lives at that time is necessary before the questions can be answered.

Nor is what looks like the almost total rejection of the Church of England easy to explain. Certainly the Church had failed to expand its provision to accommodate an increasing population. There had been virtually the same number of seats available in 1801 when the population was 45,815 as in 1851 when the population had almost doubled.[19] At the beginning of the century there had been accommodation for 43 *per cent* of the population: by 1851 this had dwindled to 23 *per cent*. Mann's optimum of 58.4 does not apply here, of course. Perhaps accommodation for about 40 *per cent* of the population would have been amply sufficient in 1801 : some incumbents in 1835 when asked to state the accommodation in their churches simply noted ' sufficient '.[20] And perhaps, in 1835, it objectively was. There are fashions in religiosity and clearly, by the mid-century, indeed a a lot earlier, there had been a change in demand. Why could not the Church supply it ? Or is that the right question ? In some parts of the country it is evident that the available resources of the church, always assuming that there was a demand for them, were quite insufficient to cope with increased needs. From the point of view of ecclesiastical governors, and these, given the nature of the establishment were politicians rather than clerics, this resolved itself into a debate about financial resources, which is why in the early decades of the century the Church began a great reconstruction of its administration.[21] What of the Church in Wales ? As a whole it was certainly not rich, but neither was it poor. Its misfortune stemmed from the fact that it was the poorer dioceses which had to face the brunt of the demands being made of it. In 1835, for instance, Llandaff[22] and St. David's were right at the bottom of the diocesan income league. Llandaff had an income of only £924 per annum, and its bishop held the deanery of St. Paul's ' in commendom ' in order to enable him to make ends meet. The enormous diocese of St. David's had a net income of only £1897.[23] Compared with these the two north Wales dioceses were well off. St. Asaph was worth £6301, and Bangor's income averaged £4464. Nor were these incomes small in relation to those of most of the English dioceses. St. Asaph was 8th in the list of 27, Bangor 12th. After 1836 when the Ecclesiastical Commissioners fixed their net incomes at £4500 p.a. both these dioceses paid a surplus into the Augmentation Fund out of which the poorer sees were brought up to the minimum (average £4200 p.a.). So far as Wales is concerned, therefore, it was not so much the absolute poverty of the Church which made it difficult for it to respond to changing needs as a maldistribution of its available resources. So this leaves us, so far as our county is concerned, with the failure of the church precisely in those areas where its financial resources were strongest.

Turning now to the diocese, let us ask, how were the resources of the Church, financial and otherwise, being distributed within it. Let us look first of all at the income of the clerics, for from the Reformation onwards it had been maintained that a chief or primary cause of the church's ineffectiveness lay in the poverty of its clergy. Here we may be on very subjective ground : medieval popes could never get enough: St. Francis managed on nothing. How do you define an adequate income ? But we can make some useful suggestions if we compare the average net incomes of incumbents in the four Welsh dioceses. The average net income of incumbents about the middle of the century was as follows :[24] St. David's—£137 p.a. ; Llandaff—£177; Bangor—£252; and St. Asaph—£271. The same degree of difference applies to the stipends of curates in the four dioceses : St. David's—£55 ; Llandaff—£59 ; Bangor—£77, and St. Asaph—£82. However one decided what an adequate income ought to be—whether one should live at a rate no higher than the poorest of ones parishioners, or that one should maintain the port of a gentleman—the disparity between north and south Wales is very striking, and on the whole one cannot avoid the conclusion that, except for the scandalous neglect of curates everywhere, the incumbents in Bangor were not badly off.

But, it could be rightly argued, it is not the average of incomes and of stipends that is relevant to our discussion, but the distribution of available income among the clerical groups. This is very true : Llandaff, along with every other industrial diocese, suffered not only from a basic poverty but even more so from an uneven distribution of what was available.[25] The poorly paid incumbents of the newly formed hill parishes constituted a kind of clerical underdog or proletariat when compared with some of their upper-class, Oxford educated brethren in the Vale parishes. Did the same apply in Bangor with a disproportionate amount of income going into a few pockets—or, more correctly, a few rich livings being very rich and with numerous poor livings being very poor ? On the whole it did not, for what is remarkable about the levels of incomes from benefices is that the variations were far less marked than in the other dioceses. For instance, there were relatively fewer poor livings—under £150 per annum—in Bangor than in St. David's or Llandaff—35 *per cent* as against 70 *per cent* and 51 *per cent*. 3 *per cent* of all Llandaff livings were under £50 per annum, 1.5 *per cent* in St. David's 1.6 *per cent* in Bangor, 0.76 *per cent* in St. Asaph. The comfortable livings, say between £200 and £400, were even more numerous in Bangor than in Llandaff and St. David's—31 *per cent* as against 24 *per cent* and 13 *per cent*. There were certainly some very fat livings : there were 12 worth between £500 and £1000. St. Asaph had one worth just over £1200 per annum. So, we are justified in concluding that on the whole there was a fairly reasonable distribution of incomes among the benefices in the diocese. The distribution of clerical incomes within the county is set out in Table 7 from which it can be seen that only about one-third of the benefices had incomes of less than £150.

Some of the higher incomes, of course, were due to the consolidation of livings and to pluralities. The 67 parochial benefices supported 49 livings, but it does not necessarily follow that this was a cause of inefficiency. Indeed, it may very well, and

most certainly did, increase the efficiency of the church by
giving incumbents of small consolidated livings a decent income. Some of these consolidations, all of which were very
ancient, could scarcely be justified however : for instance, the
rector of Llaniestyn with Penllech and Llandegwning enjoyed
a net income from the three benefices of £595, out of which he
paid a curate £80.[26] But he was the exception. It was invariably adjacent, small parishes which had been consolidated,
and this, in theory at least, should have increased efficiency.
The trouble with consolidations was of quite a different kind,
namely, the sheer physical difficulty involved in running the
affairs of two or more parishes. When the parishes were in
addition large it was relatively easy for Methodism to grow
almost as an adjunct of the Church. Methodism, it needs to be
said, was a rural movement which developed in the interstices,
as it were, of a system : it grew through the very deficiencies of
the parochial system itself.

Nor is it at all clear that pluralities were a cause of inefficiency. For one thing, there were very few in the docese ; only
three involved non-residence without licence or exemption.[27]
The main cause of non-residence was the consolidation of livings,
and the fact that more than half the glebe houses in 1851 were
not fit for habitation. How serious a factor this was is open to
conjecture, for where the glebe houses were unfit or non-existent
incumbents and curates were licensed to live elsewhere in the
parish. Nor can we point to the evil of patronage as being a
particularly serious matter in Bangor. The majority of the
rights to nominate to benefices were in ecclesiastical hands :[28]
the bishop held 35, the bishop of St. Asaph 4, the bishop of
Chester 1, and the dean of Bangor and the arch-deacon of
Merioneth 1 each. Only 10 were in lay hands. Similarly, the
proportion of livings impropriated by laymen was not high as
compared with other dioceses. In fact, out of the tithe rent-
charges as commuted at various dates in the 1840's, lay improp-
riators took only the relatively small sum of £2,507 out of a
grand total of £17,000 odd.[29] So the traditional income of the
Church was in clerical hands, from which it follows that the
tithe problem in Caernarfonshire was a clerical problem : the
resentments which it undoubtedly generated were against the

Church as tithe owners and not against laymen as tithe owners. This was true of England, where three-quarters of the £4 million value of tithes were in Church hands,[30] and it was true of Caernarfonshire where four-fifths of the tithes were in clerical hands. Finally, we might add that the Church of England in Caernarfonshire was a Welsh language church. Of the 102 services held in its churches on each Sunday in the three autumn months of 1848 only 7 had been in English. If this was an ' eglwys estron ' its language was not a ' iaith estronol.'[31]

To sum up. On the basis of this kind of information about the measurable aspects of the Church in the county in mid-century, the conclusion must be that it had lost ground to nonconformity not where it was weak but where it was strong. Scarcely any of the explanations put forward to account for the failure of the church in the new industrial, urbanized regions apply to Caernarfonshire. The basic failure of the Church was not due to the social effects of industrialisation, to the rapid and heavy concentration of demand in areas where her manpower, accommodation and endowments were weak. This was only marginally true in Caernarfonshire. Her tragedy lay rather in that she failed in areas where she was strong. And this, I suggest, is the phenomenon which the historian of religion in the county has to explain, and he will begin if he is wise, not with the Church as such but with the communities among whom the Church was an essential part.

I come finally to consider one other category of information concerning denominationalism in Caernarvonshire—namely, the chronology of its growth. The Religous Census, aided with material from other sources, enables us to trace this with a fair degree of accuracy, and to study it against the background of similar developments elsewhere. Readers will scarcely need to be reminded of the enormous growth in religious accommodation in Wales in the 50 years preceding the Census. In 1800 there would appear to have been a total of about 1369 places of worship: by 1851 this number had grown to 3805, three times as many, representing a growth rate of 178 *per cent* in 50 years.[32] Of course population had grown in the same period, almost doubling—a growth rate of nearly 100 *per cent*. Thus the provision of places of religious worship had grown at a considerably higher rate than had the population of the country. Nor need I remind the reader that this extraordinary rate of growth and this unusual amplitude of provision were due to the exertions of the Nonconformists. Some statistics will make this clear. In 1800 there had been 967 Anglican places of worship: 50 years later this number had increased to 1110. In the same period nonconformists places of worship had grown from 402 to 2695. The Anglican increase rate had been 11 *per cent*, the Nonconformists' 510 *per cent*.

The figures, of course, are the 'national' or the overall figures, and we should need to know whether there were any regional variations within the whole. Looking first at the record of the Established Church, we see that its growth varied from *nil* in Radnorshire to about 25 *per cent* in Monmouthshire and Glamorgan. Only in Flint was the rate of increase really substantial—nearly 70 *per cent*. The rural counties fared worse in this respect, and their rate of increase never exceeded 8 *per cent*. Where there was some kind of industry present the rate was usually in the region of about 10 *per cent*. Nonconformist growth was similarly uneven. Monmouthshire grew by nearly 1300 *per cent*—or 13-fold, Montgomery 14-fold, Flint 16-fold, Denbigh 10-fold, Glamorgan 6-fold. Everywhere the growth was substantial, though heavier in industrial counties than in rural counties. In Caernarfonshire the growth was about 6-fold.

These are the basic facts about Caernarfonshire—bearing in mind always that I am dealing in this paper only with the parishes of the four Unions. In 1800 there were 64 Anglican places of worship: in 1851 there were 67, an increase of 3. In 1800 there were 30 nonconformist chapels, in 1851 there were 221, an increase of 191. So the growth rate for the Church was under 0.5 *per cent*, for nonconformity over 600 *per cent* (636.66 *per cent*).

Our next question must be, when did this change take place, and by what stages? Looking first at the nonconformist contribution:[33] up to 1810 an additional 17 chapels had been built. Thereafter growth was steadier and heavier. 23 chapels were opened in the next five years (1815), 16 in the next half-decade (1820), 25 in the next, 28 between 1826 and 1830, 29 between 1831 and 1835, 26 between 1836 and 1840, 24 between 1841 and 1845, and 9 between 1846 and 1851. Thus, the great period of chapel building and reconstruction in the first half century begins after 1810, reaches massive proportions in the 1820's and continues with unabated momentum into the early 1840's. Why this chronology ? One can see that there are minor ups and downs, and a more satisfactory analysis would concentrate on accommodation rather than on buildings in order to show these variations more closely, but it is the sheer energy of this growth which is startling. Of course there were revivals in the county from time to time and place: but as I have remarked before, revivals do not explain anything, they merely add new dimensions to what has to be explained. And moreover, the sheer uniformity in this growth, its persistent rate suggest other and more basic social causes to be at work.

Answers to our next two questions might suggest what the historian should look for in the way of explanation and where, topographically, he should direct his attention. First, we must ask where this expansion was most pronounced, and second, among which denominations. As we should expect expansion was greatest in those Unions which experienced the highest growth in population and these, of course, were the Unions of of Caernarfon and Bangor where slate quarrying and its associated urban development had proceeded furthest.[34] Take the parish of Llanllechid, as a case in point. It had a population of 1322 in 1801 ; in 1811 it was 1470 (11.19 *per cent*) ; in 1821 it was 1964 (20.0 *per cent*) ; in 1831 it was 3075 (56.56 *per cent*) ; in 1841 it was 4957 (28.68 *per cent*), and in 1851 it was 5948 (22.00 *per cent*). This was an overall increase of 349.77 *per cent*. The rate of population growth was slow in the first decade, rising rapidly in the second, very rapid in the third, and falling back in the remaining decades. Its chapel building programme more or less coincides with this pattern of population growth. In 1801 it had one (Calvinistic Methodist) chapel. No additions are made in the first decade, 3 are added between 1831 and 1840, and another 4 in the last decade. Allowing for the usual time-lag, this pattern corresponds very closely : 1 chapel at the beginning, 13 at the end, not counting the Mormons in Bethesda. Llanddeiniolen, with a population increase of the same order and pattern exhibited the same phenomenon. Beginning our period

with one church only it ended with 14 nonconformist places of
worship. And the key to this lay in the Dinorwic Quarries, the
only social difference between the parishes being the growth of
a large town in Llanllechid while Llanddeiniolen continued
with its scattered village communities of quarrymen and small
farmers. Llandwrog, Llanllyfni and the other industrializing
parishes similarly expanded to the same kind of pattern if at
varying times and at different speeds (1826-35 is the great period
for these). The boroughs of Caernarfon and Bangor as well as
the small ports reflected the new posperity and the new basis for
wealth in their increased provision. Bangor ended with 17 new
or rebuilt nonconformist places and Caernarfon with 10.

But, interesting as this is, I do not think that it is the expansion of Nonconformity in the industrial parishes that is the
crucial phenomenon to fix upon, but rather the expansion in
the rural parishes, particularly the parishes of Llŷn. Increasing
population, new little urban communities which looked different from and felt different from the rural countryside, enhanced opportunities, a more liberating sense of freedom from the
closed, deferential society of the land, relatively much greater
financial resources—these social factors can be easily adduced
to explain expansion in places where economy was different.
What is more challenging is the growth in the rural areas.[35] Of
the 32 parishes in the Cricieth Union, for instance, only 6 registered no expansion at all—and in one of these there was the
makings of a chapel since there was a Calvinistic Methodist
Sunday School there. All these were inland parishes, all were
very small indeed, all were wholly dependent upon land for
their livelihood. Many of the Llŷn parishes of course bordered
the sea, and where this happened it was common for the
farmers to take to the sea for an additional increment to their
agricultural incomes—herring fishing at certain seasons of the
year. Some of them contained small fishing villages, that is,
communities for whom sea fishing was the primary source of
income. For it may be significant that the highest rate of chapel
building seems to have taken place in these maritime parishes,
Where there were fishing *townships*, as in Aberdaron, expansion
of chapel buildings was very high: Aberdaron added 4 to its
original 3. The period of greatest expansion in the Llŷn parishes

was earlier than in the industrial parishes, between 1811 and 1830, especially towards the end and beginning of that period. But this was merely the intensification of a fairly regular process which began early in the century (or late in the previous century), reached a peak in the mid 1820s and thereafter declined steadily into the 1840's: it was virtually over by 1840: by which time, as we have already shown, there were enough chapels to accommodate a larger population. Again, I would stress that it is not clear to me that this growth can be related to revivals; revivals are always symptomatic of other conditions in the social body.

The other question I suggested concerns the denominational pattern of this growth in nonconformity, for not all denominations to whom in aggregate the expansion is to be attributed, grew at the same rate or at the same time. Certainly, as we have already seen, the Calvinistic Methodists end up with a massive preponderance of chapels, no less than 103, nearly as many as all the chapels of the other denominations put together.[36] But it is apt to be forgotten that the Calvinistic Methodists started out with nearly double the number of chapels as those of the other denominations—19 as against 6 Independent and 5 Baptists. In the 50 years after 1800 the Calvinistic Methodists added 84 chapels, but the Independents added 53, the Baptists 19, and the Wesleyans 34. So the *rate of growth* of the dissenting denominations was higher that that of the Calvinistic Methodists. In the case of the Independents it was 883 *per cent*, 442 *per cent* in the case of the Calvinistic Methodists. The Baptist and Wesleyan rate was roughly of the same order—about 380 *per cent*. One cannot presume to mearure spiritual energy: but what we are saying is that the achievement of the Independents was at least as great as that of the Calvinistic Methodists, and in some mysterious ways, even greater. But the gap between the various denominations tended to widen as the century advanced. Independents and Calvinistic Methodists were building chapels at about the same proportional rate to their respective baselines up to 1815. During the next five years the gap widened as Independency seemed to lose something of its drive, but from 1820 until 1835 they were both again building at the same proportional rate until 1835—40 when again the

Independents fell back somewhat only to recover momentum again after 1840. The Baptists' rate of growth was never high and was in fact, overtaken by the Wesleyans sometime in the 1830-35 period.

Significant differences in the pattern of growth of the main denominations in the different regions of the county appear when we look closely at the threads in the pattern. If we take, for example, the three main Union Districts of Cricieth, Caernarfon, and Bangor we can locate the peak periods in their growth, and possibly relate them to large-scale social movements. Now, in the agricultural parishes of Llŷn, the Calvinistic Methodists grow very rapidly from the beginning up to 1830. They add 5 chapels in the next 10 years, then cease. The Independents, starting from a lower base, grow fairly rapidly to 1830, then stop. The Wesleyans build 5 chapels in the first decade but do not add any more until 1831 after which they continue to grow steadily until 1846. In the Caernarfon Union of parishes the model is different. For both Calvinistic Methodists and Independents the growth period here is most pronounced after 1816 or even 1821, and instead of ceasing after the mid-1830's, both denominations continue to grow, but the Methodists faster than the Independents. The Wesleyans grow very slowly up to 1830, then stop. In the Bangor Union, the gap between the Calvinistic Methodists and the Independents in their relative growth rates is less pronounced to begin with, but it is the Independents who continue to expand after the Calvinistic Methodists ceased in 1841. The Wesleyans appear to have been relatively very successful only during the 15 years after 1826 when they first appear as chapel builders in the Union. Chapel building, therefore, virtually ceases in the rural parishes of the county by the 1840's, but continues unabated up to the end of our period in those parts of the county which were beginning to support a more diversified economy. The rural parishes reach saturation point precisely at about the period when industrialization begins to attract their surplus population into the industrializing parishes. It is fair assumption that the migrant people were taking their religion with them, creating that increased demand which was so typical of the quarrying townships. This helps to explain why it was that Calvinistic

Methodism maintained in this new milieu the kind of predominance it had enjoyed in its original rural setting. In
support of this interpretation we should note also that the differences in the denominational growth pattern in Caernarfon
Union and Bangor Union suggest that Calvinistic Methodism
was most successful in those parishes where the rural base was
not entirely overwhelmed. The greater the number of industrial
townships being created by quarrying and mining, and the
greater their size and complexity, the more successful were the
efforts of the older dissenting denominations. The borough of
Bangor, with its higher proportions of tradesmen, craftsmen,
skilled artizans, and professional men, and *lower* than average
proportions of men engaged in agriculture was the dissenting
stronghold of the county so far as the number of its Independent
and Baptist chapels was concerned. It was also, of course, the
cathedral city, the seat of the bishop, the source of ecclesiastical
authority, the centre of a great network of ecclesiastical administration, the home of the Tory press: and perhaps it was no
accident that the most naked confrontation of religious ideologies should be exhibited there.

This leads me finally to remark on the nature of the Church
of England's building and reconstruction efforts—and it is
sufficient to note only one or two pertinent points. First, that
with some exceptions, the adaptation of the Church to the new
conditions did not begin in earnest until the 1840's. Only then
was there anything like a policy in high places and any objective attempt to find the necessary means. Inevitably, also, the
major effort had to be a diocesan one: the Ecclesiastical Commissioners, with a view of national priorities always before
them, were not likely to listen sympathetically to the demands
of a diocese not remotely in the same category as those which
had been caught up in the industrial revolution. One has only
to compare county by county the moneys expended by the
Commissioners for Building New Churches to see this: it went
to Flintshire and Denbighshire where the need was greatest.
Nevertheless, a considerable amount of church restoration took
place, new churches being erected in lieu of the old ones for
example at Pwllheli (1833), Llanengan (1847-8), Llanwnda
(1848), Betws Garmon (1842), Llanddeiniolen (1843), Pentir

(1847-8), Llanllechid (1846), Llanfairfechan (1849), and in six other places in Conway Union. There were also some renovations carried out, and a licensed schoolroom and a Ragged School (Twthill) opened. Thus the major effort was to make good dilapidations and to increase the accommodation of the small country churches. One wonders how well directed was some of this effort, how well adapted to changing needs. For example, the church at Llanddeiniolen was rebuilt on the same site as the old one in 1843, but as the rector remarked: ' The Parish Church is within ¾ of a mile of the lower boundary of the Parish—and is well placed as regards the old agricultural population. But the bulk of the present population which has, during the past forty years, been drawn together by the working of Mr. Assheton Smith's slate quarries, lies at a distance from the church of from 3 to 5 miles.' And he adds, as if to drive home the melancholy point, ' There arc in the Parish 13 dissenting Meeting Houses.'[37] Nor should we forget that much of the rebuilding and of the reconstruction was inspired by the Oxford Movement and embodied liturgical ideas which would have been anathema to the bulk of the lower classes. But anyway, it was too late. The religious character of the county had already transformed in those years when the Church had slumbered. Caernarfonshire had become a nonconformist stronghold. By mid century its landscape had come to be dotted with new kinds of buildings, with scores of chapels, with what were virtually centres of a new kind of culture with its own distinctive moral system, its own ideals of individual and social behaviour grafted on to the immemorial customs of the past. And in its ancient towns had arisen buildings which aspired to rise higher than the churches against whose values their own were a voluble and tangible reproach.

In this essay I have tried to describe only some aspects of a great shift in the culture of the county, and I have deliberately confined myself to one kind of measurable evidence only. To analyse this change in depth and in detail, to depict the enormous transformation which it involved, would demand the use of many other types of sources and of other techniques. But I hope that I have shown that it is the nature of the society itself that the historian of religion should look at, and that over a long period of time. And if, at the end, I should be asked what is the most striking characteristic of this denominational growth that I have tried to describe in quantitive terms, I should answer, its aggressive creativity, and that is what we need to explain.

TABLE I

RELIGIOUS ACCOMMODATION AND ATTENDANCE IN UNION DISTRICTS

619: PWLLHELI

		Denomin.	Places	Accomn.	Index	Attend.	Index
Popn.	21639	C of E	30	6809	30.11	1625	6.19
Places	107	Indept	19	3392	15.00	4098	15.61
Accom.	22613	Baptist	13	1645	7.27	2307	8.78
Index	104.50	C. Meth.	36	9518	42.09	16228	61.81
Attend.	26252	W. Meth.	9	1249	5.52	1994	7.59
Index	116.17						

620: CAERNARFON

Popn.	26910	C of E	14	4677	22.46	2238	7.10
Places	78	Indept	17	3668	17.61	6637	21.07
Accom.	20819	Baptist	6	1160	5.57	975	3.09
Index	77.36	C. Meth.	32	9894	47.52	19421	61.68
Attend.	31575	W. Meth.	8	1221	5.86	1895	6.01
Index	117.33	I. Meth.	1	199	0.95	409	1.29

621: BANGOR

Popn.	20262	C of E	10	3367	20.35	3588	13.61
Places	55	Indept.	13	3297	19.92	5982	22.70
Accom.	16544	Baptist	4	211	1.27	747	2.83
Index	81.65	C. Meth.	16	6335	38.29	11626	44.12
Attend.	26346	W. Meth.	11	3134	18.94	4230	16.05
Index	130.02	R. Cath.	1	200	1.20	173	0.65

TABLE 1—*Continued*

622: CONWAY

		Denomin.	Places	Accomn.	Index	Attend.	Index
Popn.	8640	C of E	11	3030	39.85	1529	16.47
Places	38	Indept	6	1156	15.20	2104	22.66
Accom.	7603	Baptist	4	446	5.86	874	9.41
Index	87.99	C. Meth.	12	1933	25.42	3440	37.06
Attend.	9282	W. Meth.	5	1038	13.65	1335	14.38
Index	107.42						

614: LLANRWST

		C of E	5	774	18.45	165	3.54
Popn.	3876	C of E	5	774	18.45	165	3.54
Places	18	Indept	3	554	13.21	669	14.36
Accom.	4193	C. Meth.	8	2528	60.29	3066	65.85
Index	108.17	W. Meth.	2	337	8.03	756	16.23
Attend.	4656						
Index	120.12						

NOTE: The above Table should read as follows. In the Union of Caernarfon there was a total of 78 places of worship. Of these, the Church of England provided 14, the Independents 17, the Baptists 6, etc. All the places of worship together provided a total of 20819 sittings, of which the Church of England provided 4677, or 22.46 *per cent*, the Independents 3668, or 17.61 *per cent*. etc. Of the total attendances 7 out of each 100 were to the Church of England, 21 to the Independents, etc.

NOTE 1 : where accommodation figures are not available for non-conformist chapels, I have taken the figure for the best attended service. In the case of places belonging to the Church of England, I have extracted the figures from the 1835 Ecclesiastical Revenues Commission Report.

NOTE 2 : The above Table shows the following information :

in Col. 3, the population in 1851.
in Col. 4, the total of sittings available in each parish.
in Col. 5, the ratio of sittings to population.
in Col. 6, the total number of places of religious worship.
in Col. 7, the number of places belonging to the Church of England, followed by the proportion per cent of the total sittings in the parish provided by the Church of England.
in Cols. 8 to 12, the same information for each of the other denominations.

NOTE 3 : in Col. 12, I have included 1 place of worship in Llanrûg, which described itself as Independent Methodist, namely, Ceunant [620.2.3.(8)]. I have found no confirmatory evidence that this chapel ever belonged to the Independent Methodist Denomination. Also included in Col. 12 is the Roman Catholic Church at Bangor, namely, St. Mary's [621.2.1.(14)].

NOTE 4 : Places of worship belonging to the Latter Day Saints are not included in the above Table. There were 2 such, namely, one congregation meeting in a dwelling house called Glandwr, Bank Quay, Caernarfon with standing room for 80, and another congregation meeting in a dwelling house at Bethesda, Llanllechid, which was used exclusively as a place of worship: 80 attended the evening service. Both these congregations of Mormons seem to have started in 1850; [620.3.1.(6) and 621.3.1.(8)].

TABLE 3

ACCOMMODATION

SUMMARY FOR THE WHOLE COUNTY

Union			Population	%	Places	Sittings	%
Pwllheli	..	..	21639	26.60	107	21613	31.50
Caernarfon		..	26910	38.08	78	20819	29.00
Bangor	..	..	20262	24.91	55	16544	23.05
Conway	..	..	8640	10.62	38	7603	10.59
Llanrwst	..	..	3876	4.76	18	4193	5.84
			81327		296	71772	

NOTE : The above should be read as follows :

Pwllheli, with 26.6% of the population of the county, provided 36.14% of the total of places of worship within the county, and 31.50% of the total number of seats available in the county. It provided 4.5% more seats than the total population of the Union. Etc.

TABLE 4

DISTRIBUTION OF PLACES OF RELIGIOUS WORSHIP PROVIDED
BY THE MAIN DENOMINATIONS

		Pwllheli	*Caernarvon*	*Bangor*	*Conway*	*Llanrwst*	*Total*
Church of England	.. ..	30	14	10	11	5	70
Independent	.. ..	19	17	13	6	3	58
Baptist	.. ..	13	6	4	4		27
C. Methodist	.. ..	36	32	16	12	8	104
W. Methodist	.. ..	9	8	11	5	2	35
Independent Methodist	.. ..		1				1
Roman Catholic	.. ..			1			1
TOTAL	.. ..	107	78	55	38	18	296

TABLE 5

DISTRIBUTION OF SITTINGS PROVIDED BY THE MAIN
DENOMINATIONS

		Pwllheli	*Caernarfon*	*Bangor*	*Conway*	*Llanrwst*	*Total*	*%*
Church of England	..	6809	4677	3367	3030	774	18657	25·99
Independent	..	3392	3668	3297	1156	554	12067	16·81
Baptist	..	1645	1160	211	446		3462	4·82
C. Methodist	..	9518	9894	6335	1933	2528	30208	42·08
Wesleyan Methodist	..	1249	1221	3134	1038	337	6979	9·72
Ind. Methodist	..		199				199	0·27
Roman Catholic	..			200			200	0·27
		22613	20819	16544	7603	4193	71772	

Table 6

DISTRIBUTION OF CLERICAL INCOMES
FROM BENEFICES IN WELSH DIOCESES

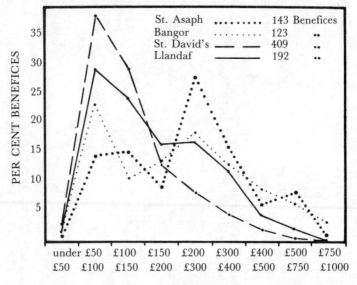

Table 7

DISTRIBUTION OF NET INCOMES OF
BENEFICES IN CAERNARFONSHIRE

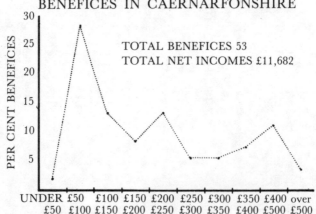

Source: Lewis's 'Topographical Dictionary' (1843 edition).

ABSTRACT OF CHRONOLOGY OF CHAPEL BUILDING 1801 to 1850

ABSTRACT OF CHRONOLOGY OF CHAPEL BUILDING 1801 to 1850

Denomination	Pre 1800	1801 1805	1806 1810	1811 1815	1816 1820	1821 1825	1826 1830	1831 1835	1836 1840	1841 1845	1846 1850	Total
Independent	6	2	1	9	2	11	8	8	3	7	2	59
Baptist	5	1	1	3	2	4	1	3	1	2	1	24
Calv. Meth.	19	1	4	9	11	9	13	11	13	12	1	103
Wesl. Meth.		4	3	1	1	1	6	6	7	3	2	34
Indept. Meth.									1			1
PROTESTANT TOTAL	30	8	9	22	16	25	28	28	25	24	6	221
Roman Cath.								1				1
Mormon											2	2
TOTAL	30	8	9	22	16	25	28	29	25	24	8	224

Table 9
CHAPEL BUILDING IN CAERNARFONSHIRE
1800-1851, BY UNIONS.

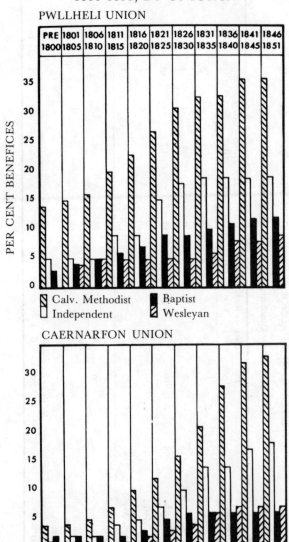

Table 9

CHAPEL BUILDING IN CAERNARFONSHIRE
1800-1851, BY UNIONS

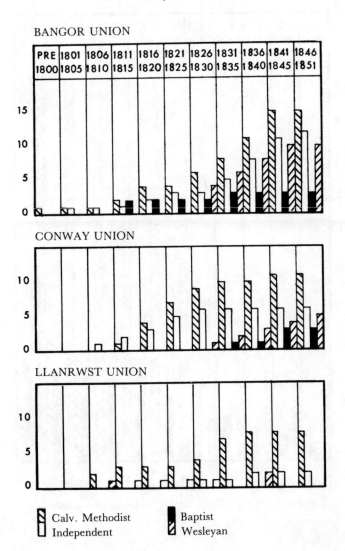

BANGOR UNION

CONWAY UNION

LLANRWST UNION

Calv. Methodist   Baptist
Independent   Wesleyan

Table 11

CHAPEL BUILDING IN CAERNARFONSHIRE
1800-1851

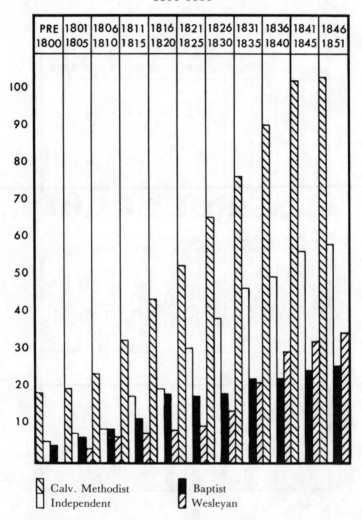

Calv. Methodist   Baptist
Independent   Wesleyan

DENOMINATIONALISM IN SWANSEA AND DISTRICT :
A STUDY OF THE ECCLESIASTICAL CENSUS OF 1851

"I climbed, one Sunday morning, on to the heights which overhang the town of Swansea, consigned on that one day, to silence and rest. Two kinds of buildings only evinced any signs of life; the high chimney-shafts, towering over the iron found-ries, gave vent to black serpents of smoke, curled round by the wind into spiral coils, chasing one another over the tiled roofs; and from the church steeples I heard the sound of bells inviting to worship. Labour and Prayer—these were the elements which seemed to float in the air over this town, spread out as it is on the edge of the resounding sea . . . Religion and Industry."[1]

To the author of that graphic and rather moving description the view of the town of Swansea from the slopes of Kilvey Hill one Sunday morning in 1867 symbolized the two major forces in the English civilization of his time. He saw not a hostile con-frontation of two opposing forces, but a harmonious and creative alliance in which the influence of religion led to liberty of thought and the enhancement of human values, while the growth of industry led to ever-increasing mastery over matter and the material conditions of life. Such expansive and opt-imistic views, though not without their critics, were a common-place in Victorian Britain, but while most historians today would agree on the importance of the two main forces, if not on their relative importance, few would be as ready to accept the validity of the equation without detailed investigation into its major elements. Hitherto, so far as Swansea is concerned, most investigations have concerned the smoke; detailed knowledge exists about the chimneys, about the industrial life of the town.[2] Its religious life still remains impressionistic, lacking even the preliminary and basic facts upon which any sociological dis-cussion of its rôle in society must of necessity be based. The object of this article is to abstract some such facts from one primary source and to present them in a systematic fashion.

*   *   *

GOWER PARISHES

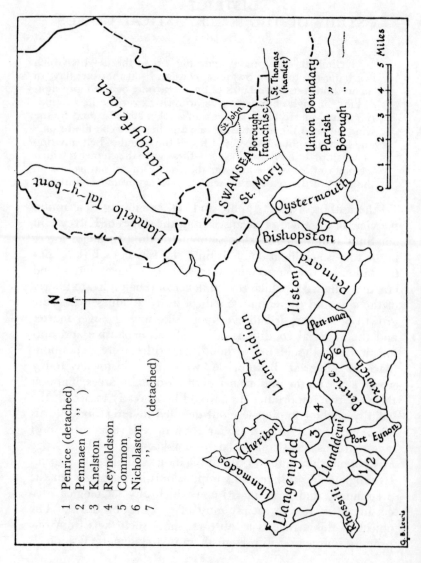

Union Boundary
Parish   ,,
Borough ,,

5 Miles

Llangyfelach

Llandeilo Tal-y-bont

St John

SWANSEA Borough Franchisca

St. Mary

St Thomas (hamlet)

Oystermouth

Bishopston

Ilston

Pennard

Llanrhidian

Pen-maen

Oxwich

Penrice

Cheriton

Llangenydd

Llanddewi

Llanmadog

Rhossili

Port Eynon

N

1 Penrice (detached)
2 Penmaen (,,)
3 Knelston
4 Reynoldston
5 Common
6 Nicholaston
7   ,, (detached)

G. B. Lewis

The tables which follow are based on the actual returns made in connection with the Ecclesiastical Census of 1851.[3] On the Sunday preceding Census Day, that is, on 30 March 1851, Mid-Lent Sunday, a count was made of every person attending religious worship in the morning, afternoon, and evening, in every place of religious worship in England and Wales. Elaborate precautions were taken to ensure the accuracy of the returns and the comprehensiveness of the census. The Census itself was the responsibility of the Registrar-General who appointed Horace Mann, of Lincoln's Inn, to supervise its organization and to prepare a Report. Printed forms, called schedules, of two kinds, one for the Established Church, the other for the various nonconformist bodies, were despatched through the District Registrars of Births and Deaths to local enumerators who, on the basis of their intimate knowledge of their assigned localities, were instructed to deliver them to the incumbents of churches and ministers of chapels or other officials of places of worship competent to give the required information. The enumerators then collected the completed schedules in the course of their duties on Census Day, 31 March 1851. Next, the local registrars worked carefully through the schedules, compared them with previously prepared lists of places of worship, and, in the case of missing returns or of deficiencies in the information asked for, took steps to perfect them. Finally the schedules were placed in numerical order under sub-district and parish (or other appropriate division), corresponding to the divisions and sub-divisions of the Poor Law Unions, and despatched to London. Here they were further scrutinized and, where necessary, perfected by means of correspondence with the local registrar of the district concerned or, if need be, with the incumbent or minister directly. The consensus of opinion among those who have studied the subsequently published enumerations and tables in the Report is that a high degree of accuracy was achieved and that the Census constitutes one of the most reliable and valuable sources for the study of British society in the mid-nineteenth century.[4]

So far as the efficiency of this central machinery is concerned, and considering the complexity of the exercise, the Census was effectively carried out in the Swansea Union. The errors which survived into the Report were comparatively few. Where possible I have accounted for them in the analysis below. Detailed by denomination these errors are as follows. One place of worship belonging to the Established Church situated in the town of Swansea is missing, and for some unknown reason this deficiency was not accounted for or rectified.[5] Pennard Parish Church appears twice. The first schedule (585.4.3.11), completed by an informant presumably at a later date, gives a total of 320 sittings and an attendance total of 500. The second (585.4.3.12), completed by the incumbent, gives a total of 130 sittings and a total attendance of 220. I have accepted the incumbent's figures. No information regarding sittings was given for Llangennydd Parish Church and obviously wrong information for Llanmadoc Parish Church. In both cases I have used in this connection the number of attendants at the best-attended service. The Independent Chapel at Felindre (Llangyfelach) was counted twice, so I have eliminated one. Siloam, Pentre Estyll made an incorrect return of sittings, and Paraclete, Mount Zion, and Tabernacle (all in Oystermouth) gave no information regarding sittings. Gerazim Baptist Chapel Llangyfelach, the Calvinistic Methodist chapels Bethel (Llangyfelach) and Babell (Swansea), and the Wesleyan chapels at Oxwich and Pitton (Rhosili) also omitted this essential information. In all these cases, as with the parish churches already referred to, I have taken the highest number attending any one service. Calculations showed that adjustments made on the basis of denominational averages seriously distorted the over-all picture.

Correcting errors or deficiencies such as these is a comparatively straightforward exercise. More serious are those errors which are unaccountable because of human ignorance, weakness, or vanity and prejudice. Church and chapel officials were instructed to make a count of the sittings provided and the numbers of individuals attending on Census Sunday, but it is very doubtful indeed whether there was any uniformity of method or agreement as to intention in the way in which the enumerations were made. In some cases it is not clear whether the figures given under the query concerning space available relate to sittings or to space measured in superficial feet. One suspects also, that enumerations are to the nearest 10, or even 100. Very often, the numbers given as present on 30 March are the same as the stated averages of attendance. In one chapel, again, the average attendance is inconceivably higher than the actual attendance given. In another place, more are given as attending than there was space. The incumbent of Trinity Church, Swansea, confessed that his average was a rough estimate only, and it is probable that some of the information given was of this character. But not all. The vicar of St. Mary's, Swansea obviously went to considerable trouble to make an accurate count of both of sittings and of attendances, and one would like to think that the majority of the figures have a fair degree of accuracy. Nevertheless, a serious doubt remains that many, if not most, of the statistics returned were estimates only which erred on the generous side. The minister of Ebenezer Independent Chapel, Swansea, was aware of this when he remarked on his schedule, "Most people would suppose we had 800 people last evening by viewing the assembly, but when numbered they were found short of 500."[6]

Another source of error which must inevitably affect the validity of the generalisations we make below concerns the Index of Attendances, or the Index Rate. This is a statistical device for measuring the comparative strength of denominations first applied by Inglis and more latterly by Goodridge.[7] It is calculated by expressing the total of all worshippers who attended in the morning, afternoon, and evening services as a proportion of the total population of the locality. The objecttions to this mode of procedure are obvious. First, it does not distinguish the numbers of individual worshippers : many individuals must have worshipped more than once. But since the Census itself made no attempt to do this there appears to be no satisfactory method of calculating the numbers of individual worshippers. Equally serious objections can be raised against any other mode of procedure: for instance, calculating on the basis of two-thirds of the total, or comparing the numbers for the best-attended service.[8] Second, this method ignores the undoubted differences in habits of worshipping as between the different denominations. Inglis and Pickering are probably right in arguing that any tendency there might be for this method to favour the nonconformists is ironed out when the scale is large enough. Working at a Union and parish level this objection appears to be more serious since local denominational customs would not be cancelled out by differing customs in widely different parts of the country. Thus, the Anglican churches in the deanery of Gower held only one service each Sunday, alternating morning and evening on successive Sundays, and generally congregations were larger in the afternoons. In the Union as a whole only the church at Llandeilo Talybont held three services on Census Sunday. The Swansea parish churches (St. Mary's, St. John's, and Trinity) and the churches of the industrial parishes held two.[9] The pattern of attendance for public worship in nonconformist chapels was different, but it was not universally three services a Sunday. Of 81 congregations, 36 met twice, 27 three times, and 18 once a Sunday. Moreover, this pattern was not a reflection of denominational habits, but rather of the differences between rural and urban customs to which all denominations, including the Church of England, conformed. Thus, townspeople worshipped oftener on Sundays whether they were Anglicans or nonconformists. All the churches holding two or more services were town churches, and all the chapels holding three services were situated in towns or in industrial or semi-industrial parishes, while the chapels worshipping only once were almost all in rural Gower or in the remote upland areas of the northern parishes. Nevertheless, it remains true that over the Union as a whole our method of comparing relative attendance rates will favour the nonconformists. With these considerations in mind we can now turn to the statistics themselves.

The geographical area of our study was one of considerable economic and social diversity. The Swansea Union had been formed in 1836 by uniting the parishes of the ancient Hundred of Swansea with the Town and Franchise and adding the parish of Llangyfelach. It consisted therefore of 21 parishes or civil divisions, including the whole of the Gower peninsula with its 17 parishes, the three Swansea parishes, and the whole of the parishes of Llandeilo Talybont and Llangyfelach. The Borough and Parish of Loughor, which was geographically a part of the area (as it had been of the ancient Hundred) was excluded in order to unite it with the Llanelli Union, and apart from the parish of St. Thomas so was the heavily urbanized eastern side of the Tawe in the parish of Llansamlet, which went to form part of the Neath Union. As an administrative unit the Union was growing rapidly in population. In the previous 20 years it had increased by 55 *per cent*—from 31,211 in 1831 to 46,907 in 1851. Compared with the growth of the other Glamorgan Unions this, if we except the Bridgend Union, was fairly modest. Cardiff (86 *per cent*), Merthyr (124 *per cent*) and Neath (92 *per cent*) had all expanded at a considerably higher rate. But it is a factor of cardinal importance to this study to realize that this increase in Swansea was taking place in virtually one portion of the Union, that, is within the Swansea town area and its immediate hinterland to the north as far as Morriston and Clydach. Thus, whereas the Gower Sub-district of the Union, which included the 17 parishes of the peninsula, grew by only 1,493 to a total of 7,044 in the period 1831-51, and Llandeilo Talybont Sub-district, which included Clydach and the lower part of Pontardawe, by only 777 to a total of 5,001, Swansea Sub-district expanded by 9,354 to a total of 23,607, and Llangyfelach Sub-district by 4,072 to a total of 11,255. Consequently there was an unevenness in the distribution of population both within the Union and within the individual parishes. Thus, the bulk of Swansea's population was concentrated within the town and franchise. Swansea Higher was sparsely populated, St. John's parish slightly less so, but the town itself contained 21,533 people, and the parish of St. Thomas another 1,089. Similarly, Llangyfelach was a large upland parish containing great stretches of moorland and waste: its population was largely concentrated—though not to the same extent as Swansea—in the industrial villages and townships developing on the western banks of the Tawe southwards from Clydach through Morriston and the northern approaches to Swansea. The same considerations apply, but on a much reduced scale, to some of the other parishes in the Union. The north Gower parishes west of the older industrial regions were beginning to experience the expansive effects of industrialization. There were pockets of industry, as at Penclawdd, and limestone quarrying was sufficiently thriving in the parish of Rhosili, for instance, to prevent that erosion of population by migration to Swansea which was the fate of most of the other rural parishes in the western parts of the Union. Parishes adjacent to Swansea on its western borders, such as Oystermouth and Bishopston, shared in the increasing prosperity of the town itself. However, even more so than in our own day, Gower was a refuge from the smoke and filth of the industrial and commercial heart of the Union. The westward movement of those who could afford to do so corresponded to the eastward movement of those whom the rural economy could not support.

The distribution of population and its movement within the Union thus exhibited a marked bifurcation corresponding to the economies of, and the stage of exploitation reached in, particular areas. D. Trevor Williams has long since shown how this was an effect of the geological divide between the north and south of the peninsula.[10] The growth areas were all north of Cefn-bryn, on the coal measures.[11] Here, new industrial communities were being formed or old farming communities transformed as collieries were sunk and other industrial undertakings created. Only in a minor and debilitated way did industry diversify the economies of rural Gower. Thus, at Port Eynon in 1851,[12] among its 70-odd heads of families there were ten quarrymen, but the majority were connected with the sea—ten mariners and nine fishermen—or with the land as farmers (11) or farm labourers (7). The remainder were craftsmen—a carpenter, a shipwright, two blacksmiths—and shopkeepers or tradesmen. Some of the parishes were exclusively agricultural, particularly the upland, central parishes. Llanddewi's population, for instance, was entirely agricultural, consisting of 19 farmers and 8 agricultural labourers and their families. In such parishes there appear to have been scarcely any concentrations of population, however small: they were scattered communities of small farmers dependent upon the craftsmen and tradespeople of adjacent parishes for those goods and services which they could not supply themselves. Nevertheless, it is important to notice that most parishes contained substantial villages where lived craftsmen serving the needs of the areas. The occupations of the heads of families in Penrice parish show a considerable diversification of trades and occupations connected with the land and sea. There were 12 farmers, 4 fishermen, 2 mariners, 4 cordwainers, a quarryman, a blacksmith, and also a hand-loom weaver, a carpenter, a thatcher, a woodward, a miller, a shoemaker, a tailor, and a gardener, as well as some professional men such as a farm bailiff, a schoolmaster, and a relieving officer. In addition, there were 7 labourers and 10 farm labourers. Such villages were the community centres of their respective parishes, small but closely integrated, self-sufficient and nourishing their local differences. It was in such communities that the chapels were to be found.

The economic divide was not the only division of social importance. Swansea Union was characterized also by a language divide. D. Trevor Williams has studied the nature of this phenomenon in some detail,[13] and it is not necessary here to do more than note its main feature, namely, that Cefn-bryn constituted a language as well as an economic boundary. To the south, the parishes were largely English-speaking, to the north, and increasingly as one penetrated into the hinterland, the language of common discourse was Welsh. Since it was in these areas that the new economic developments were taking place it meant that the growing industrial communities were Welsh, and were being continually reinforced by migrants from the Welsh-speaking areas. This is a factor of prime importance which must be kept in mind when the tables below are studied.

*   *   *

The Ecclesiastical Census attempted to measure two aspects of the religious life of the country, first, the provision of places of worship, including the number of sittings made available by each denomination, and second, the actual use made of this accommodation as measured by the number of attendants on Census Sunday. As we have already noted, the Census was organized on a District and Sub-district level, the irreducible unit on which the statistics were collected being the parish or other ecclesiastical or civil division. The published summaries, abstracts, and detailed tables of the Report were collated on the basis of Registration Districts or Unions. This was because, as Horace Mann admitted, detailed statements in parochial terms would have provided facilities "for making invidious comparisons between individual parishes".[14] The statistics given below are for the individual parishes of the Union, with the following exception. The figures for Swansea are those for the Parish of Swansea, which included the Town and Franchise, with the addition of the Parish of St. John, and the Parish of St. Thomas. Llanrhidian Parish was divided into an Upper and Lower Division for the purpose of Poor Law administration and for the decennial census, and it was so divided for the purposes of the Ecclesiastical Census. The parish of Knelston, since it had no parish church—the building having long been a ruin[15]—was included in the parish of Llanddewi. It should also be noted that Paviland, which was a detached portion of the parish of Penrice, was included for enumeration purposes with Llanddewi but for ecclesiastical purposes with Penrice.

The provision of means of worship is measureable in two ways, first by the numbers of edifices set apart for public worship, or, in some cases, of dwellings or rooms in public buildings appropriated to such use,[16] and second, by the actual number of sittings provided. Table 2 sets out the basic information, parish by parish.

Turning first to the distribution of places of worship, the first and most intriguing feature to notice is the marked difference between the heavily denominationalised parts of the Union, and the relative lack of denominational diversity in the remainder. Llangyfelach, Llandeilo Talybont, Llanrhidian Higher, Swansea, and Oystermouth all have four or more denominations. Of the remaining 15 parishes, all in the subdistrict of Gower, 7 have only one denomination, 4 have 2, 3 have three, and one has four denominations. Denominational diversity was a marked characteristic of the northern and western parishes of the Union which, as we have explained, were the industrialised and urbanised parts of the Union. A feature of this correlation between denominational diversity and urban-

isation is the actual distribution pattern of the main denominations. The Church was present in every parish (Knelston
excluded), but the old dissenting bodies (Independents, Baptists, and Unitarians) are virtually confined to the industrialised Welsh-speaking north and north-west. The only denominations present in Gower proper are the various Methodist
bodies, and here, it should be noted, the predominantly English
Methodists (Wesleyans and Primitive Methodists) alone diversify the western parishes, for the three Welsh Calvinistic
Methodist Chapels were located at the extreme west of the peninsula—an area with strong trading and cultural links with the
northern, Welsh-speaking areas of Gower, and within the orbit
of the semi-industrialized region around Penclawdd.

It does not follow from the above considerations, however,
that the industrialized parishes made a higher provision for
religious worship than the rural areas. In absolute numbers it is
true that the two parishes of Llangyfelach and Swansea between
them provided more than half the total number of places of
worship in the Union—that is, 60 out of a total of 106 (or 56 per
cent). But more than three-quarters of the total population of
the Union was concentrated in those two parishes—37,012 out
of a total of 46,907 (or 78.9 *per cent*). The full significance of
this can be seen when we compare the Accommodation Rates
of all the parishes, that is, the provision of actual sittings expressed as a proportion of the population (Table 3). While it
would require a much more sophisticated model of the sociology of religious activity than is being applied here to explain
the peculiarities of this list, it nevertheless clearly shows that the
industrialized parishes were by no means the best provided with
the means of religious worship. Despite the concentration of
resources by all the main denominations in Swansea and Llangyfelach the most that they could achieve in the aggregate was
only a little more than the optimum of 58.4 regarded by Horace
Mann as the bare minimum.[17] Swansea itself was below the
average Provision Rate for the whole Union (72.8), and Llangyfelach only slightly above it. At the bottom end of the scale
were the six parishes with less than 58.4 Provision Rate. It
should be noted that economically and demographically there

is little to mark them off from similar Gower Parishes with Provision Rates much higher than the Union average. What distinguishes them is their total dependence upon the parish churches for their means of worship. One additional place of worship in such small parishes made a difference in their Provision Rates out of all proportion to their size (Table 3).

Between them the various religious denominations provided sittings for 72.8 *per cent* of the population of the Union. Individually, the contributions of the main Christian denominations to this proportion were as follows.

Denominations				*Per Cent*	*Totals*
Church of England	..	..	..	18.9	18.9
Independents	..	..	..	20.3	
Baptists	..	..	..	11.5	
Unitarians	..	..	..	.24	34.2
Calvinistic Methodists	..	..	..	10.3	
Wesleyan Methodists	..	..	..	5.2	
Primitive Methodists	..	..	..	1.3	
Lady Huntingdon's Connexion	..	..	1.3	18.1
Roman Catholics	..	..	..	0.8	

From the above Table one can see that the old dissenting congregations together provided for slightly more than one-third of the population, and the Church of England, and the various Methodists, for rather less than one-fifth each. Allowing for the contributions of the Quakers, the Roman Catholics, the Jews, and the Mormons, who together provided for slightly more than 1.0 *per cent* of population, this left about a quarter of the total population unprovided for. Table 3 shows where these people were located, that is, in the large centres of population. Swansea's deficiency alone was 10,095 sittings, that of all the other parishes with lower than average Provision Rates totalled only 1,139. The Church of England was certainly aware of this challenge in the industrial areas, and it was by no means ineffective in the face of competition by other denominations in those parishes. It might well have been the strongest single denomination in Swansea had the vicar of St. Mary's, the parish church, been free to use its very considerable accommodation for its intended purpose.[18] As we shall see below, the reaction of the Church to the challenge of the new urbanization had been relatively recent, but it too was contributing to the building boom in the last decades of our period. Meanwhile, in all the industrial parishes it was the Independents who contributed most to the provision of sittings for the expanding population, and their distribution throughout the Union shows to what an extent they and the Baptists had adapted themselves to the new conditions and because effectively an urbanized denomination.

I have already explained the nature of the difficulties with which we are faced when we attempt to express comparatively the relative success of organised religion on the basis of the figures for attendance on Census Sunday. Bearing in mind these limitations it is nevertheless possible to arrive at tentative and approximate conclusions. The method here adopted— viz. to express the total attendances as a proportion of the total population—gives the following pattern. In the Union as a whole the Attendance Index was 71.7. This compares with an Index of 76.4 in Neath Union, 70.3 in Cardiff Union, 81.0 in Bridgend Union, 80.1 in Merthyr Tydfil Union, and 93.9 in Llanelli Union. It thus resembled that for Cardiff where there was the same basic division between one highly urbanized centre, in which nonconformity was powerful, and a large rural hinterland where it was relatively much weaker. When we grade the individual parishes in the Swansea Union according to their Attendance Rates (Table 4) we find that there is a marked correspondence with the Accommodation Rate list (Table 3). All but one of the parishes with Accommodation Rates below the Union average appear also below the average Attendance Rate. The exception is Port Eynon which had a higher than average Attendance Rate (102.5) but a lower than average Accommodation Rate (54.2). Statistically this appears to have been due to the fact that though the parish had only one place of worship—the parish Church—it was one of the very few parishes in rural Gower to hold two services a Sunday. (The others were Reynoldston and Llangennydd). Obviously, this difference can be explained only in terms of other factors which

are beyond the scope of this study to examine. But it is fairly
clear that the rural/urban discontinuity which was so marked a
feature in the religious life of the country as a whole is present
in no less marked a degree in the religious life of much smaller
communities.   Swansea, despite its 29 Christian places of
worship and the great diversity of its denominational structure,
ranks with the deeply rural, sparsely populated, poor, and uni-
denominational parishes. This characteristic is less marked in
the other heavily populated parishes : Oystermouth is only a
little above the Union average, but Llangyfelach and Llandeilo—Talybont are well above it. But in the latter two parishes
a closer analysis in terms of the rural and urban communities
which they contained would probably confirm the same kind of
generalisation.

The final Tables concern the processes by which the situation delineated above came into being. Necessarily, the statistics I have abstracted relate to a system assumed to be static,
but the historian, aware of the ever-changing structure of
society, must attempt to study its nature at any particular time
within the framework of its history. Within such a context, we
can see how greatly the denominational pattern had changed in
its recent past. Fifty years previously the numerical superiority
of the Church of England had been overwhelming. Whereas
each parish had its church (exception Knelston), the dissenting
chapels had numbered only five, and four of these (three
Independent and one Baptist) were in the upland parish of
Llangyfelach where, like the parish church, they served widespread communities. The two Methodist chapels which dated
themselves as pre-1800 were not strictly denominational at all,
but even if we admit them the total of nonconformist chapels
was still only seven belonging to five denominations. No doubt
there were off-shoots of these gathered churches meeting in
secular buildings, and from these would emerge the sister-
churches of the older congregations. Table 5 shows how rapidly
conditions changed and how effectively the creative forces
operated. By 1815 the nonconformist denominations had added
15 chapels, thus overtaking the numerical ascendancy of the
Church of England. By 1830 they had doubled their numbers,
and by the 1850s were well on the way to doubling them again.

Table 6 shows the distribution of this building among the various parishes by the major denominations. 80 *per cent* of this activity was in Swansea and the industrialized Welsh-speaking northern parishes—in fact, 55 *per cent* being in Swansea and Llangyfelach. It can be seen also that it was overwhelmingly the work of the Independents (22 chapels) and the Baptists (17). Chapel-building elsewhere in the Union was largely the work of the Methodist denominations—the Wesleyans and Primitive Methodists in English-speaking Gower, the Welsh Calvinistic Methodists in the north-western parishes.

By comparison the Church of England was much slower in its reaction to the challenge of the demographic changes which were rapidly transforming the ancient communities of the region. Some of the Gower churches were inadequate to serve the needs of even their small parishes—particularly as at the same time new, more specific and more comprehensive definitions of religious needs were coming into vogue. In north Gower the position was even worse and becoming critical, for in addition to being very inaccessible even for pre-industrial societies, the new concentrations of population made them not only inadequate but almost irrelevant. The church at Llandeilo Talybont was situated on the edge of the river Loughor and surrounded by marshes which were impassable in times of flood or high-tides. Its accommodation—260 sittings—may have been adequate in 1801 when the population was 595: it was wholly inadequate by 1850 when the population had increased to 1408 and concentrated around Pontarddulais. It was the nonconformists who supplied the deficiency. Or again, there was the problem of detached portions of parishes. Paviland was seven miles from the main part of the parish of Penmaen where the church was situated, and the rector noted that the inhabitants of Paviland never attended divine service at the parish church by reason, he said, of the distance. Our tables show that they went instead to the chapel in the village which had been erected by the Independents in 1821 with accommodation sufficient for almost double the population of the whole parish. Not until 1839 did the church begin to adapt itself to these new conditions, by which time the nonconformists had

already built 46 chapels. The first edifice to be built was the
result of private endowment, when J. Llewelyn, Esq., of Pen-
lle'rgaer put up £2,000 for a church, with 190 sittings, at
Gorseinon.[19] It was consecrated in 1839, but not endowed by
the Ecclesiastical Commissioners. Then, in 1843, Trinity
Church, Swansea, was built at a cost of £4,000, with accommodation for 1,150, but it too was not formally endowed, and
its incumbent depended upon pew rents and Easter offerings
which averaged only £50 per annum. St. John's, Clydach, with
360 sittings, built at a cost of £1,350, was consecrated in 1847 as
a new District Church, and endowed by the Ecclesiastical Commissioners with £150 per annum. Finally, a Chapel of Ease,
with accommodation for 300, was rebuilt and consecrated at
Penclawdd in 1850. This, of course, was only the beginning of
church extension in Swansea and district: by the end of the
century new parishes had been created and the more densely
populated parts of the area better provided with churches.[20]
But the nonconformists, likewise, continued to expand their
provision, and the marked disparity between Anglican and
Nonconformist provision which the Census had revealed was
never entirely removed.

*　　　　*　　　　*

Such was the pattern of denominationalism in the Swansea
Union revelaed by the Ecclesiastical Census of 1851. The
publication of the Report itself two years later sparked off,
locally as well as nationally, a controversy marked more by
political animus than by Christian charity, and it is only now, a
hundred years later, that the historian can approach the
questions there raised with some degree of objectivity. Esquiros,
in the quotation with which I opened this study, may have
exaggerated the sound of the church bells he heard that Sunday
morning in 1851: he was certainly right in seeing in Swansea a
microcosm of the religious life of the country as a whole.

TABLE I

POPULATION CHANGES IN SWANSEA UNION

(by SUB-DISTRICTS)

Source : CENSUS OF 1851.

Sub-District			1831	1851	*% increase*
Llandeilo Talybont	..	..	4,224	5,001	18.3
Llangyfelach	..	..	7,183	11,255	56.6
Swansea	..	..	14,253	23,607	65.6
Gower	..	..	5,551	7,044	26.6

NOTE : LLANDEILO, TALYBONT included the hamlets of Clydach, Mawr, and Penderry, and the parish of Llandeilo Talybont.

LLANGYFELACH included the hamlet of Clase, Llanrhidian Higher, the parish of St. John, and Swansea Higher.

SWANSEA included the Town and Franchise, Swansea Lower, and the parish of St. Thomas.

TABLE 2

PLACES OF WORSHIP, SITTINGS, AND ATTENDANCES

Parish	Denomination	Places		Sittings			Attendance	
		Total	%	Total	%	Accom. Rate	Total	Attend. Rate
Llangyfelach Population, 10,895 Density, 255.4	Church of England	4	13.7	1,358	14.8		802	
	Independent	8	27.5	3,231	35.4		5,318	
	Baptist	10	34.4	2,498	27.3		2,201	
	Calvinistic Methodist	3	10.3	988	10.8		1,579	
	Wesleyan	3	10.3	248	2.6		278	
	Unitarian	1	3.4	800	8.7		64	
		29		9,123		83.7	10,262	94.2
Llandeilo Talybont Population, 1,408 Density, 121.6	Church of England	1	20.0	260	16.7		240	
	Independent	1	20.0	420	27.1		480	
	Baptist	1	20.0	300	19.3		142	
	Calvinistic	1	20.0	420	27.1		411	
	Wesleyan	1	20.0	149	9.6		198	
		5		1,549		110.0	14,71	104.4

Llanrhidian Higher Population, 1,443 Density, 101.4							
Church of England	1	16.6	300	19.4		350	
Independent	2	33.3	848	54.7		1,220	
Baptist	1	16.6	60	3.8		67	
Calvinistic Methodist	2	33.3	340	21.9		370	
	6		1,548		107.3	2,007	139.0
Swansea, including the Town and Franchise, and the Parishes of St. John and St. Thomas Population, 26,117 Density, 1,767.0							
Church of England	4	12.9	4,021	25.0		2,717	
Independent	7	22.9	3,965	24.7		3,958	
Baptist	5	16.1	2,384	14.8		2,936	
Calvinistic Methodist	4	12.9	2,167	13.5		2,013	
Wesleyan	4	12.9	1,416	8.8		1,232	
Primitive	1	3.2	300	1.9		410	
Lady Huntingdon's	1	3.2	650	4.0		1,050	
Unitarian	1	3.2	400	2.4		328	
Quakers	1	3.2	35	0.2		35	
Roman Catholic	1	3.2	412	2.5		500	
Jews	1	3.2	72	0.4		80	
Mormons	1	3.2	200	1.2		320	
	31		16,022		61.3	15,579	59.6

TABLE 2—*continued*

Parish	Denomination	Places		Sittings			Attendance	
		Total	%	Total	%	Accom. Rate	Total	Attend. Rate
Oystermouth Population, 1,938 Density, 238.9	Church of England	1	14.2	600	37.7		208	
	Independent	3	42.8	552	34.7		872	
	Baptist	1	14.2	180	11.3		280	
	Wesleyan Methodist	1	14.2	108	6.7		60	
	Primitive Methodist	1	14.2	150	9.4		120	
		7		1,590		82.0	1,540	79.4
Bishopston Population, 513 Density, 137.5	Church of England	1	250.0	400	54.4		297	
	Independent	1	25.0	142	19.3		70	
	Wesleyan Methodist	2	50.0	192	26.1		278	
		4		734		143.3	645	125.7
Pennard Population, 348 Density, 97.1	Church of England	1	100.0	130	100.0	37.3	220	63.0

Ilston Population, 356 Density, 79.1							
Church of England	1	50.0	120	37.5		65	
Independent	1	50.0	200	62.5		36	
	2		320		89.8	101	28.3
Penmaen Population, 114 Density, 47.4							
Church of England	1	50.0	103	34.0		54	
Independent	1	50.0	200	66.0		198	
	2		303		265.7	252	221.0
Nicholaston Population, 132 Density, 115.5							
Church of England	1	100.0	60	100.0	45.4	30	22.7
Penrice Population, 398 Density, 113.3							
Church of England	1	100.0	112	100.0	28.1	67	16.8
Oxwich Population, 369 Density, 147.4							
Church of England	1	33.3	134	37.1		97	
Wesleyan Methodist	1	33.3	90	26.9		140	
Primitive Methodist	1	33.3	110	32.9		120	
	3		334		90.5	337	91.3

TABLE 2—*continued*

Parish	Denomination	Places		Sittings			Attendance	
		Total	%	Total	%	Accom. Rate	Total	Attend. Rate
Port Eynon Population, 351 Density, 197.7	Church of England	1	100.0	190	100.0	54.2	360	102.5
Reynoldston Population, 315 Density, 192.5	Church of England	1	100.0	130	100.0	41.5	120	37.7
Llanddewi Population, 174 Density, 60.0	Church of England	1	100.0	115	100.0	66.0	102	58.5
Rhosili Population, 367 Density, 95.1	Church of England	1	33.3	120	30.6		51	
	Wesleyan Methodist	2	66.6	272	69.6		292	
		3		392		106.8	343	93.4

Llangennydd Population, 398 Density, 73.2							
Church of England	1	50.0	100	20.0		200	
Calvinistic Methodist	1	50.0	400	80.0		200	
	2		500		125.6	400	100.5
Llanmadoc Population, 269 Density, 25.6							
Church of England	1	33.3	90	24.3		90	
Calvinistic Methodist	1	33.3	200	54.0		120	
Primitive Methodist	1	33.3	80	21.6		140	
	3		370		137.5	350	130.0
Cheriton Population, 312 Density, 140.7							
Church of England	1	100.0	144	100.0	46.2	67	21.4
Llanrhidian Lower Population, 563 Density, 27.8							
Church of England	1	50.0	400	53.3		340	
Calvinistic Methodist	1	50.0	350	46.6		160	
	2		750		133.2	500	88.8

TABLE 3

PROVISION OF SITTINGS AS A PROPORTION OF THE POPULATION IN EACH PARISH

Parish	Accommodation Rate	Places of Worship
Penmaen	267.7	.. 2
Bishopston ..	143.3	.. 3
Llanmadoc ..	137.5	.. 3
Llanrhidian Lower ..	133.2	.. 2
Llangennydd ..	125.6	.. 2
Llandeilo Talybont ..	110.0	.. 5
Llanrhidian Higher ..	107.3	.. 4
Rhosili	106.8	.. 2
Oxwich	90.5	.. 3
Ilston	89.8	.. 2
Llangyfelach ..	83.7	.. 6
Oystermouth ..	82.0	.. 5

UNION AVERAGE 72.8

Llanddewi ..	66.0	.. 1
Swansea	61.3	.. 12

MANN'S OPTIMUM 58.4

Port Eynon	54.2	.. 1
Cheriton ..	46.2	.. 1
Nicholaston ..	45.4	.. 1
Reynoldston ..	41.5	.. 1
Pennard	37.3	.. 1
Penrice	28.1	.. 1

Table 4

INDEX PF ATTENDANCE (or ATTENDANCE RATE) OF PARISHES IN SWANSEA UNION

Parish	Indeê	Places of Worship
Penmaen	221.0	2
Llanrhidian Higher	139.0	4
Llanmadoc	130.0	3
Bishopston	125.7	3
Llandeilo Talybont	104.4	5
Port Eynon	102.5	1
Llangennydd	100.5	2
Llangyfelach	94.2	6
Rhosili	93.4	2
Oxwich	91.3	3
Llanrhidian Lower	88.8	2
Oystermouth	79.4	5

UNION AVERAGE 71.7

Pennard	63.0	1
Swansea	59.6	12
Llanddewi	58.5	1
Reynoldston	37.7	1
Ilston	28.3	2
Nicholaston	22.7	1
Cheriton	21.4	1
Penrice	16.8	1

TABLE 5

ABSTRACT OF CHAPEL BUILDING

DENOMINATION	Pre-1800	1801-5	1806-10	1811-15	1816-20	1821-25	1826-30	1831-35	1836-40	1841-45	1846-50	TOTAL
Independent	3	2	1	2	1	3	2	3	2	2	4	25
Baptist	1		1	1	1	3	2	1	1	3	4	18
Calvinistic Methodist ..	1	1	1	2	1		1		2	3	1	13
Wesleyan	1		1	3	1	1		3		2		12
Primitive									3		1	4
Unitarians ..	1										1	2
	7	3	4	8	4	7	5	7	8	10	11	74
Church of England ..	20	1							1	1	2	25
Roman Catholic											1	1
Mormons									1			1

TABLE 6

LOCATION OF CHAPEL BUILDING 1801 to 1850

Key : I—Independent : B—Baptist : C—Calvinistic Methodist : W—Wesleyan Methodist : P—Primitive Methodist : U—Unitarian

PARISH	1801 1805	1806 1810	1811 1815	1816 1820	1821 1825	1826 1830	1831 1835	1836 1840	1841 1845	1846 1850	TOTAL
Llangyfelach	I C	I C	B	B	I B	I	I	I B	I B B B C W	B B	20
Llandeilo Talybont		B	I W				B		C		4
Llanrhidian Higher		B					I	C	C	I	5
Swansea			I W		B B W	I B B C	I	I C P	I W	I I B C U	19
Oystermouth				I W			I			I B P	6
Bishopston	I		W				W				3
Pennard											
Ilston				I							1

TABLE 6—*continued*

PARISH	1801 1805	1806 1810	1811 1815	1816 1820	1821 1825	1826 1830	1831 1835	1836 1840	1841 1845	1846 1850	TOTAL
Penmaen					I						I
Nicholaston											
Penrice											
Oxwich		W						P			2
Port Eynon											
Reynoldston											
Llanddewi											
Rhosili							WW				2
Llangennydd			C								I
Llanmadoc				C				P			2
Cheriton											
Llanrhidian Lower ..			C								I
TOTAL	3	4	8	4	7	5	7	8	10	II	67

Part 2
POLITICS

MERIONETH POLITICS IN
MID-NINETEENTH CENTURY

THE POLITICS OF A RURAL ECONOMY

MERIONETH held a special place in the affections of Welsh radical politicians in the 1860's. Its recent history, from the epoch-making election of 1859, through that of 1865, culminating in the glorious victory of '68, seemed to reflect the romantic nature of its natural scenery. The entrenched privilege of its towering landed proprietors which for centuries had over-shadowed, like massive and hostile mountains, the weak and ill-used tenantry of its narrow, remote valleys, had been defied, and the representative of a princely house had retired, beaten from the field. In the reviving historical consciousness of the time parallels between the ancient struggles of the men of Gwynedd for independence and the contemporary struggle of their descendants for their constitutional rights, were inevitably and easily draw. The prolonged contest of the '60's was seen within a context of history which, beginning with the memory of an ancient independence, had appropriated the radicalism of the seventeenth-century, and reached its fulfillment in the vicarious sufferings of the ejected tenantry of 1859, the very names of whose farms—Maes-y-gadfa and Fron-goch—seemed to typify the sanguinary nature of that epic story. The myth and its matyrology were by no means the peculiar possession of Merioneth. Cardiganshire, and, if one searched the records, other counties as well, had suffered and shared this melancholy experience.[1] But in no other county was injustice so well documented, its details so vividly portrayed, so calculated to stir the emotions. The very isolation of the struggle had lent it an heroic quality. Remote from large centres of population, lacking the new kinds of wealth which elsewhere in Wales were beginning to diversify the nature of politics, it had yet achieved a remarkable degree of political independence, and there was justice in the boast that its achievement was its own, the product of the zeal and self-sacrifice of its own organized groups owing but little to the aid or to the example of other Welsh counties. Indeed, Merioneth was the *exempla* of the new political awakening, and a generation later, in 1889, it seemed still to be providing the inspiration and the drive in the Welsh parliamentary party. There was more than a sense of poetic justice, there was the feeling of a providential ordering, when men recollected that T. E. Ellis had been born in that year of persecution thirty years earlier.[2] ' Cangen yn tyvu o'r cyf hwnw yw T. E. Ellis,' wrote the veteran Michael D. Jones, and we should certainly agree with him in his plea that ' it is necessary that someone should write the history of politics in Merioneth since those never-to-be-forgotten elections.'[3] This history, alas, has never been written, though we can be certain of what its main outlines would have been. Beginning with the election of 1859, the following decade would have been regarded as seeing the fulfilment of the attempts begun in that year to change the political representation of the county from its traditional Tory character to a kind of orthodox middle-of-the-road Liberalism. The remaining phase lasting until 1885 would have been depicted as seeing the struggle to realize fully the dreams of such as Michael D. Jones during the previous decade—to see the county represented by a Welsh, nonconformist radical. The return of T. E. Ellis in 1886 would mark the culmination of the struggle, the realization of the aspiration, the achievement of that congruence of representation and county opinion which radicals had long hoped for.[4] It was inevitable that such would have been the organizing principle in their view of their history, and we should hesitate before rejecting the history on account of its political or its ideological commitment, for this unifying theme, this structure based upon a common and a continuing experience, had in some ways corresponded with the reality. But for the modern historian, one hundred years later different question arise. He must ask why it was that the late 1850's and the decade following should have been years of political crisis, and he must explain why that poor and backward and neglected county should suddenly, but in tragic circumstances, achieve its independence.

*   *   *

The formal political history of the county in the nineteenth century up to the election of 1868 can be briefly told.[5] Its outstanding feature in the first half of the century, indeed, for the previous century and more, had been its extraordinary uneventfulness. Contested elections of any kind, whether for matters of principle or as reflecting family feuds, were as rare almost as corn on Cader Idris. Since 1792 Merioneth had been represented by only three men. Sir Robert Williames Vaughan, baronet, of Nannau and Hengwrt, had sat until 1836, a period of forty-four years during which there had been thirteen elections, all of which he had survived unopposed. This was a record to compare with the previous century when the family of Vaughan of Gors-y-gedol had provided the county's member, the seat passing like an entailed estate from father to son through three generations. Sir Robert Williames Vaughan would also have kept the seat in his family or in that of a relative's had he been able: it was certainly in his gift, and it was his nominee, Sir Richard Richards of Caerynwch (the son of ' baron Richards '),[6] who succeeded him in 1836. The contested election of that year,[7] when he opposed by Sir William Wynn, of Maes-y-neuadd, merely demonstrated in summary fashion the perpetuation into the post-reform nineteenth century of the traditions of the previous century. The return of W. W. E. Wynne, of Peniarth, in 1852, on the retirement of Richards, was similarly within the tradition, being achieved with scarcely a murmur of dissent in a county which by now was the most nonconformist in Wales. To this tradition of uneventfulness was now, by the middle of the century, added the further characteristic of anochronism, of an apparent passivity in a body of notably nonconformist voters who appeared to be content to be represented by a renowned churchman.

Yet little, if anything, was heard in the way of criticism or of complaint within the county until the eve of the famous election of 1859. This was an election memorable in its unexpected revelations concerning the political awakening within the county, memorable in its achievement, and creative in its joyless consequences. Suddenly, there was a Liberal candidate in the field, David Williams, of Castell-Deudraeth,[8] a Welshman, not a nonconformist, but, in comparison with his aristocratic opponent, a man of the people. His success, despite his failure to win the election, was spectacular. With scarcely any formal electioneering on his part he yet came within 39 votes of gaining the seat. Well might enthusiastic Liberals regard the defeat as ' a thrilling augury and sure precursor of a future victory '.[9] But six years later, in 1865, when the religious anachronism was even more pronounced, W. W. E. Wynne having been replaced by his son, W. R. M. Wynne,[10] a pronounced high Churchman if not a Puseyite, there had been no advance on the positions gained in 1859. Wynne's majority was only slightly down, and the failure was a bitter disappointment. But the explanation for it was clear. It lay in the terror which had struck at the heart of the nonconformist tenants of some of the greatest landowners of the county. On two estates near Bala it was alleged that five tenants of R. W. Price,[11] of Rhiwlas, had been evicted, and on the Glan-llyn estate of Sir Watkin Williams Wynn of Wynnstay,[12] there had been seven evictions, and a further seven who had remained neutral had had their rents raised. All those who had suffered had been nonconformists, and all had refused to vote according to the expressed wishes of their Tory landlords. Four of the evicted were relatives of T. E. Ellis,[18] of Cynlas, who had been born in that year, and his judgement, years later, as to the effect of those evictions on the communities in which they took place and throughout the county, expressed vividly the impression they had made at the time. ' It will take years,' he declared in his evidence before the Royal Commission on Land in Wales in 1893, ' to forget the thrill of horror which spread through Wales, more especially among its tenantry ' when these deeds became known. There was only one eviction in the hundred of Penllyn—indeed, in the whole of the county—after the election of 1865, and Ellis was probably right in judging that if the intention in 1859 had been to clamp down on the political aspirations of the tenantry, the attempt had succeeded. Henceforth, in Ellis's words, the tenantry remained ' submissive and subservient ' until the Reform Act of 1867 and the Ballot Act of 1872 brought them some degree of emancipation. The victory of 1868, therefore, when W. R. M. Wynne retired rather than continue a contest as costly in human relations as in cash, seems almost to have been fought at a dist-

ance, in Parliament rather than in Penllyn, in the slate quarries
of Ffestiniog rather than on the chastened fields of Maes-y-
gadfa.

*   *   *

To explain these apparent paradoxes—of an awakening which
served only to emphasise the depth of slumber, and of a victory
that tasted of the bitterness of defeat—it is necessary to look
closely at the societies in which these events were taking place.
Contemporaries were well aware that the lack of any real political activity in the county during the previous century and a
half was the expression in institutional terms of the structure of
society during that period. Politics, whether at the national or
local level, had remained, well into the 1850s, the preserve of
the landed gentry and of the great landed proprietors. According to the *Return of Owners of Land*[14] there were a total of 651
owners of one acre and upwards in the county, but the owners of
substantial states numbered only a fraction of these. There
were 87 owners of more than 1,000 acres, of whom 60 owned
less than 2,000 acres, another 17 with estates of up to 5,000
acres, 3 of up to 10,000 acres, and finally 5 at the top owning
10,000 acres. This pattern of landownership, with the bulk of
county property concentrated in few hands, was common, of
course, to the whole country. It constituted the end-product of
forces making for the consolidation of large estates which had
been taking place in Wales, as elsewhere in the British Isles,
since the sixteenth century and earlier. In Merioneth it had
produced a pattern in which nearly half (48 *per cent*) of the total
property of the county (excluding waste) was owned by some
18 proprietors of 3,000 acres and upwards. Within this group,
again, variations were enormous. Five proprietors of 10,000
acres and upwards owned one quarter (25.7 *per cent*) of the total
acreage of the county, ranging in size from the Wynnstay
estates of 20,295 acres to those of Nanney with 10,536 acres.
In other words, the New Domesday Survey showed that less
than 1 *per cent* (0.76) of the landed proprietors owned more than
one quarter of the land of the county, and that approximately
another quarter was the property of another group numbering
13, or 2 *per cent* of the total number of landowners.

Equally important for the purpose of this analysis is the geographical distribution of these great estates. In the 1840's there were a total of eight proprietors owning more than 5,000 acres, of whom five held more than 10,000 acres.[15] Of this latter group, the largest agglomeration belonged to Sir W. W. Wynn, of Wynnstay, and comprised 15,397 acres. Next, in order of extent, came the Rhiwlas estate of 14,582 acres. Sir Robert Williames Vaughan's estates totalled 11,867 acres, while those of the Nanney estate, at that time held by trustees under the will of the Reverend J. Nanney, totalled 10,536 acres. Finally, in this group, the Mostyn estates measured 10,127 acres. The three remaining estates of more than 5,000 and less than 10,000 acres belonged to the following: C. H. Vaughan, Esq., of Rûg (9,287 acres), Athelstan Corbet, Esq., of Ynys-y-maengwyn (7,956 acres), and W. Ormsby-Gore, Esq., of Glyn Cywarch (7,836 acres). It is interesting and revealing to note, that these estates, in the aggregate totalling nearly one third of the total cultivated area of the county, gave their owners, by reason of their distribution, an unchallenged supremacy within the particular regions and areas where they were located. Although most of them spread over several parishes, sometimes extending throughout almost the whole county, their nuclei were invariably compact parishes. The Nannau-Hengwrt properties, for instance, were very widespread, extending from the parish of Gwyddelwern in the north-east tip of the hundred of Edeirnion to Tywyn in the south of the county, in all covering sixteen parishes. But the bulk of the estate was in the Dolgellau area where the original Nannau estate of nearly 5,000 acres made Sir Robert Vaughan the predominant landowner and premier gentleman of the region. The Wynnstay estates were to be found in eight parish in Penllyn, Mawddwy, Ardudwy and Edeirnion. The largest single holding was in the parish of Trawsfynydd (6,731 acres), but the richest, most profitable estates were in Penllyn where he owned a total of 5,754 acres, later to be added to when he absorbed Lord Vivian's estate of 600 acres in Llanuwchllyn. Rhiwlas was the most compact and probably the richest of the large estates. Consisting of 14,582 acres, with a central core of 9,303 acres in Llanfor, all the properties were in adjacent parishes, all immediately accessible from the ancestral seat. The Mostyn lands of 10,127 acres were situated, for the most part, in Ardudwy, in the maritime parishes south of the Mawddach estuary, with the central core in the parishes of Llanenddwyn and the adjacent parish of Llanbedr and Llanfair-Harlech. In the same region, with its core in Llanfihangel-y-traethau were the properties of the Ormsby-Gore family, consisting of 7,836 acres. In the far eastern portion of the county, in Edeirnion, the Rûg estates, totalling 9,287 acres spread over seven parishes, were centred on Corwen where C. H. Vaughan had his seat and 5,950 acres. In the south of the county there were two large proprietors, namely the Nanney etsates of 10,536 acres centred on Tal-y-llyn, and the Ynys-y-maengwyn estate of Athelstan Corbet, one of the richest in the county, centred on Towyn, where he owned 6,214 acres with smaller properties in the neighbouring parishes of Pennal and Tal-y-llyn.

These large proprietors, therefore, were as a group, ubiquitous, but as individuals, their power was circumscribed by the location of their major holdings. In Penllyn, R. W. Price, and Sir W. W. Wynn were obviously the most powerful, C. H. Vaughan in Edeirnion, Sir R. W. Vaughan in Dolgellau, and Corbet and the Nanneys in Ystumanner, and the Mostyns and Ormsby-Gore families in western Ardudwy. Sir W. W. Wynn was probably the man whose influence was most widespread.

The estates of substantial owners of between 2,000 and 3,000 acres, as we have seen, were more numerous, and together they formed an impressive power group in the county. Some of these estates were very compact and rich. For example, C. T. Thruston, of Talgarth Hall, Towyn owned nearly 4,000 acres mainly in Towyn and the neighbouring parish of Pennal. Further west, John Bird, of Llan-y-Mawddwy held 3,171 acres in Mallwyd and Llan-y-Mawddwy. The most compact medium sized estate in this region, if not in the whole of the county was Peniarth, the home of the Wynne family (and later of the Peniarth Manuscripts). In 1840, this estate consisted of just over 4,000 acres and was entirely within the parish of Llanegryn. Further north, in the Dolgellau area, landowners such sa these were more numerous. One of these was Richards of Caerynwch. The Dolgellau estate was a little over 2,000 acres,

the remainder of the total of 3,986 acres being in the neighbouring parish of Mallwyd, with one small farm in Llandderfel.
Another of the lesser squires was Hugh John Reveley, of Bryn-
y-gwin, who owned a compact estate of 800 acres in Talybont
with another 2,020 acres in Llanfrothen. On the western side
of the county the leading medium-sized owners were Richard
Anthony Poole and John Ellercet Boulcott, while in the north
Mrs. Oakeley owned nearly 3,000 acres, Lord Newborough
1,895 acres, Lord Tottenham, William John Banks, and George
Casson were among the most important and, probably, the
richest, for it was here that slate-quarrying was expanding
fastest. In Penllyn, Henry Richardson of Aber-Hirnant owned
3,000 acres in the parish of Llanfor, Thomas Fitzhugh 1,848,
with Hugh Jones, Isaac Gilbertson, and T. P. Anwyl in the
same class.

Thus, to sum up, it can be seen that there were great variations in ownership within the ranks of the landed gentry of
Merioneth, and that one of its outstanding features was the
disproportionate share held by a very few families. Merioneth
was a county of small squires, but a few towered above the rest.
Ownership of extensive lands did not necessarily connote proportionate wealth. Merioneth was a poor county, and nowhere
so far as one can tell, not even in the few low-lying parishes
where intensive arable cultivation was possible, did incomes
approximate to the £1 per acre on which Bateman based his
analysis[16] of landownership later in the century. Thus according to the New Domesday Survey, only ten of Merioneth's landowners qualified for the description ' great ', that is, by having
incomes of over £3,000 per annum from their estates. R. W.
Price's 17,717 acres brought him an income of £9,386, which
was substantially more than Sir W. W. Wynn's 20,295 acres
which gave an income of only £6,800.[17] In such purely agricultural estates, much of them extensive moorland and mountain pasture, the average value of land was well below 10s. per
acre. Incomes were substantially higher than this only in those
areas where industry, in the form of slate-quarrying, was di-
versifying the economy.[18] But such areas were well-defined and
largely confined to the north of the county, in the Ffestiniog
area, to the north west, in Corwen, and south-west of Dol-

gellau.[19] Only in areas such as these could substantial rentals from minerals compensate for modest holdings of land, and increasingly as the century advanced, it was the relatively small landowners of the Ffestiniog region who were overtaking the more ancient large estates in wealth and prestige.

If such was the over-all pattern of landownership it is important to note that it was reproduced in miniature in the individual parishes. For instance, in Tywyn the Ynys-y-maengwyn estates comprised one third of the total acreage of the parish. In fact, Corbet himself and his neighbour Thruston between them owned more than half of the parish. The same two held a similar predominance in the parish of Pennal, though here there were more gentry families of middling range with, by parish standards, substantial estates. In Tal-y-llyn, the Nanney estates were incomparably the largest, while in Ardudwy there were no landlords to compare with the Mostyn and Ormsby-Gore families. Generally speaking, landownership within individual parishes was a microcosm of the county as a whole.

It is possible by using the Tithe Apportionment surveys to analyse closely the pattern of landownership in individual parishes, and, since the purpose of this study is to seek the causes of the political awakening of 1859, it might be illuminating if we look microscopically at those parishes in which political evictions took place. Taking the parish of Llanuwch-llyn first, we find that there were 14 landlords of all kinds, of whom 5 owned more than 500 acres, accounting between them for more than a half of the total acreage of nearly 12,000 acres (including waste). The largest of these was Sir W. W. Wynn's estate of 7,716 acres—two-thirds of the total acreage.[20] R. W. Price, Esq., of Rhiwlas had five farms totalling 874 acres. Next came Thomas Fitzhugh, Esq., who also had five farms totalling 741 acres. With the exception of one estate of 292 acres, all the other privately owned estates were small, the largest being 100 acres, the smallest 17 acres. Of the total of 14 estates, consisting of 40 properties supporting families, only 3 belonged to resident freeholders, and these were small farms—70,33 and 30 acres respectively. This was well below the average size of tenant holdings—about 90 acres: in fact, the farms of the largest proprietors were generally—with the exception of Lord Vivian's—considerably larger than this.[21] The Rhiwlas farms averaged 175 acres, though of course, this average conceals some wide variations. The pattern of Llanycil was complicated by the presence of the town of Bala, yet here again it was similar to that in Llanuwchllyn. The total acreage was 12,115 acres, and the bulk of the land was held by large proprietors, namely, R. W. Price, Sir W. W. Wynn, Charles Wynn, and John Davies. These four between them owned 6,772 acres, slightly more than half the total acreage of the parish, and averaging nearly 1,700 acres apiece. Apart from these, there were only three estates of more than 400 acres (average 449), two of more than 300 acres (average 340), 2 of 200 acres (average 245), and ten of 100 acres (average 146). There were 34 farms of less than 50 acres.

In the adjacent parish of Llanfor this pattern was even more pronounced. Here, nearly a half of the total acreage was owned by one man, namely, R. W. Price, of Rhiwlas, whose total holding was 9,303 acres. There was no one in the parish to compare with this extraordinary possession, not even Henry Richardson, Esq., of Aber-hirnant, who owned 3,030 acres, or Sir W. W. Wynn whose lands measured 2,250 acres. Between them, these three gentlemen owned nearly three-quarters of the available land (14,583 out of 20,030 acres or 72 *per cent*), leaving only 5,447 acres for the remaining 32 proprietors. Some of these held fairly substantial proportions of this remainder. Sir R. W. Vaughan (850 acres), Thomas Fitzhugh (588 acres), Charles Wynn (571 acres), Lord Mostyn (324 acres), Hugh Jones (341 acres), and Edward Jones (229 acres) held between them almost another 3,000 acres. The remaining 23 landowners, owner-occupiers, for the most part, held very small holdings indeed. In Llandderfel, again, three proprietors between them owned nearly one half of the total acreage of the parish—3,429 out of a total of 7,794 acres. R. W. Price, here again, was by far the greatest landowner, holding 1,556 acres as compared with the 987 acres of Lord Ward, and the 886 acres of Sir W. W. Wynn. If we add to these the total of 1,216 acres owned by another three medium sized proprietors, it will be seen that the remaining 14 were very small fry indeed. Sir W. W. Wynn was the major landowner in Llangower, having an estate there of 826 acres. R. W. Price came next with 362, with Robert Wynn and Thomas Fitzhugh owning 214 and 285 acres respectively. Of the remaining 14 proprietors, 6 were above 100 acres, and 8 below 50 acres in the size of their holdings.

It would be tedious to survey all the Merioneth parishes in this way and we can safely make the point that they all conformed, in varying degrees, to the basic pattern, namely, of a concentration of the ownership of available land in few hands. We must recall, also, that the majority of such large proprietors in individual parishes were landowners in other, usually adjacent, parishes. Their property in any one particular parish might be small, but such small properties might be representative of greater holdings elsewhere, near by, or at a distance. Sir Watkin's holdings in Llangower might be small, but behind it lay the huge estate in the county at large, and behind that, again, the 145,000 acres of his Welsh lands. The difference socially between the various grades within the proprietor class was therefore very great, and greater still, possibly, was the social difference between the landed proprietor and the small farmer, whether owner-occupier or tenant. Freeholders were, in any case, small in number in relation to the total farming community. In the parishes of Penllyn, for instance, the proportion was something like four tenants to one freeholder. Put in that way, it is very doubtful whether the true significance of the social pattern is revealed, for there was but little social difference between the small freeholder and the tenant farmer. Indeed, many a tenant farmer was better off than many of the lesser freeholders. As often as not, in their incomes and their way of life, they were well-nigh indistinguishable. Security in a hundred acres of so of land bringing in a bare subsistence with no prospect of additions to the holding might not be more attractive than a tenancy of the same acreage with the possibility of moving to a better farm. At least, there was an element of competition in the one absent in the other. But what was significant about the social pattern consequent upon the aggrandisement of most of the land in a few hands was the bifurcation of rural society into two unequal portions—the large proprietors, on the one hand, and the mass of tenant farmers and small, economically confined freeholders, on the other. Conflict of a political kind might emerge from the tensions inherent in such a situation. Moreover, given this kind of inbalance of economic power it would be likely to emerge initially within the gentry group itself where, as we have seen, landed wealth was almost as disproportionately distributed as it was between that class and the dependent classes below them.

We get a closer and more vivid impression of the structure of this agricultural society when we examine in greater detail some of the communities in Penllyn.[22] The township of Penmaen in the parish of Llanfor may be taken as typical.[23] It was a scattered community of 42 households consisting of 252 men, women and children. Rhiwlas, the ancestral home and demesne of R. W. Price, was situated in this area, a veritable palace among its surrounding farms and dwelling houses. The demesne was of 300 acres,[24] more than twice the size of any farm in the neighbourhood. The average size of these was about 60 acres, ranging from 160 acres to as little as 8 acres. 26 of the households were farms, 9 were the homes of agricultural labourers, and there were also the homes of one gamekeeper, one fuller, and two carpenters. Two of the households were the homes of widows living alone. The size of the community relative to the number of households should be noted, 42 households containing 252 persons. Families, as such, were not large. The 25 farmsteads averaged 2.9 children a household, as did the 3 small-holdings. Agricultural labourers seemed to have fewer children—1.9 per household. The largest families were those of craftsmen, which averaged 4.2 each. What swelled the number of inhabitants was the servant population. There were 25 male, and 24 female servants distributed among 14 farms. The only farms without servants were those too small to support them, or those where the children were of an age to man the farm without outside assistance. Even farms which were small-holdings—like Hendre, of 17 acres—required the assistance of at least one female servant. All farms of 50 acres and over supported two or more servants, and since, in this township, all servants appear to have lived in, the size of the households was correspondingly inflated, being about seven persons per household.

In the adjacent townships of Garn and Ucheldre, 38 households contained a total population of 246 persons, 119 males, 127 females. Of these, 150 were farmers, or the children of farmers, 48 were servants, 26 male, 22 female, living in farming households, 37 were of labouring families, 10 in the family of a wheelwright, and 3 in the house of the toll-gate keeper. Here again, the distinction between farmer and labourer breaks down, for 14 of the 28 farms were under 50 acres in size, and since some of them supported large families, it is probable that such households must have supplied labour for the larger farms, in addition to the 8 households of labourers. Some of the farms were very large. Nant-fach measured 360 acres—363 in the Tithe Award—and the tenant, David Jones, and his wife, both of them approaching seventy years of age, found it necessary to employ 4 male labourers and 3 female servants, all of whom were unmarried and living-in, in addition to the labour of a son aged 26 years and a daughter aged 29 (both unmarried). David Jones, Gydros, again, who, with his unmarried son (aged 38) and daughter (aged 33), farmed 300 acres, employed 5 male labourers and 2 female servants. Ellis Jones, Maesygadfa, aged 55, farmed 240 acres, and employed a total of 6 servants, 3 of whom were male, in addition to the labour of two of his four children (a son aged 13 years and a daughter aged 16). Such farms as these, however, were exceptionally large. In the particular districts under review, there were only 3 of more than 300 acres, 2 of 200 acres, and 3 of 100 acres. The remaining 20 farms of under 100 acres, averaged only about 50 acres each, so that the large ones must have appeared large indeed, and their occupants have a correspondingly higher status in the community. These were the aristocrats of the tenantry.

The villages in the rural communities were, of course, more highly diversified socially, but were small and closely integrated into their hinterlands. Llandderfel, in the township of Llan, for instance, was a community of 384 people living in 89 houses, and consisting mainly of craftsmen and agricultural labourers. The latter, as we have seen, were required in considerable numbers on the farms in the neighbourhood. In most townships in Penllyn, whether entirely rural or semi-urbanized, there were groupings of labourers' cottages. In Llandderfel there were 10 households whose heads described themselved as farmers but whose holdings averaged less than 10 acres and whom one assumes, therefore, to have been in fact labourers by occupation. Also, there was a slate-quarry labourer, and a lodger described as a labourer. Apart from 9 or so farmers one of whom farmed 190 acres on the outskirts of the village, the remaining households consisted of the families of craftsmen, a few professional men, shopkeepers, and paupers. There were 5 stone-masons, 4 shoemakers, 3 carpenters, 2 smiths, a plasterer, a potter, a furrier, a tanner, and a weaver. There were 2 wool-manufacturers, 2 corn-dealers, a butter merchant, a miller, a shopkeeper, 2 innkeepers, and one ale-house keeper. The professional men included a lawyer, and the rector of the parish. Finally, there were 15 paupers living alone.

Most of the villages of Penllyn were of this kind, service communities, providing a reserve of labour, the crafts necessary to satisfy basic agricultural, household and personal needs, outlets for markets and exchange, professional expertise, and, of course, places of worship. Some were larger and socially more diversified. Glan-llyn for instance, which contained Glan-llyn Hall, the residence of John Williams, land agent to Sir Watkin, who figures so largely and rarely to his credit in the Welsh Land Commission Report, had a greater diversity of craftsmen, and more specialized shopkeepers. For instance, there were two wheelwrights, a clockmaker, a draper, and a baker. There was a large woollen factory, a school, more professional people, and generally, it would appear to have been a more prosperous place than Llandderfel, reflecting the richer type of farmer and the economic and social demands of a large house and demense.

*   *   *

There can be no doubt that life in such rural communities was extremely hard. Contemporaries talked and wrote about the unremitting toil at all seasons of the year as the lot of the agriculturalist.[25] The labour of women and of girls, and even of small children was essential in the economy.[26] We have seen how, in the pre-technological age, even small-holdings required the labour of at least two men and a woman. Moreover, most of these farms in the upland areas were still in process of being tamed from the mountainsides and made fit to support cattle and a little oats. One gets the impression that pressure of population on available resources must have been acute, and though there are no recorded disasters during these years, of famine or extreme dearth, the economy of these households, including the large farms, must have been only a little above subsistence level. The farmer lived entirely on the produce of his land, and since the first charge on his income was a cash rent invariably high in proportion to his income, he was forced to live with extreme frugality. The nutritional value of the food generally eaten, lacking in foods of high protein value, has been made clear in the evidence given before the Welsh Land Commission and elsewhere, as likewise the fact that their slender profits tended to be ploughed back into their holdings in the shape of improvements or, occasionally, in the case of the substantial holdings, kept in reserve to set up their sons in farms elsewhere. The high proportion of unmarried males and females testifies to the increasing pressure of a rising population on available land.[27] The alternative to marriage late in life and relative security was probably, for the sons of farmers, early marriage and the insecurity of the agricultural labourer.[28] Or emigration. The natural gross increase in population for the county as a whole was rising throughout the early decades of the century.[29] During the decade 1851-61, natural increase was of the order of 9.17 *per cent*, in the following decade 12.88 *per cent*. The actual increase in population, however, was considerably less than this. In the decade 1851-61 it was 3.75 *per cent*, indicating a net loss of 5.42 *per cent*, or 2,780. The decade 1861-71 shows a rise in the natural increase to 12.28 *per cent*, and an actual rise to 15.55 *per cent*, indicating an in-flow of population from outside the county. This phenomenon, however, does not invalidate our thesis of a declining population in the county as a whole, for the statistics show that it was not the rural areas which were retaining their natural increase and receiving additional people, but rather, the new developing industrial regions, in particular, the slate-quarry region of Ffestiniog. The slate-quarry districts of Ffestiniog and Corwen showed an increase in population of 33.76 *per cent* and 7.67 *per cent* res-

pestively in the decade 1831-41. By 1851 this increase had
slackened off considerably, particularly in Ffestiniog (4.67 *per
cent* and 2.18 *per cent* in Corwen), and in the decade 1851-61
both showed a net loss by migration. The net loss in the rural
areas of Bala and Dolgellau during that decade was very heavy.
In the Bala region, a natural increase of 7.81 *per cent* became a
net loss of 13.51 *per cent*, and in Dolgellau a natural increase of
5.88 became a net loss of 9.65 *per cent*. This indicates that the
decade 1851-61 was not a time of prosperity in either the rural
or the industrial areas. In the previous decade, while the slate-
quarrying areas were receiving additional people from outside,
the rural areas were losing them. In fact, while Bala and Dolgellau lost 457 people, Ffestiniog and Corwen together gained
a total of 1,051. But in 1851-61, Corwen lost 446, Ffestiniog 172
Dolgellau 1,252, and Bala 910. By the end of the next decade,
1861-71, the development of the Ffestiniog quarries had grown
apace, and the parish gained 2,780 by immigration, in addition
to its high rate of natural increase, while Bala lost more than a
half of its natural increase by migration. That these migrants
moved north into Ffestiniog is a fair conclusion. They did not
move into Corwen: for this district continued to lose population,
and the Dolgellau mining areas, never as great as those of
Ffestiniog, absorbed the surplus of its own region.

Looking again at the Bala region it would appear therefore,
that in terms of population, it had been for some considerable
time, and still remained at the end of our period, stagnant. In
the 40 years since 1831 its population had fallen by 50—from
6,654 to 6,604. But its natural increase had been at the county
average from decade to decade—7.81 *per cent* in 1861, 9.27 *per
cent* in 1871. Therefore, it was producing people for other areas:
it could not support them itself. But it was precisely this area
which experienced the first political awakening in the county,
and it was this area which remained the power-house of political
ideology and organization during that critical decade after
1859. It is central to the thesis of this study that it was an economically stagnant part of the county, the breeding-ground of
frustrations rather than hope, which provided the grievances,
the ideology, the organization, while it was the expanding
industrial areas of the county which were able successfully to

activate them creatively within an existing political system, and in so doing, change that system into something new.

*   *   *

That there were grievances and social tensions present in these rural communities is undeniable. Dr. Peter Roberts, in his brilliant studies of the gentry in eighteenth-century Merioneth,[30] has concluded that the causes of the major grievances of non-residence, insecurity of tenure, lack of confidence between landlord and tenant were present by the end of that century, and we know that developments in the course of the nineteenth were such as to exacerbate them. But to what extent they were being felt as grievances, that is, isolated and objectivized, rationalized and judged against an idealized view of society, is a different matter. Much of the evidence, though not all, for believing that these grievances were deep-seated and of ancient origin, and sufficiently arduous to provoke political action comes from the evidence given by tenant-farmers or their spokesmen before the Royal Commission on Land in Wales and Monmouthshire of 1893, and from the impressive body of statistical material which its Secretary, Lleufer Thomas, appended to the *Report*. We should hesitate before accepting at its face value much of this evidence as being an accurate reflection or statement of the mind of the tenantry in the 1850's, and in particular, that this evidence afforded a fair statement of the basic relations in rural society, namely, those between landlord and tenant. It is true that some of the witnesses could remember conditions as they had been in the 1850s and 1860s with quite astonishing detail: peasants have long memories. Yet it is worth remembering that they were not merely thirty years older when they appeared before the Royal Commission, but that they had also lived through a bitter depression which had already lasted for over twenty years, and there is nothing like prolonged and deepening depression, particularly at a time of contemporaneous boom in industrial societies, to sharpen the edges of the mind and excite questions about the social order. Moreover, during that interval they had become better educated and, above all, had been exposed to an acute analysis of the ills of agriculture and of the necessary remedies in language they understood. By the 1890s in other words, they had been provided with an ideology and a programme of political action. But did these necessary elements of ratiocination and of organization exist in the 1850s ?

We must avoid falling into the contrary error of arguing that because the evidence does not seem to exist that therefore the problem did not exist. Evidence of conflict, of cleavage, or of tension between proprietor and tenant is difficult to find, but this may be because the evidence we look for is provided precisely only in times of crisis or of abnormal tension. The 1850s were not such a period. The elements of conflict were there but had not yet been rendered combustible: the tinder was dry, the powder laid, but what would provide the spark ?

Whether this interpretation is correct must await a great deal of research into the quality of rural life. We know that life for the farmers and labourers and rural artisans was hard, the lot of children and of women harsh and often cruel. Hard work from dawn to dusk on land that could never be one's own was rewarded meanly in terms of shelter, of food, and of leisure, and self-improvement was well-nigh impossible. Everywhere man was reminded of his subjection to his superiors. But this had always been so: such was the immemorial lot of the peasant. Insecurity of tenure was a reality, probably, for most tenants, though this would have been less of a preoccupation than the upward movement of rents. And always there was visible a thrusting pressure on land. Factors such as these were undoubtedly present, but one is left with the impression, nevertheless, that in fact farms remained, more often than not, for long periods, even generations, in the same families. If rents rose, landlords could not generally have acted tyrannically: quite apart from the force of public opinion, of standards of honour which counted for something, estates were not always regarded merely as economic units to be ruthlessly exploited even at the cost of destroying organic human relationships. The final grievance mentioned in the Report, that of absentee landlords, likewise, does not seem to have been excessive, nor does the familiar one of alien agents apply. Certainly, these were not the case in Penllyn. Rhiwlas lay at the very centre of the estate. Its owner R. W. Price, was never absent and the town of Bala was never without the weight of his influence in its affairs. Sir W. W. Wynn lived thirty miles away at Wynnstay, and he visited his estates in Penllyn regularly.[31] His agent lived at Glan-llyn. Both these landlords could converse with their tenants in Welsh, and John Williams, the Glan-llyn agent, was a pure Welshman. Most of the other landlords we have mentioned were Welshmen, and most were resident. Certainly, Sir R. W. Vaughan was rarely absent from Dolgellau, a Lloyd from Rhaggat, a Vaughan from Rûg, or a Wynne from Peniarth, or a Corbet from Ynys-y-maengwyn. To adopt the classification of the *Report* of owners into estate-owners and residential-owners,[32] then, the great majority of Merioneth landlords came under the first class, and were owners of ancient estates by inheritance upon which they were resident. English-speaking landowners, owners of recently formed or purchased estates, seem also to have been resident or partly resident.

What impression, then, of society, of the relation of landlord and tenant do we get from the bits of evidence available ? It was certainly a deferential society, the mass of the community reacting with proper subjection to the minute *élite* above them as they had done for untold generations. Nor, generally, was this subjection resented. It was accepted as a fact of life, and there was never any question of resolving the tensions which inevitably arose between landlord and tenant, or between the *élite* as a whole and the rest except within the terms of the immemorial organic combination. Such were the facts of rural society, and such, as we shall see, were the social implications of religious observance. One gets the impression, indeed, that relations on a formal level were good. For instance, when Wynnstay burned down in March 1858—a fire, incidentally, which destroyed priceless manuscripts—there was no doubting the genuineness of the sorrow felt throughout north Wales at this tragedy. Meetings were held up and down the country to condole with the family and to consider ways and means of expressing this regret in a practical fashion.[33] Most places, incidentally, appear to have presented the baronet with illuminated addresses, coffee sets, and elaborately bound Bibles.[34] Most of these addresses, in the inflated language of the time, expressed the belief of the people generally in ' the blessings we enjoy in this country by the wise arrangements of Providence in ordaining the subordination of various degrees '.[35] This was a belief familiar to the Elizabethan forbears of this people and by no means the characteristic doctrine of any one stratum of society or religious sect. These were the sentiments expressed by a deputation from the Quarterly Meeting of the Calvinistic Methodists held at Llanidloes in April 1858 to Sir Watkin.[36] Claiming to represent 70,000 of their adherents the deputation addressed Sir Watkin as a ' gentleman who is distinguished amongst the aristocracy of Wales, as being pre-eminently the lover of the country and the friend of his people, and who, like his father and uncle, has shown himself far removed from bigotry and intolerance, and has firmly and practically main-tained the principles of civil and religious liberty '. It might be suspected that this was flattery, a prudent diplomatic gesture, on the part of dependents becoming aware of the strength of their organization. But such a cynical view would not appear to be consonant with the facts, for Sir Watkin's record as a land-lord throughout north Wales was good.

But if we are justified in suspecting that kind of public, formal occasion by a denomination notoriously prepared to accept the powers that be, what are we to make of the Bala meeting of 25 March, 1858 to sympathize with the baronet ?[37] The meeting was designed ' to elicit the feeling of all classes, without distinction of rank or party ', and the final speaker was the Reverend Lewis Edwards. Here was a man of outstanding integrity, of intellectual power, and of great clarity and depth of vision who knew that area and its people better than most. He spoke, he said, not on the principle that political gratitude con-sists in a keen sense of expected benefits: a criticism which, as we have seen, might be applied to the formal addresses alluded to: for he was nothing to Sir Watkin, nor Sir Watkin to him. But rather because he deemed it ' his duty to come forward and bear my humble testimony to his work, both as landlord and as a man '. He judged him not on his politics:every man had a right to his own opinions: but ' by his acts: and I cannot but think that, practically, he is a more liberal man than many of these who make loud professions of their liberality: and in the present state of political parties, if I had a vote in the county of Denbigh, I should certainly give it to Sir Watkin '. He then proceeded to say some things which are extremely revealing of the true nature of the rural situation—things which might have been construed as an apologia, which may have had an ironic purpose, which almost certainly sounded a warning. Welsh landlords, he said, had to contend with great difficulties in coming to understand their tenantry fully and properly. There was the difficulty of a diversity of language, and the fact that the Welsh peasant was extremely reserved. It would be a mistake, he implied, to confuse this reserve with toadyism or flunkyism, for it was the expression of a natural dignity and innate intelligence. Moreover, they were an eminently religious people:

> ' who read their Bibles, who are taught to fear God, and to honour those who are in authority over them.' 'I know them well,' he said, ' and I speak what I know when I aver before this meeting, that there is not a class of men on the face of the earth who have a more genuine and heartfelt regard for their landlords than the tenancy of Wales. Wherever there is a landlord who has sufficient sense to treat his tenants as rational creatures, his sayings are looked upon as oracles, and every kind word from the lips of the "great man", as they call him, is a feast to their souls. And, here lies the wealth of Sir Watkin Williams Wynn. He may be rich as the owner of Wynnstay, and of countless broad acres in various parts of the Principality. He may be one of the greatest landed proprietors in Great Britain. But he is far richer in that of which no accident can deprive him—the untaught respect and affection of the people of North Wales.'

To seek to find ironic intentions in such sentiments would amount to gratuitous folly: their genuineness lies in their very conventionality.

Coming nearer, to Penllyn, one cannot, similarly, doubt the affection and respect of the tenantry for R. W. Price, of Rhiwlas, the premier landowner. He was held to be a good landlord. His estates were considered to be the best managed in the county, and his relations with his tenants were good. He was noted for his charities, and however different his religious view, it was nonconformists of one kind and another who benefited from his annual largesse, and nonconformist deacons—including one who was later to be ejected—who distributed it.[38] Hence the shocked reaction of horror when his anger was turned against them in 1859. On his side was disillusionment, a sense of betrayal, of kindness requited with contempt. On their side, the sudden realization that the old attitudes of deference and subjection extended even to politics, in particular, to aspects of politics which involved principle and the basic human rights of individual choice. It was the first indication that the immemorial combination of the country-side was breaking down.

*   *   *

The question we now have to answer is, how did politics of this kind enter into the relations between landlord and tenant ? The short answer is that as a general rule they did not. Politics were, as they always had been, the concern and preserve of the upper classes of rural society. In the event of a tenant having a vote he voted, as of course, with his landlord. Lewis Edwards, as we have seen, referred eloquently to the innate intelligence and shrewdness of the Welsh peasant. But how well informed was he on political issues ? Most of the tenantry and labourers, half a century after the time of Thomas Charles, could read: according to evidence in 1837 very few farmers were illiterate at that time.[39] But what did they read ? The denominational magazines which appear to have circulated fairly widely, carried some political reporting and comment of a very general kind, but it was always subordinated to the religious material, and in effect, amounted to very little. Some of these magazines —the ones most likely to circulate in that fastness of Calvinistic Methodism—tried deliberately, as of policy, to eschew political discussion. Some Welsh newspapers, weeklies published in Denbigh and Caernarfon, circulated, but again we do not know how far they penetrated into the hinterland of the towns. Indeed we should be wary of accepting at their face value the public statements of agitators and would-be leaders of public opinion who invariably suffered from the common error of exaggerating the effects of their own eloquence. In private, as witness the correspondence of Walter Griffith, the Anti

Corn-Law League lecturer, and others at that time, they took a far more realistic and pessimistic view.[40] Should we not rather listen to the farmers themselves ? One of them, responding to some peculiarly insensitive, stupid, and cruel attacks on the Merioneth farmers for failing to vote Liberal which Thomas Gee constantly published in his *Baner ac Amserau Cymru*, pointed out that when one reflected on the fact that many of the voters lived in remote and inaccessible folds of the mountains—as if sheltering from the riotous world—and national and international politics were entirely foreign to them, was it strange that they should be ignorant of political issues and personalities ? Such voters might sometimes have heard of the candidates: in 1859 they knew that Wynne was a gentleman who had done some good locally, but they had never heard of David Williams, his opponent.[41] Ignorance about formal politics must have been very deep and widespread in the county among the tenant farmers, and somehow a massive programme in educating them in their political rights and duties would have to be carried through before the Liberals, as the party of challenge and of change, could hope to win the county. At all times, formally ignorant of politics or not, the crucial consideration was simply that the act of political decision was not theirs to take: given the kind of society then existent, it was the function of the *élite* to govern and to take political decisions.

There was one area of politics, however, one set of issues of national concern in which they were not merely moderately well-informed, but in which also they felt themselves to be well informed not merely as individuals but as communities, and that was the politics of religion. Here, in this area, and in this area only, could the limits of obedience be measured, the extent of deference be defined. Before explaining what was meant by and entailed in, ' the politics of religion ' in a county such as Merioneth, let us first examine some facts concerning the state of religion in the county. People had recognized, even before the 1851 Census of Religious Worship provided confirmation, that Merioneth was an extraordinarily religious county. It was better provided with accommodation for religious worship than any other county in Wales, indeed, than in the whole of England and Wales.[42] Accommodation, for the county as a whole, was provided for 4.6 *per cent* more than the total population. In other words, there was room in church or chapel for almost 5,000 people more than the total population, men, women and children. Even this enormous amplitude was exceeded in Dolgellau district where there was accommodation for 16 *per cent* over and above the total population of the district. Only in Corwen was the 100 *per cent* level not achieved: and in Corwen there was seating for 93.4 per cent. And this, it should be remembered, at a time when in Wales generally—a country singled out by contemporaries as an exception to the dismal religious situation of Britain in the 1850's—the proportion was only a little above 80 *per cent*. When we ask, how many people actually availed themselves of the means of religious worship so generously provided, the statistics fail us. Nevertheless, we are probably justified in assuming that such a vast investment in religion would, on the whole, be a reaction to a felt need, and that a high proportion of the population would have been associated, either as members or adherents, with some place of worship. The index of attendance—the total number of attendances expressed as a proportion of the total population—was 93.7. The corresponding index for Wales as a whole was 81.9. There was some substance, therefore, in the boast that Merioneth was the most religious area in the most religious region in England and Wales.

This laudable condition was the result of the efforts and investments of the nonconformist denominations. So far as one can tell the established Church was not gaining numerically: the relative proportion of the population which it attracted was probably declining in these middle decades of the century, and this, despite the fact that in a religious climate it would tend to benefit from the exertions of others. Only very occasionally were new churches erected : Holy Trinity Chapel of Ease, Llanfor, was licensed in 1838 but not consecrated until 1849, and an Episcopal Chapel in Bala had been licensed in 1843: a new parish church had been consecrated at Llangelynin in 1843 in lieu of the old building, and an additional church had been consecrated in 1852 in Dolgellau: Fron-goch was to be provided with a new church in 1859. Indeed, what little church extension there was in Merioneth in these middle decades of the century was due almost entirely to the initiatives of the landed proprietors.[43]

By the middle of the century, therefore, this was a people more than adequately provided with the means of religious worship. Questions concerning the quality of the religious life experienced by them within that structure are not as readily answered. We are certainly justified in inferring that such an enormous investment in religion was indicative of its primary role at all levels of society. The rector of Llanfor in 1837, reporting to Mr. Hogg of the Municipal Corporation Commission,[44] continually adverted to the extraordinary religious proclivities of the people of Bala. There was a service, he said, almost every night— a practice he himself tried, though vainly, to eschew, as he attributed the high level of bastardy in the district to that particular institution. They were fond of festivals: at the approaching harvest the streets of the town would be teeming with people as on a fair day, except that all the shops would be shut. He thought their religion was excessively gloomy. ' They love gloomy doctrines here; they love Calvinism; they are a serious people: they love a gloomy sermon best, at least I always find it so myself.' Yet, he also observed that they were a superstitious people, visiting holy wells, and such like. They must, nevertheless, have been a prudent and pragmatic people, for the rector observed that whereas the professionally trained doctor had a good practice the untrained one also made a good living writing charms for the people to wear. Bala, of course, was famous for its ' Sasiynau ' (association meetings of the Calvinistic Methodists) when thousands of people congregated on the Green to listen to the sermons of the denomination's most popular preachers. Enthusiasm, rather than gloom, marked these charismatic gatherings, warmth of experience, a shared jubilation rather than the cold logic of Biblical exegesis. But at the same time, it was also the intellectual centre of the county, indeed, of north Wales, for here were the printing houses established originally by Thomas Charles,[45] and here also the school under the headship of Lewis Edwards who was slowly providing for his denomination, and for Welshmen in general, an intellectual justification and theoretical framework for their religion. Here also was one of the intellectual centres of dissent.[46]

It is important thus to stress the institutional strength of religion both at its centre in Bala and in the lonely, remote localities. For whatever the quality of the religious experience of the communities, however lively their attachment to the institutions of the Christian religion may or may not have been, everywhere the chapels provided centres in which their informal as well as their more formal community needs could be expressed and satisfied. The weekly services provided opportunities for the occupants of lonely farmsteads to meet their neighbours in a situation not determined by the context of work, and it was often remarked, as a matter for reproach, that special preaching services, meetings of the local associations of churches, or revivalist visitations, were made the occasions for pleasureable social intercourse.[47] The chapels were their creations, the objects of their pride, depending for their continued existence on sustained common effort. This was particularly true as there was then no settled ministry, and consequently a great emphasis on and a need for local initiative and leadership. Status within the religious community was more clearly defined and recognizable. The eldership or diaconate, since it carried such great responsibilities, gave a man a distinct position within his own community, and reinforcing this, an identity beyond the confines of his own locality. Here, the barriers of localism no longer applied, for a Methodist, in particular, belonged not only to an individual group but to an immensely strong, carefully integrated constitutional system which linked him to the greater world outside. Through him the community was given a voice in the deliberations of the denomination at large, and through him its decisions made operative at a local level. Whether consciously realized or not, this hierarchy of religion was characteristic of behaviour inside. The chapels, in creating their own values, produced men who embodied these values, and so created their own *élite*. We know very little about these *élite* groups : that they existed the facts of group activity would dictate : but the few clues we have would suggest that generally the chapel *élite* were also, by virtue of their relatively greater wealth, the agricultural *élite* of the farming communities. As we have seen, this structure was well defined, and in choosing deacons to distribute his charity, R. W. Price was merely recognizing that in some respects there existed a social organization parallel with that of which he was the foremost representative.

We can now understand the caveat put forward at the beginning of this discussion to the effect that ' the politics of religion ' needs defining in terms of the particular societies with which we are concerned. It would mean different things to different groups. For the Independents and Baptists, looking towards the academy kept by Michael D. Jones at Llanuwchllyn, or the church at Llanbryn-mair, and conscious of traditions, however tenuous, linking them with the heroic formative periods in their history, it probably did have some radical overtones. One should hesitate before assuming uncritically that the radicalism personified in Michael D. Jones[48] or in Samuel Roberts[49] were typical of Independent congregations in Merioneth generally during these years. ' S.R.' had virtually departed from the country, and had almost despaired of trying to organize his co-religionists in his own and neighbouring counties. Michael D. Jones is a lonely, enigmatic, and somewhat eccentric figure. How well-informed and politically aware the general body of Independents were in Merioneth in the middle decades of the century is open to question. The radical ideas of such ' rural ' leaders flourished best in industrial regions. It would be revealing to trace where precisely Jones's students at Bala settled after completing their studies. We shall see later in this study that the propaganda efforts of radical societies were confined and limited in their operations.

The Methodists, as we have already observed, were not politically orientated. This is not to say that they took no interest in political questions: on the contrary they were constantly making political or semi-political pronouncements, particularly when politics impinged, as increasingly they did, on their religious activities. But they were not politically motivated. They accepted the political system as God-given and outside the scope of their activities. They stressed their traditional orthodoxy both in theology and in its political implications. Loyalty to God's Word involved for them an inescapable loyalty

to the king and those placed in authority over them. As they
constantly emphasized, the touchstone of the first was the
Thirty Nine Articles, and of the second a becoming subjection
to the magistracy, which they no doubt accepted as meaning
the local dispensers of justice.[50]   But neither of these major
denominations, Methodists or Independents, seem to have
encouraged, at least until the 1850s, any kind of political discussion.   If we examine the magazines which the literate
peasants read, we must admit that the intellectual diet offered
was scarcely invigorating, and most certainly lacked the protein
of social and political comment.   Nor was the language of literature or of common discourse apt for such discussion.   Based
on the Bible and on the staple of religious commentaries, works
of theological polemic, sermons, and biographies (all of which
conformed rigidly to a type of puritan hagiography) it was
beautifully adapted to subtle theological dicussion, and Lewis
Edwards[51] was slowly, though with certain misgivings about
using a language doomed to extinction, producing a philosophical vocabulary.   But was the same true of the language of
politics?   Certainly, it was not being over-exercised.   The
denominational magazines were almost exclusively religious in
tone and content, and the sections given to current affairs and
to political discussion very limited indeed.   For the most part
they seem to have been digests of articles and such-like culled
from English magazines, and generally relegated to the back
pages and printed in a minute type which must have tested the
patience of all but the most keen-eyed readers.[52]   One gets the
impression that most editors of magazines found difficulty in
thinking about politics in Welsh.   Their language becames even
more derivative, more inflated, more circumlocutory than was
usual.   It is no wonder that it was the moral aspects of politics
which stimulated most discussion, or that it was the debate
about protestantism which was most intelligible and which
most easily moved people into an awareness of politics.   Yet
even here, in this field, it would be difficult for a monoglot
Welshman dependent only upon magazines for his information
to be able to discover exactly what were the issues involved in,
say, the Bishop Colenso controversy. By the election of 1859, we
can confidently aver, that by the ' politics of religion ' was

meant almost exclusively the local implications of the catholic-
izing tendencies within the Church of England. Questions
about the relations of church to state, of ecclesiastical endowments, of the political and party implications of sectarian
allegiance, agitated few minds and seem not to have come
within the experience of the average chapel member. They
would do so most readily only in those areas of the county where
social dependence was not so absolute as to lead to political
subservience, and in Merioneth the only areas where such a
relative independence existed were the towns. But it was the
fear of change in the religious complexion of the establishment
which indicated that the limits of religious co-existence and of
obedience might have been reached. The cry of ' No Popery '
was as potent a catalyst of political activity in Merioneth as it
had been elsewhere in the country. In such a situation of fear
and of distrust, for Methodist as well as for dissenter, the limits
of political obedience might have been reached, and given
leadership by their own *élite*, the sub-structure of society might
arise to challenge the leaders of the deferential structure at the
top.

*   *   *

Where was this leadership to be found? As we have already
explained, it was unlikely to be found in the small, rural communities: the most that the chapel-*élite* could be expected normally to achieve was to provide links in a chain of leadership
extending horizontally throughout the lower ranks of county
society. Leadership of the type required could be provided
only in the towns, and even then, precariously and inter-
mittently. It was the town of Bala which produced this group of
leaders, and its appearance was a unique phenomenon of the
late 1850s. Why Bala should have so distinguished itself is not
immediately apparent. Along with Dolgellau it was certainly
larger, richer, socially more diversified than the other Merioneth towns. Harlech, still recognized as the county town, was
a decayed, down-at-heel, nondescript village nestling under the
walls of its castle, while Corwen and the coastal towns had yet
to experience the invigorating effects of railway transport.

Ffestiniog was growing rapidly, but the period of its greatest expansion and influence was yet to come.[53] Neither Bala nor Dolgellau was distinguished by an independent industrial economy; both were closely integrated into their hinterlands, the staples of wool manufacture, tanning, etc., being mainly supported by local demands, the large scale production of cloth for export, having moved eastwards into Montgomery and the border counties. Socially, they were distinguished from the villages of the county only by being very much larger. There was the same diversification of rural trades but on a larger scale, the range of crafts being more extensive and supporting larger establishments. More noticeable was the number of specialized shopkeepers, such as drapers, various kinds of chandlers, and, above all, chemists.[54] These last named were among the most specialized of trades requiring a degree of training and education far above that of any other. There were also lawyers resident in these assize towns which were also centres of local administration. There were surgeons, printers, postmasters, bankers, schoolmasters, as well as the important groups of clerical gentlemen. In all these respects Dolgellau was preeminent. It was more populous, richer, more diversified than Bala, was situated in more fertile country, and had an industrial tradition to sustain it and the hope of industrial expansion in the future of the slate industry.

The distinguishing features of Bala appear to have been of three kinds. First, it was a religious centre. Second, and related to this, it was an intellectual centre. ' Athrofa'r Bala ', founded in 1837 by Lewis Edwards, was the only seminary in north Wales for the education of ministers for the Calvinistic Methodists.[55] In the late 1850s it was in a flourishing condition, the original antipathy of the denomination having been eroded by its success, and its financial future assured. It had two tutors. Lewis Edwards himself, the principal, and Dr. John Parry[56] who was responsible for the teaching of classics. In addition, since 1842, the Independents had had an academy at Llanuwchllyn, near Bala.[57] Originally run by Michael Jones,[58] minister of two congregations in the locality, since 1855 it had had as its head Michael D. Jones,[59] the son of the former principal and, from 1858, John Peters (Ioan Pedr)[60] as his assistant. This latter was a very remarkable person. The son of a mason, he had taught himself German and French, had lived on the continent for a time in order to perfect his mastery of those languages, had returned to Bala as a student, and shortly afterwards graduated B.A. at London University. Modern languages had therefore been added to the curriculum of the Independent Academy, and between them the Methodist and Independent seminaries were providing a remarkably liberal education for their students, and making Bala the foremost educational town in north Wales. The importance of these two features of Bala, as a religious and an intellectual centre, can be seen to good effect during the great revival of 1859.[61] It would appear that it was the students of these two colleges who were most profoundly affected. Dr. T. C. Edwards, the son of Dr. Lewis Edwards, and the first principal of the University College of Wales, Aberystwyth, later declared that it was this revival which reinvigorated the religious life of north Wales, and so far as Bala was concerned, this seems primarily to have been due to the efforts of the students at the two colleges.

The other distinguishing feature of Bala was the success of its claim to be a chartered borough. It shared this claim, of course, with many others: Wales was littered with decayed boroughs and defunct corporations. Where it differed from these was in its claim to resurrect them. This desire for a renewal of its ancient privileges and liberties was a very recent development. In 1837, when Mr. Hogg, one of the Commissioners under the Municipal Corporations Commission, visited the town to report on its structure and social complexion, no trace of these existed.[62] There were vague memories of a mayor having existed, and of a recorder, a Mr. Jones (who had been succeeded in that office by his daughter, ' Miss Jones, the recorder '), but no concrete evidence in the form of documents or any kind could be found locally. Nor, apparently, was there much enthusiasm for a civic revival. On the basis of his own researches, however, Hogg was perfectly satisfied that there were charters dating from 5 Edward II, and certain grants of the time of Richard II showing that Bala had been incorporated. His conclusion was that it was to be regretted:—

' that a free constitution which probably had long subsisted, has been permitted so lately to fall into desuetude. Respectable persons might surely have been found in the town and neighbourhood to sustain, in succession, for the credit, of the venerable borough, the light burthen of the mayoralty, of the office of bailiff, and of the other functions, which charters, or usages, have sanctioned. In a secluded and thinly peopled town, with little trade, or opulence, the immediate practical operation of its officers could be but small; nevertheless, the ultimate utility of the steady conservation of early institutions ought not to be overlooked '.

This of course, was an open invitation to the inhabitants—those ' respectable persons ' referred to—to renew this minimal form of self-government. That it was not taken up was evidence less of a lack of will among such people as of the stultifying effect upon the town of the landed gentry. An illustration of this power had but recently occurred, when the local bench of justices had refused *en bloc* to serve, as a protest against the remission of a sentence of 14 years transportation which they had imposed on two women, and more significantly, as a protest against the putting into the commision a man who was a Methodist and whose origins, education, connections, early habits, occupations, and station

' were not such as could entitle him to be the familiar associate of gentlemen, nor likely to sustain that implicit reliance upon the personal character of the justice, from which the authority of the order is in truth wholly derived '.[63]

This had had the effect of placing the hundred of Penllyn with its town of Bala under a kind of civil interdict and the Commissioners were perfectly aware that such a withdrawal from their jurisdictions would have been unthinkable with an elected magistracy. Hogg referred to it as

' so remarkable a feature of that local administration, which is the rival of and substitute for the ancient chartered government of towns '.

Indeed, he had judged that it would be indiscreet to raise the matter with R. W. Price, Esq., when he had an audience of that gentleman; and there is evidence to suppose that the leader of such an aristocratic strike would have regarded his *Report*, however guarded its wording, as an incitement to the lower orders to rebel. In fact, the moderate tone of Hogg's *Report* was probably a realistic appraisal of the state of affairs in Bala. Given such a structure of deference, and an establishment of gentry imbued with the spirit of aristocracy, and equipped by education and convention to rule, then there was an obvious utility in preserving old forms while not closing the door entirely on the possibility of men of meaner station in due course, and with proper safeguards, attaining to a share in that rule. He canvassed the possibility of a stipendiary magistracy, but in any case, recognized the existence of a closed system which he could see no particular virtue in destroying. In the meantime, Bala, as a town, might achieve a certain degree of emancipation. But for the time being it was left in a state of suspended animation.

How realistic this reading of the situation was is illustrated by the fact that twenty years were to pass before any move was made to act in the spirit of the *Report*, and it was not until January 1859 that Bala again became an incorporated borough.[64] It is necessary to stress the limitations of this constitutional change. The town had not been included under Schedule A of the first Municipal Corporation Act under which it would have been given a commission of the peace, nor under Schedule B under which it was left to the boroughs therein named to petition for such a commission. All it did was to give the resident taxpayers the right to elect a governing body of mayor and two town bailiffs—the very minimum of self-government possible. The ancient jurisdictions of the magistracy were thus left intact and their effective power scarcely modified. But in the formation of political groups it is not the limitations of such an act that are significant, but rather the evidence it affords of the existence of a source of political initiative independent of the existing power structure. These minimal institutional changes could become the nucleus around which various bodies of dissident opinion could cohere, a secure base from which sustained political activity working in other directions might spread. Thus, for instance, the question whether or not to engraft the Local Government Act, with all that this entailed in the way of local democratic administration, to the new charter, arose immediately, and as immediately brought the progressive elements in the town into conflict with the upholders of the ancient prerogatives of the gentry.[65] The regaining of its borough status was therefore an event of seminal significance in the political life of Merioneth, and not a pleasant charade played out for their own amusement by antiquarian-minded gentlemen.

Its practical significance lay in the way it brought together in one well-integrated group representatives of the two main distinguishing features of the life of Bala which we have identified, namely, the religio-intellectual and the secular-political. It brought into combination these two aspects of the life of the town, it personified them in individuals of substance and standing and provided them with an organization which might be used for more directly political ends. Indeed, since the intellectual had become one of the town's most outstanding products, the characteristic which gave it a prestige which its economic functions could not provide, the two features were in most cases combined in the same individuals. The religious leaders personified also civic pride, and pointed the way to the political emancipation of the county. We can study this focus-sing of forces in the public meeting in January 1859 for the renewing of the charter. The chairman was George Price Lloyd, Esq., of Plas-yn-dre.[66] Lloyd was a small landowner of indepen-dent means, closely related to the Lloyds of Rhiwaedog, one of the ancient families of Merioneth, but now, since the early part of the century, eclipsed by the great landowners of Penllyn. He had served as High Sheriff in 1841, and was a justice of the peace. The vote of thanks to the main speaker was proposed by Lewis Edwards, and seconded by Michael D. Jones, and the motion proposing the renewal of the charter by Simon Jones, seconded by William Thomas. Who were these men? With Lewis Edwards and Michael D. Jones we are already familiar. Simon Jones was a grocer, tea dealer and tallow chandler in the town[67] and a prominent member of the Independent Chapel, Capel Newydd, where he was the foremost deacon. He had been mainly responsible for the invitation to Michael D. Jones to succeed his father as minister of the church at Bethel, and subsequently of the other independent churches centred on

Llanuwchllyn. It was understood that having charge of the chapels would involve the principalship of the academy, and it is clear that Simon Jones was among those who had fought successfully to retain the school in Bala, and to have Michael D. Jones as its head.[68] William Thomas was a druggist, and likewise an Independent. These were the local leaders. The chief speaker was David Williams, Esq., of Castell Deudraeth, head of one of the most flourishing legal houses in north Wales. It was he who had found the original charters, having given the task to his nephew John Breese who must thus have been one of the first Welshmen to carry out such a search in the newly opened Public Record Office. And now, early in January 1859, he ceremoniously handed over copies to the townsfolk. Shortly afterwards, G. P. Lloyd was elected the first Mayor, and the following year, Simon Jones was appointed to succeed him and seems to have held that office until 1871 when the office again seems so have fallen vacant.[69]

In this way, the emergent politicians, concerned at that time only with the civic status of their borough, met the man who, for the next ten years, was to be their candidate for the parliamentary seat. That David Williams was already thinking of himself as a candidate does not seem likely: throughout the decade he did virtually nothing to present himself as a future member, and as we shall see, his reluctance to stand, when the time came, seems to have been genuine. He had been brought into the movement to re-incorporate the town mainly for his expert advice and assistance, but the giving of the charters was a gesture which must have endeared him not only to Bala people but to the county at large and given him that reputation for public-spirited generosity without which no political advance could be made. In this way, Bala created for itself a political organization at precisely the time when national politics were themselves beginning to change and to impinge on local affairs.

*   *   *

That David Williams would be thought of as a candidate was almost inevitable. The various franchise reforms being canvassed during those years, notably by John Bright, had the effect of concentrating the attention of localities upon the deficiencies in their own representation. In Merioneth the great defect was the lack of a member for the boroughs. This was a grievance with an ancient history, and attempts had been made from time to time to remedy it, the last occasion being during the debates on the Reform Bill of 1832.[70] Two reform meetings were held at Bala in January 1859, the second of which was wholly devoted to this question. Agitation was felt to be necessary in the county because Merioneth would have benefited by neither of the two plans then before the country. Bright's bill would have disfranchised Brecon and the Radnorshire boroughs, but the seats thus made available would have been given to Merthyr, and an additional representative given to Swansea. Merioneth boroughs would have remained unrepresented. Lord Derby's bill was even less promising. Of course, franchise reform was also canvassed at these meetings, Michael D. Jones calling for the ballot, but it was the question of gaining an additional seat for the county which was the main issue. These two meetings were run by the same group of people. William Thomas, the druggist, was chairman, in lieu of one of the town's two surgeons, both of whom were highly sympathetic. Resolutions were proposed by Simon Jones and Michael D. Jones, and new names appear all of whom would be found subsequently to be active supporters. The main speaker was David Williams of Castell Deudraeth. Just as it had been this same person who had been most instrumental in satisfying the new urge to some degree of local government, so also it was he who focused the new interest in politics of a more general kind, providing that necessary respectability which the local gentry refused. Again, there is no evidence that Williams had deliberately set out to foster these developments. He was responding to a local motivation which was the product of the social changes we have described.

Early in 1859, therefore, new elements had appeared in the political life of Merioneth and these were evidence of a change in the attitudes of some of its social groupings below the level of the ruling groups. It is necessary to stress the limitations of these. They were highly localized in Bala. Of the other towns only Dolgellau was represented at the 6 January reform meeting at Bala, and then, apparently, only by one person, namely D. Pugh, Esq. Other towns were to be asked to organize their own meetings to agitate for borough representation, but there is no evidence that any such were actually called at that time. Nor was there as yet any county organization in being. The nucleus of one existed. Centred on Bala, it consisted of the intellectual leaders of the community, some of its more prominent commercial men and women, and a few of the lesser gentry of the neighbourhood. It had one considerable achievement to its credit in its successful assertion of burghal rights for the townsfolk, and it was extending its interests into the realm of national politics. The driving force behind it was, at any rate on the surface, religious, and by reason of this and of its command of the chapel organizations it had links with the latent *élite* among the peasantry in the countryside. In David Williams it had a man of familiar background, connections, and beliefs who could be projected as the image of the new political leadership. It is the development of these new elements and their effect upon the political life of the county which we now have to study.

*   *   *

To bring out the full significance of the events of 1859 it is necessary to see the parliamentary election of that year within the context of the electoral history of the county since the beginning of the century. As already indicated, this was only the second contested election since 1794, and it is necessary to describe that of 1836 in order to point the contrast with that of 1859.

The first indication of a possible change in the representation of the county had come in May 1836 when Sir Robert Williames Vaughan[71] was reported to have been taken ill on his way to London and to have returned forthwith to Nannau.[72] He was approaching his sixty-ninth year, and had served as member without a break for forty-four years, since 1792, that is, when he had succeeded Evan Lloyd Vaughan of Gorsygedol.[73] As a member, he had maintained the Gorsygedol tradition of ' the old constitutional school ', a Tory of the Tories, preserving that assured independence in political affairs which stemmed from his unchallenged supremacy in county affairs. It is doubtful whether he had ever during his long parliamentary career consulted his constituents on any issue, but it is likely that his Tory views accorded well with the views of the majority of his class. He does not seem to have been present for the critical divisions on the repeal of the Test and Corporation Acts in 1829, nor those on Catholic Emancipation. He voted against the second reading of the Reform Bill in 1832,[74] and we can only infer that this would have disappointed a small number of the gentry at home. His independences of course, was an expression of his landed wealth and the power and prestige which these added to the respect in which the head of one of Merioneth's distinguished families was held. He possessed the estates of Nannau, Hengwrt, Ystumcolwyn and Meillionydd, aggregating nearly 12,000 acres and distributed through sixteen parishes. No wonder he was known as ' the Golden Calf of Dolgelley '— no doubt, as someone commented, in reference to his riches and the idolatrous regard with which he was held rather than to his ultimate fate. In fact, he seems to have been as popular as he was powerful, and the tales concerning his unaffected ways, his wit and largesse were legion, and when he died in 1843 his funeral surpassed anything ever seen in Dolgellau.[75]

The choice of a successor seems to have been left almost entirely to him. There were rumours that he had offered the seat to his son and to other relatives, to R. W. Price of Rhiwlas, and a Lloyd of Rhaggatt, all of whom declined. While these negotiations were in progress, the few Liberals among the gentry, ' hitherto ', as one leader-writer put it, ' dormant in the county ' but now restive at the way the seat was being hawked around in the Vaughan interest, found a candidate of their own in the person of Sir William Wynn of Maes-y-neuadd.[76] Sir William was the third son of William Wynn (Nanney) of Maes-y-Neuadd, who had assumed the surname Nanney upon inheriting the estates of his mother's family, the Nanneys of Maes-y-pandy. Sir William had entered the army in 1794 and attained the rank of captain in 1800. He was appointed captain of Sandown Fort, Isle of Wight, in March 1810, and knighted in the same year.[77] This post was usually given to distinguished soldiers, and certainly gave him a *cachet* over and above his county connections, and clearly it gave him the leisure to indulge what must have been a deep interest in politics. His marriage to Miss Long, daughter of Col. Long of Tubney Park, Buckinghamshire, said to have a dowry of £80,000 probably helped as well.[78] He had already attempted, but without success, to get into parliament as a liberal candidate at Stafford and at Caernarfon,[79] but though no carpet-bagger in his home county where, indeed, he had his own seat in addition to the ancestral home,[80] it was clear to the commentators of the day that his chance of gaining the seat without the backing of the major families was very slender indeed. His Address, dated 18 May from London,[81] showed him to be an ardent supporter of the reform government, particularly with regard to Poor Law administration, tithe commutation, and municipal reform, but prepared to go much further on ecclesiastical issues since he advocated a kind of state endowment of all denominations and an equality of dissent with the established Church. These were planks hardly calculated to appeal widely among the Merioneth gentry whatever their appeal might be to the town-dwellers resentful of their lack of independence. In fact, Wynn found it expedient in a later Address to modify the tone of the first and to stress the essential conservatism of his proposals.[82]

In the meantime, there were rumours of the impending candidature of Richard Richards, Esq., of Caerynwch, Dolgellau, in the Tory interest, but it was not until 31 May that a meeting of freeholders was called at Dolgellau ' to take the advice ' of Sir Robert Vaughan as to who his successor should be.[83] The meeting which was as very meagerly attended, appears to have been called on the initiative of Hugh Reveley, Esq. and the rector, and its purpose was plainly to accept Vaughan's resignation and Richard's candidature. If this was the intention, then only the first purpose was achieved, and that only partially. No sooner had a Mr. Fawden, a local landowner, been voted into the chair, than the propriety of the meeting was called in question. Conventionally, if not legally, such business as was now being transacted should have been the concern of a county meeting convened by the High Sheriff. This office at the time of the election was held by J. E. Boulcott of Hendre-

isaf, and though no Liberal, his estates all lay in the Harlech
and Llandecwyn region of Ardudwy, and so made him a
neighbour of Wynn and other known anti-Tory families such
as the Mostyns. The opposition was small, but effective. It was
led by C. T. Thruston of Tal-garth Hall, in Pennal, a very
considerable landowner in adjacent parishes, and supported by
J. Edwards of Dolserau, another, though smaller, proprietor.
These two pressed their opposition to the point of drawing up
and circulating for signature a protest addressed to Sir Robert
Vaughan, objecting to the way in which the meeting had been
convened, stressing its illegality, and affirming that the twenty-
-two[84] people who had signed the declaration accepting
Vaughan's resignation could in no wise be considered as
expressing the sense of the whole county. This protest was also
signed by a certain J. Pugh, and a physician, Dr. Williams who,
however, having been told that Sir Robert concurred with the
addresses now before them, walked out, probably preferring
neutrality in a situation which might have involved his professional interests. It is difficult to identify all the names of
those who signed the address to Vaughan. At least six were
fairly substantial landed proprietors, including Reveley, Fawden, and Hugh Jones, and it can be assumed that the reminder
were shopkeepers and tradesmen and professional men.

The protest was clearly not particularly effective, and certainly it did nothing to affect the chances of the Conservative
candidate, Richard Richards of Caerynwch.[85] Richards was
the son of Sir Richard Richards of Coed, judge, baron of the
exchequer—' baron Richards ' as he was called. His estates in
Dolgellau, Mallwyd and Llandderfel consisted of nearly 4,000
acres, and in the 1860s the Dolgellau estates produced an
annual income of about £1300. But Richard Richards was
himself a highly successful lawyer, accountant-general of the
court of exchequer, and consequently with means amply in
excess of his rent roll. Moreover, he was clearly wise to the
wiles of electioneering and not averse to taking advantage of
the law to further his own fortunes. At the nomination in
Harlech on 21 June[86]—a meeting described by the report as
' a farce '—he challenged Wynn's credentials, requiring his
opponent to take the property oath. Wynn certainly held

sufficient land—a total of 858 acres[87]—but whether this was worth a clear £600 per annum clear of all reprisals as the law required may be doubted. Certainly, Richards was not the man to act except on sound information, and unfortunately, he seemed to have had evidence also that Wynn had signed a document stating that he did not possess £20 landed property in order to evade serving the office of sheriff. There was a further instance of sharp practice when the Richards-Vaughan party but not the Wynn party, was told in advance of a change of venue for the meeting, with the result that Wynn supporters arrived too late for much effective support to be given to their candidate. But it was clear at the nomination that his support anyway would be small. Whereas Richards was proposed by R. W. Price of Rhiwlas and seconded by Reveley, the former of these one of the most powerful families in the county, the latter by no means negligible as we have seen, Wynn was proposed by Thruston and seconded by a certain Richard Humphreys described as a yeoman who, because he spoke in Welsh was ruled out of order. The poll, taken on the following Friday and Saturday merely confirmed this dismal impression, Richards polling 501 votes, and Wynn 150.

The Liberals, or the Reform Party as they preferred to call themselves, were not short of explanations for this defeat. In particular, they pointed out that the tactical advantages had throughout been with the Richards-Vaughan party, and that they had not failed to exploit them. The register of voters, it was claimed, was more imperfect in Merioneth than in any other Welsh county for the simple reason that there had been virtually no electioneering for fifty years or more. The register showed only 785 voters,[88] or 2.2 *per cent* of the population, a lower proportion than in any other Welsh county, and well below the average for the whole country which was 4.67 *per cent*. Vaughan had chosen to resign before the new register could be prepared in July, so that a large number of voters would have been effectively disenfranchised on the one occasion in half a century during which they might have exercised the franchise. Whether in fact a more up-to-date register would have made any difference is doubtful, however, for the voting pattern[89] showed that Wynn had polled only a little over 4 *per cent* of the votes cast in three of the polling areas, namely Dolgellau, Bala, and Corwen, and had had a majority in only one, namely in Tywyn. Any increase in the voting strength in the former places would have gone to Richards, for it was in these regions that his supporters were the predominant landowners. Wynn was secure only in Tywyn by virtue not of his own property there but that of his chief supporter, C. T. Thruston. Wynn's supporters were on slightly stronger ground in themselves attempting to reverse the result on a technichality by petitioning against the return of Richards on the grounds that Richards held certain offices and places of profit under the Crown. Petitions to this effect were presented on 11 July,[90] and came up for hearing on 26 July, but no parties appearing for the petitioners, the orders were discharged. The background to this episode, again, is very vague, but it seems probable that Wynn's supporters—in this case, Londoners with votes in Merioneth[91]—must have been convinced in the interval that they had no case and decided, therefore, not to press it. The representation of Merioneth by a Tory for yet another generation seemed assured.

There seemed to be adequate reasons, therefore, for passing over this election in silence. It was but a ripple on the calm surface of Merioneth politics, a slight, involuntary movement in a recumbent, sleeping figure. And yet it has some significance and some effect on the nature of the political development of the county. At the least, it showed that an opposition existed, that political activity was not entirely absent, and that something might be achieved even within the terms of a traditionally eighteenth century structure of politics. The Reformers were not entirely cast down, and the most noticeable effect of their intervention was a renewed interest in registration. The register for the following year, prepared almost immediately after the election, showed an increase of nearly 100 *per cent*—from 785 to 1336—a total which was not to be reached again until the eve of the Second Reform Act in 1867.[92] Much of this activity, of course, must have been on the Conservative side, but to have awakened the traditional political families was in itself a feat of some significance. Finally, as one leader writer put it, it was ' the planting of a tree—ths sowing of principles, which will flourish at another period '.

Twenty three years were to pass before the seed planted in 1836 bore fruit, a bitter fruit as it transpired, which set the teeth of future generations on edge. The contrast between the two elections is, indeed, enormous, and before we seek to discover what changes had taken place in the intervening decades to account for the differences, we must analyse briefly the election of 1859 in order to bring out its salient features.

Richard Richards of Caerynwch continued undisturbed in the occupation of his seat for the next sixteen years, during which time no attempt whatsoever was made to unseat him. When he retired in 1852 it was to hand over the seat to W. W. E. Wynne of Peniarth, the famous antiquary.[93] The Peniarth estate, a compact block of territory in Llanegryn parish consisted of 4,183 acres—two-thirds of the total acreage of the parish, most of the rest being owned by relatives, such as C. J. Scott and Nanney Wynne, and other large landowners like Sir R. W. Vaughan, the third baronet. The election occasioned no excitement, and scarcely any comment.[94] Wynne's candidature and Richard's resignation were announced simultaneously and Wynne's succession seemed to have been accepted without protest. The Liberals among the gentry and in the towns made no move to find a candidate to oppose one who was known to be a staunch Tory, while the Tory proprietors themselves seem to have taken no interest in the affair. So far as the formalities were concerned the nomination seemed to be exclusively a Dolgellau affair, Wynne being proposed by Sir Robert Vaughan and seconded by Lewis Williams of Vron Wnion, Dolgellau, one of the town gentry, owner of 500 acres. The entire absence of the great landed proprietors was noted, but this should be taken merely as an indication of the general apathy of the times rather than of any hostility to the candidate. The only ominous indication of a change in the political atmosphere was the remark of the candidate to the effect that ' he was sorry to say that he had plainly perceived in the county, a daily increase of democratic feeling, and less attachment to our glorious constitution.'[95] He did not elaborate, and one suspects that one would have to search hard to find the symptoms which he found alarming. The election of 1857, likewise, was uneventful, Wynne being again returned unopposed.

The contrast with the election of 1859 is spectacular. Not that this was immediately apparent. Until almost the last moment there was no certainty that there would be a contest. Not until the 23 April, nearly a fortnight after Wynne had issued his Address, and only a fortnight before the date fixed for the election, did David Williams announce his intention to stand.[96] That considerable pressure was being put upon him is obvious from the fact that twice before the dissolution he had refused to accept requisitions inviting him to do so. He contested only after completing a preliminary canvass of the county which satisfied him that more support would be forthcoming than the electoral history of the county would seem to warrant. So far as his politics were concerned he was for constitutional reform, social progress (not defined), and the development of local interests. He called for an extension of the franchise and a redistribution of seats. On ecclesiastical matters he was un-equivocally in favour of the repeal of Church rates and the redress of dissenters' grievances. Wynne, in contrast, seemed to be on the defensive. Lord Derby's reform bill, properly amended in committee, would benefit the county by the exten-sion of voting rights to ministers of religion, to various classes of professional men, and to the lower grades of landowners—the so-called ' rural ten-pounders '. He denied that he had at any time in his capacity as county member acted in a spirit of intolerance in religious matters or at variance with the dissent-ing majority in the county, but affirmed that he would main-tain the prerogatives of the church to which he belonged. Apart from issuing addresses neither of the candidates appears to have done any electioneering of a formal kind. Meetings were infrequent, the only large ones being in Bala on behalf of the Liberal candidate.[97] Further north, in Ffestiniog, there seems to have been considerable enthusiasm and sufficient heat gener-ated to alarm the authorities: but this was probably a reflection of the much more exciting struggle in the adjacent county of Caernarfon.

The poll was a small one—740 voted out of a total 1126 registered voters, or 65.7 *per cent*.[98] Of these, 389 or 52.6 *per cent* voted for Wynne, a majority of only 38 or 5.2 *per cent* over Williams. This was an extraordinarily encouraging result for the Liberals. They had had a majority of 94 in a poll of 250 at Harlech, nearly 20 *per cent* more than the votes cast for Wynne. In Bala, Williams had polled 63 to his opponent's 54. He had done well at Corwen also, where he had come within 16 votes of a majority. Even in Dolgellau and Tywyn, where Wynne's majority had been overwhelming, nearly a quarter of the electorate had voted Liberal. There had thus been a most remarkable change in the pattern of voting since 1836, when the Liberal had polled respectably only in Harlech and Tywyn. The greatest change had been in the northern regions of the county, in particular at Bala and Corwen, for though Wynne had a majority in this latter place, the Liberals had succeeded beyond expectation, and there was reason to believe that the nest election would show a 6 *per cent* swing in that area. It was said of Bala that not a single town vote had been given to the Tory candidate.[99] Here, the Liberal's victory was complete.

This success appears even more remarkable when it is re-collected that the Liberals had come late into the field in a county where canvassing for votes was still governed by the genteel conventions of the *ancient regime*, whereby landlords rather than voters were canvassed, and the permission of land-lords sought before tenants might be solicited for their votes. Of the 1,126 registered voters 423 or 7.5 *per cent* were lease-holders. In other words, roughly one or half of the total electorate could have been expected to vote with their land-lords, and it should be remembered that a majority of 570 free-holders were probably very small landowners who would like-wise normally follow the lead of their more substantial neigh-bours.[100] As we have noted, only two thirds of the registered electors actually voted, but lacking the poll books it is not possible to tell which class of voter abstained most heavily. The evidence from one estate suggests that abstentions were heavy among the tenants-at-will : but we can only speculate, in the absence of documentary evidence, as to the situation regarding other classes of voters. There were certainly well-founded rumours that tenants on all the great estates were being screwed, particularly tenants in the Bala region where R. W. Price and Sir Watkin Williams Wynn were the major landowners. At a Liberal demonstration in Bala on 3 May speakers stressed that

Price was *not* putting undue pressure on his tenants. All he had done to date was to write to each of his individual vote-possessing tenants asking them for the favour of their votes for Wynne. No one suggested that there was anything improper about such action. Soon afterwards it became known that, in response to a deputation led by Mr. David Jones of Gydros, he was permitting those who could not so favour him by voting for Wynne to remain neutral.[101] And this appears the position with regard to the Rhiwlas estate until the eve of the poll—a *modus vivendi* which appeared satisfactory to all concerned.

Then came the first blow. On 7 May, three days before the election, it transpired that Price had summoned 33 of his tenants to meet him one by one at the Bull Inn, Bala, where he had pressed them individually to cast their votes for Wynne,[102] and this despite his earlier assurance that they were at liberty to remain neutral if they so wished.[103] How effective this pressure was there is no means of telling since we do not know what the voting intentions of these tenants were. But at the poll, of these 33 enfranchised tenants, all of them £50 tenants-at-will ,14 were stated to have voted for Wynne, 19 to have abstained, and 2 to have voted for Williams.[104] Shortly afterwards it became known that 5 of these tenants were under notice to quit, and that the farms of three of them had already been promised to new tenants. Tenants on the Glan-llyn estate of Sir Watkin had suffered, if anything, more severely.[105] Seven had been evicted or were under notice to quit, and another seven who had remained neutral had had their rents raised. One of the tenants evicted was the aged mother of Michael D. Jones who had continued to farm the 30 acres of Weirglodd Wen, near Llanuwchllyn, after the death of her husband six years previously. There were no reports of evictions in other parts of the county. Bala, which had been the first place to give evidence of a new kind of political life, was thus the first place to reap the consequences of its behaviour.

*   *   *

It is not unlikely that it was the men of Bala, whom we have seen to have been prominent in the reform agitation, who had invited David Williams to stand as the Liberal candidate.

There is no direct evidence of this, but a Minute Book of the Williams Committee at Bala has survived,[106] and it is possible, on the basis of this, to describe the inner life of this same group of reformers in the developing electoral situation and the crisis which followed. It held its first meeting on 28 April under the chairmanship of John Jones, Esq., Fachddeiliog, a minor land-owner in Llangower.[107] A committee room was engaged for the duration of the election, and arrangements made for a public meeting. The committee appointed consisted of twenty-seven men—excluding the chairman—of whom the first nine had been active in the Bala meetings already described. They included Owen Richards, surgeon, Lewis Edwards, Michael D. Jones, and John Parry (ministers), Simon Jones (draper), Thomas Jones and William Thomas (druggists). The list included another surgeon, a doctor, a wine seller, two curriers, Richard Jones, the owner of a woollen factory, a painter, Peter Jones, the landlord of the Goat Inn (in fact a tenant of Wynn), and several other persons prominent in the commercial life of Bala and Llandderfel. It included also a few small freeholders, but generally the committee was one of townsfolk. Its leaders were emphatically those whom we have already identified, and whom we might describe as the nucleus of the reforming party. Not all of the men named attended the daily meetings of the committee, and from the beginning business was being per-formed and initiatives taken by a small inner group consisting of Simon Jones, Dr. Richards, Richard Jones, William Thomas, and the three ministerial members.

Of these ministers of religion, Lewis Edwards was probably a key figure. Officially, he preferred not to be involved directly in any of the formal electioneering, and at the first meeting of the committee a letter from him was read, explaining that pressure of work prevented him from making any effective contribution. But the letter itself was a brilliant and carefully composed statement of the reforming party's case. In his judgement, 'Mr. Wynne (was) one of the most unsuitable persons imaginable to represent Merioneth'. Whatever the political situation in other counties, the argument in Merioneth did not turn on the difference between either Liberals or Con-sevatives or Nonconformists and Churchmen. It had to do with the very fundamentals of the Protestant religion. ' Nor can I,' he added, ' do less than hold that whosoever votes for Wynne is guilty of betraying those principles for which Christianity in the past has suffered martyrdom rather than betray them.' Mr. Wynne had a perfect right to choose his own religion but Lewis Edwards denied that he had any right to compel any of the voters to assist him in misrepresenting them in parliament. This letter, with the author's permission, was immediately translated into Welsh and published over his name and as addressed to the David Williams Committee, in *Yr Herald* and *Baner ac Amserau Cymru*,[108] the two newspapers which circulated most widely within the county. Lewis Edwards's obvious reluctance to take an active public part in the election reflects accurately the attitudes of the Methodist leadership of the time, but likewise it reflects the increasing scale of this participation, the extent to which these old attitudes were being eroded in the acknowledged centre of the denomination in north Wales. He himself realized fully the implications of what was happening. A few years later we find him deploring this drift of the Connexion into politics, so much so that he feared it might become a political club. Laymen should be active politically, ' but certainly a political contest is no place for preachers '.[109] Thus, when arrangements for a public meeting were being finalized, for 3 May, the resolutions were drafted by Edwards, Michael D. Jones, and Roger Hughes,[110] but were not spoken to at the meeting by him. The speakers were all committee members, and the inclusion of the Reverend J. Parry, Edwards's junior at the college, suggests that his younger contemporaries at any rate were less inhibited than their seniors by the connectional image.

The committee, meeting daily, concentrated on detailed arrangements for the election. On Tuesday, 3 May, messengers were appointed to deliver circulars to sixteen voters in the Bala district. Of the eleven of these who can be identified,[111] seven were tenant farmers, and four freeholders. Most of the tenants were small: their rentals probably brought them just within the £50 franchise: but two of Sir Watkin's tenants, namely David Pugh of Cynythog Bach, Llanycil, and David Jones of Cynythog Ganol were substantial farmers, their holdings being 167 and

273 acres respectively. One of Charles Wynn's tenants in Llanycil, rented a farm of 554 acres, and another, a tenant of J. Davies, a farm of 259 acres. The freeholders, one of whom had rented out his 137 acres farm, Llwynrodyn, in Llanycil, varied in the size of their holding from 49 acres to 300 acres: the the latter was owned by David Jones, of Gendros, Llanfor, a widower, aged 72, but very active on the side of the Liberals. It is important to note that none of the tenant-farmers thus canvassed belonged to the Rhiwlas estate. This may have been due to the fact that R. W. Price had already circulated his tenants on Wynne's behalf, and as a rule tenants were never canvassed without the permission of their landlords. Why this rule should not have applied to the tenants on the Glan-llyn estate is not clear. Neither of the two tenants solicited on this occasion was interfered with subsequently, and it must be assumed that they voted for Wynne, despite the fact that one of them—David Jones of Cynythog Ganol—was approached personally by an emissary of the committee at a later date.[112] A further list of 17 was drawn up on the Thursday and circulars sent to them.[113] Of these, 12 were tenant farmers and 3 freeholders. The former were tenants for the most part of gentry of the second rank, but two were tenants of Sir Watkin, namely, David Jones of Pentrepiod, and Edward Edwards of Llwynllwydyn. Both voted for David Williams, and both were later evicted.[114] In addition, a messenger was sent to three other farmers, and another to three of the Rhiwlas tenants, namely, John Jones of Fedw-lwyd, Ellis Davies of Pentre, and Robert Roberts of Fedw-arian Uchaf. These were farms of about the average size on the Rhiwlas estate, 156, 84, and 92 acres respectively. Two of these tenants, John Jones and Robert Roberts, abstained at the election.[115]

This visit to some of the Rhiwlas tenants may have been prompted by the rumours circulating that Price was again putting pressure on his tenants by sending them messages urging them to vote for Wynne despite the assurances he had already given that they might remain neutral if they so desired. The committee took a very serious view of this, and its chairman, John Jones, Esq., visited his old friend at Rhiwlas to ascertain if the reports were true. He reported back to the effect that ' Mr. Price in the most positive manner contradicted the report and says he has sent no such messages and has not authorized any person to do any such thing in his name.'[116] Doubtless, the ' whippers-in ' were informed of this, as also the gentlemen appointed to attend the poll-booth on the day of the election.[117]   These, headed by Lewis Edwards and other members of the committee, included also H. J. Richardson, Esq., of Aberhirnant, a prominent landed proprietor in Llanfor. The inclusion of this gentleman, owner of an estate of 3,030 acres consisting of 10 substantial farms and 4 small holdings, suggests that the gentry structure was less monolithic than it appeared to be.   Certainly, he and the chairman gave the reforming party a more genteel appearance than it might otherwise have had.   But the bulk of the names of those giving public testimony of their allegiances were of the solid, burghal type whom we have already met.

Unfortunately, the Minute Book is silent for the week of the election in this critical region.   The result, however, was a sufficient indication of the success of this unique organization in mobilizing the new opinion.   In the previous election in 1836, only 5 out of a total of 142 electors had voted for the Liberal candidate.   In 1859, 63 out of a total of 117 had voted Liberal. This comparison was not made at the time: the memory of the previous contest seems to have faded out of the consciousness of the people, like an irrelevance, to be revived only years later when the legatees of 1859 came to survey their past heritage. Not a single vote in the town of Bala had been cast for Wynne, and it was the contrast between this and the voting behaviour of the other towns which struck contemporaries.   Dolgellau, Tywyn and Corwen had given relatively massive support to the Tory; only in the Harlech district had there been an equally emphatic Liberal majority.   The jubilation of having almost won the seat—only 39 additional votes had been needed—was mixed therefore with keen disappointment and chagrin, and the narrowness of the defeat was attributed to the conduct of towns which might have so easily emulated Bala.   Not even the Harlech region escaped criticism, for Talsarnau, alone among the townships of that coastal area, had cravenly voted with its landlord, Ormsby-Gore.   But most of the criticism was directed

against Dolgellau. Was it more difficult, it was asked, to vote
conscientiously in Dolgellau than in Bala? Was intimidation
more fearsome there than in Penllyn? The most usual explanation was to accuse Dolgellau nonconformists of apathy, and
here, perhaps, the commentators were right if by this they
meant the failure of Dolgellau Liberals to organise themselves.
Nothing, perhaps, illustrates so well the difference between the
two elections—between 1836 and 1859. It was Dolgellau which
had been the centre of the reforming party in 1836, now it was
Bala. But more significantly than that, the 1836 election had
represented a contest within the ruling groups ; 1859 was
witnessing a change of revolutionary proportions whereby opposition was being led by men of a lower social rank with whom
some of the lesser gentry were associating themselves. This was
a reversal of the traditional pattern of leadership, and the subsequent political history of the country would be a commen-
tary on this portentous change.

*   *   *

The significance of this change was not lost on the men of
Bala. Borne along by the impetus of their local victory they
were determined to exploit it and to lay the foundations for a
victory at a county level by extending their organization to all
other centres in the constituency. Thus it is, that when the
Minute Book starts again on 12 May,[118] the evening after the
declaration of the poll, it was to mark a new departure in the
political history of the county and, indeed, of Wales. There
were thirteen people present at a meeting then called in the
British Schoolroom, headed this time by Dr. Richards and with
Lewis Edwards taking a leading part in the deliberations. The
core of the former committee was there, professional men,
shopkeepers and tradesmen: the ministers M. D. Jones and
John Parry, Simon Jones the draper, John Jones the chemist,
J. Jones the flourdealer, the two curriers, and the town's two
medical men. It was these men who resolved that evening ' that
a Society be formed to be called "The Reform Society", having
for its objects the revision of the Register of Voters, the prom-
otion of Liberal principles in the county of Merioneth and also

taking all the necessary steps for securing the return of a Liberal member at the next vacancy in the representation '.[119]   An executive committee was formed consisting of John Jones, Esq., Fachddeiliog, chairman, Dr. Owen Richards, vice-chairman, Mr. Thomas Jones, treasurer, and William Thomas, secretary *pro tem.* This was the origin of the Merioneth Liberal Association which was to play such a vital role in the political history of the county, and in due course to provide Wales with a new generation of Liberal leaders.

The first task of the committee was to draw up a prospectus setting out the aims of the Society, and to send circulars to prominent Merioneth Liberals asking for their support. These were headed by David Williams, the late candidate, Samuel Holland, Plas Penrhyn, the quarry owner who had seconded Williams's nomination and who was later to succeed him as member. It is obvious that at this stage the Society was to be confined mainly to the county or to men fairly closely associated with the county, and that the committee wished to maintain a local initiative, for the name of the secretary of the Reform Club was crossed out.[120]   Support was evidently expected largely from the northern and eastern parts of the county where substantial gentlemen of sympathetic views resided, like, for example, C. T. Thruston of Talgarth Hall who had led the opposition in 1836 and nominated Williams in the recent election. In the south also, near the county border, was Dr. John Pugh of Aberdovey (' Ioan ab Hu Feddyg ') who was as prominent in dissenting circles as he was in literary ones.[121]   It was mainly to ministers of religion that the Society looked for support in most areas, as for instance, Dinas Mawddwy, Tywyn, Llandrillo, Trawsfynydd, and Dyffryn (Harlech). Apart from the gentry named above only Henry Richardson, Esq., who had supported David Williams at the polling booth in Bala, was written to—and his name was added as an after-thought. Most of the towns were represented in the list, including Dolgellau, W. Williams, Esq., Ivy House, being written to. A few gentlemen from outside the county, notably R. D. Jones, Esq., of Trefri, Anglesey, who had been mentioned as a possible candidate in the forlorn days of 1858, were listed. Thus, the Society was looking for its initial support in the county from among men of its own station in society. The prospectus was ready by the end of the month, and ordered to be printed in Welsh and English, an initial order for 1,000 copies being made, to be printed by the firm of Thomas Gee of Denbigh.[122]

At the same time, the rules of the Society were drawn up by Dr. Richards, Lewis Edwards and Michael D. Jones. These have not survived, but apparently members had to be proposed for nomination, there was an annual subscription of at least 2s. 6d., and people resident outside the county were being admitted to membership.[123] Subscriptions were needed to pay for the quite considerable expenses which the committee had agreed to incur during the late election, to finance registration activities, and to build up a fighting fund. The first of these responsibilities was covered by a local subscription, collectors being appointed at the first meeting. Then in June, circulars were drawn up and sent to ' the chief men ' soliciting money and permission for the use of their names at the committee of management.[124] The persons thus addressed, 35 in number, were all substantial gentlemen, of whom 16 or 17 were resident in the county, and it can be assumed that this was as complete a list of ' upper-class ' supporters as was possible to devise at that juncture. Outside the county were such prominent names as Love Jones-Parry of Madryn, Colonel Biddulph of Chirk Castle, J. H. Whalley, M.P., Colonel Morgan of Rhyl, F. G. Salisbury of Chester, and L. Pugh, the Liverpool banker. Included in the list also were quarryowners in addition to Samuel Holland— J. W. Greaves and H. S. Westmacott of Porthmadoc, and Charles Holland of Liverpool. With five exceptions, all were north Wales men.

By the end of June, therefore, the Society was well-established and hopeful of being in command of sufficient resources to be able to fulfil its main function of registration. Lawyers had been retained in the chief towns to be responsible for this, and the newspapers were kept fully informed of its proceedings. As was emphasised in the circular, registration had to be undertaken immediately as the statutory date for completion (20 July) gave them scarcely five weeks' grace. The committee were careful to point out that they had no intention of arrogating to themselves the functions of a central executive: it was merely the urgency of the business which compelled them to take the initiative. They conceived of themselves as being no more than a registration society and propoganda organization. The important political initiatives, particularly the choice of a candidate, would be the province of the projected Committee of Management which would be composed of ' gentleman of station in and connected with the County of Merioneth '.[125]

Such limited aims, however, were soon superseded by more urgent, human problems which had the effect of transforming the Society into something significantly different and with an importance far wider than the communities in which it originated. Before the month of June was over evidence began to accumulate to the effect that tenants on the Rhiwlas estate were being evicted for refusing to vote with their landlord. When rumours of these deeds reached the Society, the committee drew up a remonstrance addressed to R. W. Price and signed by 24 members headed by John Jones, Fachddeiliog, Price's old friend.[126] In this long document, they made three major points. First, they declared that they wished to do nothing that could be interpreted as an interference in relations between Price and his tenants. At the same time, however, they hoped that the rumours then circulating were groundless, for they were at variance with the excellent relations on the Rhiwlas estate. Second, they pointed out that as the late election had been about religion it had raised issues of a conscientious kind which had made it impossible for sincere protestants to vote for a Catholic sympathizer. It followed, therefore, that any such retaliation as was now taking place would quite properly be regarded as religious persecution. Finally, they insisted that enfranchised tenants had a constitutional right to excercise their votes freely: ' The rights which we maintain are rights of conscience, allowed by God and guaranteed by the glorious constitution of our country.' Along with this remonstrance, Jones Fachddeiliog sent a personal letter to Price requesting his authority to deny the rumours. Price's reply, dated from Rhiwlas 27 June, was short and unequivocal.[127] He had, he said, consistently sought to benefit his tenants, by building comfortable houses for them and assisting them in every way open to him, and he could claim to have been very kind to many of them on numerous occasions. ' In return, I expected that they would allow me one small *favour* that I asked of them.' He did not deny the correctness of the facts alleged, and, moreover, counter-attacked by appealing to the precedent which he alleged to have been set by the Liberal candidate who, it was claimed, had ejected a tenant who had voted against him. This serious allegations was soon disposed of, the secretary writing immediately to Williams who, as quickly, replied denying the fact, and declaring that any tenant who voted conscientiously against him would, on the contrary, be worthy of his resspect. All this correspondence—the remonstrance, Price's reply, and the exchange of letters with David Williams—was published in the local weeklies, and in some of the London newspapers as well.[128]

In its issue of 27 July the *Baner* published a list of the votes of all the enfranchised tenants on the Rhiwlas estate. Because the poll-books have not survived there is no means of checking this list, but as it was probably supplied by the Society and never objected to by any of the persons named in it, it must be accepted as the least unsatisfactory of the few sources available to us. This showed that of the total of 35 tenants, 2 had voted for Williams, 11 for Wynne, and 22 had abstained. Of the two who had voted Liberal, one, namely Thomas Humphreys of Berth Llanfair, was a freeholder. The other, Peter Jones of the Goat Inn, held Bryn Pader, a farm of 63 acres, and he was alleged to have been evicted at a later date, presumably for having voted Liberal and permitting his premises to be used as a meeting-point for the Llandderfel voters, by W. W. Wynn of whom he held the Goat Inn and 11 acres in Llanuwchllyn. The immediate furore, however, concerned the ejections from among the 22 voters who had abstained. The first list of ejections, published on 20 July, named 5 farms—Fron-goch, Maes-y-gadfa, Ty'n-llwyn, Nant-hir, and Tai'r-felin. By the 27th this list had been amended, Ty'n-llwyn and Tai'r-felin being omitted, and Tŷ-isaf and Tal-y-garth added. This latter farm was not mentioned in later lists, and it is certain that its tenant was not evicted as he was still in occupation two years later.

All these farms were in the Cwm-tir-mynach region, adjacent to each other, all part of a rural neighbourhood.[129] Fron-goch was the largest farm in the district—the second largest in the whole parish—and consisted of 489 acres. In 1841 it was farmed by Robert Edwards who, according to local accounts, had improved it greatly by bringing into cultivation large areas of mountain pastures. By the 1850s it was reckoned to be one one of the best farms in the hundred of Penllyn, and Edwards himself had prospered sufficiently, so it was said, to have been able to buy a farm near Shrewsbury for his only son. By 1855, however, as he grew older, the farm began to deteriorate and he was given notice to quit.[130] His successor in the tenancy was Ellis Roberts of Cynlas Fawr. This was a farm of 158 acres in the parish of Llandderfel, Roberts having obtained the tenancy, at the cost of a rent rise, on the death of his father. When he moved to Fron-goch in 1856 Cynlas Fawr went to his first-cousin, Thomas Ellis of Tŷ-cerrig, and it was here that Thomas Edward Ellis was born in 1859.[131] Now, in that same year, with the eviction of Ellis Roberts, Fron-goch was given to Owen Roberts of Rhiwaedog, a farm of 410 acres in the same neighbourhood which he had occupied since at least 1847. This Owen Roberts was said to be the son-in-law of the old Edwards who had quit in 1855, so that the farm was in fact reverting to the older family of occupants.[132] This was an irony which was not lost on the community. Nor was the fact that Owen Roberts had voted for Wynne in the late election overlooked.

Maes-y-gadfa, a farm of 237 acres adjacent to Fron-goch had been in the occupation of Ellis Jones since at least 1841, his previous tenancy having been Coed-fael-uchaf in Penmaen, a farm of 70 acres. In 1851, Ellis Jones was 55 years of age, and his household, including himself, consisted of 12 persons, namely, his wife, two daughters, two young sons, and six servants.[133] The incoming tenant, David Jones of Ddolwen, was moving from a farm of 65 acres which must have been very inadequate for such a large household.[134] He was 10 years older than the outgoing tenant but since his household consisted of 8 children (6 sons and 2 daughters) whose ages ranged from 35 years to 11 years, all of whom were unmarried in 1861, he must have been one of the very few farmers on the estate who could manage a large holding without employing additional labour. He had not had a vote in the election.

Nant-hir, Tŷ-isaf, and Tal-y-garth were smaller farms, 165, 86, and 80 acres respectively.[135] John Jones must have been a fairly recent tenant of Nant-hir, for the census of 1851 shows the farm to have been held by one William Jones, aged 30 years, unmarried, with a household consisting of an aged father, a brother aged 28 years, a sister seven years younger, two small nieces, and one female servant. The 1861 census confirms that the farm had passed into the occupation of William Jones, aged 39 years, who was married with thee children under five years, had his aged mother living with him, and employed five servants, of whom three were male. According to the *Baner*, this William Jones was the brother-in-law of the John Jones who had been evicted in 1859, so that this farm also remained in the occupation of the same family.[136] Tŷ-isaf was held in 1847 by Ellen Roberts, possibly the mother of the John Roberts who was evicted in 1859.[137] The 1861 census confirms that the farm had passed into the occupation of Evan Evans, a widower 58 years of age, who worked the farm with the assistance of two sons, one of whom was married, a labourer and two female servants. The Evans family were said to have moved from Dol-feiriog, a farm of 53 acres in the same neighbourhood. He had voted for Wynne. Tan-y-garth (or Tal-y-garth) was said to have gone to Hugh Davies of Garnedd, who, however, publicly denied this.[138] The 1861 census shows that Hugh Thomas, alleged to have been evicted, to be still in occupation of the farm. On the other hand, Ty'n-llwyn had certainly changed hands since 1859, passing from John Davies, who had abstained, to a certain Thomas Jones.

These were not the only evictions in 1859: six tenants on the Glan-llyn estate who had voted Liberal were evicted and another, Mary Jones of Gweirglodd-wen, the mother of M. D. Jones, was likewise evicted. In addition, another seven tenants had their rents raised.[139] But these still lay in the future and the Society was not immediately concerned with them. There was no doubt in the minds of the members of the committee that the evictions on the Rhiwlas estate were a retaliation for the refusal of the tenants to vote as required by their master, and that their independence in this respect was grounded in a conscientious refusal to identify themselves with a religion which they believed to be false and dangerous. Certainly, all the evicted tenants had one thing in common: they were all nonconformists. Ellis Roberts of Fron-goch and John Jones, Maesy-gadfa were elders with the Calvinistic Methodists, Ellis Roberts having followed Robert Edwards in the eldership of Mynach Chapel as well as in the tenancy of Fron-goch, for the latter describes himself as ' deacon ' in the 1851 Census of Religious Worship. John Jones of Nant-hir was a deacon with the Independents, presumably at Soar, one of the chapels associated with Michael Jones the elder, and of which M. D. Jones was minister in 1859. John Davies of Ty'n-llwyn was also a Calvinistic Methodist elder. Nothing is known about the religion of the incoming tenants. The Welsh newspapers, especially the *Baner*, were positively libellous on this topic, suggesting that the new tenants would probably accept Price's religion as well as his farms. It seems most unlikely that a son-in-law of Robert Edwards would be of a contrary religion. Nevertheless, that these men had been evicted on account of their religion was a view widely held and was the explanation most assiduously propagated by the Society. The Welsh newspapers, notably the *Baner*, pointed out that the new church at Fron-goch, built largely at the expense of R. W. Price and opened in 1858, had failed to find many worshippers in the area it was designed to serve. ' Indeed,' said the *Baner*, ' the impression in the Bala region is that the failure of Fron-goch Church has as much to do with the notices to quit as the late election.'[140] Clergymen, it explained, lay at the root of the trouble, though it was compelled to add that as yet there was no certain evidence of this. Rumours to this effect circulated and were publicized. For instance, it was reported that R. W. Price had declared that he was determined to extirpate nonconformity from Cwmtirmynach, and that John Williams, Sir Watkin's Glan-llyn agent, had stated categorically that in future farms would be let only to tenants who voted as instructed and, presumably, were churchmen. So far as the Glan-llyn estate is concerned it was later stated in evidence before the Welsh Land Commission that six of the seven farms from which recalcitrant tenants had been evicted had subsequently been tenanted by churchmen.[141] This may very well have been so, but as we have seen, this was unlikely to have happened on the Rhiwlas estate where relations between Price and his tenants had been consistently good. The Society may very well have had much to do with the circulation of rumours of this kind. It supplied the *Baner*, for example, with information, and arranged to distribute it in the locality. In their public and official pronouncements, however, they were naturally more cautious and circumspect, maintaining the religious argument but stressing also the constitutional issues—issues, that is, which were likely to appeal to a public far wider than a sectarian one.

These attitudes were well illustrated at the public meeting held in Bala on 19 August.[142] It was organized by the Society as a meeting of tenant farmers gathered together to sympathize with the evicted, Ellis Roberts of Fron-goch being present. There were delegations from Corwen and Dolgellau. All the resolutions spoken to dealt directly with the constitutional and political implications of the late election. Only one speaker— the Reverend John Parry seconding a resolution which declared that an attempt to restrict the rights of a voter was an offence against the voter's liberty—dealt specifically with the religious undertones of the current political situation. For all the other speakers the matter had become one of principle, of political and constitutional rights. The most powerful speech of the evening in fact avoided any reference to religion as a divisive factor. This was Lewis Edwards' speech pledging the meeting to use all legal means to frustrate any attempts to interfere with voting rights. He asserted that religion in Penllyn was not organized for political ends. He instanced his attitudes at the beginning of the campaign: his refusal to take part directly either as speaker or canvasser. If he had erred, he said, it was in not doing enough. It was Price who had made religion an issue by believing rumours concerning the political activities of chapels which, as he himself could testify, had no basis in fact. Unfortunately, Price had acted in accordance with those arrogant assumptions concerning the rights of the disposal of property which characterized landed proprietors everywhere, namely, that because the franchise has nothing to do with conscience, and conscience nothing to do with the election of an M.P., there could be no offence in compelling dependent tenants to vote in a certain way. Any tenant who refused to do so must be guilty, therefore, of wanting to injure his master. Why not, asked Lewis Edwards, apply the same logic and reverse the proposition? Should not twenty-four tenants, the possessors of an aggregate of twenty-four votes, be within their social rights in expecting their landlord, the possessor of *one* vote, to exercise it in their favour? If obligation be the cement of the society it must be mutual and the rights of both sides in the combination be respected. To claim a right to dispose of votes as well as of property would lead to the enslaving of the tenantry. It was their constitutional right as freemen to resist such a tendency. In asserting these rights they were not adopting warlike postures. ' It is not we who started this conflict,' he declared, 'but we cannot make peace except on the basis of justice. We cannot sacrifice principle. Whatever the consequences, we are under an eternal obligation to defend the right of conscience, and to maintain the rights of our neighbours. If war there must be, then we cannot but say, "God defend the right".' One has only to compare this speech of Lewis Edwards with the speech quoted earlier to appreciate the nature of the change which had transformed political discussion in the space of a few months. The underlying cause may have been religious: the language of the conflict was about politics.

But there was evidence that at a yet deeper level there were social and economic grievances, not a sharp or well-defined as religion but nevertheless sufficiently sharp to exacerbate the situation. For instance, it was well-known that the frequent tenancy changes at Fron-goch and other farms were always accompanied by a rent rise, sometimes very substantial ones. More revealing of the acuteness of tenant grievances was the evidence of one of the evicted, John Jones of Nant-hir, which the Society recorded for the benefit of its Liverpool sympathisers.[143] In this, John Jones explained how he had laboured over the years to improve his farm at his own expense, bringing 15 acres of mountain into cultivation, planting new hedges, laying drains, and paying for the transport of all materials needed in the building of a new stable. These three grievances —frequent rent rises to take advantage of increased productivity, loss of invested capital, no compensation for improvements—were to become the staple economic grievances of the 1880's and '90's. They were present in the 1850's. So also that other grievance—land hunger. The ready way in which the farms of the dispossessed were disposed of from within the neighbourhoods was an indication of social tensions cutting across even family relationships and religious loyalties. Looked at from outside—from the comparative security of an expanding publishing business—this was the nastiest and most reprehensible feature of all. Wrote the *Baner*, ' The lust of these men for land, their lack of understanding, their heartlessness, and their lack of self-respect for themselves as men, is utterly fearful.'[144] The lack of understanding of Thomas Gee, that prophet of Liberalism, must strike us as even more terrifying, and inspire in us pity for those who were taught by such as he not to distinguish between religious grievances and social inequalities and deprivations. The material seeds of conflict were already sown, and the election saw their first growth.

It is important also for the purposes of this analysis to realize that the evicted were not necessarily small farmers or from the lower ranks in rural society. They were peasants, surely, but leading men in their communities, substantial farmers, the heads of large households.[145] Of the 22 tenants on the Rhiwlas estate who had abstained, only 4 held farms of less than 100 acres. 10 of the farms were between 100 and 200 acres, 5 between 200 and 300 acres, 2 between 400 and 500 acres, and 1 above 500 acres. This was an inverse relation to the general pattern of farm size, for of the 96 farms belonging to Rhiwlas in the parish of Llanfor, for example (excluding the demesne of 508 acres), 70 were under 100 acres, 15 of between 100 and 200 acres, and only 11 of 200 acres and above. On the estate as a whole very nearly 72 *per cent* of the farms (118 out of a total of 164) were below 100 acres in size, and of the remainder nearly one half of the tenants had abstained. As we have already seen, three of the five evicted farmed some of the largest holdings : they were chosen, probably for that reason, from among the top ten *per cent* of the farming community, the group most looked up to by their fellows, from among whom the parishes sought their servants, the chapels their deacons, and, indeed, the Bala Union its Guardians, and the Guardians themselves its vice-chairmen.[146] If the object of R. W. Price had been to stamp out any incipient political independence among his tenantry, then the individuals whom he had singled out to suffer his wrath and to provide examples could not have been better chosen.

The alarm if not terror provoked by these evictions compelled the new Society to act in entirely novel ways. From July onwards a new purposiveness, a new drive, is discernable in its operations. G. P. Lloyd, Esq., of Plas-yn-dre, became a vice-president and donated £5.[147] New members were admitted without formal election, and local gentlemen now gave substantial sums to further its work. As a result, it was able to extend the range of its activities. Delegates were sent to other county towns, such as Corwen and Tywyn, in order to assist them in setting up similar movements. Also, it initiated an intensified propaganda campaign in the county by means of lectures and public meetings, and particularly through the medium of the Welsh newspapers. Its major preoccupation became educative, therefore, for before any of the aims could be realized the ignorance of the majority of the peasants would have to be broken down. Politics of the kind now being advocated were not, and never had been, a normal constituent of community discussion in the way that religion had become. The task of the Society was to achieve this kind of transformation using the means and techniques of communication open to it. As one letter-writer put it, ' You bards, cease for a while hymning the flowers and birds, and sing to the Ballot. Writers, lecture and write about the franchise and taxation. Musicians, tune your strings to sing the praises of our humble heroes ',[148] and so on. However improbable this might sound, in fact this would involve the capture of one of the most important cultural activities of those rural communities, namely, the literary societies which, though often closely associated with chapels nevertheless existed independently of religion. For its part the Society tried to interest Thomas Gee in commissioning a series of front-page articles on political subjects, particularly on the franchise, and invited popular lecturers to tour the county with similar topics. Education, therefore, became a primary aim of the Society but the original purpose of the Society was not forgotten, and with the subscriptions which now began to flow it was able to engage professional men in the all-important task of registration and to keep at all times the image of David Williams as the prospective Liberal candidate in the forefront.

It can be seen, therefore, that the events of 1859, centred around the town of Bala, constituted the turning-point in the political history of Merioneth. It had been a traumatic experience for those engaged in it, from the farmers who had suffered to the townsmen who had led and directed the change. The county had been aroused, a new leadership had emerged, social grievances blended with religious conviction and fervour had provided an emotional drive for a constitutional argument, and above all an organisation embodying all these elements had been created. These were all new elements in the political life of the country and, as we have shown, were expressive of changes taking place in the social life of the county. It was in the nature of things, therefore, that they should have been limited in their effects and circumscribed in their operation. The experience had been a local one, but conditions were not such as to make it probable that it could be capitalized upon a county basis. For this to happen the movement would have to shed its local character and be identified with wider political movements : the events in Bala would have to lose their particularity in order to gain a greater significance and intelligibility within a wider movement of change. Such a shift was beyond the competence of the group we have studied: they lacked both the financial means and the sophisticated techniques of management and organization that such an advance would involve. These could be supplied only from outside the county, and in changed circumstances such as would favour their success. When we ask, therefore, why success should have come nine years later at the general election of 1868 we can identify the critical factors as follows. First, there were the accumulative effects of further changes in the economic and social complexion of the county. Second, the intrusion into the county of a powerful political organization, namely, the Liberation Society. Third, the effects of franchise changes after 1867 on the political classes, and fourth, the primary role of a religious argument in the contest of 1868.

The first of these factors was the rapid growth of the slate industry in the north of the county, in particular, in the parishes of Ffestiniog and Maentwrog. Slate quarrying was an old-established industry in that region,[149] and its general configuration had already been laid down in the boom years of the 1830's and '40's. There had been a decided retraction in the decade 1845-55, but thereafter there had been a very considerable expansion which was particularly marked in the middle and late 1860's.[150] By then there were some 18 separate undertakings in the parish of Ffestiniog, most of them owned by limited liability companies which had invested large sums of money in the new machinery and improved communications. There had been a corresponding growth in the population of the parishes involved. The population of the Ffestiniog Union in 1831 was 11,558.[151] By 1871 it had more than doubled to a total of 24,141, the actual increase in the latter decade being at the rate of 32 *per cent*—double the county average for the same period. In the decade 1851-61 there had been a net loss by migration of just over 1 *per cent*: in the decade 1861-71 there was a net gain by immigration of 2,780, or 15.2 *per cent*.

The result of this population growth was a relatively enormous expansion of the small towns and villages which had been established in the boom years at the beginning of the century. The largest of these settlements were the creations of the nineteenth century: the characteristic quarry towns of Ffestiniog were new urban centres established sometimes by the quarry owners but more often by the immigrant workers themselves. Blaenau Ffestiniog was the most important and typical of these, built largely by the men through their own building societies, and by the quarry owners.[152] These communities were entirely Welsh in character. The capital reorganisation of the industry which was taking place in the 'fifties and 'sixties[153] would not appear to have altered profoundly the originally local and Welsh character of the industry, and by this time the leading immigrant capitalists who had directed the expansion of the early decades of the century had been assimilated into county society. Holland, Greaves, Casson—these were men who, by virtue of their controlling influence in the industrial life of the parish, occupied a status in these communities comparable with that of the rural gentry in the county towns to the south. They were all landed proprietors as well as industrialists, and as such bestrode the two worlds of the rural and industrial economies. Older-established landed families, such as the Oakeley family of Tan-y-bwlch, had made the transition earlier than these immigrants by involving themselves, either directly or as lessees, in the new economy. In any case, there was a community of interest among this gentry class in the Ffestiniog region which marked them off from the other gentry in the county, and which increasingly made them the natural leaders of the new social communities which their enterprise had created. At the more immediate level of management,[154] change in ownership made scarcely any difference at all, for only exceptionally was this critical aspect of the industrial economy in the hands of immigrant Englishmen. Agents and managers were almost exclusively Welsh, and drawn usually from among the working classes themselves. Finally, it must be emphasised that these were nonconformist communities, some of them exclusively so. Blaenau Ffestiniog, for instance had grown around the existing Independent chapel[155] and it, and the chapels and schoolrooms of the other denominations remained the focal points of the communities. In places such as these it was the Church which was compelled to conform to the customs and ideals of societies in whose origins and growth it had had but little part to play.[156]

The second factor making for change was the coming of the Liberation Society into the county.[157] Liberationist activities on a local level had hitherto been virtually unknown in the county. Until 1859, not a single Merioneth man or organized body of men had contributed to the central funds of the Society. Very occasionally, in the early years of the Society, Merioneth had been represented in one form or another on its Council, but this had been minimal and formal only, reflecting the aim of the Society to have every county in the country represented. There had been one representative in 1847 and another in 1850, but there is no evidence that they did anything to further the aims of the Society, and they certainly never contributed financially. Nor had the Executive Committee made much of an effort to till this unrewarding soil. Delegations visited Bala and Dol-

gellau in 1851, but if membership of the Society and contributions to its funds can be taken as an indication of its success
then its labours must have been entirely unfruitful for not a
single contribution was made in the years following. The turning point came in 1860 when one person subscribed 10s. 6d.,
and significantly enough, that contribution came from Bala.
For the next three years Bala remained the only place in
Merioneth providing financial support. In 1861, 11 contributions totalling £2 11s. 0d. were made, in 1862, 9 amounting
to £1 15s. 6d., and in 1863, 3 totalling £1 3s. 6d. The following
year, in 1864, 13 Bala people contributed a total of £2 2s. 0d.,
and 5 in Tywyn a total of 11s. 0d. Bala was thus virtually the
only place in the county providing support for Liberationist
policies. Equally significant is the fact that the individuals subscribing to the Society were precisely the men whom we have
identified as the leaders of the new political movement.
Throughout these years it was committee members of the
Merioneth Reform Society who contributed most generously
and most regularly. Thus Lewis Edwards, Michael D. Jones,
John Parry and John Peters sent their annual 5s. 0d., Dr.
Richards his half-guinea, and Simon Jones his half-crown or
five shillings. There is no evidence to show that there was any
formal connections between the two societies at this date: it
would be highly improbable that there should be: but the
sudden commitment of so many key individuals to support of
the national Society suggests that one major effect of the
experience of 1859 was a readiness of the town *élite* to identify
themselves with political views and policies far more extreme
than those which had hitherto characterized the political life of
the county. If the election of 1859 had been a chastening one
and a disillusionment it had also been a clarifying one.

The subsequent history of the Liberation Society within the
county was one of rapid growth and increasing influence. In
1865—the year of the election—13 Corwen people contributed
£2 16s. 6d., and the Tywyn contribution increased. In 1867,
Dolgellau people began to subscribe, 19 individuals contributing a total of £3 19s. 0d., while the Bala subscription rose
to £3 7s. 6d. The following year saw the adherence of Llandderfel and Llandrillo, bringing the total of contributors to 70

and the amount subscribed to more than £11. Clearly, this indicates a significant shift in the political life of the county, and it is important to make two points in relation to it. First, that initially, as we have already explained, the change was a response to local factors. The chronology is unmistakable. Even as it had been the experience of 1859 which had made some of the individuals most closely involved to be receptive to Liberationist policies, so it was the disappointment following the 1865 election which turned more people in fresh areas in the same direction. The attempt to win that election with local resources only had proved a failure and demonstrated finally the need for support by an outside body possessing the financial resources and the electoral knowledge and expertise to organize opinion. The Liberation Society could make headway only where it was able to capitalize on local discontent and frustration. Secondly, and more obviously important, was the fact that the Liberation Society did decide to become active in north Wales. As we have explained elsewhere,[159] it was not until 1866 when a series of north Wales conferences was arranged by the Society that this occurred, and it was by reason of this coincidence of need on the one part and of effort on the other that 1866 seems a great enhancement of the Society's appeal and influence in Merioneth in that and subsequent years.

The North Wales conferences were held at Newtown, Denbigh, and Bala during the month of September 1866.[159] Newtown and Denbigh chose themselves as venues for such meetings. They were county towns in shires where Liberationist support had been consistently strong over the years, but in this respect almost any of the other towns in those counties might have served equally well. It was the ease of access provided by the recently opened railways which was probably the determining factor. Bala was chosen as the venue for the Merioneth meeting for the simple reason that only there was there any support for Liberationist objectives, and any organized body to which the arrangements could be assigned. Despite the late harvest of that year the Bala Conference, held in the British School Rooms on the 26th, appeared to have been a great success.[160] There were two formal meetings addressed by the delegates from the Executive Committee, namely, John Carvell

Williams, Edward Miall, and Henry Richard, and care was taken to invite representatives from some of the other county towns to support the formal resolutions. But it was the Bala people who were prominent. One of the chief supporting speakers was Michael D. Jones, the chair was taken by Dr. Richards, and the final speaker was Lewis Edwards. Most of the other founder-members of the Merioneth Reform Society were on the platform, but most significantly, it was the presence of between 20 and 30 students from the two Colleges which struck contemporaries. Some of the future leaders of Methodism in North Wales were thus being encouraged to identify themselves publicly with Liberationism—to stand shoulder to shoulder with politicians whom their fathers had distrusted and feared.

All the conferences conformed to a pattern. The three delegation members spoke to the main resolutions which enunciated general principles concerned with the special obligations resting on Welsh nonconformists to support the disestablishment movement and to organize themselves politically to this end. A local man was then called upon to read a paper on the history and present state of the representation of his particular county, and finally, a resolution would be passed calling for the setting up of a County Committee to give practical effect to the previous resolutions, involving also the setting up of Local Committees in all the county towns. In other respects the meetings were quite dissimilar: the Bala Conference was notable for the intensity of its emotional involvement. However sedate and respectable the formal proceedings might be, underneath was the feeling that the situation being discussed was a human one—that underlying the statistics was a tale of human suffering. Whereas the main supporting speakers at Newtown and Denbigh had stuck elegantly to their briefs in their papers on the religious and parliamentary statistics of their respective counties, at Bala Michael D. Jones delivered a speech singular in its biting sarcasm, in its invective, and in its searing hatred, and passionate enunciation of principle.[161] Its theme was the misrepresentation of Merioneth and its social consequences. If by representation was meant the representation of property, then Merioneth was most efficiently represented :

' A great proportion of the land belongs to the Tories; and our Tory member represents land, game, dogs, horses, sheep, cattle, goats, fowls, turkeys, ducks, geese, and every other kind of property. Our Conservative member, we know , will do all in his power for the rights of land. We are sure that the game, dogs, and horses will not be neglected . . . The fowls, the sheep, the cattle, and goats of Merionethshire need no Aesop to call upon our Tory member to attend to their interests. They are well represented in Parliament. Complaints come from other sources. It is the men of Merioneth that are unrepresented and misrepresented.'

But even allowing that men are given representation by the constitutional machinery of the country, very few have a share in that representation. Tenant farmers have the vote: but the franchise is exercised by the landlords, and extending the franchise by lowering the qualification would merely magnify the evil. The wealthy classes assume or claim that they know more and are more virtuous than the lower classes and that this justifies them in managing the affairs of the country. In Merioneth ' they say, allow us to take out your eyes, and we shall very kindly lead you by the hand '. Who then are represented? Wynnstay, Rhiwlas, and a few other places of less importance. And of course, the clergy who, since the landowners are Tory, are themselves Tory.

' The moon is bright because the sun shines. The clergy generally in Wales are with the gentry, and against the peopl, as it is in Merioneth . . . The clergy really are the officers of the aristocracy generally appointed and promoted by them. They are a body of spiritual constables or police, in black instead of blue clothes.'

The gentry do all in their power to defeat the representative system because they know that potentially, since it is the basis of the constitution, it is destructive of their power.

' It is no wonder the gentry hate it so thoroughly. Ahab and Jezebel finding that Naboth alive would not serve their purpose, resolved to convert him into a dead body; and the Merioneth landocracy, finding that representation is inconsistent with their illegitimate sway, have ruthlessly strangled it into a corpse, shutting their eyes to the grand doctrine of the resurrection . . . They are the enemies of our specific form of government . . .

They are traitors to their country. They make a free country into a feudal soil. Some of our barons convert Wales, as far as they can, into a Russia.'

But in doing so they injure themselves, cultivating selfishness, pride, and avarice.

' Every fish and fowl must be under their sway, or they are not satisfied, and were smaller birds and flies of any use, they would soon demand an extension of the game laws. They degrade themselves in becoming hated oppressors, when they might be revered leaders of freemen. They breathe from their very birth an air of flattery, and in mature years they stand less chance of hearing the truth.'

Pari passu, the tenantry are degraded, terrorised, corrupted, and their landowners are blissfully unaware of their true social conditions.

' The slaveholders of America had a contempt for their slaves, which made them careless of the negroes' comforts. The Tory landowners of Merioneth are similarly blinded.'

Buildings on some farms look as if they were intended for some backwoods of a colony.

' There are hardly any huts in Ireland inferior to some of the dwellings of Sir Watkin's tenants, who dispirited and heartless, wallow in filth.'

The decencies of privacy between the sexes cannot be observed in these barbarously constructed houses. Farming also suffers.

' Since the application of the screw to the Rhiwlas tenants, farming has declined rapidly. There is not that good understanding and co-operation between landlord and tenant that prevailed in times gone by. The tenants are on the high road to poverty; and another enemy to good farming has latterly appeared on the Rhiwlas estate, in addition to the screw, namely, game.'

He claimed that Mr. Thomas, the druggist, bailiff of the county court,[162] had lately informed him that two-thirds of the business of the court came from the tenants of Sir Watkin. In his peroration he brought his listeners back again to the theme which was uppermost in their minds, and to which he returned again in the evening of his life and which is the theme of this essay.

> ' It would be a great help if some powerful pen could be employed in England to write the history of our battles, our sufferings, and our martyrdoms. John Jones, Maesygadva, was a moral hero, of whom Merioneth ought to be proud. The deaths of Owen Roberts, Vrongoch, and Mary Jones, Weirgloddwen, are not to be forgotten. They all died gloriously for they derived strength from God's sanctuary, true to their religion, and the liberty of their country.'

This speech deserves careful study and extensive quotation. Its logic and its language, its identification of political ills with social distress express passionately the extent to which old assumptions had been rejected, and the almost desperate readiness of the people concerned to embrace a new political philosophy and adopt new methods of agitation. Compare the speech with others quoted earlier in this essay and the difference is apparent. As Lewis Edwards, speaking later at this meeting put it, ' They (i.e. Miall and Richard) are like veteran soldiers; and, if necessary, we will join them on the fields of battle.'[163] The coming of the Liberation Society to Merioneth was a call to battle, and it put forth no uncertain sound at Bala thanks to the experience of Bala men.

The third factor which helps to explain the victory of 1868 is the effect of the Reform Act of 1867 on the electorate of the county. Unfortunately, it is impossible to be precise about the exact nature of the franchise changes of that year because the poll books have not survived. Also, since the 1868 contest was not pressed to the poll there are no voting statistics to compare with those of previous elections. Bearing in mind these limitations, however, it is possible to come to some fairly reliable conclusions as to the magnitude of the numerical change in the electorate as a result of the Reform Act of 1867.

TABLE A

POPULATION AND ELECTORATE

Year	Pop.	% Change	Electorate		Increase	Increase %
1831	35,315		(in 1832)	580		
1841	39,332	+11.0	(in 1840)	1025	445	76.7
1851	38,843	—1.0	(in 1851)	1027	2	Static
1861	38,963	+0.3	(in 1866)	1527	500	48x6
1871	46,598	+20.0	(in 1868)	3185	1658	108x5

TABLE B

ELECTORS TO POPULATION

1832	1 in 61	or	1.6% of the population
1840	1 in 38	or	2.6% "
1851	1 in 38	or	2.6% "
1866	1 in 32	or	3.9% "
1868	1 in 15	or	6.8% "

Between the First and the Second Reform Acts the total electorate grew from 580 in 1832, or 1.6 *per cent* of the population, to
3,158 in 1868, or 6.8 *per cent* of the population.[164] This represents a growth-rate of more than 500 *per cent*—considerably
more than the average growth-rate in most rural counties in
Wales. It can be seen, however, from Table C (below), that
this is an inflated figure, and that the true increase was more
likely to have been of the order of 300 *per cent*—much more in
line with the order of increase in the country as a whole. The
580 electors registered in 1832 probably represent something
like the maximum number possible under the old unreformed
constitution. It was, as we have seen, the contest of 1836 which
stimulated party organizations to see to the register of electors,
and the figure of 1336 at the registration of that year following
the election can be taken as representing the maximum number
of electors possible under the Act of 1832. As can be seen, this
was an increase of about 76 *per cent* over the pre-1832 electorate:
about 1 in 38 people had the vote as against 1 in 61 before the
Act. Thereafter the proportions remained fairly constant until

the early 'sixties. The reason for this is evident: it is not simply that there was no political activity, but also that population and wealth remained fairly static during those decades. The substantial rise in the early 1860s reflected the increased political activity following the election of 1859. Under the leadership of the Merioneth Reform Society registration was again a major preoccupation of the political organizations in the various localities, and the proportional rise in the numbers of registered voters reflects this activity. The increase of 500 on the register represented a growth-rate of over 48 *per cent* in the 12 years from 1852 to 1865.

Table C shows clearly that this was not gradual but a phenomenon confined to the second part of that period. Moreover the rise continued steadily as the decade advanced, through by the middle years of the 1860's the tendency of the rise in the electorate to be far in excess of the rise in population had been halted, for by then population was increasing at a rate of about 20 *per cent* while the electorate had a growth rate of about 36 *per cent*. By the time of the Second Reform Act, therefore, about 3.9 *per cent* of the population had the vote as against 2.6 *per cent* in 1832—or 1 in 32 of the population as against 1 in 38. The effect of the legislation of 1867 was to more than double the numbers registered.

It is when we seek to discover the effects of the franchise changes upon the social composition of the electorate that our sources fail us. Table C (above), which is based on statistics obtained from Parliamentary Papers, is less informative than it appears to be. Without the poll books it is not possible to analyse by social class or occupation over a period of time the various categories of voters distinguished in the Table. The three main categories were the freeholders, the lessees, and the occupying tenants, and it is vital consideration to know what numerical relation existed between them, but this cannot be done when, for instance, the vast confusion of freeholders is included under the same blanket term. It is fairly certain that in Merioneth very significant numbers of freeholders qualified by land were also tenants in respect of other lands occupied by them. Furthermore, as we have already argued, there were rarely any differences socially between small

TABLE C

REGISTERED ELECTORS, 1832 TO 1868

Year	Population in census year	% rise or fall	Free-holders	Lessees	Occupying Tenants	Trustees	Offices	Qualifications	Others	TOTAL
1832	35,315									580
1835			350	37	394	3			1	785
1837			711	103	504	17			1	1,336
1840			239	74	598	92	3	19		1,025
1843	39,332	+11.0%	341	96	679	84	6	23		1,229
1847			601	73	461	12	29		4	1,180
1851	38,843	+1.0%								1,027
1852			502	76	397				31	1,006
1856			557	125	432				49	1,163
1857			570	84	423				49	1,126
1863	38,963	+0.3%								1,475
1865			758		530	50	37	47	105	1,527
1868	46,598	+20.0%	1132	—12 occupiers. Others—2053						3,185

freehold farmers and the more substantial tenant farmers. And finally, Merioneth was unique in that its towns were not enfranchised, with the result that town dwellers could qualify to vote only on one of the county franchises. It is this latter feature which explains the curious and untoward fact that the Parliamentary Returns, as used in compiling Table C, show a preponderance of freeholders over tenant-at-will. The following Table D, based on the one set of Returning Officer's Registration Lists which have survived,[165] demonstrates clearly that the statistics conceal the all-important fact that a substantial proportion of the freeholders enumerated were town-dwellers and not freehold farmers.

TABLE D

ANALYSIS OF VOTING LISTS FOR 1841

Parish	Freeholders	Lessees	Occupying Tenants	Others	Total
Llanfawr	21	3	48	1	76
Llanycil	64	5	27	1	97
Llandderfel	16	2	24	1	47
Llanuwchllyn	16	5	37	1	59
Llangower	9	2	9	1	21
Total	126=42%	21=7%	145=48.3%	8=2.7%	300
Ffestiniog	9	21	6	1	37
TOTAL	135	42	151	9	337

The critical parish in this respect is Llanycil where the town of Bala was situated. Here 64 freehold voters are listed, but the Overseer's List for the parish as printed with the authority of the Revising Barrister shows that only two of these freeholds were in respect of land only. The nature of the qualification in all the other 62 is given as ' Freehold house and land ', or ' Freehold house and garden ', or simply ' Freehold house (or houses) '. This immediately reduces the number of so-called freeholds in the five parishes from 126 to 64. Put proportionately, the published statistics would appear to show freeholders as constituting 42 *per cent*, tenants 48.3 *per cent*, and leaseholders 7.0 *per cent*. In fact, the rural freeholder—the farmer—constituted only 21.3 *per cent* of the electors of the five parishes. A similar calculation can correct the statistics in respect of the leaseholders. Of the 21 shown as leaseholders in Ffestiniog parish no less than 20 held leases on their houses: only 1 appears to have been a farmer. In other words, the leaseholders of Ffestiniog were likewise town dwellers and evidently quarry-workers by occupation. Corrections such as these would probably apply to the whole of the county were the information available. As it is, we can do no more than venture a guess and state that generally speaking the numbers of freehold electors shown in Table C who were farmers probably numbered about one half of the stated numbers. The remainder were townsmen —shopkeepers, craftsmen, and the like. The sudden rise in the number of freehold voters in 1836 and again after 1859 may thus be made more intelligible. It is extremely likely that it was accounted for by increased registration in the *towns* rather than in the countryside, and that it was this element in the population which responded to the work of the Reform Society. Equally significant was the slightly less sharp increase in the numbers of occupying tenants registered. It needed no Society to stimulate this. It was a function of landownership so to do, and even as the numbers of voters remain fairly constant in the 'forties and 'fifties so, after 1859, they rise sharply, reflecting not a resurgence of political interest on their part but a hardening of the political attitudes of the landowners.

As a result of the Reform Act the electorate doubled, rising from 1527 to 3185. Not all of this increase would have been due to the extension of the franchise to the £12 occupier. A proportion of it would have reflected the increasing population and the rising prosperity of certain parts of the county. In the decade 1861-71 population increased by 20 *per cent* compared with the 0.3 *per cent* of the previous decade. As we have already indicated this upward swing probably began towards the middle of the decade and was concentrated in the slate-quarrying districts of Ffestiniog. It is probable, therefore, that considerable numbers of quarrymen must have qualified as leaseholders in respect of their properties—their houses and gardens. There is no means of ascertaining this properly. Nor, since there was no poll in 1868, can we be quite certain that the increase in the electorate took place principally at Ffestiniog. The lowering of the occupation franchise would have operated everywhere and brought additional small farmers and craftsmen on to the electoral roll. Yet it was certainly the impression in the county that the increase in Ffestiniog would be critical. We should readily agree with this judgement, for it was not merely the numbers of additional voters registered which were important politically, but the concentration of relatively large numbers of votes in well-defined, homogeneous communities. The addition of a few hundred votes among the scattered tenantry on the great estates would scarcely affect the social power of the landlords:they would be too dispersed to matter. At the Revising Court in Blaenau Ffestiniog in September 1868 it was stated that 200 new claims had been made on behalf of the Liberals. Not all were admitted, but it was claimed after the registration that as a result of this Court there would be 300 votes in Ffestiniog as compared with 80 in 1865.[166] It was on the basis of calculations such as these that the Liberals in Merioneth estimated that at the coming election they would have a majority of 439—a degree of precision and of optimism which was never put to the test, but, which we may fairly aver, was not far off the mark in Merioneth in 1868.

Finally, it was of inestimable importance that the election of 1868 was being fought, so far as Merioneth was concerned, on one issue only, namely, the question of the disestablishment of the Irish Church. As we have already argued, this was virtually the only aspect of politics which the body of electors and the populace in general could understand as an issue of principle and to which they could engage themselves. The fact that the Liberal Party as such, under the leadership of Gladstone, was committed to such a measure helped to break down that feeling of isolation and of parochialism which had hitherto characterized them. Moreover, it activated an interest in other political questions and drew their attention to secular affairs. Thus, under the exigencies of the election, the quarrymen were beginning to think of themselves as belonging to an industrial class, to express their solidarity with workers in the same

industry elsewhere, and to think of their future in terms of their
new political rights. This was the burden of a message drawn
up by them at a Liberal Meeting in Ffestiniog,[167] which was
chaired by Samuel Holland, for the benefit of their fellow
workers in Caernarfonshire. Thinking about the Irish Church
taught men to act in accordance with their rights.

These, then, were the four factors which were critical in the
changed political climate of the late 'sixties. In combination
they created a new political situation, generated a new political
spirit, and in so doing marked a decisive break with the past.
All, we must note, were relatively sudden in their operation,
and their effects all concentrated within the three years after
1865. It was in these years that the growth of population and
the concentration of an industrial class in Ffestiniog first
became, within the slow-moving and conservative economy of
a backward county, massive and portentous. It was in 1866
that the Liberation Society organised itself in the county in a
purposeful way, and in 1868 that the effects on the electorate of
the 1867 Act, which, until the last moment could not have been
foretold, became calculable. And finally, it was in 1868 that
local men could transmute into the terms and language of their
own experience, the rhetoric of Gladstone and of Bright.

*　　　　*　　　　*

How clear a braek with the past this was is evident when we
compare briefly the two elections of the 'sixties. The 1865
election had all the flavour of the old tradition but with a new
bitterness added.[168] W. W. E. Wynne announced his resignation on 7 June, and the same day hiss on, W. R. M. Wynne,
announced his candidature. As in 1836, so now there was no
officially convened county meeting, no formal requisitions:
simply the Addresses from Peniarth. The same day, David
Williams issued his Address, but as in 1859 scarcely moved a
finger to organize support. The Conservatives canvassed ener-
getically in the time-honoured way. For example, the young
candidate was taken on a round of visits to the tenants on the
Rhiwlas estate by its new owner, the young and bustling
Richard John Lloyd Price who had inherited the estate from his

grandfather in 1860. Perhaps he was also shown the game on these visits, for this had been one of Price's first innovations in his now fashionable mode of life.[169] Superficially, the Liberals appeared to be better organized. They had a Central Committee of 5 headed by T. Price Lloyd, of Nannau, and including such staunch figures from the past as C. T. Thruston, of Talgarth Hall, and Charles Edwards, of Dolserau.[170] These, it should be noted, were for the most part, the gentlemen to whom the original Bala Society of 1859 had looked to for support. But there were very few public meetings, and this, for the Liberal cause, was virtually to do nothing, and to ignore the most effective way open to reformers of propagating their views. Worse, it was a tacit admission that the so-called Tory way of winning elections was the only way. A Tory party could afford to be without an organization: a reforming party could not survive without one.

More serious was the tone of defeatism everywhere in evidence. Typical of this was the lack of spirit among the Liberals at Bala. Only one meeting appears to have been called,[171] and that was a grim affair when it was not formal and cliché-ridden. Michael D. Jones's speech was that of a man *de profundis*. What shall we do? How can we forget the sufferings of 1859? Could the Rhiwlas tenants be expected again to defy a master who was incorrigible where his predecessor had been merely misguided, and who was already giving evidence of his harsh determination to support Wynne to the uttermost? M. D. Jones's advice was simply to act as they had done in 1859. ' Penderfynwch ddweud y gwir '. But this was a counsel of perfection, and it needed no prophet to foretell that Bala would give the Tories a majority. The landowners had learned their lesson, and the screw was being turned more tightly than before. According to Michael D. Jones[172] *all* the Rhiwlas tenants in fact voted for Wynne, and it was this which decided the election. David Williams was not exaggerating or taking refuge in the coventialities of disgruntled, defeated candidates when he proclaimed after the election that it had been obvious that large numbers of tenant farmers had been coerced, ' that a new element of coercion developed itself in the acts of persons of position '.[173] With the exception of Harlech, all the polling

districts gave Wynne substantial majorities,[174] and the fact that
he gained the seat by almost as great a majority as his father
had in retaining his in 1859 was testimony not to his own popularity or that of his party, but to the effectiveness of landlord
control when it was exercised with vigilance and determination.

How different was the election of 1868! The spirit of the
election is new, more akin to that of 1859 but now far more
widely dispersed. The Liberals were first in the field,[175] holding
public meetings in all the main places, and by September it was
already being rumoured that Wynne would retire rather than
face a contest. David Williams, as ever the reluctant hero,
cautiously refrained from publishing an Address until the
results of the registration under the new Act were known. By
then, 1,400 electors were said to have signed the requisition
inviting him to stand, and by October it was virtually certain
that he would win the seat.[176] Bala once more came into its
own, the pioneers of 1859 being again prominent after the eclipse
of 1865. But it was Ffestiniog which was now generating most
spirit and showing the greatest enthusiasm. From landed gentry and quarry-owner to workman and farmer, in church and
chapel, there was a unanimous voice in favour of David Williams. Samuel Holland (speaking in Welsh), chaired some of
the meetings and took a prominent part in all. Usually, there
was a brass-band present—a sure sign that ' Y Blaenau '
regarded itself as a ' new town '. There was no Conservative
organization. Given that unique uniformity of opinion between
its ' natural leaders ', its gentry and clergy, and its prepond-
erantly working-class vote it was almost unthinkable that such
an organization could survive. It may be true that had cirum-
stances been different and the gentry and quarry-owners been of
a different political complexion from the workmen that coercion
might have produced a different result at Ffestiniog. It is more
probable that such an aliented, disjunct upper class would have
hesitated out of mere prudence to apply the ' screw '. Michael
D. Jones maintained that the quarry workers were far more
independent than the farmers of the country, and that on an
issue like disestablishment they would have maintained their
independence. Their very numbers made it most unlikely that
they could be intimidated, and their town of Blaenau Ffestiniog

gave them a physical, tangible solidarity unknown to the small dispersed communities of the agricultural areas. No reasonable landlord or quarry owner would deliberately set out to create a mob. As it was, the local gentry were Liberal and all the chapels solidly behind Gladstone. Even the rector, it would appear, reflected these Liberal views.[177]

It is impossible to prove that it was these developments in the north of the county which convinced W. R. M. Wynne that he could not retain the seat. But insofar as they were symptomatic of changes elsewhere in the county we can understand that his decision was a realistic one.[178] From our vantage point a hundred years later we can, perhaps, see some significances more clearly than those who lived through the events we have tried to describe. The centre of gravity in the political life of the county had moved from the south where it had lain for so many generations. For a short while it had lain at Bala, and had come to rest finally in the north. This had been a qualitative change. Bala had generated the new spirit: it was there that new ideals had been born in suffering. It was Blaenau Ffestiniog which provided the kind of society in which it could flourish creatively in the future.

‘ Mae Castell Deudraeth ar ei draed,
A Pheniarth mewn adfeilion. ’[179]

APPENDIX

POPULATION MOVEMENTS IN THE REGISTRATION COUNTY OF MERIONETH, 1831—1871†

Registration District	Population					Increase or Decrease 1831-41		Increase or Decrease 1841-51	
	1831	1841	1851	1861	1871	Actual	%	Actual	%
Corwen ..	14,014	15,089	15,418	16,107	16,451	1,075	7.67	329	2.18
Bala ..	6,654	6,953	6,736	6,352	6,604	299	4.49	—217	—3.12
Dolgellau	12,912	13,211	12,971	12,482	14,311	299	2.32	—240	—1.82
Ffestiniog	11,558	15,460	16,182	18,289	24,141	3,902	33.76	722	4.67
Registration County Merioneth	45,138	50,173	51,307	53,230	61,507	5,575	12 35	594	1 15

Increase or Decrease 1851-1861

Registration District	Natural	%	Actual	%	Gross Gain(+) or Loss(—)	%
Corwen	1,135	7.35	689	4.47	—446	—2.88
Bala	526	7.81	—384	—5.7	—910	—13.51
Dolgellau	763	5.88	—489	—3.77	—1252	—9.65
Ffestiniog	2,279	14.08	2,107	13.02	—171	—1.06
Registration County Merioneth	4,703	9.17	1,923	3.75	—2780	—5.42

Increase or Decrease 1861-1871

Registration District	Natural	%	Actual	%	Gross Gain(+) or Loss(—)	%
Corwen	1,707	10.59	344	2.14	—1,363	—8.45
Bala	589	9.27	252	3.97	—337	—5.30
Dolgellau	1,166	9.34	1,829	14.65	+663	+5.31
Ffestiniog	3,072	16.80	5,852	32.0	+2,780	+15.20
Registration County Merioneth	6,534	12.28	8,277	15.55	+1,743	+3.27

†Based on the decennial Census Reports. I am indepted to Mrs. Janet Jones for assistance in drawing up this Table.

CARDIGANSHIRE POLITICS IN THE MID-NINETEENTH CENTURY

A STUDY OF THE ELECTIONS OF 1865 AND 1868

THE elections of 1865 and 1868, though separated by three years, exhibit so many features in common that they deserve to be regarded by the student of politics as twin manifestations of the same general changes in the political life of the county and of Wales as a whole. They require to be studied within such a wider context not merely because they would, in themselves, be unintelligible except in such a relation, but also because the emergence of what can be called a ' national ' view of Welsh politics, with a consequent breakdown of the ancient particularism of the counties, is the feature of politics in the 1860's which most insistently demands our concentrated attention. If one asked what, from the point of view of Welsh politicians of the time, was the feature most to be deplored or commended (depending on the point of view held) in the nature of politics at that time, the answer would surely be this, the intrusion into the counties of political ideologies and techniques which claimed a kind of national validity and scope, and which perforce challenged the traditional values and parochial arrangements of the old political classes in those ancient societies. It was the conflict between two differing cultural views—between the politics of deference, the remote exercise of the prerogatives of leadership based in a society expressive of degree and station, on the one hand, and the politics of numbers, of *vox populi, vox Dei*, on the other, which gave to the reform movement of the middle sixties its peculiar tensions and, often, bitterness. These tensions are present almost wherever we look in Welsh politics at that time. But not everywhere equally, for there was nothing cataclysmic in the changes we have to observe, and everywhere they were determined and shaped by the balance or interaction of social forces. Looking at the elections of those years over the country as a whole, we can readily see that, with the possible exception of Merthyr Tydfil, the victories of the new over the old were

165

practical only, the outcome determined by the extent of the changes in the basic social configurations of the localities. Only where the growth of industry, and its concomitants, the creation of new types of communities and new leadership patterns, had changed the fundamental social relationships was the victory complete. Such were Merthyr and Denbighshire, and in these three constituencies (particularly the Merthyr Tydfil and the Denbigh boroughs seats) the return of Henry Richard and Watkin Williams and Osborne Morgan should be regarded less as victories, of battles fought and won, than as the recognition of established facts, the bringing into a state of congruence the underlying social realities and the political arrangements appropriate and corresponding to them.

But if, on this view, Merthyr Tydfil and Denbigh boroughs exhibit the victorious recognition of facts, how are we to explain the changes in Cardiganshire? In this paper I shall argue that the elections themselves, and, therefore, the underlying social changes, marked a transitional stage in the development of the new kind of politics. To adopt the metaphor of a Cardiganshire man before the Land Commission of 1893, it was the cracking of the ice; no more than that, but carrying with it the promise that in due time, and ineluctably, the waters would flow unimpeded along their destined course.

The *locus classicus* for the election of 1865 in Cardiganshire is, and always has been, the account written some three years afterwards by the Reverend James Rhys Jones (Kilsby).[1] As a piece of journalism it is first-rate: far superior, one would judge, in point of style and presentation, in vivid immediateness and understanding of contemporary modes of political action to the pompous, inflated semi-translations of English reviews which masqueraded from time to time in *Y Traethodydd* as political commentaries. Kilsby's account is regarded as authoritative, and it is worthy of consideration because, like the Apostle John, he describes what he had seen and heard. Kilsby had himself taken a leading role in the electioneering, having attached himself almost from the beginning to the bandwagon of David Davies, lending not only his authority as a Calvinistic Methodist minister but also his notoriety as a popular and out-spoken lecturer to that unusual candidate. Moreover, Kilsby was the close confidant of some of Cardiganshire's leading Nonconformist Liberals. In addition to John Matthews, a prosperous grocer of Princess Street, Aberystwyth, he was on terms of intimate friendship with John Jones (' Ivon '), another grocer and Methodist deacon.[2] ' Ivon ' was prominent among the leading figures in that small coterie of intellectuals, mainly commercial men, shopkeepers, craftsmen, and apprentices, who had made of Aberystwyth something of a cultural centre before the coming of the University College.[3] Kilsby and ' Ivon ' had corresponded for many years, sharing not only a passion for the poetry of Williams Pantycelyn, but also a preoccupation with, and a concern for, the political representation of Wales and of Cardiganshire in particular.[4] Kilsby was thus in a position to have access to information not otherwise available, and it is clear from this article that he wrote from inside.

To accept his account of what happened in 1865, however, would be naïve in the extreme. However intimate his knowledge of events, it was partial, and despite his avowed objectivity—his determination ' to write without vitriol, vinegar, or wormwood' (ingredients rarely absent from his most temperate and appetizing brews)—his sympathies were engaged all on one side, and his purpose was a polemical one. It is his assumptions, his ironies, which give the game away, and we can learn a great deal about the deeper layers in the election and about Cardiganshire politics if we examine these.

The course of events is set out clearly enough in Kilsby's article. It had been understood for some twelve months in county political circles that the Tory member for the county, W. T. R. Powell, of Nanteos, who had been returned in 1859, would not again contest the seat.[5] He had suffered ill-health for some time, and had let it be known that he wished to retire. The Liberals, who had contested the seat in 1859—if, indeed, ' contested ' is the word, since there had been no Liberal association in existence—and whose organization was thought to have improved in the meantime, had looked towards the house of Bronwydd for deliverance, and it was understood that Sir Thomas Davies Lloyd would contest the seat against any Tory on Powell's retirement. In fact, a few weeks before the dissolution, Powell declared that, his health having improved, he would again offer himself, whereupon Lloyd of Bronwydd promptly published a letter in the local papers stating that under no circumstances would he contest the seat against the sitting member.   This caused consternation in the Liberal ranks, but scarcely as much as was caused by the almost simult- aneous appearance in the county of two men who were pre- pared to do so, namely, Henry Richard and David Davies. Appearing out of the blue—or rather, out of the hills of Car- diganshire and the smoke of London—Cardiganshire Liberals now had to decide on which candidate to accept. A meeting between these two and their retainers was arranged to take place at Aberaeron on Thursday, 6 July, but a few hours before this confrontation Powell announced his retirement and, as a consequence, Lloyd his renewed candidature. Thereupon, and before the nomination meeting had taken place, Henry Richard withdrew, giving as his reason for so doing a desire not to split the Liberal vote, the Conservatives having failed to find a candidate of their own. David Davies, however, refused to do likewise, announced his candidature, and proceeded to fight the election. In the event, he was defeated, Lloyd being returned with a majority of 361 in a total poll of 2,659 votes.[6]

Why did Lloyd win? Kilsby and Davies, representing, as they would argue, the Nonconformists Liberal party in the county, had a simple answer to this question which it was the purpose of Davies's farewell Address to the voters and Kilsby's *Traethodydd* article, as well as numerous comments in the national journals, to propagate. This was first, that Lloyd would not have been returned without the realities of gentry power to aid him, and second, that the Nonconformists of the county had failed to unite behind Davies.[7] The first of these reasons is, of course, polemical, but like all good polemics it has some regard for the truth, if not for the whole truth. It might for instance, be significant that Lloyd had his majorities in four of the six polling districts—in Cardigan, Aberaeron, Llandysul, and Aberystwyth—and of these, three were in the south of the county. where his influence, since there was no Conservative standing, was great, if not predominant. His majority at Aber- ystwyth, as Davies so often pointed out, was due to the influence of the house of Gogerddan which was implacably opposed to him. David Davies, for his part, did best at Tregaron and Lampeter, districts through which his railways were to run, and which were therefore likely to benefit immediately from his investments. One wonders how the Cardigan district would have voted if Davies's plan to open up the Cardigan coast had included a railway linking Cardigan to Lampeter along the Vale of Aeron.[8] But to argue that this factor of gentry coercion —or, for that matter, the blandishments of capitalist investments—was the *sole* reason for the result of the election, or even that it was exercised in the ways described by the nonconformist publicists, few of whom were actually resident in the county, was to over-simplify the situation, and to ignore social factors of great importance. This explanation makes assumptions which we must examine. Similarly, the second reason concerning the failure of the nonconformists to act in the ways expected of of them makes assumptions about the nature of nonconformity in the county which need to be questioned. Kilsby and Henry Richard alike deplored their obvious failure to vote Liberal Nonconformist. But why did they not do so? Was it realistic, in social terms, to expect them to do so? To these two questions I now turn.

The political representation of Cardiganshire in the nineteenth century—and this is a truism—reflected the social configuration of the county. In this, there are two main features which need to be examined; first, the pattern of landownership, and second, the existence of the towns. So far as landownership, was concerned the basic pattern was extremely simple. If we accept the analysis in John Bateman's *The Great Landowners of Great Britain and Ireland*,[9] which was based primarily on the information contained in *The Return of Owners of Land*, 1873, or the *Domesday* as it was called,[10] we find that the structure was pyramidic with a tendency for the outline to bulge a little above the medial line of substantial squires. There was only one peer, and he owned 42,890 acres with an income (according to the *Domesday*) of £10,579 *per annum*. This was the Earl of Lisburne, and his estates, though not the largest in the county, were commensurate with and probably sufficient to maintain his port and station as the premier landowner in the county.[11] Below the

Lisburnes in rank came a group of great landowners, four in number, who were commoners owning at least 3,000 acres with a rental of at least £3,000. At the head of these was the Pryse family of Gogerddan with estates totalling 26,684 acres and an income of £10,634, the lands covering much of the northern part of the county and bordering on those of Trawscoed. The Powell family of Nanteos owned 21,933 acres with an income of £9,024, the estates being rather more scattered, extending from the north of the county towards Tregaron in the south-east, which borough had traditionally been included in the Nanteos fief. J. B. Harford, of Falcondale, in the Lampeter region, had an estate of 5,782 acres, and an income of £4,256 *per annum*, and the Alban Gwynne family of Monachty, near Aberaeron, 3,794 acres with an income of £3,678 *per annum*.

A feature of the above analysis is that these five landowners held between them roughly one-third of the total acreage of the county (excluding waste), and that three of them—Lisburne, Pryse, and Powell—held by far the greater part of this.[12] These men were, therefore, heads of the county's premier families. The nature as well as the extent of their estates needs to be understood if their social standing and political power as a governing group are to be appreciated. The estates of the top-most three were all in the upland region extending like a crescent from the north to the south and south-east, and including the lead-bearing hills as well as the relatively good agricultural valleys. The Harford and Gwynne estates were somewhat different in character, depending less on mineral deposits, and typical, therefore, of the profitable estate-farming of lowland mixed agricultural economics—much nearer to the £1 an acre annual value to which landlords of this type aspired. The houses of these gentry—centres of estate management—reflected their status in society, and, if we may judge by the amount of rebuilding, their aspiring ambitions as well. The old ancestral homes had either long since been demolished and rebuilt or, as at Trawscoed, incorporated into more magnificent buildings set in parkland and surrounded by walls to keep in the game and keep out the lower orders.

Below these was a much larger group of squires, families with estates of from 1,000 to 3,000 acres, or quite often very much more, but whose rentals did not exceed £3,000 *per annum*. According to Bateman, there were forty-eight of these in Cardiganshire in 1885 owning an aggregate of just over 81,000 acres. The *Domesday* of 1873 shows there to have been six squires with incomes ranging from £2,000 to £3,000 *per annum*, and twenty with incomes ranging from £1,000 to £2,000. This first group contained many ancient large estates, as those of Abermaid (6,891 acres), Allt-yr-odyn (5,416 acres), Betws Bledrws (4,782 acres), and Llanaeron (4,397 acres). These were in the southern part of the county for the most part, in the coastal region, or eastwards towards Lampeter, areas of mixed farming. Similarly, there were some very extensive estates and famous names among the group of twenty with incomes from land of up to £2,000 *per annum*. Llidiart, Highmead, Hafod, Mabws, Bronwydd, Glanrheidol, Alltlwyd, Llanfair, Llanina, for example, come within this group, many of the owners being of ancient lineage, their estates having borne the same family name for many generations. Below these again was a slightly smaller group of eighteen with incomes from £500 to £1,000 *per annum*. Again, many of these were very old—Neuadd, Tyglyn, Pigeonsford, Tyllwyd—but their owners scarcely ranked high in the social hierarchy, yet it is still the class from among whom J.P.'s were chosen, containing army men, landed clerics, and the like, above the yeoman or substantial farmer, sometimes pricked for the shrievalty, occasionally producing a deputy lieutenant.

Thus, a total of forty-five families in these groups owned another third of the total available acreage.[13] The rest of the land—excluding that owned by corporations—was held, for the most part, by farmers pure and simple, and small-holders. There were about 1,500 holding up to 100 acres, another 300 odd farms of 100 to 500 acres, and of these rather more than 1,500 had incomes from land of under £50 *per annum*. This is the class which appears in the census returns as 'farmer employing one or two servants', or 'small-holder', the ones at the very bottom of the land-owning class, the least prosperous of them, no doubt, supplementing their livelihoods as agricultural or mining labourers.

I should be the last to pretend that this is a sufficient analysis of county society, but it does serve to show that this landed society was dominated, in terms of wealth, by a very few families. It needs scarcely to be said that they exercised a social power commensurate with it. I should estimate that about fifty families in all were of any consequence in the political structure of the county—that is to say, supplying the office of justice of the peace, of sheriff and lieutenancy, chairing the quarter sessions, the boards of guardians of the poor, and so on.[14] But within this larger group was a very small group, whom we may term the governing families, whose leadership, however it might be contested and resented, was, nevertheless, paramount. In particular it was this group which supplied the office of lord lieutenant, the *custos rotulorum*, and, above all, which provided the parliamentary families. From the eighteenth century onwards Lisburne had contested Pryse, and an uneasy balance of forces between these two houses (and the intricate network of families related to them) had resulted. Pryse, Powell, Lisburne—these are the dominant names because those are the county proprietors. Only John Lloyd Davies of Allt-yr-odyn breaks the pattern, and he, having climbed meteorically to wealth *via* the law, and having been doubly successful in his marriages, had been accepted in county society, and represented the boroughs for one parliament (1855-57) as a Tory.[15]

The other aspect of Cardiganshire pertinent to our investigation is the existence of the towns. They have never been looked at closely, their growth studied, the nature of their integration into the county as a whole ascertained, and, above all, their populations analysed on the basis of occupation, wealth, and religious and political affiliations.[16] The first thing that strikes one about these towns is the pre-eminence of two, Cardigan and Aberystwyth. These were, and had been, the county towns, with Cardigan claiming a statutory right to superiority which Aberystwyth, due to its increasing share in the wealth of the county, which the railway was immeasurably to enhance, was successfully disputing. In addition to these, there were the ancient boroughs of Lampeter and Tregaron—the latter by prescription—and the decayed borough of Adpar, and lastly, the small but thriving ports on the bay such as Aberaeron and New Quay. All these towns —with the exception of Adpar —were busy places, and supported populations very different from those of their hinterlands. They were communities of tradespeople and craftsmen and mariners ; centres of local government and entrepôts for the basic requirements of agricultural life. They tended to be highly mixed communities as well, rich and relatively poor living side by side, though as, for example, Aberystwyth grew in size there would appear to have been an increasing tendency for the classes to move apart— there was a recognized ' working-class district '[17]—and for the dominant trades to occupy distinct parts of the town. Cardigan can be taken as typical of the other towns in the extreme diversity of trades occupying the same streets. For instance, Panty-cleifion Street contained a schoolmaster, tailors, dressmakers, a mason, washerwomen, a cabinet maker, fishermen, mariners, a gamekeeper, a soldier, a butcher, a variety of shopkeepers, and Richard D. Jenkins, Esq., the mayor, J.P., alderman, captain in the volunteers, who occupied two houses. He was a solicitor by profession, farmed 410 acres, employed fourteen labourers besided an unspecified number of women, and, in addition to his family of four, gave bed and board to a governess and domestic, coachman, footman, cook, nurse, housemaid, and kitchen maid.[18] In all the main towns there were substantial men such as Jenkins, either professional people such as lawyers or surgeons, or tradesmen, builders, shipbuilders, living cheek by jowl with scores of other lesser tradesmen in these tight, various, diverse communities, aware of their skills, jealous of their rights, precise in their knowledge of the functioning of their towns and of their place within them. Compared with the countryside, therefore, the sheer numbers and diversities of trades and degrees of wealth within the same circumscribed communities are striking. Relatively speaking, they were also freer communities, and their freedoms were likely to be commensurate with their size. It is true that even the largest of them, Aberystwyth, could not have escaped, even if it had wished to do so, the entrenched privileges and omnipresent influence of the Gogerddan and Nanteos families. The system of town government, but slightly modified in its externals since 1834, was still liable to the ' diktats ' of those families, and although, since 1832, they could no longer obtain their ends by mere nomination to the chief offices, the sheer weight of tradition and the facts of power determined that their wishes on crucial matters, particularly those of a political nature, could never be ignored.

Quite different from these towns were the communities of lead miners in the hills. These remote and rugged places, on the frontiers of civilization almost, lacked totally the delightful variety and complex social organizations of the lowland towns. Take, for instance, the large district of Ystumtuen. In 1861, the township contained 189 houses, 487 males, and 527 females. Of these, 163 of the men were lead miners, there were 49 female and 23 ore-dressers, 8 mine labourers, and 14 other men directly employed in the mines. There were 21 small farmers, the usual shopkeepers, a schoolteacher, an innkeeper, and a book distributor (probably an itinerant). In fact, here was a community wholly dependent upon one industry. In the parish of upper Llanfihangel-y-creuddyn, which included the Cwmystwyth lead-mining township, and had a total population of 494, all the men and some of the women were directly engaged in lead mining. The only tradesmen (apart from the technical tradesmen engaged in the mines) were a shoe-maker, a shopkeeper, two drapers and a grocer, and a silk and cotton and wool weaver. It is necessary to stress that they were not only uniform economically, but small, remote, cut off by distance from the lowland centres, struggling communities where life was hard, and where the women and the children from a very early age were expected to contribute their labour to the harsh, unhealthy business of extracting lead from the mountain-sides.

I have devoted this space to an analysis of the structure of county society because the evidence suggests that here we have two types of society profoundly differing from each other and producing, therefore, two different kinds of political life. The difference is between the closed society of the rural areas and the relatively open society of the towns. There can be no question but that in the rural areas, and including the small townships and the lead-mining communities, society was founded on degree and place, and on the traditional values which were, as likely as not, to be unchallenged, accepted along with the necessity to work in accordance with the immutable succession of the seasons. It was the outsiders who thought of Cardiganshire as ' always the breeding-ground of Toryism '. It was the city-bred politician, likewise, who referred with scorn or astonishment—but rarely with pity and understanding—to the slavish, menial attitudes of the tenantry in relation to their lords.[19] We are prone to accept these value judgements, and then, by a natural progression, to search for explanations of these phenomena in the economic plight of the small farmers and labouring classes, and so to justify them. It is true that there is evidence enough in governmental reports on health, pauperism, and education to support these contentions, and literary evidence galore. ' Mae rhy fach o wahaniaeth yn awr rhwng y bugail a'i gi,' wrote Gwilym Marles the Unitarian in 1865,[20] of the shepherd boys of south Cardiganshire, and this can be taken as generally applicable not only to the farming communities in their scattered homesteads, but to the boys and girls who, from a very tender age, sorted the lead ores in the mining communities. What political activity could they know, except what their forefathers had known, the formal, sometimes frolicking, visits to the polling booths on the very rare ' diwrnod lecsiwn ' to watch their betters cast their votes? The descriptions we have from the pens of such as Kilsby and Henry Richard and the eloquent local correspondents of newpapers and magazines are all written from a point of view totally and utterly alien to the deferential societies they observed. Slavish meniality, looked at from the inside, becomes a form of behaviour rooted in the soil, expressive of ancient social values and conventions, and sustained by religious doctrine as old as the system itself—from Elizabethan homily and beyond to Methodist sermon and hymn. Of course, this is a statement in moral terms of economic and social realities. What relation other than that of social inferiority could exist when a tenant confronted the absolute owner of thousands of acres, whose livery, perhaps, his forefathers had worn? Moreover, there would seem to be no cogent reason why one should doubt that, at the time we are writing of, and generally speaking, the relation was held to be a good one. One reads oftener of the affection which the Pryses and Powells and Vaughans elicited than its opposite.

The dependence of tenants on a good conscientious landlord was not thought to entail servility on the one side or tyranny on the other. Wealth and the ownership of large acres brought great privileges; but it also entailed high responsibilities, and the relation between high and low was held to be reciprocal.

The secrets of such organic deferential societies could not be understood by the outsider. They were likelier to find the tensions and relationships they were accustomed to in the towns. Here, and here only, for the most part, was there an indigenous political life, and here only could the language of contemporary political dispute find a response. Again, this reflected the different economic and social realities. The craftsman, master of his trade, the commercial man, the professional man, owners of property, with money invested in their business and, it might be, in ships and mines, were aware of the competitive element in life, and town government, like the managing of their affairs, or the perfecting of their crafts, was a process of which they were aware and to a share in which they aspired. Town life breeds individualism; and respect and eminence are given to him that earns it rather than by hereditary descent. Moreover, implicit in the history of the chartered boroughs was conflict: the burgesses believed that their liberties had been granted them after negotiation, and negotiation implies, at least, a kind of equality and freedom where rights are concerned. In fact, the Cardiganshire towns were not outstanding for the quality of their political life; they were too small for the most part, their rate of growth too gradual, they were too integrated in, and dependent on, the life of the countryside, to be largely independent, and all had a history of gentry control. It was unthinkable in 1865, as it had been for generations before, that Aberystwyth should produce its own genuine burgess member of parliament. There were men rich enough to carry the cost of a contest, but the highest political service they could reasonably aspire to was what their forefathers had done —propose or second the nomination of a Pryse on election day. The reason is clear: Aberystwyth did not have a tradition of political independence. Its constitutional framework had survived largely to serve the needs of the house of Gogerddan. ' In respect of local government,' wrote the editor of the local newspaper, ' it has a town council, with property, but without public functions.'²¹ This, again, was not necessarily a symptom of servility or of a lack of civic pride. It was the measure of the innate conservatism of a people beholden to the great agricutlural interest they served and from whom they were recruited.

However much alien politicians might deplore these social facts and attitudes, in practice they had to recognize the reality of the situation. Thus, when Henry Richard, backed by the Liberation Society, came down to contest the seat in 1865, the first thing he did was to consult Gogerddan and opinion in the towns. Later, after his agents had visited Bronwydd to learn what the baronet's intentions were, he retired.²² His reason for so doing must be accepted; under no circumstances was he to split the Liberal vote. But judging by his subsequent statements, and from other evidence, the decision of Sir Thomas to stand merely gave the ' coup de grâce ' to Richard's pretensions. It was the failure of Cardiganshire nonconformists to show any independent spirit whatever which forced him to withdraw so unceremoniously and in such a bad humour. No candidate, it was thought, could afford to stand without at least the passive assistance of the landed proprietors. The voters would tend to measure the extent of this rather than weigh conflicting ideologies in deciding where to give their support.

But, you will object, David Davies stood. Precisely; and it is this outrageous, unpolitical action of his that is new in the election, that gives the parliamentary history of the county a new twist. Davies did not consult Pryse; he consulted no-one; he merely sent two of his associates, David Howells, a solicitor of Machynlleth, and a one-time partner, Ezra Davies, to the house of John Matthews to tell that highly-embarrassed man that he was in the field.²³ A little later he informed the hastily convened meeting of startled nonconformists in Aberaeron that he would contest the seat against either Lloyd or Powell and break the grip of Toryism on the county. It was Davies's intervention and not Richard's as stated by the majority of commentators, which caused Powell to retire, for it was Davies's money alone which could break the gentry grip. If Richard's first action had been to consult Pryse, David Davies's first action had been to deposit, so it was said, £10,000 in an Aberystwyth bank—' ale money for the battle ', as John Matthews commented. Indeed, from this point of view, the election begins to look like a contest between two kinds of wealth, the affluent railway contractor pitting his ready cash and ruthless commercial methods against the sedate and comfortable but strained resources of the rural gentry. His strongest and most sustained appeal was to the town-dwellers, to those who could best understand his language, who would be less liable to resent his methods, whose interests were bound up with his own. This is certainly the impression we get from the speeches he himself delivered, and those made by his supporters. Thus, in the nomination speech made by Jones of Llwyn-y-groes, the wealthy Aberystwyth nonconformist, the emphasis, almost to the exclusion of everything else, was on the candidate's investment in the county, on the benefits this was conferring on the county. Davies himself dilated on this theme, presenting himself as the philanthropic employer of three-thousand workmen.[24] He was called a thorough Liberal, but no one defined this. On the other hand, Sir Thomas Davies Lloyd scarcely needed to be presented, and for his part, he attacked Davies by implying that he was a bird of passage, and that his investments in the county were by no means disinterested. Lloyd had much to say about politics, and gave some specific pledges on some issues likely to arise in the next parliament. He made no pretence to being a radical; he was a Whig turned Liberal who would judge administrations and measures on their merits. On the one issue which radicals thought to be pre-eminent in the election, namely, the question of the ballot, neither candidate would change the present system. It is, in fact, difficult to see what the election was about if not about personalities and the confrontation of the old traditional society by an oblique, somewhat confusing, impression of new and scarcely understood forces of industrial wealth.

This is not to say that there was not an ideological factor present in the situation; there was, and this was represented by nonconformity. Professor David Williams has already published a study of the Census of Religious Worship of 1851 relating to Cardiganshire, and it is not necessary to repeat his

conclusions here exept to emphasize that by 1851, and probably
for some considerable time before that date, the county was
overwhelmingly nonconformist.[25] What is important for our
purpose is the denominational pattern. It was believed to be a
Calvinistic Methodist county, and with some justice; they
were the strongest single denomination. But they were not
distributed equally throughout the county, the line of division
running from east to west, the Methodists being strongest in
the Unions of Aberystwyth, Aberaeron, and Tregaron, the
older dissenting sects in the southern Unions. In the south,
also, were to be found the fourteen Unitarian chapels, five in
Lampeter district, four in Aberaeron, and five in Newcastle
Emlyn (including parishes in Pembrokeshire). No-one has
investigated this curious division. One suspects that it might
have something to do with the quality of leadership displayed
during the classical period of expansion by such worthies as
Dr. Phillips, of Neuadd-lwyd, or Azariah Shadrach, these
patterns of leadership reflecting social differences within the
county which we can but guess at.[26]

More to our present purpose are the questions, what rôle was
organized religion expected to play in 1865, and what rôle did
it in fact play ? Both Henry Richard and David Davies
anticipated overwhelming support from the nonconformists.
Henry Richard was thought to have the advantage of being a
well-known Congregationalist, who had started his career as a
minister, and was also the son of one of the apostles of Calvinistic Methodism, born and bred in that stronghold of Methodism, Tregaron. He could appeal, therefore (so it was averred),
equally to all nonconformists. David Davies appeared as a
Calvinistic Methodist deacon, and it is certain that his appeal as
such was a strong one, though again, it is impossible to confirm
this.[27] It is the experience of Henry Richard which affords us
some clues to the extent to which voluntaryism as a political
creed had interpenetrated Cardiganshire nonconformity. As
already stated, the real reason why he withdrew so unceremoniously from the contest was his bitter disappointment at the
quality and extent of the support he expected to find. He had
been more sanguine than the facts merited, and the facts, I
thing, were these. Nonconformity in Cardiganshire was not, at

that stage, a political movement, not even to any marked extent in the south of the county. The Liberation Society, which arranged Richard's candidacy, supplying him with agents, had never been even moderately successful in its operations as compared with the rest of the country.[28] Up to 1860, from the foundation of the Society nearly sixteen years previously, there had been an intermittent dribble of subscriptions and donations varying from half-a-crown to £1.18.0, all from Independent churches in the south—from Llechryd, Wern, Cardigan, and New Quay. Not until 1860 did Aberystwyth people begin to contribute, and then in insubstantial sums ranging from a little over £3 in 1860 to £7 odd in 1867. In some years there was no contribution made. Talybont seems to have been the only other place sufficiently interested to contribute to the Society's funds.[29] If this can be taken as a measure of the response of Cardiganshire nonconformists to the most radical and active section of political dissent, then the conclusion is obvious. But there is further evidence which points to the conclusion that many of the leading ministers, even among the older denominations, resented the intrusion of politics into religion. The *Baner* reported that nonconformists campaigned against Davies, and singled out as a rare exception the example of a young Independent minister who had worked for Davies despite the pressure of his older colleagues.[30] The explanation for this situation is, I think, a social one, that nonconformity itself conformed to the social pattern, adapted itself to the social ' mores ' current in the different localities. How else can we explain the attitudes of the Unitarians in the south, generally held to be radicals of an extreme kind? It is not, I think, the fact of the existence of Unitarianism as such that is important, but the locale in which it is found. It is true that a radical theological creed can sometimes carry radical political views of an extreme social kind, but only where social conditions are such as to generate them. Or consider the peculiarities of Capel-y-Drindod; there is no doubt how the Congregationalist-Methodists, or Methodistical-Congregationalists, voted; they were ' not unappropriately ', said John Matthews, designated ' Guinea Pigs '.[31] Capel-y-Drindod was not the only example of an imposed ecumenism. Bwlch-y-groes, in Llangunllo parish, was somewhat similar in its origins.[32]   Put at its lowest, the situation was that described by the Reverend John Jones, of Blaenannerch, a Methodist, who said that Calvanistic Methodists would vote for any landowner who gave them leases for chapel building; or, on a higher level, the refusal of John Matthews, a deacon at Tabernacle, Aberystwyth, to do anything in the election which might endanger the chapel lease, granted by Powell of Nanteos, which was due for renewal.[33] Was the question of church-rates now, or at any other time, a burning issue in Cardiganshire?   Or was the situation in Llangunllo, where Bronwydd was the dominant house, typical— where the churchwarden was an Independent, and where Independents rated themselves?[34]

Too much should not be made, therefore, of the post-election pronouncements of the two nonconformist candidates.   Henry Richard stated that he now realized what a mistake it had been to withdraw, since all the county's nonconformists were united in his favour.[35]   David Davies, thanking the electors for their support, claimed that the election proved the county to be overwhelmingly Liberal.[36]   I hope that enough has been said to doubt these statements; neither was true at the time.   Nevertheless, much had been accomplished, and there was, perhaps, some factual basis to Davies's contention that the county would never go Tory again.   At least, history has more or less justified him.   But if it were to go Liberal, what kind of Liberalism would it be?   That it should remain the Bronwydd type of Liberalism —what Kilsby Jones aptly described as a half-way house between Toryism and nonconformity—was more than likely, since this was fairly representative of the Whiggism of the land-owners.   The desirable objective for such as Richard and the nonconformist wing was that the county should be represented by a Welsh Liberationist.   To achieve such an end, however, was a task of incredible difficulty, and was possibly far too much to hope for by reason of the tremendous inertia of rural life. Richard Cobden, writing to his friend Henry Richard in 1851, had remarked that all new or radical political bodies faced the problem of how to make their power felt at the hustings.[37]   This was still the problem fifteen years later, particularly in rural counties undisturbed by the transforming power of industry

and population growth. One does not need to be told by dis-
illusioned editors of contemporary journals that there was a
terrible and enervating lack of interest in political questions in
Cardiganshire in those years; one feels this, reading their
magazines, to be true. Even during elections there was very
little real discussion of issues; the hustings were a facade only.
Kilsby noted shortly after the election, when he had had time to
reflect, that there were fewer Liberal landlords in Cardiganshire than he had expected, and that those few were not radical.
Kilsby, be it noted, was thinking not of the great proprietors,
or the large squires, but of the lesser landlords. Hence, it
follows that if the nonconformists' aim was to be realized,
reliance would have to be placed on the urban middle-class
element in the population. Coming from Kilsby, this is ironic,
for the whole purpose of his famous article was to demonstrate
that the election had not been about social questions, but about
political ones. Now, at the time of writing the above letter, it is
a social analysis he has been forced to make, and this corresponded very closely to the conclusion reached by hard-headed
Aberdare Liberationists at about the same time, namely, that
what was needed in rural Wales was a strong middle class to
stiffen the lower tenancy.[38]

What, then, was done? Obviously, the constituency could be
nursed. Both Davies and the Liberation Society did this fairly
assiduously. The former, in characteristic fashion, proceeded to
make substantial gifts to chapels—£100 to the new one at
Borth, £100 to the new English Independent chapel at Aberystwyth, and £300 for the British Schoolroom.[39] He was
anxious, wrote John Matthews, to do something for the people
along the coast—that is to say, the places through which his
railway ran, and which Lloyd had taken by small majorities.[40]
In this way, Davies refurbished his nonconformist image, and
softened-up the constituents. The Liberation Society, in a more
round-about way, did this also, Mr. Samuel Morley, the
eminent nonconformist philanthropist, coming to the aid of
various chapels with expanding fashionable congregations but
slender resources.[41] Far more practical was to see to the register,
and this the Liberation Society did by employing their chief
spokesman in Cardiganshire, Thomas Harries, of Llechryd.[42]

Both these types of operation were necessary, but what use were they if the people remained politically unawakened, or apathetic? Hence the concurrent drive of the Society to improve its organisation and intensify its propaganda in the county—particularly in the coastal towns. There can be no doubt that these activities together made some impression.

More revealing as to the nature of the problem confronting politicians in Cardiganshire, and of the nature of politics at that time, are two schemes which did not succeed. I refer to the attempt to establish a newspaper at Aberystwyth in opposition to the *Observer*, and the plan to create a Welsh Land Freehold Society. Kilsby Jones initiated both of these, and to his honour it cannot be said that this was the reason for their failure. The idea of a Welsh Freehold Society was new, though not unexpected, for a pattern existed in the National Freehold Land Company, which Cobden had founded in order to create freehold votes for the Anti-Corn Law League, and which still existed in a moribund state.[43] Also, there appeared to have been a similar Company at Llanfyllin in the 1860's.[44] Kilsby's idea was to establish a joint-stock company with a capital of £100,000 which would be invested in mortages yielding about $4\frac{1}{2}$ *per cent*—as profitable as any railway debentures, thought David Davies—and which would be used to assist people to build on their freeholds—to give the common people, farmers and the like, a stake in their counties. £20,000 to £25,000 of this would be allocated to Cardiganshire, and provided that it was regarded and run as a commercial venture, David Davies promised that he would invest considerably more than £1,000 in it. There would be national directors, including it was hoped (too sanguinely as it turned out), Mr. Corbett of Tywyn, Chairman, Mrs. Jones, of Llwyn-y-groes, David Williams of Penrhyndeudraeth, candidate for the Merioneth seat, David Davies and his partner Mr. Savin. Cardiganshire names mentioned included Mr. Jones of Borth (the cousin of Jones, Llwyn-y groes), Robert Edwards of Aberystwyth, and John Jones (Ivon), the last-named acting as some kind of agent as well as being on the directorate. In addition, Dr. Pughe of Aberdovey, a prominent radical, was to be co-opted on the Cardiganshire side. Kilsby wanted the Company to be strongly Methodist in

composition, but alas, it failed to attract the substantial
Methodists of Aberystwyth, and Kilsby then sounded out
London Welshmen, though he still wanted the headquarters
of the Company to be in Aberystwyth, in the Skinners' Arms,
then up for sale. Hugh Owen appears to have embraced the
scheme with enthusiasm, and took over the organization from
the despairing Kilsby, and it was probably Owen who convinced Kilsby of the impossibility of interesting the Welsh
squirearchy in it, and that it would have to be carried out by
men of business of the upper middle class.[45] After all, this was
the year when Hugh Owen and Dr. Nicholas were trying to
persuade the National Eisteddfod to help in the creation of a
similarly financed and run joint-stock Welsh Grammar School
Company for the production of middle-class youths for their
middle-class University.[46] Like the Grammar School scheme
this one, too, died in the hands of Hugh Owen, and nothing
more was heard of it. Why? Because there were no middle class
farmers or commercial men in Cardiganshire prepared to
risk their capital in a political scheme masquerading as a
business venture.

The scheme for a Liberal newspaper suffered a similar fate—
antenatal social anaemia and financial malnutrition. Its fate
was closely involved in that of the Land Company because it
had, so to speak, been conceived in the same stable. It had its
origin in what Kilsby regarded as the scandalous partiality of
the *Observer* in the late election, and its main function was to
circulate among the Methodist majority of the northern part of
the county, and create a public opinion among them on
political questions. On the face of it, the scheme was a modest
and realistic one. Kilsby discovered a certain Mr. Hughes, who
was employed by the London firm of Mackenzie as their Welsh
reader and compositor, who was prepared to do the printing.
The initial investment in machinery and type was not expected
to exceed £400, and the Skinners' Arms would provide admir-
able premises as well as be the headquarters of the Land
Company. Why did this modest undertaking fail? It is
impossible to tell, but one suspects that sufficient backing by
the right kind of men could not be found in Aberystwyth. It
seems that some of the most well-to-do Methodists, like Mr.

Jones, the Ropewalk, were not entirely sympathetic, and anyway, one doubts whether Aberystwyth could possibly have supported yet another newspaper which would have to exist mainly on local advertising support.

From this it will be observed that, from the point of view of reforming politicians, the problem of Cardiganshire was both a social and an educational one. People needed to be taught politics, or rather, taught to extract from their religion the political doctrines thought to be implicit in it, but the primary task must be to free them of the nexus of social inhibitions in which they were imprisoned. Landlords could always use the powers they possessed to coerce into conformity the few individuals on their estates who wished to act independently of these masters. Such powers had rarely been used in the county, and it is virtually certain that little pressure was exerted in 1865. It is interesting, also, to note that in the opinion of some observers it was less the landlords directly who coerced the lower tenancy than the lawyers, many of whom held small mortgages on their farms. Someone estimated in 1860 that £5,000 would free most of the small-holdings of these encumbrances, and therefore their holders of the possibility of being screwed.[48] What evidence for this exists, I do not know, but it is not improbable. Coercion was not used in 1865 because, in a way, the Tory squires had made a tactical error in failing to contest the seat themselves. They had lacked leadership, had looked towards Trawscoed for a sign,[49] and when none had been forthcoming, had fallen into the error of discussing the merits of the two Liberal candidates—trying to define the undefinable. And if Liberalism was undefinable at that time, so was Toryism. It was said that some Tories had found Davies more genuinely Conservative than Lloyd, and they had acted accordingly,[50] showing, perhaps, in this a rare perceptiveness, as if foretelling the future inclinations of that politician. But this indecisiveness had been the nonconformists' opportunity, and the taste of freedom had been sweet in some mouths. Yet, what would the situation be in a future election on a wider franchise with a thorough-going and acceptable Tory in the field? It was not to be expected that the leading Tory families would again permit both seats to be held by Liberals, and it was certain that they would fight hard to return to the old tradition whereby the two seats had been shared by the two parties.

It is curious, nevertheless, to mark how tardily the Tories prepared for the coming election. They had no public organization whatsoever, no registration society, and it seems that they relied throughout upon an unofficial organization of their voting power by traditional means, that is to say, by recruiting all the available lawyers in the county, and employing estate agents as party managers in the localities. Of course, the Liberals used these means also, but behind them lay effectively organized party caucuses, both ' county ' and nonconformist, backed by the prestige of the two sitting members, the expertise of the Liberation Society, and the funds of David Davies and Samuel Morley. Moreover, both Pryse and Lloyd were shedding their Whiggism, and they could claim by their votes in parliament to be in some respects more advanced than Gladstone himself.[51] Both declared themselves wholeheartedly in favour of the disestablishment of the Irish Church, while keeping the Liberationists at arm's length. This phenomenon we can take as indicative of the growth of Liberal opinion in the county, for in these respects the two representatives were not so much giving a lead to county opinion as responding to it. This was particularly true as 1868 approached, for the main issues before the country—the Irish Church question and nonconformist grievances—would be decided on a much wider franchise, the effect of which would be to bring within the county constituency those sizeable sea-ports, such as New Quay, and inland townships, such as Pon-rhyd-fendigaid, where nonconformity was strongly entrenched and well organized, but which had been only partially represented in the past.

There is no space to describe in detail the election of 1868, but some important features must be discussed. First of all, the choice of candidates. The leading Conservatives of the county met at Aberaeron on 19 May, and there decided to invite Edmund Mallet Vaughan, a nephew of the Earl of Lisburne, to contest the seat. No other candidate was seriously considered, for though the best that could be said of him was that he was young, and the worst that his digestion was stronger than his intellect, no stronger candidate could be found since he would automatically have the support of two of the great proprietors, Lisburne and Powell, the remaining Tory squires traditionally following the lead of these two. On the same day, a Liberal caucus met at Cardigan to discuss the representation of the boroughs, the sitting member, Colonel Pryse, having let it be known that he would retire if a suitable candidate could be found to succeed him. In the meantime, Lloyd of Bronwydd, the county member, had also declared that he was not prepared to stand the cost of yet another contested election, but that he would, if invited, accept nomination for the borough seat in the event of Pryse's resignation, where he would be virtually certain of an unopposed return. Hence, on the 26th, Pryse formally announced his retirement, and Lloyd was nominated to succeed him, these arrangements being confirmed at a meeting at Aberaeron in July where the Liberals of the other boroughs pledged their support, and at which it was made known that he would have the support of Nanteos. This settled the affairs of the borough seat.[52]

This left the county seat without a Liberal candidate. Henry Richard, for whom the Liberationists had been nursing the seat, had long since transferred his interests to the more congenial constituency of Merthyr Tydfil, while Davies was still not *persona grata* with Gogerddan. Hence the choice, late in August, of Evan Matthews Richards, of Swansea, to contest the seat as a Welsh Nonconformist Liberal.

Much can be learned about the shape and strength of opinion in the county by studying the candidature of this man and the contest which followed. There were clear resemblances between him and his predecessor, David Davies. In the first place, he was rich. Money, in large quantities, was essential in order to compensate for the serious deficiencies of being non-resident and not a landowner. In fact, the election cost him the comparatively modest sum of £2,084—or £1 a voter—almost £1,000 less than Vaughan's expenses, a discrepancy to be explained by the fact that the Lisburne interest, having been earlier in the field, had already engaged practically every lawyer in the county on their side.[53] A more interesting resemblance between the two lay in their appeal to the middle classes by reason of their commercial interests. Davies's investments in railways were tangible contributions to the wealth of the county, the results being already evident, so it was said, in the rebuilding of places like Lampeter, in the development of the watering-places along the coast, and the transformation of places like Tregaron. Richards held out the promise of investing money in new techniques of ore extraction to be used in his Swansea lead and silver works. This kind of appeal could not be disregarded, as it was everywhere believed that Cardiganshire was potentially one of the richer counties in Wales if only ways and means could be found to exploit its mineral resources.[54] This was the theme of many speeches and articles, and there can be no doubt that the townsfolk, many of whom had county voting qualifications found the appeal irresistible.

But the differences between the two men are equally revealing. There had been something eccentric, an element of defiance, and more than a suggestion of fortuitousness in Davies's candidature. Richards's by contrast, was carefully contrived, and a nice, calculated balance preserved between the old and the new. In the first place, nothing was done without the active concurrence, if not participation, of the house of Gogerddan. Thus, in July, the Liberal caucus at Aberystwyth made official approaches to Pryse on his behalf. Shortly afterwards, Lewis Llewellyn Dillwyn, Liberal member for the Swansea borough, Richards's partner in the spelter works at Swansea, and a man of considerable standing in Glamorgan county society, communicated with Colonel Pryse, and finally, in early August, Richards travelled to Aberystwyth to meet the head of the house. Only then, on 18 August, did he issue his *Address* to the electors.[55] No candidate, whatever his qualifications, could have hoped to do even reasonably well without assuring himself of this support. Throughout the subsequent campaign, and wherever he went, inside or outside Gogerddan territory, Richards proudly displayed this support, presenting himself almost as a favourite son, while the Pryses, on their part, chaired his meetings at Aberystwyth.[56]

More revealing than this, however, were Richards's relations with nonconformity. Here, the ranks were divided almost as badly as they had been in 1865, between the Liberationists on the one hand and the more orthodox Liberals on the other.

These latter were in a great majority. The anti-Liberationist party, be it noted, was the Liberal party; its most bitter and vociferous opponents were not county Tories but town-dwellers and leading Liberal squires like Colonel Wagner of Aber-eifed, near Cardigan, Mr. Hughes of Castell-du, Mr. Jones of Llwyn-y-groes, the lawyer Asa Evans, and such like. Their attitude was based partly, no doubt, on resentment of the fact that the Liberation Society was usurping the functions of the old Liberal leadership in the county. They objected to the social pretensions of Mr. Harries of Llechryd and the Cardigan minister, William Jones, who called the meeting at Aberaeron in May to discuss the representation of the county, and which initiated action by approaching Colonel Pryse. They resented, too—as as they had done in 1865—the importation of strangers, paid servants of the Society, into the affairs of the county, and they viewed with bitterness and dismay the spectacle of an alien body parcelling out the rest of the county for its own nefarious political purposes.[57] It is clear that this resentment was inter-mixed with ideological considerations. Part of the social situation was the fact that the doctrines of the Society were not acceptable in, and felt not to be applicable to, rural life. We must not forget that the Liberation Society was identified not merely with the separation of Church from State, but with political doctines of an extreme kind. These do not appear to have been propagated in Cardiganshire, and, it seems to me, would have received little or no response anyway, because the Society's intellectuals thought in terms of an urban context. The social problems in the county were of a different kind, and only later, during the great agricultural depression, would radical espouse levelling ideas and begin to talk in terms of absentee landlords keeping open an exhausting drain of money from the poor agricultural districts. Social tensions were reduced here by the fact of migration—migration on an increasing scale, in some places, almost double the rate of natural increase. Here, as elsewhere, the rise of industrial towns in South Wales acted as a safety-valve for rural dis-content. Disestablishment was not for most of the people of Cardiganshire a real issue, because it was not a social issue— or was not yet seen to be a social issue. Hence Richards's care-

ful repudiation of the Society in explicit terms wherever he
went, and in whatever was said or published on his behalf.
'Without,' as he put it, 'wishing to throw dirt on the Society,'[58]
he carefully pointed out that his surname was Richards—with
an ' s '—not Richard. Clearly, a confusion between him and
Henry Richard was likely to lose him votes. For Henry Richard,
the importance of Irish disestablishment was as establishing a
precedent, a preliminary to Welsh disestablishment; for what
was good for Ireland, there being no essential difference
between the two situations, was *parri passu* good for Wales.
Not so E. M. Richards. This worthy Baptist who, despite his
protestations, had consistently supported and co-operated with
the Society in Glamorgan, now gave a clear undertaking that he
was not at present prepared to vote for the disestablishment of
the Church of England in Wales. There can be no doubt that
in this he was acting in accordance not merely with undertakings he had probably given Colonel Pryse, but also responding to Liberal opinion in the county.

Yet, however equivocal Richards might in fact have been on
the political objectives of extreme Dissent, he most certainly
felt himself to be, and wanted the voters to feel themselves to be,
a part of that movement of the political consciousness of the
Welsh people which was manifesting itself in the contest at
Merthyr Tydfil and in Denbighshire, Merioneth, and Anglesey.
This was partly the reason why he brought the Glamorgan
members of Parliament—H. A. Bruce, Sir Henry Hussey
Vivian, and L. Ll. Dillwyn—to Aberystwyth to speak in his
favour at a meeting chaired by Sir Pryse Pryse. In this way,
the political isolation of Cardiganshire was being broken down,
and the events of the election being given a wider significance.

And the Conservative candidate? Compared with the
Liberals he scarcely campaigned at all. His Address, a per-
functory, ill-composed, platitudinous document, might have
been sufficient in any pre-1865 election. It was greeted now,
even by men sympathetic to him, with derision, and he was
compelled to publish a slightly more explicit one.[59] The contrast here is between two different attitudes to local politics and
electioneering. It seemed as if the Vaughan party did indeed
think it sufficient merely to employ virtually all the lawyers of

the county, and to rely on the persuasive abilities of landlords. What could they rely on but these traditional methods? As the contest developed it became clear that coercion would be used more blatantly than ever before, and that on some estates many tenants would be faced with the option of voting with their landlords or suffering eviction. In his evidence before the Hartington Committee in 1869, Thomas Harries claimed to have investigated two hundred cases of notices to quit being sent to tenants, and alleged that undue influence was exerted by Tory landowners acting in concert against village shop-keepers from whom their custom was withdrawn, of parish officers being removed, and congregations turned out of their rooms. It is clear that not all of these instances were in Car-diganshire—Carmarthenshire and Pembrokeshire seem to have suffered equally—but some of his attested examples concerned south Cardiganshire farms. One particular example, for which evidence was produced, showed how pressure began to be exerted as early as the rent-day in 1865 (25 March) when the landlord enclosed a letter with the recipt pointing out that an election would take place before Christmas, and expressing the hope that the tenant would vote on the same side as the land-lord. This was followed in November by another letter re-gretting the information which had reached the landlord to the effect that the tenant was wavering in opinions, and followed in March 1869, after the election, by a notice to quit. Harries insisted that the majority of evictions were probably for political reasons. The difference between the election of 1868 and previous ones was that the Irish Church question made it difficult for nonconformist tenants to vote with their landlords, Harries remarked, ' We have been very stagnant in politics in Wales; it is only within the last few years that we have come to feel a little more interest in the subject ' and that it was the religious issue in 1868 which stimulated controversy and hard-ened attitudes.[60] Richards and his supporters deliberately fostered these anti-social attitudes, as the Conservatives would have regarded them, appealing to the tenants to vote according to conscience and by conviction whatever the consequences. It may, indeed, have been those who listened and had the aston-ishing courage to act accordingly who won the election for

Richards. His majority was only 156 in a poll of 4,000.[61] Only in Aberystwyth was his majority fairly substantial (16 *per cent*), and the explanation for this is not difficult to find. After all, it was not merely Richards who had consulted the territorial magnate before presenting himself. Involved in this exercise in deferential politics were also his presumed supporters, the Nonconformists who had failed to support either Henry Richard or David Davies in 1865 rather than offend Gogerddan. Only in the north of the county, therefore, where freedom to vote according to conscience really meant freedom to vote with Gogerddan, was the Liberal majority assured. In Cardigan district the Nonconformist-Liberal majority was only about 9 *per cent*, in Aberaeron 6 *per cent*, and in Llandysul about 8 *per cent*. In Lampeter and Tregaron Richards was in a minority, and these were the districts which had given Davies majorities over Lloyd in 1865, and these were the areas where undue influence and coercion were exercised in their most naked forms. Well might Welsh Nonconformists-Liberals establish a fund to support the sufferers—' Fund y Gorthrymedigion '—however doubtful the political morality implied in such a movement. To speak, therefore, of a Liberal victory in Cardiganshire in 1868 is in some senses inadmissible. The ice had been broken, and in the process people had suffered, but it would still be some time before the changes initiated by David Davies in 1865 would be brought to fruition and Cardiganshire would describe itself as the most Liberal county in Wales.

THE ELECTION OF 1868 IN MERTHYR TYDFIL: A STUDY IN THE POLITICS OF AN INDUSTRIAL BOROUGH IN THE MID-NINETEENTH CENTURY

At the General Election of 1868 in the two-member constituency of Merthyr Tydfil, Henry Austin Bruce, who was shortly to become home secretary in Gladstone's first administration, was returned at the bottom of the poll, being beaten by the nonconformist radical, Henry Richard, and a local ironmaster, Richard Fothergill.[1] Bruce's return for one of the seats had been confidently predicted on the basis not merely of his acknowledged eminence within the Liberal party and his popularity in the country at large,[2] but also by reason of his standing in the constituency itself, which he had represented continuously since 1852.[3] Many had argued that, whereas in comparable borough constituencies the extension of the franchise introduced an unknown factor into the calculations of electoral agents and party managers, in Merthyr Tydfil, which now, by reason of the Second Reform Act, had become a predominantly working-class constituency, Bruce's association with such Radicals as John Bright, John Stuart Mill, G. J. Goschen, J. D. Coleridge, and W. E. Forster—"the vanguard of the Liberal Party"[4]—made him peculiarly acceptable to the new class of voter, so that the franchise changes would operate in his favour. Moreover, it was pointed out, Bruce enjoyed the advantage of being a local man, interested in the industrial life of the constituency not only as a senior trustee of the great Dowlais iron works but also as a substantial landowner controlling extensive and lucrative mineral rights.[5] These factors, it was believed, made him well-nigh invincible.

In the event, Bruce polled less than one-third of the votes cast, being defeated by a total outsider in the person of Henry Richard, whose politics had been confined to the activities of the Peace Society and of the Liberation Society, and by the local ironmaster, Richard Fothergill, who had been a political nonentity. Contemporaries saw in these unlooked-for results evidence of the massive strength of nonconformity and of the perpetuation of local influence and connection into the new order of things.[6] But these factors, while accounting satisfactorily for the victory of Richard and perhaps for the return of Fothergill, do not explain the rejection of Bruce, since the nonconformists of the constituency were by no means antipathetic to him, and he enjoyed the same kind of local advantages as the ironmaster. The purpose of this article is to discover what other factors were present, and in so doing to contribute to an understanding of the nature of politics in an industrial borough at the time of the passing of the Second Reform Bill.

Merthyr Tydfil in 1868 remained what it had been in 1832 when it was first enfranchised, the largest borough constituency in Wales and one of the largest in Great Britain. It embraced two of the most heavily industrialized and densely populated valleys in the country, which were separated by a mountain ridge hindering communication and which were for most purposes, other than that of parliamentary representation, distinct and individual communities. The eastern half of the constituency included the great industrial centres of Merthyr Tydfil and Dowlais, with their dependent townships, and in the western half lay the industrial centre of Aberdare with its dependent communities.

Industrially the two valleys had much in common. The townships in both depended upon the ironworks, mines, and collieries around which they had grown. But the valleys differed in the relative importance of iron-production and coal-mining in their economies. In the Merthyr valley iron predominated, coal-mining being ancillary to it, and the economic and social life of its communities depended upon the famous ironworks of the Guest family at Dowlais and that of the Crawshays at Cyfarthfa. In addition there was the smaller Plymouth ironworks situated in Merthyr which had been acquired in 1862 by Richard Fothergill, and the derelict Penydarren works also owned by him. All these works, with their ancillary industries, gave employment to about 14,800 individuals, and, since their owners together thus controlled practically all the valleys's industrial undertakings, the social and political power which they wielded was enormous. In Aberdare, on the other side of the mountain, the balance within the economy was reversed, with coal predominating. The largest ironmaster was this same Richard Fothergill, who employed between four and five thousand hands in his Aberdare ironworks and in the collieries dependent upon it. Coal was, however, the major industry there, with some forty collieries producing steam coal for export; the coal proprietors had no formal affiliations with the ironmasters to whose interests their own were often antagonistic. Wages in the Aberdare steamcoal collieries were higher than in those of the ironmasters, and in Aberdare the colliers were not obliged to accept the customary position of inferiority to the workers in the iron industry.[7]

The constituency of Merthyr Tydfil, as enlarged by the Reform Act of 1867, had a population estimated to be 105,000. The southern part of the Aberdare valley had been added to the old constituency,[8] and there large coal proprietors were exploiting the rich steam-coal deposits which lay under lands owned, for the most part, by the family of H. A. Bruce. This addition to the district was expected to strengthen enormously Bruce's hold upon the constituency.

Such changes in the physical extent of the constituency were politically important but of minor significance compared with the Second Reform Act's grant of the vote to properly qualified resident householders. The old electorate, the "ten-pounders" of the 1832 Act, were swamped. The majority of voters on the old lists were the professional men, the prosperous tradespeople, and the highest ranks of works' officials. Out of a total of 1,387 voters[9] only 126 were described as belonging to the working classes (as defined by the Poor Law Board), and it is probable that a fair proportion of these did in fact belong to the lower reaches of the class next above.[10] A study of the overseers' registers over a period of years would probably show that there was a constant ebb and flow over the £10 line of demarcation of some 200 electors to whom the vagaries of changing economic circumstances gave or withheld the franchise.

The effect of the Act of 1867 was to increase the number of voters tenfold, from 1,387 in 1866 to 14,577 in 1868.[11] Both the skilled and unskilled labourers in ironworks and mines were enfranchised, with the result that the old, essentially middle-class electorate was submerged and the old tradition of representation broken by the emergence of hitherto ineffective political forces. Previously, the borough had been in the pockets of the ironmasters, which had meant that the Guest interest had been able to control the occupation of the single seat.[12] Bruce had held that seat for sixteen years. Traditional methods of control, however, had depended upon the existence of small electorates. Now the new conditions had created a vast new electorate, which might not be so amenable as the old to the usual forms of coercion and influence and which might remain insensitive to the appeals of an old tradition from which they had been excluded.[13] The grant of an additional member by the same Act was likewise of enormous importance, since it enabled the new class of electors to create for themselves a new tradition of representation, parallel with the old and as expressive of their political beliefs and aspiration as was the old with the politics of the upper and middle classes.

As soon as it became certain in 1867 that by the terms of the Reform Bill then before parliament Merthyr would be granted an additional member, election activity began. By the middle of the year, three candidates for this second seat had appeared. Two of these, E. M. Elderton, a London solicitor, and B. T. Williams, a barrister on the south Wales circuit, lacked what were then considered to be essential qualifications, the advantages of local connection and the backing of some powerful political organization within the constituency. The most formidable candidate was the ironmaster Richard Fothergill. A Fothergill Election Committee, consisting of influential voters from both valleys, had prepared a requisition for presentation to Fothergill in June 1867, but his address appeared before the deputation had in fact formally approached him.[14] The power of this committee depended upon the candidate himself and upon the influence which he possessed as a large employer of labour, ranking next to the Guests and the Crawshays in the industrial hierarchy. Although he was more powerful in Aberdare where his major holdings were situated, he was by no means negligible in the Merthyr valley. The fact that his Penydarren works there were derelict could be used to his advantage, since in the depressed state of trade at the time he could be presented as a great potential employer of labour. His "stake in the community" might seem sufficient to make his return a foregone conclusion, and he was hailed as the great and benevolent capitalist whose return to parliament should be regarded not only as his merited reward but as an act of calculated self-interest on the part of the community. His address declared him to be an impeccable Liberal, a follower of Gladstone in economic, financial, and religious matters, and stated that he was prepared to go even further than Gladstone on the question of the ballot.

Fothergill's support came from the middle commercial classes. A lawyer and mineral agent led his supporters on the Merthyr side of the constituency, and of the 1,200 who signed the requisition inviting Fothergill to be a candidate about 400 came from this area and were traders of the valley or officials in Fothergill's works. Aberdare, as we should expect, provided nearly double this number of signatures, and they came from the same social class. That the Aberdare communitee members were perhaps less spontaneous and more calculated in their support is indicated by the fact that part of their compact with the candidate provided that his Abernant Truck Shop should be closed.[15] In the early stages of these alignments, Fothergill's fellow ironmasters adopted a quietly evasive and noncommittal attitude. Although W. T. Crawshay went so far as to add his signature to the requisition and even on one occasion to chair the committee, his was an unenthusiastic adherence, limited to the support of Fothergill for the second seat only and claiming the right to withdraw should his active support tend to discomfort or in any way endanger Bruce, the sitting member.[16]

One of the most active and, to all appearances, influential members of the Fothergill committee was Dr. Thomas Price.[17] If we are to understand the nonconformist and working-class vote, we must consider his earlier influence and his attitude during the contest. Price's authority and influence were based upon his unique standing in his denomination in the Aberdare valley. He was the leading Baptist in a constituency in which Baptists were in the majority, and that they were so was due in part to his assiduous missionary work in the growing and often isolated mining communities which had sprung up rapidly during the past twenty years. His chapel and home at Aberdare were the centre of a radiating influence effective among the Baptists in the two valleys. Because of his almost apostolic authority in his denomination, he held a position of outstanding prestige in political and social life. He typified the aggressive, self-confident leadership of dissent. He had been the chief leader in forming the Representation Society, a large nonconformist group which concerned itself with political matters. For the past twelve years, Price had edited various Welsh newspapers and periodicals, and was in 1867 in his seventh year as editor of *Seren Cymru*, a denominational monthly which circulated widely in Wales. Under his editorship it was never merely a denominational magazine. It devoted more space to the discussion of current political issues than did most of its comparable contemporaries, and it generously reported parliamentary affairs, especially the activities of the Welsh members. In 1862 the Liberation Society, which had been founded in 1844 by Edward Miall with the aim of insuring for all religious classes equality before the law by breaking down the entrenched privileges of the Church of England, had turned its attention to Wales, and from that moment Price had enthusiastically supported its activities. Price's peculiar contribution to the society's propaganda, so far as it related to Wales, had been to contend that its analysis of the extent and nature of Anglican-Tory control of the rural constituencies, a control based upon "feudal" traditions maintained by means of coercion and corruption, applied equally to the industrial constituencies. The ground landlords and the iron and coal proprietors could, he had declared, "screw three out of four of the electors from Cardiff to Holyhead".[18] He had therefore consistently preached over the years the need for uniting on the basis of religion and class against these evil influences. What individual voters could not do, the united body of nonconformists could surely succeed in doing and to this end he had been largely instrumental, early in 1867, in establishing a Representation Society designed to organize the nonconformists of the two valleys on political lines. With the Reform Act on the statute book, Price found himself in a situation where the conditions necessary for a political victory of the kind he had envisaged had been realized. The electorate was almost exclusively nonconformist and working-class, and the great question now was whether the new voters would accept his guidance in their dual capacities. Price, who had been closely associated with Fothergill at two previous elections (1852 and 1857) and who now supported Fothergill for mainly personal reasons and on grounds of expediency, calculated that they would. As his other candidate Price supported Bruce. Price believed that the new voters would rally behind these candidates. That he was proved wrong was due to two factors: the activity of the Liberation Society, which he had been largely instrumental in forming, and the emergence of a working-class industrial and political organization with its own independent ends and methods.

At first the Representation Society was hesitant in defining its attitude to the election. An Aberdare solicitor, C. H. James,[19] and his brother were at its head, and there were four secretaries, three of them Unitarian ministers, the other a Baptist. Affiliated with it were the eighty-one nonconformist congregations of the two valleys, representing an overwhelming numerical superiority of the voters. If the electoral campaign were fought on issues upon which nonconformists were united, and if a suitable candidate could be found, they could carry the election. In the spring of 1867, however, neither of these conditions seemed to exist. Not until March 30, 1868 were Gladstone's reolutions on the Irish church formally presented to the House of Commons, and none of the candidates, least of all Fothergill, measured up to the qualifications formerly set by Price. It seemed that the choice of an ironmaster would dictate the ways in which the election would be fought, and these ways involved techniques which Price had so vociferously condemned over the years. Moreover, Fothergill was the choice, if indeed he had been chosen, of a caucus, and this again was in defiance of the democratic methods of selection heretofore desired by Price. For more than two months the Society hesitated. Then finally it renounced Fothergill and Price and proceeded to chose its own candidate. The first tentative moves were made in Merthyr where, after a series of meetings, it was decided to invite Henry Richard, secretary of the Peace Society, to contest the seat as a nonconformist-liberal. By the end of July the

Aberdare nonconformists had joined in the movement, and both valleys were agreed that Richard should be invited to stand "as a Welshman, advanced Liberal, and Nonconformist".[20]

What the Representation Society was now attempting was unprecedented not only in Merthyr Tydfil but in the whole of Wales. The candidate they had chosen possessed in an eminent degree the virtues and characteristics most admired by the sects, and enjoyed considerable popularity and influence in dissenting circles generally, but he was not particularly conspicuous as a politician. He had had only a short experience in electioneering, and his record as a candidate in 1865 in Cardiganshire was not wholly in his favour.[21] Above all, he was not a rich man and had no connections with the constituency. Richard himself realized the weight of these objections and was reluctant to commit himself without first visiting the constituency to discover the nature of the opposition and to test the extent of the support he had been promised. He also desired time to consult his London friends, some of whom, such as Samuel Morley, might be prepared to assist him financially.[22]

Thus to emphasize a cautious and independent attitude was a shrewd move on the part of Richard. At once it pointed to the contrast between him and Fothergill, the one being apparently reluctant to stand, the other rushing in with a blunt disregard of the niceties of local politics and traditions. Moreover, a series of preliminary public meetings would have the double advantage of demonstrating to Richard the nature of the support he would receive and to the nonconformists as a body the fact that their strength lay in the solidarity of their numbers. The meetings could serve Richard in another way, for, whereas the numbers who attended Fothergill's meetings could be construed as merely an expression of calculated self-interest or even of fear on the part of an electorate consisting of his work people and therefore amenable to his influence and likely to be organized as a political body by the industrial organization which he commanded, Richard's support could be shown to be free, spontaneous, and organized by a machinery created by the people themselves for purposes unconnected with secular ends. As this preliminary series of meetings showed, the Representation Society was an organization perfectly adapted for electioneering, since the chapels, in addition to providing in most villages the only places in which meetings such as these could be held, could function also as centres for the dissemination of literature in an atmosphere of religious duty and fervour.

All of Richard's meetings were large and enthusiastic. He expounded his political creed and explained its necessary relation to his hearers' religion. He was no mere tyro in politics, he claimed, but he had, on the contrary, benefited over a period of eighteen years from an intimate friendship with Richard Cobden,[23] so that there was therefore some justification for the view that on such practical issues as religious freedom, education, trade, the press, and elections, his was the authentic voice of his mentor. His references to the Irish church were not the remarks of a would-be politician seeking the shelter of the Gladstonian umbrella, for this was an issue with which Richard was identified in the public mind, particularly in Wales, where, since 1862, he had led the campaigns of the Liberation Society[24] and had assiduously propagated the belief that disestablishment in Ireland was a necessary prelude to a similar measure in Wales. Furthermore, now he dealt with the question of the parliamentary representation of Wales authoritatively. Finally, it was as the champion of a religious majority suffering the disabilities of a persecuted minority that he accepted the nonconformists' invitation to stand as their candidate, always giving this aspect of his candidature a more than local significance by relating it to the wider problem of Welsh representation in general.[25]

Consequently, the Representation Society, henceforth to be known as the "Henry Richard or Nonconformist Committee" (without, however, losing its original identity as a religio-political pressure group), had every reason to be satisfied with its choice and with the reception accorded its candidate in both valleys. Richard had been promised over 7,000 votes in Aberdare, and, if the ironmasters refrained from exerting pressure at Dowlais, about 8,500 in the Merthyr valley.[26] Too much should not have been made of these figures: the election still lay in the future, the Fothergill party had yet to be organized on a combative basis, and the influence of the other masters revealed. But the computations convinced the candidate and his committee that, provided no undue influence were exerted, Richard's election was fairly certain.

The coming of Henry Richard had altered completely the balance of political forces within the constituency. It put an end to the assumption that the senior member would continue to be H. A. Bruce. Previously none of the other candidates had desired to say or do anything which might damage his interests. On specific but minor points they might disagree with him, but never in such a way as to suggest that he was not—by virtue of service, intellectual ability, moral worth, and standing in local and national politics—worthy of continuing to represent the borough. The advent of Richard changed all this, and Bruce, from being beyond criticism, now became the centre of a violent and protracted argument in which his views on current questions as they affected the locality were closely scrutinized and found wanting, and his past record revealed not as the basis but as the solvent of his prestige and popularity. The resounding success of Richard with the new class of voter, with whom the ultimate power lay, made it certain by October 1867 that the contest for the second seat would be not between Richard and Fothergill but between Fothergill and Bruce.

Closely associated with the power of nonconformity in the process in which Bruce was displaced as the favourite for the first seat was another movement which had developed side by side with it, and sometimes antipathetically to it, namely, an active tradition of working-class radicalism. The connections between the two were informal and personal, closest in the old dissenting denominations, remotest in the various Methodist connections.[27] A radical group, which had been extremely active during the parliamentary Easter recess, continued to hold meetings independently of those organized by the nonconformists. At these radical meetings, old Chartist doctrines were propagated, and the more recent works of the Chartist leader, Ernest Jones, discussed.[28] The conveners of these meetings were also staunch supporters of Richard and were thus enlisting in his behalf a body of radical opinion which need not, of its own volition, have gravitated to him. Richard was *par excellence* a nonconformist; the structure, texture, and impulse behind his thinking was religious; while the tradition represented by the Chartists tended in a secularist direction. This blending of the traditions did not make Richard into a working-class candidate. But it did begin the crystallization around him of a working-class sentiment which had a solid nonconformist centre with an as yet ill-defined periphery of secular working-class cohesion.

How did all this affect the candidature of Bruce? Until November 1867 he was content to observe events from a distance, for, apart from one local newspaper, the press in both both valleys agreed with the London and other provincial papers that he was utterly secure in the tenure of a seat in which he had so distinguished himself.[29] Actually, he had little cause to be complacent. It was not clear that the nonconformists, now that they had the vote, the numbers, and their own candidate, would confirm the choice of previous generations of electors. Bruce was a churchman, a landowner, and an Englishman in training and sympathy, and there were issues between him and his constituents which platform reassurances of confidence and loyalty could not entirely or for long conceal. Moreover, Price's support of Fothergill, which had involved his defection from the nonconformist cause, seemed likely to have the unforseen result of weakening support for his other candidate, Bruce. Price's constant defence of his position in the columns of his paper stimulated his former followers to re-examine the bases of their political faith and to become increasingly critical of any attachments that fell short of the ideal. Thus, Bruce's refusal to pledge himself to vote for the secret ballot, his conditional acceptance of nonconformist views on education, his "traditional" views on the relation of church to state, and his denial of the existence of any specifically Welsh problems, began to be mooted as sufficient excuses for rejecting him.

Of far greater importance in defining the attitudes of the new electors was the gradual hardening of opinion among the working-class voters against Bruce for purely industrial as distinct from quasi-religious and political reasons. At the time when the preliminary alignments were being made, writers who claimed to be expressing an independent working-class opinion adopted a vaguely negative attitude to all that was happening. By the time Richard had entered the field, however, they were prophesying the rejection of Bruce and elaborating reasons for their antipathy to him.

These views originated among the colliers, and the gravamen of their charge was that Bruce was unsympathetic to them and had permitted himself to become a mere tool in the hands of the masters. The miners found their evidence in the part Bruce had played in the last great strike in the coalfield in the winter of 1857-58. On that occasion, at the beginning of the post-Crimean-war slump, the miners had struck against a 15 *per cent* reduction in wages. The strike had been peculiarly bitter, and Bruce appears to have stood aloof until the situation had so deteriorated that troops had been quartered in the town of Aberdare. At this point he had intervened, persuading the home secretary to withdraw the troops, the men of Mountain Ash (his own district) to return to work, and the masters to refrain from imposing a further penal reduction of 5 *per cent*. Finally, Bruce had addressed a mass meeting of the colliers at Aberdare at which he made two speeches. In the first he carefully analyzed the economic situation and claimed that on this occasion the masters were not guilty of injustice, which, in his view, was the only justification for a strike. The colliers were familiar with these arguments, and possibly, since similar arguments had been effective in all other parts of the south Wales coalfield, they would have accepted them and returned to work, had not Bruce made a second speech. The effectiveness of the first speech was destroyed by the second, obviously unpremeditated, which amounted to a passionate denunciation of the Aberdare colliers. As a direct result of the resentment the second speech elicited, the strike continued until resistance had been broken by the importation of "foreigners".[30] Now, ten years later, this episode was remembered with bitterness, and Bruce's part in it recollected, distorted, and made into an issue in the election. Here was evidence that in the fundamental affairs of the constituency Bruce would be not a neutral concilliator (as he pretended) but a spokesman for the masters.

In the 1868 election, the politics of the constituency were conditioned by two major factors, the current slump in the coal and iron trades and the problem of safety in the mines. Trade had not recovered from the financial panic of 1866. The depression which had begun in the winter of that year continued, with only a light easing, throughout the summer, and now, in the winter of 1867-68, it was becoming deeper than ever. That wages had not been reduced was due to the fact that the winter depression of 1866-67 had affected the iron and the coal industries unequally. The ironmasters, who were the hardest hit, had been unable to decide on a reduction for fear of losing their men to the sea-coal collieries, which were enjoying a brief, unexpected period of comparative prosperity.[31] But now the depression of 1867-68 was affecting both industries equally, so that the situation, so far as it concerned the masters, seemed to be relatively simple, and agreement on the terms of the reduction now to be made, easy to reach.

The matter was complicated, however, by problems of safety and of working conditions, which had lately become acute. The former had been growing more insistent as the miners went deeper, and both sides of the industry had been giving this question a great deal of attention since 1849, when fifty-three men had been killed in an explosion at the Lletty Shenkin Colliery, Aberdare. Since then nearly three hundred men had been killed in the Aberdare and Merthyr collieries,[32] and both masters and men now saw that the law relating to safety would have to be amended. The subject gained an awful and spectacular prominence on November 8, 1867, when 168 men and boys were killed outright in an explosion at the Blaen-llechau Colliery, Ferndale, in the neighbouring Rhondda valley. A wave of horror and fear swept through the coalfield, and a protracted debate began on the exact measures which should be brought forward in the next session of parliament. Here was a political issue which would divide the voters, for the masters and men were diametrically opposed on the measures deemed necessary.

These political implications soon became even more urgent. Their impact on the politics of the constituency became unavoidable when John Nixon, head of one of the most powerful groups of collieries in the Aberdare valley and chairman of the coal-owners' association, proposed to make the question of safety a means whereby the northern or doubleshift system of working could be imposed upon the colliers of the soft-coal areas by statutory action. He had long been advocating such a system of working the mines, mainly for economic reasons, and the colliers had as consistently opposed him for social reasons.[33] That Dr. Price, to whom the colliers would normally have turned for advice, seemed to be supporting Nixon served only to make more explicit the reality of the political differences which now separated them from Price. His adherence to Fothergill and his support of Nixon's proposal strengthened the colliers in their determination to follow an independent political line.

Parliamentary action would have to await the reassembly of parliament. In the meantime, however, the depression presented an opportunity for imposing the double-shift system locally in the associated collieries, and the method adopted was calculated to bewilder and divide the colliers. Early in December, notice was given that the colliers were to do one of three things: agree to abandon their present system in favour of a more intensive method, adopt a full double-shift system, or accept a wage reduction.[34]

The response of the colliers to this announcement, which they regarded as an attempt to take advantage of their weakness in order to impose a system which they believed antipathetic to their best interests, was one of dismay and incredulity. It was not the wage reduction that they feared, since that could be regained when trade improved, but the proposed changes in working conditions, since these, once adopted, might never be reversed. Gradually, during January and early February 1868, when work in the collieries ceased, the miners worked out the strategy to be pursued. The question of wage reduction was to be kept separate from the major issue of working conditions and to be dealt with in the traditional ways on a local basis by committees locally appointed. But the colliers' way of dealing with the major grievance was a new and significant departure. A committee responsible to delegates from the whole coalfield was appointed and charged with the preparation and presentation of a petition to parliament against the introduction of the double-shift system.[35] By the middle of February, the committee had analyzed reports from all parts of the coalfield, on the basis of which it was later to publish in pamphlet form a comprehensive and detailed statement of the colliers' case. By May two petitions, one against introducing the double-shift system, the other proposing certain changes in the Mines Inspection Act, had been prepared and given to H. A. Bruce to present to parliament at the earliest opportunity. Copies of the pamphlet were sent to members of parliament and widely circulated elsewhere.[36]

From the standpoint of the politics of the constituency something positive and of great importance had been achieved. The newly enfranchised workmen had not only expressed themselves on an issue which touched them closely but had created, independently of any existing political bodies, an organization whereby this opinion could be made politically effective. In the exigencies of a contested election they were being educated in their political rights and duties, and inevitably their cohesion about their particular rights and interests would play a dominant part in the electoral life of the constituency when this stirred into activity again in the spring.

That new issues were arising was not immediately apparent. Outside observers concentrated only on the traditional elements and attempted to analyze an admittedly confused situation in terms of the response of the various sections of the electorate to the conventional party issues. Few realized that the really decisive attitudes towards Bruce had become fixed during the winter and that the election would be decided on local issues.

To all appearances, when electoral activity began in earnest in the summer, there was every justification for the old view. One of the issues in the general election was the disestablishment of the Irish church, and Welsh nonconformists felt this to be a matter of extreme urgency not merely because of abstract moral considerations or political expediency but also because of its immediate practical relevance to the political situation in Wales. The three major grievances in Ireland which demanded redress—the establishment, the land laws, and representation— were, it was argued, closely paralleled in Wales, and the Merthyr nonconformists' organization, functioning in its dual capacities, continued without intermission throughout the summer to urge the necessity of the first reform and the desirability of the others.[37]   As a pressure group they organized meetings and collected signatures for a petition on Irish disestablishment for presentation to parliament,[38] and as an election committee they were able to exploit to the full the fact that their candidate, Richard, both as an individual and as a leading member of the Liberation Society, had been actively engaged in teaching the necessity for such measures of religious and political freedom as the Liberal party under Gladstone's leadership now saw to be expedient.[39]

The other two candidates could not enjoy such an unequivoocal position in relation to the nonconformist convictions of the electorate as could Richard.   Bruce was most vulnerable, perhaps, on the subject of education, for some of the decisions taken during his tenure as vice-president of the committee of council on education could be construed by his enemies as favouring church schools in Wales at the expense of those of the dissenters. Nevertheless, the numerous attempts made to attack him on this score were largely ineffective, for in the meantime Bruce had taken the precaution of having the terms of a new bill he had prepared, which he hoped to present in the new session of parliament, approved by a representative meeting of the inhabitants of the two valleys.[40]   His parliamentary record with regard to dissenters' grievances was one of which he was justifiably proud, and was not likely in normal times to arouse the resentment of his constituents. On the Irish question, likewise, his pronouncements were regarded as for the most part satisfactory, although they went scarcely far enough to please his more radical audiences, especially as he consistently refused to agree that the disestablishment of the Irish church was to be a prelude to a similar measure applied to Wales. At no time in the election, did these become fundamental issues, so far as Bruce was concerned, however, despite some efforts to make them so.[41]

The main cause of Bruce's rejection must be sought in the nature of his relations with the new class of voters, particularly with the colliers. Apart from the specific differences between them and their representative in parliament, there was a long-standing and deep-rooted tradition of distrust which made a mutual understanding almost impossible. Bruce's honest and noble desire to see the social life of the valleys transformed, and his individual contributions to that laudable end were vitiated by his complete inability to communicate his ideas to those most involved in their realization. The newspapers which opposed him (the radical *Merthyr Telegraph* and the Chartist *Merthyr Star* in particular) fastened on every statement of his which might be construed in a fashion derogatory to the working classes,[42] and drove home the lesson: "From education, habits, and national prejudice, it was difficult for a man in his position in life thoroughly to understand the wants of the working man."[43] Bruce constantly underestimated the tradition of working-class politics which had survived the agitation of the 1830's and 1840's, and the degree of class consciousness and cohesion which remained. Members of the reform societies, however, were actively preaching the need for the completion of the original Chartist programme, especially the need for the ballot.[44] This was also a main plank in Richard's platform, but whereas the justification of his demand for the ballot was conceived mainly in rural and quasireligious terms, the workmen were conscious mostly of the realities of intimidation in an industrial setting and thought mainly in terms of power. At the same time, Bruce's supporters were asking the workers to continue in the occupation of his seat one who was popularly believed to be the nominee of the ironmasters, and a man whose fortune was based upon coal royalties rather than coal production and whose wishes, therefore, the old constituency of professional men and tradespeople had found it expedient to adopt without cavil.[45]

During the summer of 1868, the colliers heard reports of Bruce's activity in parliament which confirmed their suspicions that he would oppose their interests on the issues of safety in the mines and on the double-shift system of work. On June 4, Bruce presented the miners two petitions, the one on safety and the other on the double-shift, and in the following week he initiated a debate calling the government's attention to the report of the Select Committee on Mines of 1867.[46] So far as the question of inspection was concerned, this report had recommended an increase in the inspectorate but had emphatically rejected the miners' proposal for the creation of a system of sub-inspectors. Bruce, who had been a member of the committee, heartily approved of its conclusions, and in his speech elaborated his reasons for so doing. The main objections to the colliers' scheme, he said, were: (1) there was a shortage of trained men to serve as sub-inspectors, and (2) the necessarily small salaries of such officials would expose them to the temptation of accepting bribes.

The question of double-shift working was the subject of the miners' first petition and Bruce discussed it also. Here he appeared to be outspokenly in favour of those masters who were agitating for the statutory establishment of the double-shift system throughout the coalfield, and he suggested an ingenious way in which that could be done. Parliament, he pointed out, could not legislate directly on methods of coal-getting, but, since it had been demonstrated that the double-shift system was the method most economical of lives, parliament could impose it as a safety measure. *Hansard* reported the concluding sentence of his speech: "It [the double-shift system] was, however, greatly opposed by the colliers where it had not taken root. He would suggest the appointment of a skilled commission to inquire into this subject, and to report its result in security, economy, and safety."[47] The *Times* reported a substantially different concluding sentence: "He did actually propose the appointment of a Commission . . . but he felt assured that a great good would be the result of the introduction of such a system as he had mentioned."[48] Bruce hastened to correct the *Times* version in a letter to the newspaper, declaring that he had expressed no personal opinion on the merits of the system.[49]

It was the *Times* report of this speech that the colliers read, and to them it confirmed what they already suspected, that once again Bruce was an interested party in the controversy between them and the coal masters.[50] This belief of the miners stimulated them into taking a more active part in the election. Early in October, they determined to issue an address to be circulated throughout the Welsh coalfield, drawing attention to the issues involved, to the power which the workers now possessed as voters, and to the importance of electing to parliament men who would be sympathetic to their views on inspection and the double-shift system.[51]　Moreover, the Aberdare colliers now launched a full-scale attack on Bruce, which put him on the defensive. He attempted to justify himself in public meetings, but increasingly they tended to degenerate into uproar and riot even in those areas where his influence was strong, as in Mountain Ash and Dowlais. He issued a written defense of his parliamentary record with regard to colliers' grievances,[52] but it likewise was of no avail since the colliers themselves, aided by Fothergill's party, could equally well propagate their own interpretations.

Late in October, another event occurred which aroused the suspicions of the workers. The Guest interest openly entered the fray on Bruce's side with a directive to their workmen to give him their second vote.[53] A little later, the Cyfarthfa interest issued a similar directive to the voters of their dependent township of Cefn-coed-y-cymmer.[54] Now the workers' very real fear that the new electorate, despite its size, would be subject to the same pressures which had weighed upon the old and had led the voters to favour the masters' interests seemed to be realized. The Guest directive created such an outcry in the constituency at large that it had to be withdrawn in favour of a statement promising complete freedom, but that of Cyfarthfa came so late that opinion could not be organized against it.[55] The extreme sensitivity of the voters to these directives was an expression less of the realities of the situation (there seems to be no evidence that either the Guest or the Cyfarthfa interest was preparing to use coercion in behalf of Bruce) than of those basic but necessarily vague and imprecise feelings of distrust which now had a chance to rise to the surface and to speak in political terms. These feelings became politically effective because there were specific industrial issues between Bruce and the colliers around which there existed an organization providing the means whereby they could be translated into deeds.

In the meantime, Bruce continued to defend himself in public meetings.[56] Finally, a week before the poll, he met deputations of the colliers from both valleys and from outside the constituency, who mercilessly cross-examined him in a session which lasted through a long evening.[57] On the question of the double-shift he was forced reluctantly and with an ill grace to agree that its introduction into the Aberdare area was neither possible nor desirable. But on the subject of inspection he remained adamant, preferring to lose his seat rather than to eat his words in regard to it.

This meeting virtually put an end to any uncertainty regarding the result of the poll. As the colliers put it, if Bruce, as a matter of principle, refused to support their petition for a sub-inspectorate, they, too, would stick to principle and send someone to parliament who would represent their views in this and in similar matters. No amount of influence could now elect him, for, apart from the almost insuperable difficulties of coercing such great numbers of men, the ironmasters had renounced any intention of doing so, and the colliery proprietors had at no point interfered.

In this way working-class issues had been brought to the forefront in the election, coming to dominate the other issues and forcing the other candidates to clarify their attitudes toward them. The other candidates benefited from Bruce's discomfiture, and both hastened to take advantage of it.

Fothergill was now certain of gaining the second seat, and he hastened to exploit the workers' grievances by appearing as the champion of their views. Reading his speeches some ninety years later and noting how curiously vague and uninformed his pronouncements were on the other political questions, one must conclude that these industrial question were the only ones on which he and the colliers could see eye to eye. In addition, of course, these issues served to deflect attention from some of the questions at variance between him and his own employees.[58] Fothergill's party led the outcry against the alleged interference of the Dowlais management with their workers' freedom of choice in the election, and these tactics diverted attention from the subtle pressure being exerted on Fothergill's own workmen in his own interests.[59]

Henry Richard likewise found it expedient to stress the more radical planks in his platform. The religious vote was assured; in the later stages of the electoral campaign he concentrated on the "class" and "nationalistic" aspects of Welsh nonconformist dissatisfaction. In a far less equivocal fashion than Fothergill he could claim to be a "working-class" candidate in that he was a Cobdenite radical and the choice of an organization which depended for its support of working-class people. He made much of his humble origin, contrasting his own moderate income with the affluence of the other two candidates, and suggesting thereby that wealth, influence, or connection had not obstructed, and were not likely to obstruct, his consistent vision of the good of the populace as a whole.[60] His Chartist allies made much of this theme, developing the point that a propertyless man such as Richard was more likely to understand and to represent the ideas of a propertyless electorate than were powerful ironmasters or *rentiers*, particularly in the parliaments that lay ahead when questions vital to the people's welfare would be raised. More and more his meetings came to resemble those vast demonstrations of workmen which were often held on the hillsides in times of stress. As the poll drew near, Richard's meetings left the chapels and halls to occupy the valley slopes where great concourses of men could express their solidarity. Moreover, all these meetings were conducted in Welsh, and all of them ended in outbursts of patriotic fervour. Richard clearly understood what had happened. His radicalism became more marked, and he combined it with nonconformity and nationalism into a kind of "philosophy" of Welsh politics, involving both a rejection and an affirmation. He rejected an old order of society with landed gentry and churchmen at its head, and he declared that their place had been taken by the "national" leaders of a new civilization which had developed apart from them.

The return of Henry Richard at the head of the poll with an overwhelming majority over both of the other candidates was rightly regarded at the time as a great victory for the nonconformists of the borough. He had received one of the two votes of each elector in the constituency, whereas the heaviest voting in favour of Fothergill and Bruce had been confined to those localities where their influence was greatest. But I have attempted to show in this paper that factors other than nonconformity were present in the election, and these must be taken into account if we are to understand the nature of the new tradition of political activity which was thus inaugurated. The rejection of H. A. Bruce for industrial as distinct from religio-political reasons was as positive an achievement by the new working-class electorate as their return of Richard. The concentration of contemporaries on the factor of nonconformity to the exclusion of those arising out of industrial grievances[61] should not obscure the true significance of the election. Henry Richard realized this significance, when soon after he described himself as "emphatically the advocate of the cause of the working man and of Welsh nonconformity".[62]

Part 3
EXPLANATION

RELIGION AND SOCIETY IN THE FIRST HALF OF THE NINETEENTH CENTURY

In a lecture before the Royal Statistical Society in 1854 Mr. Horace Mann, who had been responsible for the Census of Religious Worship of 1851 and who had written the Report which had been published two years later, made the following observation. ' Scarcely anything,' he said, ' is more curious or puzzling than the attempt to trace the cause why particular doctrines or religious parties should find one soil favourable and another adverse to their propogation and success. But at all events, as far as facts are concerned, England furnishes a striking picture of sects and creeds supreme in one part and absolutely unknown in another.'[1] By ' England ', obviously, he meant ' England and Wales ', and as an illustration of the phenomena he had in mind he instanced the Calvinistic Methodists who provided sittings for 27 *per cent* of the population of the whole of the six counties of north Wales, but less than one per cent in the other 27 *English* counties where they also had congregations. One might object that he was scarcely comparing like with like: the Calvinistic Methodists he was referring to was the *Welsh* Calvinistic Methodist denomination whose congregations, if we except those to be found in the cities and large towns of England, were confined to the Principality.[2] It might also be objected that it was scarcely fair to exclude the seven counties of south Wales from his equation though, as a matter of fact, this would have made no difference to his argument, for even in south Wales the difference in the proportion was still very great—14 *per cent* as against 27 *per cent* for north Wales. Mann also noted how the largest denominations, the Wesleyan Methodists, the Independents (or Congregationalists), and the Baptists, though present in virtually every part of the country, varied enormously from region to region and from place to place in the relative numbers of sittings they provided. Nor was the Established Church an exception to the rule. The provision it made in England varied between a low of 17.6 *per cent* of the population in Durham to a high of 58.1 *per cent* in Rutlandshire. Mann offered no explanation and put forward nothing in the way of a theory to account for these differences, but he did suggest that any such explanation would need to be based on a close investigation of the nature of society in a multiplicity of localities.[3] As a matter of fact it is only now that such research is being carried out,[4] and this is partly because denominationalism, and indeed religion generally in England and Wales, no longer arouses the jealousies and animosities that once appeared to be one of its main ingredients. Apart from one or two very remarkable studies, the Report provoked but little of that objective analysis that Mann would have approved of.

The main reason for this was that the Census was itself the product of the debate between the Church of England and the Nonconformists concerning the nature of the Christian Church and of its role in society, and the widely held belief that the Established Church had no right to the wealth and privileges that it possessed. Underlying this was the belief, more or less supported by observation, that a substantial part of the population had no formal connection with any organized religion, and that secularist and even atheistic movements were becoming increasingly influential among sections of the population which orthodox religions could not or would not reach.[5] Indeed the primary purpose of the Census was to discover the size of the worshipping population by establishing precisely how many places of worship there were and how many people had attended them on the last Sunday in March 1851. Unfortunately, the way this Census was organized left much to be desired, and the publication of the Report in January 1854 sparked off an ' arithmetical war ' that lasted for many years, making it impossible for a more accurate and objective census to be taken in later years. But though one cannot be confident about the accuracy of detailed figures, whether of sittings or attendances, one can rely on them if what one is seeking to do is to compare the religiosity of regions one with another or, as in this study, comparing the religious statistics of two countries, England and Wales.

According to the Report England and Wales together had a total of 34,467 places of all kinds, providing an aggregate of about 9.5 million sittings. [6] The population of the two countries was about 18 millions. Obviously, not every individual could be expected to be present at a religious service on any particular Sunday; the very young and the very old, for example, the sick and the maimed, and the many thousands of people who were expected to work on Sundays. Mann estimated that about 7.5 millions came into the first category leaving 10.5 millions, or 58 *per cent* of the population, who were able to attend, or not prevented from attending, divine worship. If this calculations were correct, then it followed that there was a shortage of over a million sittings, and Mann was of the opinion that about 2,000 additional places of worship were required, especially in the large towns where, as the Report so clearly showed, the deficiency was greatest.

It was not in Wales that the deficiency was to be found. Here there were 4,006 separate places of worship containing a total of 1,005,410 sittings for a population of 1,188,914. If we accept Mann's estimate of the proportion of the population able to attend, that is, 58 *per cent*, then the figures for Wales show that there existed more than a million sittings for a notional 700,000 worshippers. So, in the two countries together there was a deficiency of over one million sittings, but in Wales a surplus of over a quarter of a million. As Mann observed in the Report (p. cxxvii), ' It will be noticed, indeed, how favourably Wales in general is circumstanced—nearly all the districts having a surplus of provision ', ' fortunately basking ', as he put it, ' in excess of spiritual privileges '. He made this observation in the context of an analysis of the figures for the country as a whole showing that provision varied as between rural areas with accommodation for 67 *per cent* of population and industrial areas with accommodation for only 34 *per cent*. The detailed tables in the Report—that is, the series of tables showing provision in each Registration District—clearly showed that there was some kind of relationship between the relativities of provision and the economic and social characteristics of the regions themselves. The deficient Districts were all in industrial areas, in large towns and cities. It was in the towns that the millions dwelt—according to Mann, more than 5 millions—' who every Sunday neglect religions ordinances . . . of their own free choice '.[7] There was nothing new in this general conclusion. A few years earlier, for example, Edward Miall, editor of *The Nonconformist*, had observed that ' The bulk of our manufacturing population stand aloof from our Christian institutions. The operatives of these realms, taken as a body, and the still more numerous class whose employment is less regular, and whose temporal prospects are still more discouraging and precarious, must be described as living beyond occasional contacts with the institutions of Christian faith and practice.'[8] The strategy of the reformed Church and the institutions designed to carry out that strategy, such as the Church Building Commissioners and the Incorporated Church Building Society, was based on the same understanding. What was new was this great body of statistics, more or less reliable, gathered from from every parish in the land, where before there had been partial observation, rough guesses, and the subjective impressions of individuals.

How did Wales fit into the pattern thus disclosed? Putting aside for a moment the over-arching problem of why the *whole* of Wales should have been so markedly different from England, one conclusion is inescapable. It is that, as in England so in Wales, differences in the provision of facilities for religious worship corresponded to differences in local economies and societies. In those counties where industry had developed most extensively and rapidly provision was relatively least favourable. Generally speaking, in industrial and mining counties, provisions was made for about 70 *per cent* of the population. It was highest in Merioneth and Brecknockshire, in both of which counties provision exceeded the total populations. The same was true of the Registration Districts. Provision was greatest in the rural Districts: for example, Machynlleth (124 *per cent*,) Dolgellau (116 *per cent*), and Llanfyllin (105 *per cent*): and it was lowest in the industrial Districts, or heavily urbanized Districts, such as Newport (68 per cent), and Merthyr Tydfil (58 *per cent*). So, and taking the provision of sittings as the basis for comparison, though Wales was far in advance of England, she was not an exception to the unvarying rule that it was in the industrial regions, particularly in the large industrial towns, that organized religion was least successful, and perhaps, in comparison with rural areas, likely to become progressively weaker.

Unfortunately, we cannot rely on the accuracy of the statistics in the Report purporting to give exact numbers of attendants. For one thing, it was chapel and church officials that were responsible for counting the numbers of worshippers present in the various services, and the actual enumerators ' returns show that many of them must have been wildly optimistic and that most of the officials estimated rather than counted the numbers of worshippers. For another, it was congregations that were counted and not individual worshippers, and since in most places there was more than one service it is impossible to tell how many individuals had been present in more than one. Mann's way of arriving at an estimate of the numbers of individual worshippers was to add to the numbers attending the morning service, one half of those attending the afternoon service, and one third of those attending the evening service. This inevitably favoured the Church of England for morning service was invariably the best-attended Anglican service. But to base the calculations on attendants at evening service would *pari passu* favour the nonconformists. In what follows, therefore, I have based the calculations on the best-attended service whether it was morning, afternoon or evening.

The resulting statistics reinforce the conculsions arrived at on the basis of accommodation: Wales was not only better provided than England but also made more use of its superior accommodation. The proportion of the population of the two countries together which attended was 24 *per cent*: for Wales alone it was 34 *per cent*. This is to say that, in very general terms, about one third of the total population attended a religious service on Census Sunday [361,543 attendants in a population of 1,005,721]. The proportion was higher in the north Wales counties (38 *per cent*) than in the south (35 *per cent*), and higher in the rural Districts than in the industrial Districts. For example, in the Districts of Aberystwyth, Machynlleth, Cardigan, and Bangor more than a half of their populations attended, but in Newport, Swansea and Neath slightly less than one third were present. The proportion was slightly higher in Merthyr Tydfil, Pontypool and Bridgend, but still very significantly lower than in the rural Districts.

One can therefore conclude with a fair degree of certainty that, in comparison with England, Wales was extraordinarily successful both in its provision for religious worship and in the use made of it. But it is equally clear that, like England, Wales was subject to those same social forces that shaped the pattern of religious adherence in both countries alike, and there was an organic relation between the external evidences of religious behaviour and the society of which that religion was an essential part. In particular, the relative success of organized religion depended very largely on the nature and extent of industrialization and the amount and type of urbanization to which industrialization had given rise.

It is important to distinguish between the nature and size of industrialization on the one hand and the nature and extent of urbanization on the other. Looked at from the point of view of provision, it was not industrialization as such that was necessarily antipathetic to religious growth: on the contrary, industry created the wealth that was invested in the places of worship, in maintaining the fabric, in supporting the ministry, and in financing school building and so on. This was true of the rural areas as of the manufacturing and mining areas, for industry benefited agriculture by providing an expanding market for the food it produced and a refuge for the surplus population that would otherwise be a drain on their resources. It was the social consequences of industrialization in the large towns that were so antipathetic to religious organizations. In Britain by mid-century the population of the large towns (i.e. towns of more than 20,000 inhabitants) was growing at a faster rate than that of the country as a whole. By 1861 a total of about 5.5 millions lived in 72 towns with populations of 10,000 and above[9]— nearly 3 millions in London alone, 500,000 in Liverpool, 400,000 in Manchester, 300,000 in Birmingham, 200,000 in Leeds, and 155,000 in Bristol. Towns in this category were growing at a rate of 18 per cent per annum, and it was mainly in these, and particularly in the largest ones, that religious deprivation was most in evidence.[10] This was but one aspect of their more general social deprivation: indeed, as Charles Booth and other social investigators were to discover later in the century, the spiritual needs of the inhabitants of the large industrial towns and cities were commensurate with their physical needs.[11]   These towns were expanding haphazardly and the flood of new immigrants from surrounding rural areas and further afield had the effect of overwhelming all the religious and cultural resources that the towns may have provided before the onset of rapid growth.[12]

Industrialization did not take place in precisely that fashion in Wales nor were the social effects the same. The basic pattern was similar: identical forces were at work: but the scale of development was not the same. There were only three ' great towns ' in Wales, namely, Merthyr Tydfil, Newport, and Swansea. And when we examine the structure of these carefully they turn out to be not towns on the pattern of Liverpool or Manchester or the wool and cotton towns of the Midlands, but rather congolmerations of industrial villages nucleated around ironworks, non-ferrous smelting works, and iron and coal mines. This applies equally to the new settlements in the mining and manufacturing districts on the coalfields of the south and north as to the older commercial towns, such as Swansea, Neath and Aberafan, that were being transformed at the same time.[13]   There were enormous structual differences between these different category of towns. In effect, they were all collections of small villages or towns and their social life, despite the extraordinary speed of their growth and its haphazard nature, was very different from that of, say, Liverpool. This is not to say that these Welsh towns, both the old transformed ones and the newly planted ones, did not have terrible social problems to contend with. There were slums of classical character in all of them, places of appalling social conditions, of cruelty, inhumanity and despair.   But ' China ' was not Merthyr, and social reformers, including both evangelical clergy and the advocates of ' town improvement ', were becoming increasingly sensitive to the evil reputation which such places could give to otherwise well-behaved and respectable towns.[14] What was true of the relative magnitude of the urban element on the steam-coal and iron-ore fields was certainly true of the newly emerging pattern of settlement on the anthracite coalfield in West Glamorgan and East Carmarthenshire then beginning to be exploited. While it is important, therefore, to stress the unplanned nature of the new industrial towns, to mark their lack of proper systems of sewage disposal and of adequate supplies of clean water, their lack of amenity buildings, the gross overcrowding that was so characteristic of them, and their universal lack of good governance, it is also necessary to stress their small size, the fact that their individuality bred community and practical co-operation, both in their places of work and in the streets of homes. In the anthracite area many of the emerging industrial towns were forming around existing agricultural villages, and the new developments were taking place at such a relatively slow pace and in such a way within the old societies as not to destroy competely their ancient character. Almost anywhere on the coalfield town and country seemed to be in balance and the quality of interpenetration to be such as to create a new culture rather than to produce conflict between the new and the old.[15]

Another important difference between the English and the Welsh towns was their different social structure, and especially their class structure. It was often said that the industrial towns of Wales were working-class towns. This was certainly the opinion of visitors from England and it was the opinion of the inhabitants themselves when they chose to think in such categories.[16] Between the iron-master or the coal proprietor and their workmen, it was said, there was no middle-class of any substance: there were only a few men of private means, professional men, tradesmen and large shopkeepers. This state of affairs corresponded to the distribution of wealth in society. The master owned the capital and the worker (sometimes) his tools, his skill and physical strength. Without seeking to analyze this remarkable state of affairs it should be observed that this elementary form of social structure in the new towns was of the very essence of their development. They had been simple in their original formation and simple the resulting structure remained. They lacked a strong, visible middle class to carry the responsibilities of government, to invest in cultural overheads, to secure and to defend an official form of religious culture, a middle class into which members of the working class could aspire to ascend.

These considerations are important. At the time in England there was a great deal of discussion about the causes of the irreligion of the working classes. ' All the writers of the bourgeoisie are unanimous on this point,' wrote Engels, ' that the workers are not religious and do not attend church.' In 1847, round about the same time, one of Engels's ' bourgeois writers ', Edward Miall, was expressing his conviction that one of the obstacles that Christianity had to face in its efforts to convert the people was what he called ' the spirit of aristocracy ', by which he meant precisely those narrow, hard class divisions in society.[18] He noted how the middle classes shaped religion in their own image and in such a way as to express their own snobbery—their own version of aristocratic exclusiveness—and at the cost of excluding from their places of worship the poor among the working classes. Mann's $5\frac{1}{2}$ million irreligious were not to be found in the upper and middle classes, for membership of church or chapel was an essential part of their mode of living and an essential indicator of respectability, but rather among the millions of workers—his ' unconscious Secularists ' or, perhaps more realistically, ' non-believers '. Most of these, it is safe to assume, would have received some little instruction in Sunday school or in day schools in the elements of Christianity, ' but, no sooner do they mingle in the active world of labour than . . . they soon become strangers to religious ordinances as the people of a heathen country . . . as ignorant of Christianity as were the heathen Saxons at Augustine's landing '.[19]   Mann offered an explanation for this state of affairs, and his reasons were very similar to those of Miall, namely, the fact that the churches and chapels maintained and even accentuated the evidences of social differences, the apathy of the churches concerning the condition of the poor, the belief among the lower classes that the message of the ministers of religion was irrelevant because they received stipends for their labours, and the undoubted fact that the physical condition of the poor overpowered and stifled any and every effort on their part of understand the things of the spirit. The reaction of the prosperous middle classes—chapelgoers as well as churchmen—

to the creation of slums in the hearts of the towns was to escape into the countryside and there create suburban communities complete with their own chapels anc churches to testify to their respectability.[20]

To what extent does this pathology of social morbidity apply to Wales? Almost certainly developments followed a different course in those middle decades of the century: later they would run parallel with those in England. As we have seen, already Wales lacked that middle class that was the engine of social change in England. But in any case that fecundity of religious life, that amplitude of places of worship, had not been provided by the middle classes. It had not been middle class people who had directed the vast expansion of the previous half-century but the ordinary people themselves. Moreover, because social mobility within the new towns, given their social uniformity, and, to a lesser extent, within the old towns, was less marked than in English towns there was a correspondingly weaker motive for transferring from one chapel to another, or from one denomination to another, in search of greater respectability. Hence, it was the shape and structure of society which partly accounted for the outstanding success of religion in Wales and that, be it remembered, at a time and in places when organized religion could scarcely be expected to flourish at all.

But while considerations as to the nature and structure of society are fundamental to any explanation of the relative differences in the provision of religious accommodation, such considerations do not necessarily explain its extraordinary amplitude. It is individuals and groups of people who recognize a need and who will the means to satisfy it, and the most puzzling question of all is, why they should have provided so much? Part of the answer becomes clear when we consider the pattern of denominationalism revealed in the Census. This again, as I have already suggested, was very different from the pattern in England, and the differences are worth noting. In England and Wales as a whole 41 *per cent* of all places of worship belonged to the Anglican Church, the remainder to the other denominations—a fact that was eagerly seized upon as illustrating the extent to which the Established Church had lost its ascendancy in the religious life of the country. But measured by the numbers of sittings the Church was by far the largest providet, having no less than 52 *per cent* of the total available. The Church was also ahead in the ratio of sittings to population provided by the different denominations. For each 100 persons the church provided 30 seats and the nonconformists 28. In Wales, however, the differences were much wider and favoured the nonconformist bodies, taken as a whole, rather than the Church. Of the total of places of worship of all kinds, 29 *per cent* belonged to the Church and 71 *per cent* to the other denominations. For each 100 persons the Church provided 26 sittings, and the others between them 58 *per cent*. Of the total of 983,653 sittings 30.5 *per cent* belonged to the Church and 69.5 to the nonconformists.

Differences in the patterns of denominational adherence were even greater. In England and Wales together almost as many worshippers attended the services of the Church as attended those of the nonconformists—47 *per cent* and 49 *per cent* of the total respectively. But in Wales alone only 9 *per cent* had been present in Anglican places of worship and 87 *per cent* in the chapels. These proportions varied greatly, it needs scarcely to be stressed, from place to place. The Anglican Church was strongest in the rural, anglicized Districts, especially along the Border, and weakest in the industrial, Welsh-language speaking Districts. For example, 70 *per cent* of the attendants in Monmouth District went to Church, 43 *per cent* in Knighton, 10 *per cent* in Abergavenny, 9 *per cent* in Neath and in Swansea, 7 *per cent* in Bridgend, 6 *per cent* in Merthyr Tydfil, and only 1 *per cent* in Bala District. One cannot over-emphasize the fact that the relative weakness was most pronounced in the rural areas. The problem for the Anglican Church lay not in the towns alone or even primarily, but in the Welsh speaking parts of the countryside.

It is clear, therefore, that the masses in Wales had rejected the Established Church and that the measure of that rejection was their astonishing success in providing themselves with places devoted to alternative forms of worship. Wales was a nonconformist country, and there are two aspects of this massive preponderance that need to be emphasized. First, its docrinal orthodoxy, and second, the simplicity of its denomational structure. There were only 21 Roman Catholic churches in the whole of the Principality and most of these were in the ports and industrial towns where there were large communities of immigrant Irish constantly being renewed from the mother country. The exceptions were places like Holywell and some Border towns in the south where indigenous Catholicism maintained a tenuous tradition. To all intents and purposes the only sect, in the strict meaning of the word, were the Mormons, or Latter Day Saints, who had 31 congregations, mainly in the industrial south, centred on Merthyr, and in the industrial north-east. When we consider that Horace Mann listed no less than 35 denominations and sects—excluding what he called ' isolated congregations '—it is important to remember that this multiplicity was not to be found in Wales. Orthodox Protestantism was the religion of the Welsh people.

Similarly, her denominationalism was every bit as monolithic and formal. It is the simplicity rather than the complexity of the pattern that is striking. Among the old dissenters, the Independents were the most numerous, followed by the Baptists, with the Unitarians, who had about 50 congregations, coming a poor third. As I have already suggested, although there were elements of sectarianism more or less present in all of them it is their ' denominationalism ' that needs emphasizing, and likewise the great deal that they had in common. Membership was confined to those who accepted the particular theological standpoint of the congregation, but it is clear that most of the denominations by mid-century expected to recruit, and were so organized as to recruit, mainly from and within families. The proportion of ' hearers ' in their congregations ebbed and flowed with changes in the religious climate of revivalism, but they also constituted a kind of reservoir from which the memberships were renewed. The existence of this class of ' hearers ' testified not, as has sometimes been suggested, to the relative failure of the denominations but on the contrary to the esteem in which they were held by society at large. For though all the denominations, particularly those old denominations for whom ' voluntaryism ' was a *raison d'être*, rejected any official connection with the state they had by no means rejected ' the world ' as such. Indeed, they accepted the world, and the continued adherence of ' hearers ' in substantial numbers was evidence of their success in inter-penetrating society and the best hope they possessed of eventually transforming it. All of them, in their relations to formal political movements, advocated constitutionalism and all had abandoned any revolutionary characteristics that at one time they may have possessed. Millennialism was no more prominent in their theology and in their behaviour than was normal in the contemporary evangelical forms of Christianity, and it was invariably held that the Millennium, to which all aspired, would follow rather than precede, the Second Coming of Christ. Beliefs such as these, when embedded in a strong structure of denominationalism based on the family and operating within the close-knit communities of town and country, were not conducive to extreme attitudes on political issues, but on the contrary tended to nurture a reliance on the gradual achievement of social improvements, a spirit of moderation, a readiness to accept working compromises, and an emphasis on organized participation in public affairs.[22] All this was possible because of the remarkable theological consensus that had already been achieved. The Unitarians apart, all were moderate Calvinists; the Welsh Baptists were Calvinistic, and there were very few General or Arminian Baptists in existence.

Much the same was true of those new nonconformists, the Methodists. Nearly twice as many people attended the chapels of the Welsh Calvinistic Methodists as attended those of the Wesleyan Methodists, and the numbers of chapels stood in roughly the same proportion. But what is typical about both, and especially of the Welsh Calvinistic Methodists, is their extraordinary strength and resilience as denominations. When one considers the divisions, the fractionalism, the secessions within the original Wesleyan Connexion from 1797 onwards, and the numerous and sometimes powerful denominations that were formed by the various secessions,[23] it is remarkable how little the Methodist movement in Wales appears to have been affected. The Methodist New Connexion, the Primitive Methodists, the Wesleyan Association, the Bible Christians, and the Brethren—these, with the exception of the Primitive Methodists were scarcely present in Wales at all. The Primitive

Methodists, had about 100 congregations, many of them using temporary or rented premises or meeting in private houses, all of them small and seemingly insecure. Most of them were located in industrialt owns along the Border and most probably consisted of English immigrants. There are two main reasons to account for this peculiar feature of Welsh Methodism. The first is that the modified Presbyterian form of church governed and developed by the Welsh Calvinistic Methodists—the indigenous form of Methodism—did not encourage or stimulate secessions based on constitutional and internal political tensions characteristic of English Methodism. Second, Welsh Methodism still retained that intense evangelicalism and revivalism that characterized its formative period in the eighteenth century, and consequently gave no scope for any internal movements of frustrated evangelicalism. While Welsh Calvinistic Methodism preserved the spirit of the fathers there was no demand for Primitive Methodism: Welsh Methodism was ' primitive ' enough.

This analysis of the simplicity and strength and homogeneity of Welsh denominationalism is complete only if I stress the second of the two characteristics to which I drew attention, namely, its theological orthodoxy. All of them, including the Established Church, only a minority of whose clergy and adherents were of the High Church persuasion, were evangelical in their theology. Moderate Calvinism was the characteristic theological belief of the vast majority of Welshmen. Within this body of belief—and it was of relatively recent growth—there was plenty of room for differing emphases and for doctrinal variations, but from the point of view of this essay, what is significant is not the strength or frequency of theological controversy but, on the contrary, the universal consensus that existed. There was a community of belief that was of the utmost practical significance, for it is difficult to see how the denominations as a whole could have developed so powerfully, without internecine warfare and with virtually no secessions, had they not shared in a fundamental concurrence of belief and uniformity of practical theology. *Odium theologicam* there was, but it was never on such a scale as to disrupt the universal consensus or render impossible the holding of common attitudes to the world or the achieving of common aims. It is undoubtedly true that the role of ideology and denominational differences in Welsh religious life have been exaggerated at the expense of the fundamental community that existed, and it may perhaps be a characteristic error on the part of hisorians, who tend rarely to wander beyond the study or out of the manse, to believe that the esoteric ideas and the subtly-spun differences of trained theologians should be of much relevance to the average worshipper. In English Wesleyanism, it was the conviction on the part of ordinary lay members that too much emphasis was being placed upon formal learning and not enough on the instilling of spiritual warmth and a thirst for souls that led to the first and most damaging secession. In this respect, at any rate, the Welsh Calvinistic Methodists were closer in spirit to the Primitive Methodists, to Hugh Bourne and William Clowes, than to Jabez Bunting.

This general principle is true also with regard to differences between the denominations on constitutional questions and church government. The debates, of course, were invariably theological in substance and based on the New Testament and on an appeal to history, but the actual geographical distribution of the main denominations leads one to the conclusion that factors other than purely ideological ones must have been present. Generally speaking, it is clear, for example, that the most heavily populated urban and industrial areas favoured congregational forms of church government while the rural areas favoured modified forms of Presbyterianism. The distribution pattern was the product of history, and one should never minimize the role of individuals in the planting and the spread of particular forms of religion, but at the same time one cannot but question whether the extraordinary strength of Calvinistic Methodism in the Bala District and in north Wales generally was entirely due to the influence of Thomas Charles. Michael Jones and his son also laboured in Bala, but it was the industrial valleys of the south and the towns on the north east coalfield that provided the soil most congenial for the spread of their characteristic ideas on theology and church government.

The relative success or failure of denominations cannot be explained in terms only of individuals and personalities. It is necessary to understand also, if this is possible, the ways in which the various religious causes fitted into the social nexus of which they were organically a part. The ways they fitted into the modes of production of the various places, into the characteristic amusements and forms of play and structure of family life need to be understood as well as the more obvious and formal religious connections they may have had. It was accepted that the denominations existed at one level in competition with one another, but this competition was not unlimited or anarchic: it took place only in accordance with accepted norms of corporate behaviour. But at the levels that really mattered the denominations presented a united front to the world. This was particularly true in periods of relative decline, when the tide of religion was at the ebb or, contrariwise, when revivals held out the promise of great conquests or significant gains. Facing a world that was fundamentally irreligious they knew that they were in a minority and that the Gospel they preached in common was what gave them distinctiveness and that it was more important than the things that divided them. The former was the essential thing that differentiated them from the God-less world around; the latter were the inessentials that were basically matters of style rather than belief. All knew that the modes of religious experience that they provided occupied the highest place in the societies of which they were part, local and national. It was industrialism that had brought, and continued to bring, the people together in great towns and urban settlements: the denominations believed that it was the force of religion that was primarily responsible for transforming them into particular and defined communities sharing basic beliefs and holding to specific modes of behaviour. In rural areas religion had developed in and through the relations of kith and kin, working organically within and as part of the inescapable facts of life for farmers, craftsmen and labourers. In this sense, the denominations represented creative adaptations of the religious and cultural ideals of the people and the ineluctable realities of their economic situations. When one considers the stupendous changes that took place in rural society as a result of the growth of population it is difficult to see how those ancient societies could have adapted themselves relatively peacefully were it not for the role of religion. In this context its role was precisely to defend the communities against the forces that threatened to destroy them. Only in this sense can one accept the notion that Methodism saved society against revolution. Calvinistic Methodism was a conservative force in society because it believed society to be its own creation and that it had a primary duty therefore to preserve it against attacks from without and anarchy from within.

The social role of religion in the mining and manufacturing areas was not so very different. There, in the new urban settlements, the challenge was not so much the preserving of the old as the creating of new communities in entirely novel situations. We are prone to forget that all the denominations alike, church as well as chapel, faced the same basic social problems even though they might differ one from the other in the quality of the apprehension of it, namely, the problem of maintaining their integrity and of extending their influence in the wild and lawless communities in which they found themselves. These were culturally ' frontier societies ', and we should listen carefully to descriptions of them that we find in contemporary writings—the observations of the inhabitants themselves as well as governmental reports of one kind and another. Because these communities, by reason of the very facts of their geographical situation and the nature of their growth, were subject to only the most elementary forms of control from without or, indeed, from within, their inhabitants themselves had to order them in accordance with their own notions of social good. That, in effect, is what the popular movements of the time were about, and it was that necessity and those ideals which, in times of troubles and of stress, produced ' communitarian ' movements for, for example, the equable distribution of justly priced bread or for a fair price for labour. It is in that context that the role of religion must be understood: the denominations were one instrument in the hands of a people seeking to adapt creatively to their environment, and in so doing shaping that environment, or those parts of it that were not entirely beyond their control, in accordance with their own highest cultural aspirations.

This was particularly the function of the nonconformist denominations because of the unmistakeable failure of the Established Church to do so. Whatever the factors were that account for that failure—the constitutional and legal rigidity and the inherent conservativism of its hierarchy, in particular, that made it difficult for the Church to accept the changes that were revolutionizing society in the industrial regions—what requires emphasis is the undoubted fact that its failure pre-dated industrialization and urbanization. This is the significance of the rise and growth of Methodism. It was never the intention of its leaders to secede from the Church of their fore-fathers, and formal secession took place almost twenty years later than that of the English Wesleyans: but once they had begun to organize ' societies ' as independent groups within the local communities, then secession became virtually inevitable. The aim of the Methodist Revival was to revitalize the Protest-ant Reformation in Wales and to give it the kind of popular reality that its proponents a century earlier had hoped for, but given the historical nature of the Established Church and the failure of all attempts at comprehension, the creation of some-thing like a new denomination became a necessary and unavoidable part of that process.

Another aspect of that same historical process was the fact that the Revival had been, and continued to be, based on education and a drive for literacy. In its early stages the Church was deeply involved as the main patron of the education provided by the Circulating Schools of Rev. Griffith Jones of Llanddowror, but it was not primarily ' Church education ' as such that was being offered to the people, and the Church Catechism that the old and young were taught to read was for the sake of their immortal souls and the knowledge of saving grace. It was the S.P.C.K. that tended to think in political terms and whose mission it was to produce a type of Christian who would *ipso facto* be a loyal citizen. This kind of social control, while by no means foreign to Griffith Jones's con-ception of the purpose of his schools, was not in the forefront of his mind, and its relative unimportance helped to explain why he insisted on using the language of the people not as a temp-orary measure while they asborbed English but as the proper and sufficient method for learning Gospel truths. This tradition was maintained in the Methodist societies, was taken over by the dissenters and came to full fruitition in the Sunday School movement. Auto-didacticism became the characteristic mark of Welsh education. This was religion's supreme contribution to Welsh culture and justifies entirely their claim that they lay at the heart of community and gave it meaning, coherence, and drive. The ' pay-off ', of course, was rich and unforseen, for out of this came not only religious organizations as such, but secular ones as well—friendly societies, literary clubs, eisteddfodau and political movements, and, more indirectly, unions and philosophical and rationalist societies. Henry Vincent and O'Connor were listened to as well as preachers, Morgan Williams of Merthyr, the Chartist leader, as well as Thomas Williams of Gwaelod-y-garth, the Nonconformist Liberal, and *Utgorn Cymru* as well as *Seren Cymru* were read. The tradition of literacy based on voluntaryism that was so eagerly promoted by all the denominations combined creatively with the older traditions of radicalism nurtured by the dissenters to produce a new culture which enabled the country at large to survive the destructive forces unleashed by the new industrialism of the second half of the century.

It is along such lines as these that one should think as one contemplates the patterns of religious worship revealed in the 1851 Census. It is the uniqueness of Welsh religion as a whole that is striking, and it is precisely that quality that goes far to explain why religion should have been given such a pre-eminent place in the nationalism characteristic of the time. Because religion was organically a part of society and not something defined by others from above and imposed from without by force of law, it became the means of preserving old traditions and of creating new ones and thus of binding the present to a vivid and meaningful past. ' Curious and puzzling ' indeed it was, and curious and puzzling the distribution and growth of religious organizations remain: but no Welsh historian can afford to ignore such important phenomena or avoid proposing his own explanation.

THE LIBERATION SOCIETY AND WELSH POLITICS, 1844 TO 1868

WHEN A. H. Dodd described 1868 as an *annus mirabilis* in Welsh politics he was subscribing to a view of the events of that that year which has passed into the mythology of Welsh political and historical thinking. For Dodd ' the wholesale dethronement of. . . great parliamentary dynasties ' justified the appellation ' wonderful ',[1] and if we exclude the exaggeration of the word ' wholesale ' we must agree that it is here that the importance of the general election of that year lies. Other historians and politicians from Henry Richard onwards have descanted on the same theme, but there has been curiously little serious effort to assess its significance in an objective and disinterested manner and, in particular, scarcely any attempt to analyse the nature of politics in the preceding generation or so. Yet such studies are obviously crucially necessary, for wonderful changes in the world of politics do not occur *in vacuo*, are not unprepared, do not emerge fully fledged out of the minds of men. We cannot understand such changes until we know something of the operation of the forces which produced them. Such a knowledge of antecedent changes, of the causation of significant events must obviously be comprehensive if it is to be meaningful: it should concern itself not only with the mechanisms of politics, but with changing economic and social conditions, and take account of intellectual developments, of man's attempt to adjust himself to, and to control, the forces of change active in society. To attempt such a task within the compass of this paper would be impracticable, but something of profit along these lines might be attempted if we confined ourselves to thinking about one of the political agencies by which a new public opinion was created in Wales in the two or three generations preceding the elections of 1868. There were many such agencies, of course: the complex, disorganized body of Welsh nonconformity in its relations with English nonconformity; the educational movements of the age; nascent party machines; the press; working class organizations, both industrial and political. But involved in all these, and coming gradually to play a more formative rôle in their development and inter-actions, was a great religio-political society, namely the Anti-State-Church Association, or, as it later became known, the Society for the Liberation of Religion from State Patronage and Control. To study the operations of this body is not a fringing issue, for in the nineteenth century the maintenance of what were called ' religious interests ' was dependent on the existence of sectional societies, a state of affairs which had grown out of the realization by dissenters round about 1837 that neither of the two great parties could be relied upon to support their just demands. It will be argued that it was the Liberation Society, more than any other agency, which was responsible for shaping those political attitudes in Wales which in 1868 produced such wonderful fruit.

Welsh nonconformists publicists in the '60s were fond of declaring that English nonconformist Radicals were merely teaching their countrymen principles which Welshmen had been familiar with since the days of Samuel Roberts and earlier.[2] The kind of assumptions implicit in such judgements reflects the self-confidence and assurance of the nonconformists of the '60s: as descriptions of historical fact they are in error. For however powerful a pressure group the Liberation Society may by then have been, and however influential its leadership in Wales may by then have become, it had attained to this position only as the result of constant and careful exertion, and through a conscious effort to preserve and develop and adjust these elements in the dissenting tradition which appeared to it to be fundamental. An essential preliminary therefore to a description of the history of the Society in Wales, and of its influence in reshaping the tradition of Welsh dissent, must be a sketch of the history of its predecessors in this field.

*　　　*　　　*

It is important to realize that when the Liberation Society began its work in the provinces in 1844 it was nowhere entering into a virgin territory. Both as regards the geographical location of its supporters, and in the work which it set out to accomplish, the soil had in some measure been already turned. In Wales we shall see that during the first critical years of its existence it could expect to find a fairly vigorous spirit of co-operation primarily in those parts of the country which had had closest relations with previously existing pressure groups or quasi-political organizations centred on London. Leaving aside for the moment purely religious organizations such as mission-ary societies (though these had their political affiliations) or denominational bodies, and movements such as the anti-slavery societies, there had existed a number of purely political dissenting societies which had had Welsh affiliations. By ' political ' is not meant organizations organically connected with the established parties, whether Tory (which in this context was unthinkable), Whig, Liberal, or Radical. It happened, for certain fairly clear reasons, that these dissenting bodies consisted for the most part of men who found more to support and to hope for in the Whig-Liberal party: but such individual persuasions, as every political crisis from 1793 onwards showed, were unofficial. The societies as such were political only in so far as political action seemed at times to be necessary to protect or to advance dissenting interests; indeed, it was they who gave some reality to the technical term ' Dis-senting interest '. But it is necessary for the understanding of early nineteenth-century politics to appreciate that they were political only in the broadest sense.

Of these societies two are important for our purpose. The first of these—the Protestant Dissenting Deputies—was hardly a society in the accepted usage of the word.[3] It was a rep-resentative organization of the congregations of the three denominations situated within ten miles of London. It origin-ated in November 1732 when certain of the leading London dissenters, among whom Welshmen were prominent, met to consider an application to parliament for the repeal of the Corporation and Test Acts. No such appeal was made on that occasion, but an organization was created consisting of a com-mittee annually elected from the general body of delegates representative of London dissenters—Presbyterians, Cong-regationalists, and Baptists. Since 14 January 1736, such choice of deputies had been made by the London congregations at

regular intervals ' to take care of the Civil Affairs of the
Dissenters ', and it is with the activities of this body that we are
now concerned. It is unnecessary to trace the history of the
Deputies in subsequent years. What we have to remark is that
this task of taking care of the civil affairs of dissenters involved
them in two different but related kinds of activity. In the first
place, it involved them in political action, since the basic
concern of the Deputies was the repeal of all penal legislation
affecting dissenters. The committee retained a solicitor to
watch over their interests, and appointed a treasurer to receive
the subscriptions which were solicited to finance their often
expensive agitations and negotiations. The nature of their
agitation was such that it could not remain a merely metropolitan society: it claimed to speak for dissenters everywhere,
in the colonies as well as in the United Kingdom, so that it soon
extended its activities into the provinces. After 1745 especially,
and in the last three decades of the eighteenth century and the
beginning of the nineteenth, it systematically circulated addresses and manifestos on political issues, co-operating with
reform organizations, striving to arouse the consciences of
dissenters everywhere. By 1789, after the failure of an attempt
at repeal in the previous year, it felt sufficiently influential and
representative to address all protestant dissenters in these
terms: ' we express your sentiments when we express our own
. . . We feel alike as fellow-citizens unjustly deprived of civil
liberties and are equally sensible that what we claim is not a
favour, but a right '.[4] Books and pamphlets were circulated,
county meetings organized in favour of repeal, but, the French
Wars intervening, the committee met for the last time in 1794
until reconstituted in 1810.

The second function of the Deputies was the defence of the
existing rights of dissenters as defined in the statutes, and called
forth, therefore, a different kind of activity. There were many
ways in which individual dissenters and congregations could be
deprived of their rights; assaults by hostile communities and
mobs, interference with meeting houses, the refusal of magistrates to execute their offices in granting licences as required by
law, the refusal of parochial clergy to perform their duties as by
law required, and so on. In such cases—and they tended to

become more frequent, especially during the American and French wars—the Deputies, with their superior resources of legal knowledge, finance, and metropolitan influence, could take upon themselves the defence of the injured and aggrieved. They could prosecute the brutal, overcome recalcitrant magistrates by appeals to higher courts, and take action against defaulting clergy in the ecclesiastical courts.[5]

In these ways the Dissenting Deputies became the main instrument in the creation of a cohesive body of dissenting opinion in the country. London was bound closely to the provinces, isolated congregations made aware of their united strength. There can be scarcely any doubt that this was the effect on Welsh dissenting congregations. Wales seems to have been peculiarly the seat of Tory hatred during these years.[6] Up to 1810 alone, more than thirty cases out of a total of about 250 concerned Welsh congregations.[7] What needs to be stressed is this, that there existed during those difficult years bridging the two centuries a relationship between Welsh dissenting congregations and their London and provincial brethren by which ideas could be disseminated and action on political matters concerted. It is necessary to stress this, because so many historians of this period have assumed that such connections either did not exist or were at best tenuous and personal merely. Considerations such as these should make us pause before accepting such a view.

The other precursor of the Liberation Society was the Protestant Society for the Protection of Religious Liberty.[8] Founded, by John Wilkes mainly, in 1811 it existed until 1857 when it was wound up and its assets transferred to the Deputies.[9] Its effective life was considerably shorter than this, however, for its last annual meeting had been held in 1839, three years after the death of its founder, with whom also the society may be said to have expired. In many ways the aims of this society, and the methods it adopted to further them, resembled those of its older contemporary. On a parliamentary level it aspired to ' the repeal of every penal law which prevented the complete enjoyment of religious liberty ', and at a local level it busied itself with the defence of particular congregations throughout the country in exactly the same way as,

but with greater publicity than, the Deputies. Where it differed
was in its organization and in its composition. In both it was
altogether more comprehensive, since the emphasis in its title
was on ' Protestant ', and it sought to unite members of the
Established Church, mainly the Evangelical wing, with dissenters in the extension of religious freedom. This gives us the
essential clue to its nature, its strength, and its weakness. More
so than the Deputies it was the child of political fortune: it
could not have existed at an earlier period and, as we have
already indicated, it was largely defunct by 1839, defeated by
political realities. From its inception it was closely identified
with the Whig party and it was customary for Whig magnates
to preside over its annual meetings. This kind of alliance was
obviously of benefit to the Society; without the co-operation of
the Whigs no measure of religious liberty could hope to pass
through parliament or any obnoxious measure be opposed. But
equally the politicians had much to gain. At a time of party
conflict the society could place its organization at the disposal
of the Whigs, while the newspapers which it published or was
associated with—*The World* and *The Patriot*—provided cheap
and reliable forms of propaganda for the party. In addition, the
society appealed to the substantial middle-class-merchant-
industrial classes with large resources at their command. While
this kind of alliance lasted—and it would last only so long as it
suited the Whigs—the society was likely to flourish.

Another difference concerned the composition of the Protestant Society. Whereas the Deputies' Committee was confined in
its membership to, and largely dependent for financial support
upon, the London congregations, the Protestant Society sought
its membership in, and looked for support to, every congregation in England and Wales. Every English congregation
subscribing £2 annually, and every Welsh congregation £1
annually, was entitled to the support of the society and empowered to send two delegates to the annual meetings. Individuals, of any religious persuasion, could become members
on subscribing £1.[10] Welsh subscriptions were never considerable, totalling only about £55 up to 1834 (though the
evidence is incomplete). More interesting for our purpose is the
distribution of subscriptions. Twelve places were officially

associated with the society, six in Monmouthshire, two each in Glamorgan and Denbighshire, and one each in the counties of Pembroke, Carmarthen, and Cardigan. Again on the basis of incomplete evidence, only eight cases of particular grievances were dealt with during its existence, ranging from Caernarvonshire and Montgomeryshire to Brecon, Carmarthenshire, and Monmouthshire.[11]

This does not, at first, appear to be a very impressive record. But the work of this society should be seen within the context of the age. It was the first of the great dissenting societies (as distinct from the pre-existing Deputies) to make a sustained attempt to organize dissenting opinion on political lines in the the provinces, as it was certainly the first to be aware of the rather special circumstances prevailing in Wales. This was undoubtedly why the Reverend Thomas Charles of Bala was almost from its inception added to the committee and made a member of the deputation called to protest against Lord Sidmouth's Bill of 1811 which would have placed severe restrictions on the licensing of dissenting ministers.[12] Had this bill been allowed to pass into law the expansion of Methodism in Wales, depending as it did almost exclusively on lay evangelization, would have been severely handicapped in the most crucial years of its history. On an issue like this the Protestant Society taught old dissenter and new nonconformist the value of united action on political matters.

But evidence such as this would still not enable us to assess the contribution of this society to Welsh political life. The propaganda agencies available to it were of necessity primitive, for during the greater part of its existence there were few Welsh magazines in which its work could be publicized. This is why it depended so much on personal contacts, and the law still forbade the creation of auxiliary or corresponding societies in the provinces.[13] Nevertheless, these contacts were powerful, and it was through its sympathisers that its literature was disseminated, and its petitions signed and despatched. Indeed, when we study the course of political agitation in Wales during the '30s we must perforce marvel not that so little was done but that so much was accomplished, such sure foundation laid with such inadequate materials and primitive machinery.

Up to the late '30s these two societies were the most influential organizations for the furtherance of dissenting aims. After 1837 their influence declines, and other societies of a more radical nature, culminating in the Liberation Society, take their place. Why was this? To answer that question would require an analysis of British politics during those years—a task outside the limits of this paper. But some general considerations may be suggested which will throw light on the place these societies occupied in Welsh political life during these decades. Looking first at the Deputies and the Protestant Society we can see that their efficiency was considerably impaired by their failure to adjust themselves to the changing political climate. Their very moderation, and the tradition of co-operation with the Whig party became a hindrance. We can trace the evolution of this change. There had been complete unanimity—if a little jealousy—in 1811,[14] and again in 1828 when repeal had been the fruit of co-operation in a United Committee,[15] when identity of purpose had enabled them to pool their resources, and to co-operate as one in the task of organizing dissenters behind the parliamentary campaign. There was a common strategy, and common means, and a use in common of the network of ministers in the countryside who acted as agents in collection of petitions and so on. At the height of the Reform Bill agitation, again, there was no hesitation in either camp in raising funds to pay the electoral expenses of Lord John Russell in Devon: even Carmarthen contributed £5 15s 0d. towards this fund, and an additional £11 which went into the coffers of the Deputies.[16] But even as early as this there were indications that the middle-class leadership was beginning to become uneasy at the implications of such involvement in purely secular politics. In March 1831, during the Reform Bill agitation, the Deputies found it necessary officially to resist the pressure being put upon them ' to interfere as a seperate body in a matter purely political ', even though they have ' no doubt that Dissenters will be almost universally found in their Individual and Parochial capacities among the foremost to support the laudable endeavours of the Whig party '.[17] But the more extremist dissenters were already co-operating with Liberals and Radicals, finding in the self-same fundamentals of dissenting thought a justification for making political demands far in excess of anything the Whigs were likely to concede, and prepared moreover to make use of the existing machinery to press these demands. It was the refusal of men such as these to restrict themselves to moderate political aims which led directly to the Liberation Society.

This had become clear by the late '30s, for by then circumstances were favouring the Radicals. In January 1834 a United Committee, formed the previous year and consisting of the Deputies, the ministers of the three denominations, the Protestant Society, and the United Secession Presbytery, dissatisfied with the progress being made in the reformed parliament towards the redress of grievances drew up a statement of what they considered to be the just demands of dissenters.[18] The details of this need not detain us: the demands for the civil registration of births, deaths, and marriages, for marriages and burials in accordance with rites of their own choosing, for unrestricted entry to the two universities, and for the abolition of church-rates—these are familiar enough, for they remained the basic demands of dissenters until removed by piece-meal legislation in the course of the century. Discussion arose and differences developed as to the theoretical implications of the principles which underlay these demands.

In the view of the United Committee these principles, stemming from the Reformation, asserted ' the sole and exclusive sufficiency of the Holy Scriptures, the Right of all Men to judge for themselves in the interpretation and use of that Divine standard, and the correlative Right to Act according to their judgement in matters of Religion, so long as its exercise interferes not with the Right of others . . . As such Rights do not originate in human Laws, no human Laws can justly abridge them '. From this it followed that ' the exertion of political power ' for religious ends was presumptuous and unjust, subject to no limitations, and partial in its operation in that it was bound to favour one denomination at the expense of all others. With this most dissenters would agree. But the statement then went on to declare that equal rights and justice could be secured only by a complete separation of Church and State. Now, this represented an advance on the older position, and explained why the Wesleyan body had refused to join the United Committee. Disestablishment had never before gained such respectable backers. Indeed, the most 'respectable' among the dissenters, including the secretary of the Deputies, shortly after resigned on the grounds that dissent was becoming identified with extreme views on the establishment question.[19] In fact, this swing to disestablishmentarianism was itself symptomatic of the breaking up of the old alliance with the Whigs and of the hardening of political affiliations along religious lines.

For the time being the alliance continued and the moderates maintained their ascendancy: agitation was to be temperate, petitions were to be directed to the redress of practical grievances and extreme demands to be avoided. Governments, whether Whig or Tory—and party differences tended to become less pronounced—were extremely reluctant to grant anything but the most insignificant of reforms, while, contemporaneously, there was an increasing tendency for dissenters to distil extreme demands out of their principles. What greatly accelerated this tendency and destroyed the ascendancy of the moderates was the realization, in 1837, that the Whig refusal to support any church-rate abolition bill in parliament spelled the end of the old tradition of alliance and that henceforth dissenters would be compelled to proceed independently of either Whig or Tory.[20] Here was a difficult situation. It appeared to many, and was accepted as inevitable by some, that nevertheless the connection must be maintained. But increasingly others saw that dissenters must move farther to the left in the direction of alliance with the Radicals. It is at this point, in the late '30s and early '40s, that that alliance of the left wing in dissenting politics with radicalism in secular politics took place which was to be increasingly influential in British politics, and which was to give to Welsh nonconformity its distinctive tone.

The man most responsible for this alliance—the creation of a new nonconformist orthodoxy in political affairs—was Edward Miall of Leicester, who, in 1841, came to London and established *The Nonconformist* newspaper.[21] This paper was devoted to a more radical exposition of the agreed principles of dissent with a view to stimulating dissenters into consistent lines of political action on the question of the relationship of Church and State. The novelty in Miall's political creed was its essential simplicity: he saw that there was ' little prospect of a radically improved system of legislation upon ecclesiastical matters excepting the legislature itself were reconstituted, and therefore, side by side with the ecclesiastical, [he] urged the question of political reform, not, however, merely as a means to an end, but as, in itself, a just and necessary step '.[22] It was this attitude which enabled him to bridge the gulf between an essentially middle-class movement vainly attempting ecclesiastical reform with archaic means, and a working-class political movement as vainly attempting its own enfrachisement using revolutionary techniques. Moreover, his association with the Christian Chartists, and his attempt, with Joseph Sturge, to unite Chartism with the Anti-Corn Law League assured him of support wider than that of the other societies.[23] Both as a Chartist and a Leaguer he understood the need for a simple programme of reform and for massive organization.

It was not until 1843, however, that Miall proposed to give practical expression to these views in the formation of a new society. The time was propitious: the old societies were defunct or divided, the most recent ones ineffective, while in the world of politics Graham's Education of Children in Factories Bill [February 1843] seemed to all dissenters to be an undisguised attempt by the government to hand over the education of the population to the clergy. There was alarm at the growth of Tractarianism, rejoicing at the success of the Scottish secession movement, and the Anti-Corn Law League was an inspiration and a guide. The new venture began with a meeting on 7 December 1843 of seventy Midland ministers at Leicester which passed a resolution declaring ' that the present juncture of events distinctly and loudly calls upon the friends of the voluntary principle cordially to unite and earnestly to labour, in the use of all peaceable and Christian means to accomplish, as speedily as possible, a separation of the church from the state '. A conference was to be called at London to launch the movement on a national basis. Three secretaries were appointed (among whom was Dr. Thomas Rees, historian, and editor of *The Electric Review*), a provisional committee of 200, and an executive committee of twenty-one. The conference was to take place in May, and to consist of delegates from congregations, colleges, and properly organized public meetings.[24]

How did Welshmen respond to this? It is clear that the secretaries corresponded widely with ministers in Wales, and that they could rely on the magazines of the Independents and Baptists in particular for publicity.[25] Existing denominational organizations were asked to co-operate, and it is significant that these preparations coincided with the perambulations through south Wales of Henry Richard and another delegate from the Congregational Union charged with the task of persuading local associations of congregations to join the central body.[26] This would not perhaps be important were it not for the fact that Article IX of the Union, accepted in 1833, affirmed that ' the power of a Christian Church should in no way be corrupted by union with temporal or civil power '.[27] It is interesting to note how frequently local associations visited by the delegates proceeded to pass resolutions affirming the principle of disestablishment and their readiness to assist the new movement.

As a result of these exertions, Welsh representation at the founding conference was strong. Twenty-two delegates attended, distributed thus: from Monmouthshire 8, Glamorgan 4, Montgomeryshire 4, Carmarthenshire 3, Denbigh 2, and Merioneth 1. The other counties were unrepresented, and we may infer that the main appeal of the newly-created Anti-State-Church Association was in the border counties and south Wales. Welsh representation on the Council of Five-Hundred was more extensive though still heavily weighted in the same way, but the five Welsh members of the executive committee of fifty were all from south Wales. The evidence provided by the first subscription points in the same direction. Of the puny sum of £8 7s. 6d. subscribed during the first year, £6 2s. 6d. came from Monmouthshire, the remainder from Denbighshire (£1), Pembrokeshire (10s.), Carmarthenshire (10s.), and Montgomeryshire (5s.).[28] Nevertheless, the association had been founded, and had elicited a good response notably in those areas with the oldest dissenting tradition, which enjoyed the easiest communications with England, and where the Protestant Society and the Dissenting Deputies had been most active.

*   *   *

Before we can attempt to assess the influence exerted by the new association on the course of Welsh politics between 1844 and 1868 it is first necessary to see how, and in what directions, the association developed in Wales.[29] This can be attempted statistically on the basis of the subscriptions contributed annually to the funds of the association. Such information will enable us to mark any flunctuations in growth of membership, and in its geographical distribution. Generalizations based on such evidence must necessarily be crude, but at least they may enable us to ask fresh questions about the nature of Welsh politics during that obscure period.

Looking first at the finances of the association, income as a whole increased six-fold in the period 1844 to 1869—from £1,178 to £7,558. Welsh subscriptions during the same period increased fifteen-fold, from £14 to £217. The trend in both cases is clear, and within it the flunctuations are similar (except at one point), corresponding roughly to fluctuations in the trade cycle. Contributions slump in the first three years of the '50s, rise rapidly to 1856, fall sharply the following year, then rise fairly consistently to 1864, before plunging again during 1864-66. The year 1867-68 sees a peak level. At one point, namely in the middle '60s, there is a marked lack of correspondence between the British and Welsh trends. Where between 1864 and 1866 Welsh subscriptions decline sharply, income as a whole continues to rise, and steeply in 1865-66. At this point Welsh subscriptions rise while gross income falls. It is necessary to draw attention to this phenomenon, since the explanation, as we shall see, lies not only in changing economic conditions (the slump following the American Civil War), but was determined on the Welsh side by political changes. So far as Welsh subscriptions are concerned we can generalize by saying that, normal fluctuations apart, the volume of Welsh support increased at a fairly consistent rate keeping pace with total income, but rising appreciably in the years after 1862.

When we look at the geographical distribution of Welsh membership, the features which we saw to be characteristic of support for the association's predecessors remain valid up to and including 1862. At the first triennial conference in 1847 the pattern, by counties, was as follows: in Caernarfonshire, Denbighshire, and Montgomeryshire one each—a total of three places in north Wales. In south Wales ten places subscribed, as follows: six in Monmouth, two in Glamorgan, and one each in Carmarthenshire and Cardiganshire. In subsequent triennial conferences up to 1862 the geographical spread is mainly in south Wales and less pronouncedly in the northern border counties. More exactly, by 1862 the north Wales counties of Montgomeryshire (5), Denbighshire (3), and Merioneth (1) have a total of 9 places contributing. The south Wales counties (excluding Radnorshire, which had none) have 22 places, fairly evenly distributed, making contributions. After 1862 the pattern changes significantly. In the north, between 1863 and 1868, the number of places rises from 9 to 55. In the south it rises from 45 to 54.

When these distribution changes are looked at more closely, they appear to be highly significant—more so than anything revealed by the financial returns. Looking first at south Wales, the year of expansion is obviously 1862-63 when the number of places rose from 22 to 45. Expansion was greatest in Glamorgan (6 to 17), Monmouthshire (5 to 10), Carmarthenshire and Pembrokeshire (4 to 7 in each). Cardiganshire remained constant at 2 places, and Breconshire increased from 1 to 2. This is to say, the greatest expansion takes place in the industrial areas which of course, were also the regions of maximum dissenting density. This pattern, on the whole, is sustained to the end of our period. When we look at the actual places within the counties the same tendencies are repeated in microcosm. In Glamorgan it is the towns in the industrial belt which provide the support—Swansea and its valley, and the sweep from Neath to Hirwaun across to Aberdare and Merthyr, and down to Pontypridd and Cardiff. The Vale is totally unrepresented. The same is true of Monmouthshire, and, after 1864, of Carmarthenshire. Even in rural Cardiganshire it is the seaports which are conspicuous. This is not to say that the Society made no impression on rural Wales: it merely indicates that its greatest support, in so far as this can be measured statistically, was to be found in the most heavily industrialized areas.

Turning to North Wales, the period of expansion begins not in 1862 but in 1863-64 and 1867-68. In 1863 there were ten places contributing: in 1864 there were 21: in 1867 this had risen to 32, and in 1868 had reached a peak of 55. 1864 is a conspicuous year because the outstanding feature of the dist-ribution change is not a great increase in those counties already associated with the Society. Montgomeryshire, Denbighshire, and Merioneth increase by only 3—from 10 to 13. What must be carefully marked is the spread of the Society into counties hitherto almost totally innocent of Liberationist cells. In 1864 Anglesey has 1, Caernarfonshire 3, Flintshire 3: previously there had been virtually none in those counties. In 1867-68 it is these counties which show the greatest increase: the total of 55 was made up thus: Anglesey 5, Caernarfonshire 9, Denbighshire 13, Flintshire 9, Merioneth 11, Montgomeryshire 8. Again, the correlation between the spread of Liberationism and industrial-ism holds good. This is true whether applied to the iron and non-ferrous centres of Flintshire and south Denbighshire of Caernarfonshire and Merioneth, or the almost defunct indust-ries of Anglesey.

This changing pattern of distribution corresponds fairly accurately with the conclusions drawn from a study of the finances of the Society: there is an upsurge of contributions in 1862-63 and again in 1866-67. But it is a rough correspondence only, since the percentage increase in the numbers of places contributing is considerably higher than that in the other. The explanation is, of course, simple, but nevertheless of great importance in the understanding of the nature of the growth of the Society in Wales. It is this: more people in more places are subscribing smaller sums than hitherto to the central fund. It would be tedious to examine the statistics, but the evidence supports this conclusion, that the average amount declines while the numbers of people contributing go up. We might anticipate and conclude further, that the social class attracted by the Society had changed during the period.

Unlike the Protestant Society, therefore, the Liberation Society succeeded in establishing itself and in growing at a steady rate throughout our period. Why was this? To find an explanation we need to examine more closely the nature of the Society—its policy, the machinery at its disposal, its reaction to political change. We shall then be in a position to understand its impact upon Welsh political life.

Surveying the history of the Society from its foundation in 1844 to the climacteric of 1868 we can discern four fairly distinct stages in its development. These are, firstly, a period of consolidation from 1844 to 1847; secondly, a period of exposition and the perfection of organization which lasted until 1853; thirdly, a period of intensive parliamentary activity until 1861; and, finally, a period of readjustment when activity was redirected to the constituencies as the corollary of further parliamentary agitation, for church rate abolition and reform culminating in the general election of 1868.

Between 1844 and 1847 the new association was struggling to establish itself in the country and to create an effective central organization. Constitutionally, authority was vested in the Council of 500 chosen triennially, and executive authority delegated to a committee of fifty chosen from the council members. There was, and for long remained, an air of unreality about this cumbersome and imposing body, and clearly in most respects it was merely a way of associating as many people as possible with the public appearances of the association. A large proportion of its members do not appear to have subscribed: presumably they had been nominated by local enthusiasts.[30] The executive council likewise, though intended to be geographically representative of the whole country [15 from London, 7 Scottish, 5 Welsh, 2 Irish, in addition to the English], consisted effectively of the London members. Its meeting were rarely attended by more than eight or nine in addition to the secretaries. The secretaries consisted of three honorary secretaries who shared the work between them, which must have been very considerable. The treasurer was Dr. Thomas Rees— a man whose memory is insufficiently regarded in Wales. In the localities the association was represented by registrars whose duty it was to collect funds, distribute literature, arrange meetings, and so on. This was realized to be an unsatisfactory arrangement, but was the best available for the time being, since the establishment of branch or auxiliary societies was still prohibited by law.

The activites of the association in these opening years were thus limited by deficiencies in its organization, in particular by the lack of a paid secretariat at the centre, and of agents domiciled in the main centres of population. Without these, the purpose of the executive committee could not be translated into action, or the almost complete dependence of the association on the ephemeral enthusiasms of local partisans be lessened. It was limited also in another way. Dissenters at this time were being encouraged to take an active part in the agitation against the Corn Laws,[31] and it was essential to avoid any action which might weaken the effectiveness of the Anti-Corn Law League, or, conversely, cause the association to be regarded as but an auxiliary of the League. Under such circumstances, considerations of expediency demanded that the appeal of the association should be primarily religious, be directed principally at dissenters, and that it should be concerned with the solidification or the uniting of existing materials among voluntaryists rather than the diffusion of the ideal of disestablishment into areas or among other bodies which were known to be antipathetic to such an ideal.[32] In short, the immediate purpose of the new movement was to teach those of the dissenters whose traditions were already voluntaryist that the influence of the Established Church had increased, was increasing, and should, if civil and religious freedoms were to be preserved, be diminished. Politically, this meant that the association had to look forward to some years of intensive propaganda which, it was hoped, would lead to the creation in the localities of powerful dissenting caucuses. The most difficult part of such a task would be to persuade dissenters that the old tradition of co-operation with the Whig party was now sterile, and that dissenters, as individual electors, must concentrate on the long-term policy of returning their own members to parliament even at the cost, it might be, of harming their erstwhile allies. In the House of Commons itself, where the association had only one member,[33] it could scarcely hope to exert any influence on legislation. The prerequisite of successful parliamentary action was the creation of a powerful, well-organized body of independent opinion in the country. The political dualism of parliament must be undermined, in the first place in the constituencies.

So far as activity in Wales was concerned, the one event of significance took place after the foundation of the association. At a meeting of the Montgomeryshire Independent Association in August 1844, resolutions supporting the new venture were passed, and a working committee formed to call a conference later in the year at which their solidarity with the aims of the association should be given practical expression.[34] This took place at Machynlleth in September, and was composed almost entirely of delegates from the north Wales counties. A member of the central executive committee was present, and, if we may judge by the numbers who attended and from the resolutions passed, the conference was highly successful. The association's policy of dividing counties into districts and appointing registrars was adopted and partially initiated, and a sub-committee formed to supervise the translation of Anti-State-Church tracts into Welsh.[35] But the tangible and permanent results of the conference, once the initial fervour had died down, were negligible. For years—until his departure for America—Samuel Roberts of Llanbryn-mair remained virtually the only subscriber in the whole of Montgomeryshire.[36] As we have seen, it was not until the '60s that the association made any significant advances in north Wales. The same is true of south Wales: few permanent organizations were set up,[37] and no intensive efforts were made to begin the association's policy of steady indoctrinization. For the most part the Welsh magazines, *Y Diwygiwr* and *Seren Gomer* in particular, printed abbreviated reports of the association's annual meetings, and the Rev. David Rees especially welcomed articles on the theme of disestablishment. The association itself, its resources stretched to the limit, could afford to send its lecturer, Kingsley, to Wales only very occasionally, and then only to the densely-populated parts of the southern counties. No tracts appear to have been made available in Welsh, and this, coupled with the fact that none of the established English weekly newspapers published locally were favourable to the aims of the association, necessarily meant that its work in south Wales was gravely hampered.[38]

During the six years between the second and the third triennial conferences—from 1847 to 1853—the association made considerable progress both in the country and in parliament. As an organization it increased in membership, and its growing resources were an indication of its greater effectiveness and of the leading position it had gained in the estimation both of its friends and of its enemies. Its income rose from £1,178 to £1,723 in 1850, though it had fallen, because of the depression, to £1,623 by the third triennial conference.[39] Partly, this growing success may be attributed to a more efficient organization. In the first place, there was now a full-time, salaried secretary, and an office staff.[40] The man appointed to this key post in 1847 was a London Welshman, John Carvell Williams, a person of great administrative abilities, a fluent speaker, and controversialist—a man who devoted himself to the work of the association with such vigour and singel-mindedness that he soon came to be identified with it in the public mind.[41] In the second place, the old system of honorary registrars was dropped in 1848, and replaced by a new system whereby local committees empowered by the executive committee, and responsible to it, were established.[42] This new policy proved of permanent value, and was undoubtedly a source of great strength since the committees thus formed were better adapted for the essential propaganda work of the association, were more flexible and pervading than the old system, and, most important of all, could constitute whenever the need arose dissenting caucuses in the constituencies. Thirdly, it now became the policy of the association to appoint full-time and part-time lecturers who toured the country in accordance with carefully prepared itineraries. In addition, collectors were appointed, usually part-time, who were paid small salaries and a commission on the amounts collected. As a result of these and other changes the organization was greatly improved, so that by 1853 the executive committee was sufficiently confident of its eventual success to embark on a radical change in policy.[43]

Before enquiring into this it is necessary to mark the effects of these organizational changes on the fortunes of the association in Wales. The appointment of a secretary with Welsh antecedents and connections, and of a full-time lecturer, certainly made a difference in that henceforward meetings were held more regularly in the Principality. Attempts were made to send either the secretary himself, or a lecturer, or a member of the executive, to Wales at least once a year.[44] In fact, south Wales was visited twice in the three years up to 1850, and again in 1851 and 1852.[45] North Wales was visited in 1850 only.[46] In addition, soirées—that typical Victorian institution—were arranged at the request of certain Monmouthshire gentlemen in South Wales in the autumn of 1852.[47] These visits were intended, of course, not only to stimulate interest in, and provoke discussion of, the association's principles, but also to organize the setting up of local committees and to collect subscriptions. In neither objective, during this period, were their efforts very successful. By 1853 there were still very few local committees, and subscriptions actually fell.[48] But it appears not to have been the policy of the association, thus early in its history, to concentrate its resources on Wales. It was more profitable to concentrate rather on the heavily populated Midland areas and on London, visiting the outlying parts of the country only as frequently as was deemed necessary to keep alive existing organizations. Wales presented difficulties which were not present elsewhere. For example, the language was a positive hindrance, but more serious was the lack of a sympathetic press. Apart from the denominational Welsh press the English-language weeklies were almost all hostile or, at best, indifferent to the existence of the association. Apart from *The Principality*, founded at Narberth in 1851, there was virtually no weekly in which the association could be certain of being given generous space.

Nevertheless, the association was becoming increasingly influential in British politics. At each election after 1847 it had taken an active part in organizing dissenting opinion in certain carefully chosen constituencies, with the result that its leaders could claim in 1853 to have been partly responsible for the appearance in the new parliament of that year of a group of nearly forty dissenters or dissenting sympathizers.[49]   It was this accession of influence within the legislature backed by a disciplined and vocal opinion in the country which persuaded the executive committee to embark on a new policy in 1853. The recent election in particular had demonstrated its strength, so much so that the established parties, though they still coupled it with extreme radicalism, were no longer disposed to ignore its existence, and were even ready to concede that it had achieved an impressive degree of respectability.   It was for this reason that it was felt to be prudent to change the name of the association to ' the Society for the Liberation of Religion from State Patronage and Control ' as being less liable to misapprehension, less offensive, and in other respects more desirable than the negativity of ' Anti-State-Church Association '.[50] This, indeed, was part of the new policy which Miall now proposed at this third triennial conference. The society should now aim ' at the accomplishment of an exclusively political change ' based on the affirmation of the old religious principles as interpreted by the Society and which it had been actively propagating with success in the country during the previous decade.   Since the political change envisaged was a change in the law, and since any but moral and constitutional means were repudiated, and that only in parliament could such legal changes be made, the aim of the society could be ' practically narrowed to this point—the return of a House of Commons in which the majority of members shall hold, and be willing to carry into effect, our views '.   Somewhat sanguinely, Miall thought that this was not an impossible ideal, and the steps he now proposed that the Society should take were eminently practical.   In the first place, the society could now embark on a cautious parliamentary career designed to lead, rather than, as in the past, merely to take advantage of adventitious parliamentary circumstances. To this end he proposed the setting up of two sub-committees, a parliamentary and an electoral sub-committee, consisting of three to five members each (not necessarily members of the executive) with power to sit as one when necessary. The first of these, which would be headed by a permanent salaried lawyer, would watch business in both houses, scrutinize all bills, inspect notices of motion, receive all parliamentary papers.   It would deliberate weekly, discuss strategy, communicate with members, and concert action on specific measures. In short, this standing committee would act as a kind of unofficial whips' office, unobtrusively impressing upon the proceedings of the Liberationist sympathizers a certain continuity and persistency of action which would in time make its authority known and respected in party and government circles.[51] The electoral subcommittee was to be a separate body but intended to work in association with the parliamentary, and its task was to direct the political activities of the society in the constituencies. It was to have a separate budget, and it was empowered to employ electoral agents as the need might arise. An important part of its work was the collection and analysis of electoral statistics for each borough and county constituency throughout the country —the creation of a body of facts which could be used not only for propaganda purposes but which would provide the executive committee with the necessary up-to-date information on which to plan its campaign in the country.[52]

Reporting these changes at the end of the year in *Y Diwygiwr*, David Rees commented thus: ' Ymddengys yn eglur bod y Gymdeithas hon a wawdid ac a ddirmygid fel peth ffôl yn ymgeisio at ryw ddyfeision utopaidd, wedi dod yn ffaith led fawr '[53] (' It seems clear that this Society, which was mocked and scorned as a foolish affair aiming at some utopian schemes, has now become a fact of some importance '). The echo of *The Times* comment on the growth of the Anti-Corn Law League is unmistakable, and indeed, in some respects the achievements of the Society in the years which followed were even more remarkable than those of its great predecessor. Its machinery was now ' almost perfect ', for in addition to the two standing committees already mentioned and the network of local committees throughout the British Isles, the Society was now its own publisher,[54] issuing under its own imprimatur not only tracts and pamphlets but substantial controversial and historical works as well. In addition, 1855 saw the foundation of its own periodical, *The Liberator*, which soon gained a wide circulation and which could be printed in very substantial numbers in times of emergency and distributed at comparatively little cost over the whole country.[55] There appeared thus to be every justification that the Society could now embark on a policy of cautious advance in parliament with some hope that its increasing influence in the country would sooner than later enable it to take the offensive in the very citadel of the entrenched privileges of the establishment.

The third stage in the history of the Society is the story of increasing success in the country matched by an almost correlative failure in parliament. There were many measures which the Society considered its own, and which the parliamentary sub-committee carefully watched over in their often depressing passage through the houses. But the measure nearest their heart was the perennial and venerable Church Rates Abolition Bill which, entrusted to one or other of the Society's supporters, annually made its appearance on the table of the House. Friends and foes alike regarded the fortunes of this bill as a barometer of the popularity and effectiveness of the Society. Up to and including 1854, it had never got beyond the second reading. After that date it consistently passed that stage but failed in the Lords. Until 1859, moreover, the majorities in the Commons in favour tended to get larger: after that date they declined, until in 1862 the bill was lost on second reading by the casting vote of the Speaker.[56]

It would be interesting and illuminating of the nature of parliament during those years to trace the detail of this curious story, but space does not permit. For our purposes what is important is the reaction of the Society to this decline in its parliamentary fortunes. Despite increasing evidence that both the major parties were opposed to unconditional abolition and prepared to make use of it for purely tactical reasons with only an almost cynical disregard for feeling in the country, the Society persisted in pressing its demands on parliament. The effect of this was to drive the parliamentary committee further to the left into closer co-operation with radical groups of members who had their own peculiar reasons for desiring the destruction of the deadly dualism which so effectively strangled reform.[57] Liberationist members were now to be found acting in unison with dissident groups vainly working for parliamentary reform and the ballot, with the result that in the country the Society was coming to be identified with the reform movements. At the same time agitation in the country was stepped up, and an all-out effort made in 1857 to secure the return of more radical members. But this cost money, and the deficit by 1858 was running at the rate of £700 per annum.[58] Consequently, it was more than ever necessary to canvass the country in order to raise additional money. Special delegations were sent to most of the industrial areas, including those of south Wales, as a result of which subscriptions rose sharply.

The activities of these years both in parliament and in the country bore but little fruit. This was the age of Palmerston, of massive indifference to any kind of reform, and the Society suffered a loss of influence along with most other reforming movements. The results of the 1859 election could not be regarded with complacency since the gains which followed 1857 were lost, for not only had Liberationist candidates been defeated but the popular party, with whom also the Society so closely worked in parliament, had likewise been reduced.[59] This was reflected in the voting on the Church Rates Abolition Bill of 1861: for the first time since the Society had taken over this measure it had lost its Commons majority. The session exhibited an almost unbroken succession of defeats, and this despite the almost unprecedented intensity of effort in the country. 'The present House of Commons is too evenly balanced, and too strongly reactionary, in all questions affecting religious equality, to admit of the hope that we can secure a majority in favour of the measures we have heretofore urged upon its adoption.' Consequently, parliamentary activity of a direct kind was to be abandoned as unprofitable, the agitation against Church rates transferred to the localities, and the Society's efforts concentrated upon securing the return of a parliament more amenable to legislation on voluntaryist principles—in short, the aim of the Society should now be ' to convert the House of Commons into a more efficient instrument for our designs '.[60]

A fourth stage in the history of the society began therefore in 1861 with the initiation of a policy designed to bring pressure to bear on a parliament liberal in its professions, but hostile to reform in both Church and State. In this final stage Wales was to play a notable part. In a minute dated 27 September 1861,[61] it was resolved that since parliamentary work was now to be in abeyance and electoral activity in the country intensified, special attention should be paid to the Principality. ' Looking to the great preponderance of Nonconformity in Wales, and to the fact that it is at present scarcely represented in Parliament, we think it important that a special and decided Electoral effort should be made in that part of the Kingdom.' One or two gentlemen well acquainted with Wales, who would be able to suggest and, more or less, carry out such measures as might be proposed, ought forthwith to be engaged, and a campaign quickly initiated. Consultations with Welsh friends began almost immediately, and by the middle of January it had been decided in principle to hold two conferences in Wales during the year, one in the south in May or June, the other at a later date in the north. Henry Richard was to be asked to join a deputation from the society consisting of Miall and the secretary, and the movement's organization in Wales perfected by the appointment of a full-time agent.[62] Later, in June, Richard became a member of the executive, and the arrangements for a high-powered conference in south Wales completed.[63]

There had been some doubt of the wisdom of such a drastic change in policy when it had first been mooted. Now, the utter disregard for Liberationist aims in the new session confirmed the Society in the rightness of the course it was pursuing. In another respect, also, the emphasis on local agitation and on south Wales in particular proved to be fortunate. The depression in the cotton industry excluded the possibility of any lucrative activities in Lancashire:[64] subscriptions from that area could be expected to fall: and it is clear that one motive in turning to south Wales was that Welsh subscriptions could be so raised as to make up the deficiency.

The Swansea Conference of September 1862 extended over two days, and was attended by 200 delegates from the southern counties with a few from North Wales.[65] The various speakers were all prominent dissenting laymen or ministers, the one exception being L. Ll. Dillwyn, the member for Swansea, and a prominent Liberationist in parliament. He explained that he was able to co-operate with the Liberation Society because it endeavoured ' to maintain and enforce the great principle that the Established Church of this country is not a corporation existing for the benefit of any particular section of the community, but that it belongs entirely to the people; and that they have a full right at any time to resume its possessions or reform its doctrines, as they have done in times past, if a majority of the nation should so determine '.[66] This, as John Batchelor of Cardiff explained, was precisely what they were now about—the conference had been called ' to decide upon the best mode by which the Welsh people can assist ' in creating such a majority in favour of disestablishment. Later speakers carefully analysed the present position of dissent in the country, and there was unanimous agreement that the lack of correspondence between their numerical and what was called their moral superiority on the one hand, and the character of their representation in parliament on the other, was a standing reproach to them as dissenters. Miall and the other two delegates were extremely forthright. Judging by the members returned by Welsh electors, Wales was ' an almost perfectly unanimous nation of State Churchmen '. Yet the statistics showed nonconformists to be victorious, and therefore able ' to do as you please '. There was not, moreover, the social clash which inhibited English nonconformist political action—no middle class which, when it attained wealth, fell away into the fashionable church. Carvell Williams, armed with statistics gathered by his agents, drove home these truths, and argued that ' the division lists of the House of Commons . . . showed . . . that Welsh Dissenters were either unconscious of the latent power at their command, or were strongly neglectful of their duty '. He attributed much of the laxity of Welsh Liberal members to ' abstinence from out-door agitation', and argued from evidence supplied by the parliamentary sub-committee that even unsatisfactory members could be compelled to vote in ways favoured by their constituents. Henry Richard spoke in the same strain, and moved a resolution urging dissenters to carry their principles to the polling-booths and supply Dillwyn, their greatest champion, with supporters in the House, so that members might say, ' Here comes Dillwyn with his Welsh reserve '.

Perhaps some of those present recalled the similar enthusiasm displayed at the 1844 Machynlleth Conference, and the apathy and neglect which followed. This was not again to be the case, for the Society, which at the time had been attempting a new thing, had over the years gained a vast amount of experience. None understood better the nature of politics in parliament and in the constituencies than Miall and Williams, and both, despite their impossible aims, were eminently practical men. The Society did not expect revolutionary results to issue from this conference, but they saw to it that measures were immediately taken which would inititate the kind of changes they hoped for. A committee for south Wales, with headquarters at Cardiff, was immediately established, and a district agent appointed.[67] The proceedings of the conference were published in English and Welsh and widely distributed along with specially-written tracts in Welsh and a selection of English ones in translation. Of great importance was the appointment of an electoral agent in south Wales. This was made in October 1865 when it had become evident, after the general election of that year in Cardiganshire, that with adequate preparation Henry Richard could be expected to be returned for that constituency at some future election. A local man was chosen for the post, and it was his task, carried out with great success, to nurse the constituency for Richard at the Society's expense.[68] Henry Richard himself paid regular visits to the area, and though at the next general election he chose to contest the much safer seat of Merthyr Tydfil, Cardiganshire was in fact won for, if not in the name of, the Society by a Welsh nonconformist. It was during these years from 1862 onwards that Richard became a leading member of the executive and the Liberation Society's expert adviser on Welsh political affairs.[69]

It is important to emphasize that this activity in Wales was an essential part of the new policy of the Liberation Society. It was clear that the leaders had now realized the importance of the outlying areas, and of the Celtic fringe in particular.[70] The Lancashire distress may, to a certain extent, have compelled them to look away from the areas of primary support: more likely, the change was based on deductions based on a study of the electoral facts which the Society's agents had been collecting over the past six years or so. The whole emphasis was on electoral action. The Society did not think of itself as a party, though it is probably true to say that its machinery was as perfect, if less powerful, as any of the existing party machines. It thought of itself rather as a distinct pressure group, allied officially with no party, and prepared, in the present juncture of politics, to act independently of party. Indeed, in 1865 it seemed to the executive that the most they could expect of the Liberals under Russell's leadership was for them to keep their ascendancy in parliament but use it only as the Conservatives should please. In such a situation, it was clearly vain to work for Liberal gains in elections: the policy should be rather to demand the co-operation of local Liberal caucuses in those constituencies where Liberationists or Liberationist sympathizers were in a majority on the register. Local action was therefore imperative—the building up of strong Liberationist caucuses loosely allied to Liberal parties but prepared, if need be to act independently. For such a policy the Welsh constituencies, both on religious and sociological grounds, were peculiarly suited.

Not until September 1866 did the society attempt a similar assault on North Wales. The original intention had been to initiate systematic efforts there at the same time as those in South Wales, but this had been postponed presumably on the advice of the society's supporters in those areas.[71] In the meantime, north Wales had not been forgotten entirely: efforts were made to interfere in the Montgomeryshire elections in 1863;[72] but it is clear that for the time being the Society could expect to make no headway there. South Wales, with its now highly organized and smooth-running committee and agencies, and, of course, its greater numerical and financial resources, was a far more profitable enterprise. It is significant, also, that when the society did turn its attention to north Wales, it was in response to the suggestions of the south Wales committee meeting at Pontypool that a series of six county conferences should be held in the autumn, three of which should be in Denbighshire, Montgomeryshire, and Merioneth.[73] Urgency was given to the request, and a favourable response elicited from the executive, by the change in the political situation. The defeat of the Liberal government on the question of reform indicated either a change of government or a dissolution, and the Society's electoral machinery, always held in readiness for such an emergency, was quickly put into action.[74] It was, perhaps, the realization that such electoral activity could scarcely be effective in areas where there existed no local machinery to manipulate, which finally persuaded the executive to begin a large-scale operation in the northern counties. The Liberal defeat had been followed by a change of government only, but, like most political observers, the Society's leaders were convinced that a general election could not long be delayed. Moreover, it was in the interests of the Society to do everything possible to help put an end to the frustrations of successive minority governments.

In July, therefore, it was decided that Miall and Richard should attend a series of conferences in north Wales in the autumn. The following month Miall reported that he had visited the main towns in the counties of Flint, Denbigh, Merioneth, and Cardigan, and had arranged for four conferences to take place in September at Newtown, Denbigh, Bala, and Aberaeron. There were to be further meetings in the Cardiganshire towns during the following month and, depending on the response to the conferences, further meetings in the other counties later on.[75] It is quite clear that the Society did not expect a repetition of their success in south Wales in 1866: the deliberations of the executive were those of cautious and not oversanguine politicians. In the event, the success of the conferences exceeded their expectations. At Denbigh alone there were more delegates from the county than those furnished by the whole of south Wales in 1862, and there were gratifying attendances at Bala and Aberaeron, despite poorer communications and a late harvest.[76] This must be attributed to efficient preparation—to the fact that during the previous three years the south Wales organization had been running smoothly and that a great deal of experience had been accumulated which was now at the disposal of the local committees again

coming into existence in north Wales. In both series of conferences the theme was the same, that is to say, the political
ineffectiveness of a majority religious movement. ' Whatever
the shortcomings of English, Irish, and Scotch Dissent,' said
Carvell Williams, ' it shapes public opinion. Its influence is
traceable in the conduct of the public press. It is an element in
the decisions of cabinets and in the calculations of politicians.'
But, it was argued, Welsh nonconformity did not occupy a
corresponding place, and this despite the fact that the wrong
inflicted by the Church of England was greater than that
inflicted on the Irish. This was the theme, and in each county
delegates were presented with electoral facts and figures which
demonstrated beyond cavil the anomalies in the Welsh representation of the counties concerned. County electoral histories were prepared, contests analyzed, or the deplorable lack
of contests accounted for. On the whole, the speakers agreed
that the situation resulted from apathy, or traditionalism, or a
feeling of helplessness in the face of an unscrupulous use of the
advantages which economic power conferred on the parliamentary families. The Rev. Michael D. Jones of Bala, in
particular, made a speech of peculiar force and bitter irony on
the theme of the misrepresentation of Merioneth. He dealt
scornfully with the so-called justifications for oligarchic rule:
the wealthy say to the working classes, ' Allow us to take out
your eyes, and we shall very kindly lead you by the hand ':
delineated the moral, social, and economic consequences of
' influence ', and ended on a note of passion which must have
been unforgettable for those who heard it.[77]

These conferences resulted in the setting up of a network of
committees in the counties concerned[78]—committees which
were charged with the task not only of spreading the doctrines of
disestablishment but of building up a political organization in
readiness for the forthcoming general election. Controlling and
co-ordinating the activities of these committees (and of those in
south Wales) was a sub-committee of the executive formed on
the return of Miall from a series of meetings in Cardiganshire
which had rounded off the north Wales conferences. It consisted of Miall himself, Richard, Williams, and the editor.[79]

The inclusion of the editor was significant, for not the least important of the Society's labours was the production of literature in Welsh. By August 1867 the Welsh sub-committee was of the opinion that an agent for north Wales should be appointed, his area to include all places on the Cambrian Railway as far as Aberystwyth. The post was offered to the Rev. Dillwyn Davies of Llanfyllin at £30 per annum—raised later to £50 after a correspondence with the candidate.[80]

There thus existed by 1867 an organization covering almost the whole of Wales, a staff of agents and of political experts, the whole efficiently directed from the centre. We have already noted the striking advances made throughout the Principality, but especially in north Wales, after 1855.[81] This must be attributed to the tremendous drive of the Society, its ability to generate, and to channel into political action, the enthusiasms latent in Welsh nonconformity. Neither did the Society have to wait for any tangible results. It lent its support, both financial and otherwise, to newly founded political organizations, as, for instance, when a South Wales Liberal Registration Society was formed at Carmarthen in July 1867,[82] and a Welsh Reform Association in July 1868.[83] More so, perhaps, than any other evidence of growth, movements such as these demonstrated the enhanced influence of the Society and of its effectiveness. Surveying the results of their work in Wales, the executive committee in May 1867 reported that the conferences held in Wales had proved successful beyond their most sanguine expectations. They were convinced that in Wales the society had found ' a soil which will ultimately repay diligent culture, and that that country, when it is energized into political life, as it is influenced by religious feeling, will not let its voice be unheard, and its power be unfelt, in the Legislature '.[84]

Nevertheless, the success was only indirectly the fruit of the Liberation Society's exertions. For the times were propitious, conducive to great advances, and both the great parties, under the leadership of Gladstone and Disraeli, were passing into a phase of constructive reform, the very antithesis of Palmerstonian conservatism. The Liberals, in opposition, were again disposed to take up questions of ecclesisatical policy, while both parties found themselves unable to resist the popular movement for parliamentary reform. The Society took up again an active parliamentary programme. A Church Rates Abolition Bill, sponsored by it, after a lapse of seven years, again passed the Commons by a substantial majority, only to be lost at third reading in the Lords.[85] But the Society had the satisfaction of knowing that Gladstone would introduce an official Liberal abolition bill early in the next session, and, above all, that the election would be fought on the question of the disestablishment of the Irish Church. Moreover, parliamentary reform, as the statistics collected by the Society's agents showed, would inevitably benefit the Society, and nowhere more so than in Wales. It was essential that the Society, while co-operating closely with reform organizations, should also make its own dispositions, and it is vitally important to realize that so far as Wales was concerned it was the Liberation Society which was mainly responsible for reform agitation rather than either the Reform League or the Reform Union. These latter had their supporters, particularly in the industrial valleys where the League was active.[86] But in Wales, and partly due to the exertions of the Liberation Society, parliamentary reform had a religious or ecclesiastical, rather than a secular, flavour. It alone had a powerful organization, and it alone enjoyed the confidence of the leaders of that peculiar culture which the forces of industrialization and a numerically resurgent nonconformity were rapidly creating in Wales.

This paper, did it aim at a comprehensive analysis of Welsh politics at the end of the period with which it is concerned, would end with a study of the ways in which the organization thus created functioned in the Welsh constituencies at the general election of 1868. Such a study would not show, except possibly at Merthyr Tydfil, the overwhelming success of Liberationist candidates. Indeed it would show, on the contrary, at least one example of an avowed Liberationist candidate repudiating any connection with the Society rather than endanger his candidature,[87] and even in Merthyr Tydfil, where the Society's supporters most vociferously claimed their greatest victory, it would clearly demonstrate that other factors were equally important in the return of Henry Richard.[88] Nevertheless, such an analysis would show to what an extent and in what ways the nature of Welsh politics had changed in the previous twenty-odd years. In particular, it would show that Welsh nonconformists were now more prepared to give political expression to their religious sentiments. Here was a change of great significance not only to Wales itself, but to the larger political unit of which Wales was a part. If the year 1868 was indeed an *annus mirabilis*, that it was so was due in no small part to the work of the Society for Liberation of Religion from State Patronage and Control.

THE DYNAMICS OF POLITICS IN
MID-NINETEENTH-CENTURY WALES

The term ' dynamic ' carries normative, qualitative overtones, as when we say that change at a particular time was
dynamic, or full of energy or force as compared with other
times. I want, at least initially, to avoid this adjectival usage,
and to use the word in a more neutral, technical sense, meaning
the social forces, the impulses, cultural in the widest sense,
which shaped society, gave it its special quality by which it can
be distinguished from any other period in the history of that
society. Politics is the very essence of this approach to the past
because of the organic relationship between, on the one hand,
political systems and political behaviour, and on the other economy, society, culture. The precise nature of this relationship in
so far as it involves abstract concepts or models of society I leave
to the political philosopher and the sociologist. As a social historian—and the historian of Wales can be no other—political
systems and political behaviour are essential and inseparable
parts of the total social situation. My brief, therefore, is to
examine some of the salient features, distributive and qualitative, of the structure of politics and of political behaviour at a
particular time in the past so as to isolate those main forces
which determined the shape of that structure and the tendencies
of that behaviour.

The period I wish to examine is a short one. It covers the
generation or so from 1850 to about 1870. It is sufficiently
long for one to detect significant changes taking place, and of
sufficient brevity for these changes to be assessed in their total
relations. It is also a very distinctive period of time. Contemporaries felt this: those among them who were old enough to
remember and to make comparisons had no doubt at all that
they differed enormously from any other period of time in their
lives. Compared with the first fifty years of the century, for
instances, these were years of progress, of an enormous shift in
the productive capacity of the country, in the movements of

people, in the accumulation of wealth, and, possibly, of its more equal distribution and its investment in social overheads, like sanitary reform, education, etc. This question of the distribution of wealth—of an increasing fund of wealth—was a matter for debate: it was what politics could be about even if, to some people, they appeared to be about other, less relevant, things. But at least it was a matter for debate and not for disturbances as in the past. Corn riots, Rebecca, the tremendous upheavals characteristic of the '30s and '40s, physical force Chartism, the millenial movements of those decades—these appeared to have sunk into the dark backward of the nation's experience and Wales to be settling into its proud image of 'gwlad y menyg gwynion', respectable, religious, petty bourgeois in style and aspiration. Likewise, those who lived on into the '80s and '90s, who felt again the incipient violence of those revolutionary times, looked back to these two decades as somehow unique. Quite rightly they traced the origin of the struggle for disestablishment, for equality of opportunity, for greater social justice to those years, and in looking back at them found a constant source of assurance and of inspiration. Only rarely did they write about those years, and then never as history—something to be worked over, constantly reassessed in the light of evidence—but always polemically. While Liberalism still retained its appeal and maintained its hegemony the 1860s remained a kind of contemporary politics, a romantic memory, matter for peroration and eloquence. The aged and venerable Michael D. Jones, one of the heroes of the mid-century struggles, wished towards the end of his life, like some Moses standing on Pisgah, with the fulfilment of his dreams unfolding before his eyes, that the history of those times should be written. In a sense it was impossible that it should be, for it survived as myth, and only now perhaps are we in a position to understand the social reality of the times. Therefore, what I propose briefly to do is to ask first of all what the politics of those years were really like, in what ways and why they were changing, and to what effect. It is the context rather than the content of politics that I am concerned with in this paper, and I shall seek to examine the formal structure in order to expose

some of the more important aspects of the social reality underlying it.

*   *   *

Let us look first of all at the system of parliamentary representation as it existed in 1850. There are two questions here:
first, what was the formal, constitutional structure of the
system, and second, how did it work? On its structural side the
system was the ancient one surviving from the Act of Union as
amended by the First Reform Act which had become operative
eighteen years previously. The legislation of the sixteenth
century had given Wales 27 members, and the Reform Act of
1832 had raised this to 32, gaining 5 of the 88 seats which had
become available for redistribution. The additional seats had
gone to the counties with the largest population—Glamorgan,
Carmarthenshire, and Denbighshire, and in addition the Glamorgan boroughs had been split into two groups, and the town of
Merthyr Tydfil enfranchised for the first time. So, in 1850,
there were 32 members for a population of 1,163,139, or 1
member per 36,000 persons. This ratio varied greatly, of
course. Radnorshire had 1 member for 12,000 people. Monmouthshire 1 for 52,000. But generally speaking the variations
in the ratio were not harsh, though they were considerably
wider in 1850 than they had been in 1832, and, of course, the
dynamic behind this changing ratio was the movement of population in response to economic changes. The counties with
relatively unfavourable ratios were the counties in which
industrialization was most advanced—Monmouthshire, Glamorgan, Caernarfonshire.

Of greater importance in this analysis was a feature of the
system which was also carried over from the *ancien régime* and
which only far-out radicals had wished to abolish in 1832—
namely, the distinction between county and borough constituencies. This was a feature with a built-in inequality not
abolished until 1884-5. There were 17 county constituencies
containing an aggregate population of nearly 850,000 [849,
623], so that each county member represented, on average, just
under 50,000 people [49,977]. This ratio again varied, and

again it was the heavily populated counties, that is to say, the counties whose industrial economies were attracting population which were worse off. The member for Radnorshire represented 18,000 people, the member for Caernarfonshire, 66,000. The grant of one additional member each to Glamorgan, Carmarthenshire, and Denbighshire reduced their ratio, but even so the growth of population in these counties, as in Monmouthshire [1 for 65,000,] was tending to reproduce the inequalities of the unreformed system, and to give reformists an argument from numbers which traditionalists, of whatever party, were loath to accept.

Much more complicated was the system as it affected the boroughs. There were 15 borough constituencies, 5 in north Wales, 10 in the south. The towns and ancient boroughs of Merioneth had never been represented—a grievance deeply resented and aired from time to time by its political classes, but, as if to compensate, Haverfordwest in Pembroke remained enfranchised, and the dividing of the Glamorgan boroughs into two, and the grant of a member to Merthyr Tydfil, had shown a special regard for numbers. On the face of it, therefore, there was a fair balance between the two types of constituency—far in advance of the balance achieved elsewhere in Great Britain. This, of course, corresponded to the theory of the constitution current in 1832 and still maintained in 1850, to the effect that the territorial interest was socially and politically superior to any other kind of interest, and therefore to be protected and its continuity and well being ensured. In fact, as Norman Gash has shown, so far as the system was concerned the counties were grossly under-represented in comparison with the boroughs. In Wales the disparity was less than in England: there were more county seats than borough seats, and the ratio of county and borough electorate was more equal in Wales. In practice, however, the balance was vastly in favour of the county seats, and in Wales it was the borough seats which could claim to be suffering an injustice. For what was unique about the system of borough representation in Wales was another feature which it had inherited from the past and which the reformers of 1832 had not abolished, namely, the system of enfranchisement of contributory boroughs. What this meant in practice was that the fifteen borough members represented between them not fifteen boroughs but sixty spread unevenly over the whole country. There were only two single-town constituencies— Brecon and Merthyr, and Merthyr consisted not of the town of Merthyr only, but of all the towns and townships of the parishes of Merthyr and Aberdare, with the town of Cefn-coed-cymer in the parish of Penderyn added. This system of enfranchisement of contributory groups of boroughs had the effect of giving the vote to certain of the inhabitants of virtually all the main urban centres in Wales and of many minor ones. Four towns in Anglesey were enfranchised, 6 in Caernarvon, 4 in Denbigh, 8 in Flint, and 6 in Montgomery. In South Wales, 3 of the main towns in Monmouthshire, 9 in Glamorganshire, 7 in Pembroke- shire, and 6 in Radnorshire. There were strident anomalies: for instance, the iron towns in north Monmouthshire, and Aber- gavenny itself, but when one looks closely at the repatterning which was taking place in the distribution of population such anomalies abound and one need not have been a prophet or a Chartist in 1850 to predict that it was precisely at this area that the system was most vulnerable to criticism.

This leads to another feature of borough representation, namely, the size of the constituencies. On average the ratio was 1 member to 19,000 population. But here again the variations were very wide. Brecon had a ratio of 1 in 6,000, its neighbour Merthyr, 1 in 63,000; or Radnor 1 in 7,000, Swansea 1 in 45,000. There had always been such variations, but never as wide as they were in 1850 with every indication of their becoming wider. One in 14,000 had been about right in 1832 when only Merthyr and Swansea in the south had had pop- ulations of over 20,000 (which was the Victorian minimum for a large town). No one in 1832—not even the Boundary Com- missioners—could have forseen the *scale* of the massive pop- ulation shift which would take place in the next 20 or 30 years, nor could anyone accurately have foretold the economic run- down of the once-thriving urban centres of the mid and north Wales region. The representative towns of mid Wales were minute: but they played precisely the same quantative role in the system as the vast heaving industrial towns of Glamorgan and Monmouthshire, and the expanding industrial towns of

Denbighshire and Flintshire and Caernarfonshire. The balance in the system between rural and urban territorial and commercial, agricultural and industrial was thus more apparent than real, and the system heavily weighted in favour of the landed gentry. This was as it always had been. The distinction in Wales between county seat and borough seat had been a theoretical and political one and not based on any sociological differences. The Welsh towns before the Industrial Revolution had been too small to create economies substantially different from their hinterlands. They had never dominated their surroundings, never generated a commercial class powerful enough to challenge the representation. They had survived from the Middle Ages as chartered towns or as boroughs by prescription because it had suited the political interests of the gentry that they should continue to exist as political entities. Their sole *raison d'être* had been a political one, and now in 1850, the majority of them could imagine no other existence but that of serving the political interests of their masters.

This general conclusion is confirmed when we turn from the constituencies to the members. Did the two types of constituency return different types of members? We should expect the county constituencies to return landed proprietors or their scions, and of the seventeen knights of the shire, secure in the enjoyment of their social primacy, only one did not belong to an ancient political family. This was Richard Richards of Caerynwch, a judge and son of a more famous father who had founded the family fortunes at bar and bench: but since this remarkable family had allied with one of the premier Merioneth families, not even Richards is an exception. All the county representatives were of ancient lineage, very wealthy, and all resident as proprietors in the counties they represented. In 1850 the Wynns of Wynnstay, the Bulkeleys of Baron Hill, the Pennants of Penrhyn, the Mostyns of Mostyn, the Rices of Dynevor, the Emlyns, Adares, Talbots, Powells—these, and others were there where their ancestors had been in some cases for more than two hundred years. But precisely the same upper-class landed families monopolized, or very nearly so, the borough seats as well. Here we have the Pagets of Plas Newydd, the Plas Coch, Owen, Hanmer, Gogerddan, Frankland Lewis families, and so on. Whatever the structure of the sixty representative towns, whatever their commercial function, their sociological framework, the members they returned came almost exclusively from the same monolithic aristocratic class.

The exceptions to this rule in 1850 were few, sociologically ambiguous, but highly suggestive of portentous changes in the structure of politics. The outstanding exceptions were the two Glamorgan borough representatives, Sir J. J. Guest sitting for Merthyr, and Henry Vivian sitting for Swansea. Both these members were leading industrialists, technocrats, owners of two of the greatest industrial concerns in Great Britain. In 1832, when both had been returned, they had specifically stood as representatives of industry. As such, they were the products of a kind of political understanding between the territorial and the industrial interests in the county whereby the seats were to be shared. This understanding had dated from around the 1820s, since when the two greatest industrial seats in Wales had returned industrialists. All had served their county well, and particularly the industrial interests, in parliament, and whatever their politics or party affiliations may have been to begin with they had moved steadily in a Peelite or Liberal—even radical—direction ever since. But equally important is the fact that all were not merely, or even aggressively, industrialists: they were also landowners. Vivian was not only Vivian and Co., Copper Smelters, but also the Vivian family of Singleton Park in Swansea. Guest was not only the owner of the Dowlais Iron Co.: he was also Sir John, baronet, married into the aristocracy, possessed of wide estates in Berkshire, and a socially ambitious wife with aspirations towards the peerage.

What I wish to emphasize is this, that whatever the position may have been in 1832, however keenly demarcated the difference between landed wealth and industrial wealth, by the 1850s, and increasingly as the decades went by, there had been a convergence of the two kinds. Social mobility horizontally was typical of the middle age of industrial wealth whether or not the owners aspired to parliamentary honours. The Crawshay dynasty experienced this, as did the Fothergills, and all the others: the large house, the estate far away in the rural solitudes, the enjoyment of the leisure of the landed, the adoption of the port of, gentlemen. Nor was this horizontal movement a one-way traffic: landed gentry moved into commerce and industry and learned quickly how to exploit the hidden wealth, the unseen potentialities, of their estates. The gothic glories of Penrhyn or of Margam or of Cardiff Castle—those resplendent homes, those blank cheques to conspicuous consumption, were built on the profits of industry, their builders among the shrewdest business men of the age. The system of representation, therefore, was eloquent testimony to two related facts: first, to the monolothic control of political life at that level by a relatively small group of aristocratic dynastic families, and second, to the convergence in practical politics as in style and manner of life of the two major sources of wealth. The conflict in the body politic might appear to be between two kinds of wealth: in fact, the significant conflict was between wealth and its opposite. As ever, the conflict would be about equality.

But parliamentary politics involve not only representatives and constituencies: they also involve constituents and electors. What kind of pattern emerges when we look at the system of representation from this angle, from the bottom up, as it were? Here, we need to distinguish between constituents and electors: the former was inclusive, embracing the whole of the population of any particular constituency, the latter exclusive and embracing only that portion of the population qualified to vote. The franchise was a trust, a responsibility exercised by those whose property gave them a stake in the country and who by virtue of their possession of property could be presumed to be more intelligent and trustworthy than the porperty-less. Even as a member of parliament exercised his privileges as a trust on behalf of his constituents, so that portion of the population entrusted with the vote exercised it on the behalf of the community at large. That, roughly, was the theory underlying the constitution and the justification for the inequalities which in practice ensued. For the enfranchised portion of the population was small, and unequally distributed both geographically and by social class. On average, about 4.9 *per cent* of the population had the vote, or roughly 1 in 20. The counties, in respect of this ratio, were better off than the boroughs—1 in 18 as against 1 in 23. In the counties, too, there was distinctly less variation as between constituencies. Apart from Merioneth which was bound to suffer since it had no borough constituency, and Radnorshire which was favoured by the smallness of its population and its abundance of small rural towns, there were no serious or outrageous variations. In the borough constituencies by contrast, the variations were outstanding. Thus, Merthyr Tydfil with its population of 63,080 had only 1,102 voters, or 1 in 57: Swansea, likewise, with over 45,000 inhabitants had only 1,698 voters, or 1 in 26. The ratios were only slightly less in the Caernarfon district and in the Flint district. Nor is the general conclusion unobvious, for what these borough constituencies had in common was their industrial economies, and it is clear that the heavier the extent of industrialization the greater the political inequalities. It should be emphasized that these are rough generalizations only, for they are based on the numbers of electors registered in 1850, and the number registered was undoubtedly fewer than the number who might have qualified. Even so, this would make less practical difference than one might imagine for in the exigencies of a snap election only those persons registered would be allowed to vote.

It is important to note also that these inequalities were built into the system, and that there is evidence to show that by process of time they were becoming more pronounced. Taking the second point first: if it had been intended or foreseen in 1832 that there should be a fixed relation between numbers of population and voters, then the proportions of the one to the other should have remained steady as population increased. In fact, while the rise in population was of the order of 28 *per cent* in the twenty years after the Reform Act, the rise in the proportionate numbers of electors was only marginal. In 1832, the ratio had been 5.4 *per cent* voters to population, or 1 in 8; in 1851 it was 4.9 *per cent*, or 1 in 20. For the reason I have already given, too much cannot be made of these figures except to reiterate that the tendency was for inequalities of political rights to widen as time went on. By the eve of the Reform Act of 1867, almost at the end of our period, the situation was even more disparate. Population figures had leapt forward to nearly 1½ million, but the numbers of registered voters had increased proportionately less. Population grew in the twenty years after 1850 by 23.8 *per cent*; numbers of registered voters by about 10 *per cent*.

Part of the reason for this lay, obviously, in the way in which the right to vote had been distributed among the population. Since the right to vote had been attached to the possession of property its unequal distribution was a direct reflection of the unequal distribution of property among the population. In the counties the right to vote was restricted to certain type of freeholders, leaseholders of specified kinds, and to the tenants of properties worth £50 or more per annum. These franchises, drafted as they had been by amateurs, were of incredible complexity and only the lawyers, who grew fat on applying them to the vastly diverse conditions of different localities, mourned their passing in 1885. On the face of it, the borough franchise was much more straightforward, the Reform Act having introduced one uniform qualification—occupation of a house or premises of the annual value of not less than £10. The existing borough freeman franchises which had been virtually universal in Wales from the seventeenth century onwards were to continue in being during the lifetime of their possessors. Thereafter, there would be only one class of voter, namely, the £10 householder. As we shall see, this last point was of cardinal importance in determining the social type of borough voter in Wales. In addition to these property qualifications both types of franchises were hedged around with severe restrictions. In boroughs, for instance, all local rates due during the previous year must have been paid, and the receipt of any assistance from the rates during the year brought automatic disqualification. Also, the voter had to be properly registered, and in addition had to be prepared to face a possible challenge to the inclusion of his name at the annual revising barrister's court. Finally, he had to pay for the privilege of being registered. To sum up, not only was the franchise by reason of its property demands restricted to certain social clasees in the populations of counties and boroughs, but the complexity of the system itself was a real deterrent to the development of anything approaching a democratic state.

It was an economic representation, therefore, a representation of property rather than numbers. What is difficult to determine is the precise distribution of property among the electorate itself. It is fairly certain that the county electorate was more homogeneous than the borough electorate. Both the freehold and the various leasehold qualifications were, in terms of the income which their holders might be expected to have, pretty stiff. They would certainly exclude the small cottager and the bulk of farmers, especially those in the deep agricultural counties where productivity and prices were relatively unaffected by adjacent urban markets, and where the level of farming was by custom rarely above the level of subsistence. On the other hand, the £10 leasehold of not less than sixty years might bring into the electorate a class of workman whose way of life was essentially urban. For instance, it would enfrachise a fair number of craftsmen in unenfranchised rural towns living in small properties on lease from a local landlord. Shopkeepers in such communities might come into this category also, and it was undoubtedly the existence of substantial numbers of such urban leaseholders in the quarry towns of Ffestiniog which turned the 1868 Merioneth election in favour of the Liberals. What seems quite clear is that the occupying tenant franchise was less important than was at first imagined. This class of voter, enfranchised under the so-called Chandos Clause, was the yearly tenant, the tenant most dependent upon his lord, most liable to influence because most unprotected in the security of his tenure. In the middle '60s his class constituted 24 *per cent* of the county electorate almost equally in all counties —the only exceptions being Merioneth and Montgomery (34 and 39 *per cent* respectively). Thirty years earlier it had constituted 28 *per cent* of the county vote, and this decline in the relative ratio of this most dependent class of voters suggests that we ought perhaps to look again at the old explanation of why counties always voted Tory before 1868, and, as we shall see later, the £50 tenant qualification in Wales meant not a small farm but a large one, not an impoverished peasant but a relatively prosperous one. It is not possible to tell with any certainty either precisely what property levels were included in the class of freeman elector. What is certain is that the franchise was not restricted to property in land; it could be a freehold in virtually any kind of property. Moreover, the 40s. freehold had become devalued by the nineteenth century. The most cursory analysis of mid-century county poll books dispels the old illusion of the freeman voter being the backbone of the county elect- orate. Most of the freehold farms in Welsh agricultural counties which had survived the depressions of the early part of the century were probably too small to qualify for the vote anyway. Most of the substantial farms, as I have already indicated, were by mid-century, leasehold, and we should look for the county freeholders in the small towns and villages and find their possess- ors among the small shopkeepers, the tradesmen, craftsmen, country artisans. These, with the substantial tenant farmers, were the ' gwerin ' of the Welsh countryside, rather than the labourers, cottagers, and dependents. It was this class which formed the backbone of local administration, which constituted a kind of upper class in the lowest stratum of county society, the class productive of its own distinctive, independent elite.

The social structure of the borough electorate is more difficult to determine, partly because of the continued existence of the old franchises along with the new one introduced in 1832, and partly because of the more immediate and more profound social changes taking place in some of the towns and urban communities. The new franchise, as we have seen, was the so- called £10 householder qualification. This was likewise a property qualification restricting the vote to the occupiers, as owners or tenants of one landlord, of buildings of the annual value of £10. At the same time the ancient freehold or burgess qualification remained in being during the lifetime of their possessors, and a generation would be required before their extinction and the evolution of one uniform property qual- ification. In 1832, immediately following the Reform Act the proportion of these two classes—£10-ers and freemen—was exactly equal in the country as a whole: roughly 6,000 in each class. But the proportions varied from borough to borough and it is instructive to look at the variations. Only in the old close boroughs, in which the franchise had been restricted to very small self-perpetuating corporations of aldermen, were the old franchises overwhelmed by the new. Beaumaris and Brecon were the two examples of this, and in those two boroughs the Reform Act broke the monopolies of centuries. In Carmarthen,

Caernarfon, Denbigh, Flint, and Haverfordwest the ancient rights franchise had been of the scot and lot type—that it is to say, restricted to payers of local rates and taxes, to holders of property within those boroughs. In all these boroughs the pre-reform electorates had been relatively large, and it is reasonable to assume that sociologically they would have belonged to the same class as the new £10-ers. Probably a majority of the potential electors in those boroughs had a choice of registering under the old or the new, and a substantial proportion must have chosen the old, more prestigious qualification. But this would have depended on the scale of the local taxation: in some of the boroughs it may well have been so low as to make its incidence well-nigh universal, in which case in such boroughs there would have been virtually a household suffrage—in terms of the age, a democratic franchise. It is impossible to be precise either about the extent of the old freeman franchise defined in terms of rights rather than of property. The freedom of a borough could be gained in a number of ways, and borough charters defined the term in different ways. In some boroughs it was restricted to men who had served an apprenticeship to another burgess, in which case the rights of burgess-ship were defined in terms of occupation and confined to tradesmen or craftsmen. In other it was conferred by birth, in which case it was automatic; in others by marriage, and in most, before the Municipal Reform Act, it could be purchased. These variations are obviously important in our attempt to define the character of the electorates in boroughs, for the simple reason that they defined strictly the distribution of the vote. In boroughs where the freedom was automatic there was virtually a household franchise: Aberafon and Llantrisant were examples, and in such boroughs the extinction of such freehold qualifications in favour of the £10 qualification would in course of time severely restrict the electorate and change its character class-wise. For instance, it could mean, and did mean, that a substantial portion of the working class would be deprived of their vote.

That a substantial shift in the character of the electorate did take place in the course of the next thirty or forty years is undeniable. One indication of it is the decline of the freeman vote: by the middle '60s freemen voters constituted only about one-fifth of the total borough electorate. The total electorate itself had grown by about a third during the same period. The population of the boroughs as a whole had doubled. Fewer people were therefore qualifying for the vote, and conceivably significant numbers who had had the vote when it had been relatively less dependent upon property were now excluded. The general conclusion must be that the electorate was maintaining and even defining more closely its middle-class character. It is true that in 1866-7 when the second Reform Act was under discussion politicians had been surprised at the high proportion of working-class men enfranchised, and certain historians have made much of this as indicating an inherent shift towards greater democracy, even under the old system. Thus, it could be shown that in 1866 nearly 40 per cent of the borough electorate in Wales was returned as belonging to the working class. But when we look into this we find that ' working class ' was defined as including not merely wage earners but also small handicraftsmen employing labour themselves—men whom we would put into the lower middle class. In nearly all the Welsh boroughs the £10 house holder—that is the male occupiers of houses of a gross estimated rental of £10 and over —constituted a minority of occupiers, and without going into the exact statistics, and while allowing for variations in house value from place to place, it is a fairly safe generalization to conclude that the borough electors consisted mainly of professional men, the managerial groups where there was industry, tradesmen, and the more substantial shopkeepers, artisans, and those members of the working class in receipt of good wages and in regular employment.

This latter point is important and deserves some elaboration. In the population of any representative borough, there would be, in any particular year, three main political classes, namely, the enfranchised, the unenfranchised, and the disenfranchised. The enfranchised I call those whose income was sufficiently high to ensure their registration. This group might include what social historians have called the ' aristocracy of labour ', that is to say, the skilled artisans, the highly paid craftsmen, the mechanics who were coming to constitute an increasingly important part of the working class in industrial boroughs. But it might also, in some such towns, include quite ordinary work-men above the level of labourer, for what made men poor in the mid century was not low wages particularly or even mainly, but irregularity of employment. Some industries, and some sections of particular industries, were more prone than others to violent and rapid fluctuations of demand. Ironstone mining, for instance, was a more regular employment than coalmining and so it was always the case that ironminers were better off than coalminers even though their rate of wages was rather less. Contemporaries were all agreed that as a class of workmen iron-miners were steadier, thriftier, better behaved, more sober, better husbands and fathers than coalminers—in short, more respectable. The non-ferrous smelting industries centred around Swansea and Llanelli provided steady and regular employment, and it was remarked that the wages of a copper-smelter were the equivalent of a salary. By comparison, the iron-smelters of Merthyr and the Monmouthshire iron towns suffered sudden and drastic interruptions to the flow of employ-ment. Demand flunctuations were unpredictable, as were the prices paid for labour which could vary enormously from place to place and from time to time. The sociological, cultural differences between the Swansea-Neath area and the Merthyr-Aberdare area were not due simply or mainly to differences in the settlement patterns, or their diverse histories; they reflected these deep differences in the patterns of employment current in each. We should expect to find, therefore, in the towns of Llan-elli, Neath, Swansea, Aberafon, as in towns of a similar industrial base in Flint, for instance, that the enfranchised in the population would have a solid, regular base consisting of these aristocrats of labour. The unenfranchised group would consist of the poor, the labouring class, probably a majority of the working population. At its topmost level it would merge into my third group, namely, the disenfranchised, meaning by this those men who came just below the necessary qualification, and those whom, it might be, illness or partial unemployment had deprived of the vote. This was the class of frustration, of resentment, of envy, and of anger—in fact, potentially a political class. Added to this class of significant deprivation was yet another, even larger class of workmen equally deprived, equally resentful, namely those resident in large towns or communities of an industrial character whose growth had antedated the arrangements of the Reform Act. By the 1860s, in north Wales as in south Wales, industrial towns had developed at a faster pace than the towns of the first industrial revolution. The Caernarfonshire slate towns—Bethesda, Ffestiniog; iron towns of the second growth, like Maesteg and Cwmafon; and industrial suburban extensions to enfranchised towns outside the borough limits, as in Swansea, Neath, and in parts of Denbighshire. Add to these certain older industrial centres, such as Abergavenny and Pontypool, and you have communities of many thousands almost completely unenfranchised, whose only hope of representation lay in the county constituencies but of which, by definition, they could not belong. The county franchise was of a character inimical to those communities: only a small fraction of their inhabitants could be brought within the pale, and although those numbers could and did make a significant difference, in structure, wealth, and social tendency they belonged with the boroughs, and in terms of political attitudes they were to be numbered with that middle spectrum of frustrated aspiration in the representative boroughs.

Paradoxically, the existence of these urban people in rural constituencies and of rural people in urban communities decreased the possibilities of their sense of grievance from being expressed. The representation of ' interests ' would be best served when the two kinds of electorate were homogeneous, distinct, and separately organized for political ends expressive of their own particular community needs or aspirations. This could not happen when an electorate which would normally respond to the appeal of a candidate attractive to them was swamped or heavily diluted by an electorate naturally belonging to the contrary interest. For example, after 1857 it was inconceivable that any Tory, however well born, however rooted in the county, could gain one of the Glamorgan county seats from the Liberals Talbot and Vivian: the urban-based, industrial vote could always be marshalled against him, as Nash Vaughan Edwards-Vaughan of Rheola discovered to his cost in 1857. Edwards-Vaughan's attempt was doomed to fail anyway because, as we have seen, the two Glamorgan county members

were both industrialists and landowners and so satisfactory to
both interests. It would work the other way as well, in the
boroughs. The Liberals of Cardiff felt that they had a real
grievance in that they were represented by a Tory landowner,
and this was the reason why Walter Coffin, the Unitarian coal-
owner, stood in 1852, gaining the seat by a mere thirty-six votes,
hardly any of which, by the way, he polled in rural Cowbridge.
In fact, the outstanding characteristic of parliamentary politics
in Wales during that generation was its uneventfulness. Contested elections were the exception rather than the rule: in the
five general elections between 1852 and 1868, and ignoring
by-elections, there were only about thirty contested elections
out of a possible 158. One of the reasons for this almost certainly
lay in the acceptance by the local leaders of the political classes
in the constituencies of this idea of a necessary congruence
between the two types of constituency and their social composition, the rural and the urban. Strains were appearing in
this convention by the '6os, as we shall see, and they were due
to the fact of increasing industrialization, to the fact that urban
growth took no note of political arrangements designed to
accord with the social simplicities of a past age.

Looking deeper into this phenomenon of the rarity of contested elections we can observe yet another characteristic of the
political system, and the operation of forces making for change.
Contested elections were rarer in rural constituencies than in
urban constituencies, and most rare in those rural constituencies
where there was scarcely any industrial development to diversify
their economies. There were no contests between 1852 and
1868—more precisely, no contests pressed to the poll—in
Anglesey, Montgomeryshire, Breconshire, and Radnorshire.
The only exceptions to this rule were Cardiganshire, where
there were three contested elections, and Merionethshire, where
there were two, but in both of these constituencies there
were significant social changes taking place, or personalities
involved who refused to accept the normal conventions of
county politics. In all the borough constituencies, with the
exception of Radnor, there were contested elections, in some
cases regularly and persistently. The question arises, why this
differences in political behaviour between the two types? Why

should the deep rural constituencies be conspicuous for their
lack of political activity in contrast to the urban constituencies
where, for the most part, political conflict was to be expected as
something normal?

The answer lies in the differing social structures of these
contrasted types of constituency. The rural constituencies
remained pre-industrial, that is to say, societies stratified
hierarchically into estates rather than in classes, with a strict
correspondence between status and ownership of land. The
social structure in its formal patterning was therefore extremely
simple. The vast inequalities between proprietor and occupier,
between landlord and tenant, corresponded exactly to the
inequalities of wealth between these two extremes. If we were
to construct a model of the distribution of wealth in rural Wales
it would resemble the Students' Union building on Penglais, the
bell-tower representing the minute proportion of estate owners,
and the podium of the Union itself the rest of the population—
that is to say, about 4 per cent of the population owning more
than half of the land available for exploitation. In Merioneth,
in no way untypical, a total of twenty-one proprietors owned a
half of the total acreage.   Economically, the relationship
between ' rentier ' and tenant; socially it was one of deference,
that is to say, a relationship in which differential levels of
income and of standards of living, and differential status
situations were accepted and rarely, if ever, questioned. For
the relationships between the unequal groups were not contractual ones, but customary and reciprocal ones. It was not an
individuated set of relationships but an organic complex of relationships in which the essential component parts were knit
together as closely and as intimately as by kith and kin. And
custom rather than legal restraints and the sanctions of law
organized what the economy anyway demanded—the recognition of the interdependence of the parts and the co-operation
of the whole for the survival and good of all. Knowing one's
place, recognizing one's obligations and rights—these were
attitudes that one was born into and educated into. In a sense,
it is well-high impossible for conflict to disrupt such harmony:
where deference operates reciprocally, where rights and duties
are observed throughout the community, the upper strata can-

not exploit the lower nor the lower be resentful of the superior way of life of the upper stratum. Now, if one means by politics the free exercise of individual rights in the choice of alternative ends, then it is obvious that politics cannot exist in such a closed system. Where power is so unequally distributed among the community, those strata in it which possess least must either acquiesce or rebel, and the acquiescence or the rebellion must involve the whole of the community: there can be no middle way. In essence, this is what happened in rural disturbances: the Rebecca Riots are a prime example of what happened when intolerable economic conditions caused whole communities of tenant farmers—the communities most conscious of deprivation —to strike against the system itself. At a more political level— the level of political rights—we can see how communities of farmers in Merioneth in 1859 or Cardiganshire in 1865 put themselves into what was virtually a state of rebellion by breaking the age-old compact that communities on estates voted as communities with their lords. Events in those two counties are politically significant for that reason: they mark the intrusion into rural communities of ideas and modes of individual initiatives utterly at variance with the norms of those communities, and therefore ultimately socially destructive of those communities.

It is highly significant also, that the source of such unprecedented acts of defiance at the expense of the social solidarity of the community was never to be found in the deep farming communities themselves. They were invariably generated in the rural towns and spread from thence via craftsmen, tradesmen, and the large tenant farmers, i.e. the upper stratum of the dependent class. Overtly political acts always originated and spread thus. The slate towns of Caernarfonshire, the coal-and lead-mining communities of Denbigh and Flint, the ports of Cardiganshire, and almost everywhere the market and administrative towns—it is in such as these and not in the deep rural areas that political movements (as distinct from blind social upheavals) are generated, organized, and carried through. And it is clear why this should be so: the towns were more open, more mobile, stratified differently, openly accepting the competing rights of conflicting interest groups, having a style of life far more complex, modes of behaviour more idiosyncratic, pursuing a wider range of intellectual pursuits, and receptive to the flow of ideas from outside. In arguing thus I do not want to suggest that the rural towns had always been thus and, by implication, centres of significant political activity. That is far from the truth. Some of them had had a political experience of sorts, but rarely an experience of politics growing out of the social tensions of the towns themselves. They had adopted political stances, worn political colours, as it were, but only at the bidding, and usually at the expense, of rival political lords. Generally speaking, in the post-reform period, most of them had slumbered in the protection of a dominant family, or been bribed or befuddled into a state of acquiescence and apathy. Not that Welsh boroughs were corrupt, for they were not. Bribery and corruption were not typical ingredients in their political life, not because they were inherently ' cleaner ' but by reason of the comparative rarity of contested elections. But that is not the point I am making: it is their potentiality for politics of a real and significant kind that I wish to emphasize in contrast to the different possibilities in their rural hinterlands. And this period between 1850 and 1870 saw the awakening of such possibilities, the intrusion of novel factors into the situation. As someone remarked in 1868, ' Liberty is like guncotton, safest when it is spread ', adding that the debris of revolutionary explosions had fallen on Dolwyddelan.

The communities of the coalfield were functional communities, not organic, and held together, not by the complex of kith and kin relationships, communal work patterns, the subtle interrelations of demesne and small-holding, palace and cottage but by the impersonal demands of the industries which dominated them. Whereas the farmers' relations to the estate were ' natural ', involving families rather than individuals and, as often as not, having a long, continuous history, the relationships of the inhabitants of the towns to the industries which gave them existence were mainly economic and contractual and brief. They were communities stratified above all by ' class ', and the key difference between these industrial communities was the existence of class consciousness. There was no mistaking the existence of the upper class—the ironmaster, coal-owner, landlord, royalty owner, any more than that of the estate owner. His life was as conspicuously different from the bulk of the population as that of the landed proprietor was as different from that of the tenant farmer. His power was probably greater, more naked, and less subject to the constraints of custom. There was also a distinctive middle class consisting of the lawyers, surgeons, and salaried men, engineers, and accountants—men who more and more were coming to occupy key positions not only in the industries themselves, but in towns which were rapidly being reshaped and reorganized. In the industrial processes these were years of rapid technological change, and these were the men raised up or trained to carry them through. But they were also years of significant advances in urban technologies—in social medicine, sanitation, health, and education, of gas and light companies, railways, and assembly rooms, and these were the men in the van of such changes. There were also the large shopkeepers and the agents and bankers who were proliferating in those years of prosperity. This was a class fairly easily identifiable by their style of life: they live in large houses, keep servants, have a carriage and pair, and aspire to ape the manners (the morality as Victorians put it) of their social superiors. Below them were the amorphous working classes, the wage earners, the labouring men, the great bulk of the population.

This analysis is necessarily crude; it ignores significant gradations within the classes themselves, and particularly the extent of mobility between the upper reaches of the working classes and the lower middle classes. The aristocracy of labour meaning by that the artisan and ' engineer ', the well-paid craftsman, educated and alive to the possibilities of individual self-improvement, certainly aspired to and often reached a higher standard of comfort than the bulk of the working men. But in the context of politics it is not this kind of individual mobility only that is significant at this time, but also the more general convergence, as it were, of middle class and working class. Class conflict was not of the essence of the situation, although the conditions necessary for such a conflict were being laid down: the socio-economic aspects of proletariatization were grimly present—the exploitation of the worker in terms of the reward for his labour, the aculturization of the migrant peasant. While, in the expansive years of the middle '50s and '60s, the real wages of most workers went up, in relative terms they almost certainly went down. Nor should we assume that there was an automatic correlation between levels of income and living conditions among the working classes. If it is true that there was a slow, fairly regular rise in real incomes there was almost certainly a decline in housing standards and a lack of health-giving and health-preserving public amenities in some of the old towns and in many of the new ones. This was certainly the overwhelming impression of workers themselves. But if there was little or no convergence economically, there was a real convergence of the classes in a relational and normative sense. The formal and informal relationships with the middle class outside the context of work became more intimate, especially in the religious and the political fields where, in parliamentary politics, the working class no longer attempted to organize itself as such and to operate independently, as in the past, but was prepared to co-operate closely with representatives of the middle classes. Henry Richard was returned by an alliance of middle-class radicals and working-class activists. And this was evidence of a kind of ' normative ' convergence, that is to say, the acquisition by the working classes of standards of behaviour and of an out-look resembling that of the middle classes. This made it possible for the middle class to provide leadership in those areas where the working class could not provide for themselves, and more specifically, in formal parliamentary and local politics. This did not mean that the working classes were thereby absorbed, as it were, by the middle class; on the contrary, these were decades of creative growth in distinctively working-class movements with which the middle classes generally were not in sympathy— specifically, trades unions and some forms of political agitation surviving from the age of Chartism. In most other social move-ments typical of the working class the convergence was almost complete: Friendly Societies, benefit clubs, for instance, or that most revealing of Victorian crusades, the temperance move-ment, and finally, of course, in religious organizations. It would be wrong to speak of class conflict, therefore, except in the most general of terms. But class consciousness can exist without overt class conflict, and nothing is clearer in the literature of the time than this. Colliers and ironworkers constantly compare their situation with that of the capitalists (the term carried no socialist connotations), their comparative poverty with the excessive riches of the owners, their inadequate social conditions and the lack of investment of any of the wealth being created by their own labour in social overheads. And this led to feelings of resentment, openly expressed, and often of hatred. ' The attitude of the new manager,' wrote *Y Gwron* about the Maesteg Iron Works in 1858, ' suggests that on his appointment he had sworn an oath to impoverish all living things in Maesteg.' They feel that they are an oppressed class in society, that they have grievances unique to themselves, and which can be redressed only if they organize themselves powerfully for political ends. By the end of the '60s, therefore, ' y dosbarth gweithiol ' had come to have distinct political overtones, and in local politics as well as in the exigencies of contested elections, they had come to constitute either in alliance with the middle classes or independently of them, a real and positive political force.

*   *   *

I have contrasted these two types of constituency in these bold terms because we are apt to forget that such divisions existed in Welsh society a hundred years ago. But contemporaries could not ignore such elementary facts. They knew that the centre of gravity had moved from the country to the town, that Wales, like England, had become a nation of town-dwellers, that more people lived in the industrial counties of south Wales and Denbighshire than had lived in the whole of Wales fifty years previously, that more people dwelt in the two parishes of Merthyr and Aberdare than in the whole of Breconshire and Anglesey, or Cardiganshire and Merioneth combined. And they could see this enormous shift as a continuing process, observe the steady movement of people away from the country to the industrial areas, and they understood it for what it was, a movement from penury to comparative wealth, from restrictive

societies inhibitive of personal initiative to the enhanced freedoms of competitive, mobile societies. There were features of
these urban societies which they found highly distasteful.
' J. R.' of Conway, accustomed to the rural solitudes of the
valleys of north Wales and not entirely reconciled even to the
slate towns of Caernarfonshire, thought of Merthyr as an
abomination and Maesteg, for all its splendid chapels, an
excrescence on the fair face of the countryside. But even he
recognized that it was these places which were determining the
slope of social progress in Wales. The industrial areas, said one
acute observer in 1861, were one grand laboratory. They were
experimental places, crucibles in which a new culture was being
forged. Nor did any politician or social reformer doubt that not
only would this new culture inevitably extend itself into the
countryside but also that it would be a positive good that it
should so extend itself. The physical means were already
apparent, for the railways were visibly an extension of the urban
culture into the rural parts of the country, tangible evidence that
the transformation of Milford into a new Hull, Pumlumon into
a kind of Klondyke, and Aberystwyth into a second Swansea
need be no idle dream. And with the new wealth would come a
new structure. ' What Cardigan needs,' said the men of Aberdare in 1865, ' is a middle class.' Arrogant perhaps, but if, as
was generally held in those days, the function of a middle class
was to break the social distance between the high and the low,
to bridge the gulf between proprietor and farmer, then this was
precisely what was lacking in the rural societies—a middle class
sufficiently independent to break that monopoly of power possessed by the proprietorial class, and to lead the deluded
peasants into the land of promise. And this was exactly what
the politicians and social reformers set out to do: they deliberately set out to create a rural middle class as the social
prerequisite for the initiation of the changes they sought·

The question now arises, how did they propose to do so?
What elements lay at hand? What machinery could be devised
for this extraordinary project? To comprehend their understanding of the situation we need to look again at our analysis
of rural society. We saw that by the criteria of wealth the
stratification of rural society was of such a character as to

exclude a middle region between the wealthy and the poor, or at least to allow the existence of only lower grades among the gentry themselves—hardly a middle class in the sense required of the times. But if we apply criteria other than wealth a different picture emerges. Weber teaches us that stratification can be by social prestige and honour, and that such stratification can cut across the class divisions of wealth and possessions. Looked at thus we find that the lower stratun of rural society was not monolithic in the slightest. It had produced its own elite, men whom the community honoured for their superior intelligence, or for other marks of socially acceptable excellence. Herein lies the social importance of the chapel and of religion generally in rural (and in industrial) Wales during those years. The preacher, the college lecturer, the chapel deacons—very often men of outstanding gifts, educated and literate most of them to a higher degree than that of the generality of their communities, in the highest sense the legislators of their times. Moreover, for the most part, in so far as one can tell, these were invariably the most prosperous among the lower classes: as I have already said, they might be tenants but they were always large tenants, enjoying the confidence of their landlords, and usually the most direct line of communication between the landlord and the rest of the estate. That is, they were already fulfilling some of the functional roles of a middle class. They might also be craftsmen, secure in their trades and beholden to none. It is this elite, I suggest, flourishing in the home-grown religious institutions of the countryside which constituted the raw materials out of which a middle class was to be forged.

But how to forge this material into a viable middle class? Clearly what was sought was the inculcation of a middle-class consciousness into this elite, and how could this be done except by education? The education required was of two kinds, formal and informal. So far as the first was concerned the educational technocrats of the time—men like Hugh Owen and Dr. Thomas Nicholas—found a great lack here. The education of the lower classes could safely be left to the National and British and Voluntaryist systems. Hugh Owen had done his work well, and Welsh educationists, like most English educationists of the

middle '60s, were smugly satisfied that the working classes were
sufficiently provided for. What was lacking in Wales was what
Thomas Nicholas called ' educational symmetry '—meaning
by this a closed, self-contained, hierarchical system of schools,
elementary, middle class, higher colleges, and a university.
Only the first was provided. Now, in the '60s, the motto was
' Educate the middle classes and you obtain an enlightened and
powerful people ', and Hugh Owen added, you provide feeders
for the projected university which, in their conception, would
likewise be a middle-class institution. The hard, calculating
utilitarianism of these prophets of higher education is everywhere evident, involving, as one critic put it, the sacrifice of
language and traditions and history on the altar of utilitatian-
ism. We can be more than thankful that such as these were not
entirely successful in their efforts, and that the University
College of Wales founded on more humane principles than the
repellent philosophy of Thomas Nicholas.

More to the point were the informal means available of
educating this rural elite. Here, the machinery was, first, the
press, and secondly, those great political societies which began
to proliferate at this time. The function of both was to teach
politics, to inculcate political attitudes, to teach the values of
citizenship, and the rights of man. The incipient rural middle
class—the elite—was already literate. Their religion demanded
this minimum of them, and the different denominations had
long been providing reading matter for them in the religious
magazines. What they did not provide was what was needed—
an education in politics, for the vast majority of them had little
or no interest in politics, and devoted a minimum of space to it.
The '60s, following the repeal of the Taxes on Knowledge in
1854, and Gladstone's repeal of the duties on paper in 1861,
saw an enormous efflorescence of periodical literature at a price
well within the pockets of most people, and from scores of presses up and down the country: it made possible the appearance
of newspapers. This is the great turning-point in Welsh political
life—the availability of a great variety of newspapers reflecting
all kinds of political attitudes and allegiances, and in Welsh and
English, circulating widely throughout the country. *Baner ac
Amserau Cymru* is the prime example, but by the end of the '60s

every county and almost every town and locality had its newspaper in which were to be read detailed accounts of meetings,
verbatim reports of speeches, columns of letters, and hard-
hitting leaders. It is impossible to exaggerate the importance of
this change which was beginning to take place in the reading
habits of the people. These newspapers were different in kind
from the old denominational magazines: this is the age not only
of the county newspaper but of *Yr Herald, Y Gwron, Tarian y
Gweithiwr, Y Gwladgarwr, Seren Cymru*, and literally dozens of
others, and we should not forget either that *The People's Paper,
The Beehive*, papers of a radical purpose, were circulating in the
industrial towns of north and south Wales. When Aberdare
claimed in 1867 that ' what we think today, Wales will think
tomorrow ' she was not idly boasting. Aberdare and Merthyr,
Swansea, Caernarfon, and Denbigh had become what the great
English towns had become—provincial capitals, and this by
reason of their presses and their opinion-forming newspapers.
And not only newspapers, but magazines, critical quarterlies,
not always religious in tone, and the vast mass of pamphlet
literature which poured from the scores of red-hot presses up
and down the country and which now lie in the National
Library awakening feelings of awe in the researcher.

Allied to this extension of newpaper publishing and of
publishing generally were the great national political societies.
I have written above [Chapter VII] about the most important,
the most effective, of these—namely, the Liberation Society,
and now I need only underline the fact that this radical, anti-
establishment anti-aristocratic, middle-class society, with its
organization present in every locality, its ample resources, its
own presses, and its own newspaper did more than any other
agency to educate the people in politics. Its political doctrines
were not unique to itself: the doctrine of disestablishment was as
old as dissent itself, and made familiar to Welshmen of generations previously by some of their religious magazines. What
was unique was its propaganda technique, the completeness of
its philosophy, and its rigorous, unrelenting penetration of the
whole country. There were other societies as well: the Peace
Society, the United Kingdom Alliance, and other temperance
societies, all were active during these years, and all political in

that their objective was the capture of party and the exerting of direct influence via the electorate on Parliament. Add to these the operation of the great Reform League with its lecturers and demonstrations and you have a tremendous force operating in the direction of educating people in the nature and ends of political responsibility. This educational activity covered the whole country, but its effect was particularly directed to the countryside, and the measure of its success was the overwhelming victories gained in 1868, for these were evidence that in the county constituencies men had voted as individuals rather than, as in the past, as elements in communities taking their direction from their lord, or alternatively that they had voted as religious communities, or as communities of workmen.

Such were the main elements in the situation as it was developing in the 1860s, such were the social forces at work within the formal structure of the constitution. But our analysis cannot end there, and I wish finally to draw attention to the way in which, right at the end of our period, the structural features and the ideological changes came powerfully and creatively together. First of all, the second Reform Act of 1867, by lowering the qualifications in the county constituencies and introducing a virtually universal household franchise in the boroughs, brought within the pale of the constitution precisely those elements or groups in the population most sensitive to the new influences we have been discussing. The rise in the electorate was considerable—about 50 *per cent* in the counties and 250 *per cent* in the boroughs. In the boroughs its impact was immediately apparent. In Denbigh, for instance, where the rise was of the order of 300 *per cent*, it enabled a very radical member to gain the seat. The outstanding fact about that election was the way in which the new working-class voters, mainly colliers, organized themselves as a distinct political movements. For these, the oldest trade union groups in Wales, franchise reform came as a real emancipation and their electoral activity was the political aspect of their attempts at industrial union in a time of economic depression. In Cardiff, too, where the vote had doubled, the Liberals had the enthusiastic support of the Trades Council in beating off the attacks of the Cardiff Castle Tory interest. The story of

Merthyr Tydfil, which overnight became the most democratic borough in Great Britain, is told above in Chapter V. Here the working classes not only returned Henry Richard, but also dismissed the aristocratic H. A. Bruce. In the counties, too, these changes had equally profound effects on the voting behaviour of their electorates. A large proportion of the farmers, that rural elite was now enfranchised, as also the urban men of the country towns and the rural industrial communities. We can see how critical was the change in voting patterns in Merioneth, Caernarfonshire, in Denbighshire, in Anglesey, and in Carmarthenshire. It would be tedious to relate their stories, to analyse one by one the contests of 1868; suffice it to say that it was the new electorate, the old disenfranchised in borough and county, by now sensitized and activized by the years of intensive education, which sprang to life, exulting in their new-found freedom to act decisively and, if necessary, to suffer, as many of them did, for the sake of their ideals.

For, finally, it was ideas, hopes and aspirations that were involved. This analysis has been in terms of the structural factors in the situation; but ideas know no frontiers, and recognize no class barriers. The main issue on which these men voted —the question before the country—seemed to them far more simple than it does to us today, namely, the disestablishment of the Irish Church: a technical matter involving abstruse questions of ecclesiastical law, deep considerations of policy. But to that generation of men it was supremely a question of justice, of morality, of the fitness of things. And they voted as they did because they felt the analogy between themselves and the Irish, between *that* alien church and *this* alien church, between *that* system and *these* blatant inequalities, to be profoundly true. The peasant and the collier, the craftsman and the ironworker, occupying grotesquely different social situations, had things in common to which their eyes had been opened. Their vote was against a prime example of injustice and social wrong in a neighbouring country, and it was a vote for a more equal society in their own. The passion they brought to the conflict was the force of their own suffering, the inspiration they found in their own experience as a people, their solidarity in their language and in their own democratic institutions of chapel and

club, eisteddfod and school. They saw in the men they had
returned to parliament men after their own hearts, and they
continued to listen to them and to follow those among them who
most clearly and sensitively expressed their own deepest aspirations. The fruit of all this in process of time, was a new
culture, radical, humane, and democratic.

NOTES

DENOMINATIONALISM IN CAERNARFONSHIRE

1Charles E. Glock, ' The Religious Revival in America ', in N. Birbaum and Gertrud Lenzer, *Sociology and Religion* (New Jersey, 1969), pp. 397 ff.

2Census of Great Britain, 1851. Religious Worship—England and Wales : Report and Tables, 1852-3, LXXXIX. The returns themselves are in PRO, HO129 (Ecclesiastical Returns, Census of 1851).

8On the nature of the Ecclesiastical Census and its reliability as a source, see *The Religious Census of 1851. A Calendar of the Returns Relating to Wales*. Vol. 1 South Wales, Edited by Ieuan Gwynedd Jones and David Williams (Cardiff 1976), pp. xiii ff, and refs. therein.

4For a description of the method adopted, see the Report from Horace Mann to the Registrar General, in *Census of Great Britain. Religious Worship—England and Wales* (London, 1853), pp. clxix-clxxvi.

5Specimen forms are reproduced in *The Religious Census of 1851, op. cit.,* Appendix A.

6*Religious Census, op. cit.,* Vol. 2 (North Wales), p. 309.

7*Ibid.,* p. 354,

8*Ibid.,* p. 332-3.

9The missing Caernarfonshire parishes included in the Ffestiniog Union are as follows (populations are given in brackets) : Beddgelert Parish (1253), Llanfihangel-y-Pennant (665), Dolbenmaen (382), Penmorfa (1109), Ynyscynhaiarn (2347) and Treflys (103). *Religious Census,* Vol. 2. pp. 277-81

10What follows is based on the *Report, op. cit.*

11*Ibid.,* pp. cxx ff.

12For a discussion of this, see Ieuan Gwynedd Jones, ' The elections of 1865 and 1868 in Wales, with special reference to Cardiganshire and Merthyr Tydfil '. *T.H.S.C.* (Part 1, 1964).

13These figures are based on the published *Report, op. cit.,* and it is important to note that the statistics therein relate to *Registration* Counties, and not necessarily to the ancient or geographical counties. Similarly, the Sub-districts into which the Unions were divided, might include parishes or townships in adjacent geographical counties. Thus, I have included the Union of (614) Llanrwst (Denbighshire) in my analysis because the following parishes were in Caernarfonshire even though, for the purposes of the *Report,* they were included in Denbighshire : Township of Maenan (406), the Abbey ex-parochial (30), Gwydir (382), Trefriw Parish (428), Llanrhychwyn Parish (586), Betws-y-coed Parish (478),Dolwyddelan Parish (727), Penmachno (1251), and Ysbyty Parish (892). Note also, Caernarfon Union included the five parishes of Llanidan Sub-district in Anglesey, and that Bangor Union included the whole of the Beaumaris Sub-district, also in Anglesey. My detailed analysis excludes all communities not in the ancient county, and includes all communities excluded by Union boundaries. For detailed population see *Religious Census,* Vol II.

14See Table 2.

15This paragraph is based on information taken from the Enumerators' Returns, Census of 1851. PRO, HO 107/2514.

16This analysis is based on the published *Report, op. cit.*

17See Tables 4 and 5.

18See Table 1.

19These figures are based on an analysis of the Ecclesiastical Revenues Commission, *Report of the Commissioners of Inquiry into the Ecclesiastical Revenues of England and Wales,* 1835 (P.P. 1835, XXII, pp. 110, *passim*).

[20]E.g. the incumbents of Cricieth with Ynyscynhaiarn and Treflys, and of Llanwnda with Llanfaglan.

[21]The standard work on this topic is C. F. A. Best, *Temporal Pillars : Queen Anne's Bounty, the Ecclesiastical Commissioners and the Church of England* (1964). See also Olive J. Brose, *Church and Parliament* : the *Re-shaping of the Church of England, 1828-1860* (1959).

[22]On the situation in Llandaff see E. T. Davies, *Religion in the Industrial Revolution in South Wales* (1959), Wilton B. Wills, ' The Established Church in the Diocese of Llandaff, 1850-70 ', *Welsh History Review*, 4, No. 3 (1969), pp. 235 ff, and, in more detail, the same author's dissertation, ' Ecclesiastical Reorganisation and Church Extension in the Diocese of Llandaff, 1830-1870 ', M.A. (Swansea, 1965).

[23]These statistics are taken from *Ecclesiastical Revenues Commission, 1835, op. cit.*

[24]*Ibid.*

[25]See the graph with Table 6.

[26]P.P. 1850, XLII (226), p.4.

[27]*Ecclesiastical Revenues Commission, 1835, op cit.*

[28]*Ibid.*

[29]This conclusion is based on an analysis of the Tithe Apportionments for Caernarfonshire in the N.L.W.

[30]See W. R. Ward, ' The Tithe Question ', *J. Eccles. Hist.* XVI (1965).

[31]P.P. 1850 XLII (4).

[32]These calculations are based on the published *Report, op. cit.*

[33]See Table 8.

[34]See Table 9.

[35]See Table 10 for chapel building parish by parish.

[36]See Table 11.

[37]*Religious Census*, Vol. 2, p. 324.

DENOMINATIONALISM IN SWANSEA AND DISTRICT

[1]Alphonse Esquiros, *Religious Life in England* (1867), p. 188.

[2]See, for example, R. O. Roberts "The development and decline of Copper and other Non-ferrous metal industries in South Wales", *T.H.S.C.* (1965), and references therein. Also, D. Trevor Williams, *The Economic Development of Swansea and of the Swansea District to* 1921 (1940).

[3]See *The Religious Census of* 1851, *op. cit.*, pp. 248-175 for a calendar of the returns.

[4]See especially the article by W. S. F. Pickering, ' The 1851 Census—a useless experiment ? ', *British Journal of Sociology*, XVIII, No. 4 (1967).

[5]I am inclined to believe that the error lay in the preliminary list which was not corrected when the statistics were collated.

[6]585.3.1.15, *Religious Census, op. cit.*, p. 262.

[7]For references see note 3 above.

[8]For a full discussion of the difficulties involved see Mann's *Report*, and *Religious Census, op. cit.*, pp. xi ff.

[9]A return of the Ecclesiastical Commissioners in 1850, "Churches and Chapels (Wales)", P.P. 1850 (90), *XLII*, 22, shows that of the 23 churches in the Union 18 held one service on Sunday (including in this Oystermouth which held two in the summer months). As explained in the text, the schedules give different information with regard to Llandeilo Talybont.

[10]D. Trevor Williams, *op. cit.*, and especially *idem.*, "Gower : a study in linguistic movements and historical geography", *Arch. Camb.* (1934), pp. 302-27. See also J. Parry Lewis, "The Anglicization of Glamorgan", *Morgannwg*, IV (1960), pp.28ff.

[11]See Map 1, p. 54 in D. Trevor Williams, *op cit.*

¹²This section is based on the Census Enumerators' Returns, PRO HO 107/ 2645-7.

¹³D. Trevor Williams, *art. cit.*

¹⁴*Report*, p. clxxi.

¹⁵S. Lewis, *Topographical Dictionary of Wales*, vol. 1, (1833), *sub.* Knelston.

¹⁶Thus, one congregation of Wesleyan Methodists used a dwelling house and another hired a room in the market in Morriston, while the Mormon congregation at Swansea worshipped in the Trades Hall, High Street.

¹⁷*Report*, pp. cxix, ff.

¹⁸The vicar of St. Mary's returned as space available 418 sittings free and 953 otherwise appropriated, and remarked as follows : "Of these 953 ' other sittings ' in this Church the whole of the North Aisle which contains 120 sittings is *claimed by one individual*. The North Gallery containing 150 sittings is private property. The Chancel containing 150 sittings is the property of the Lay Rector. So that out of 953 sittings 424 sittings are not under the control of the Church-wardens and those parts of the Church are comparatively empty while many of the Parishoners are applicants for sittings in vain". For the background to this situation see Rev. David Walker, *A Short History of the Parish Church of Swansea* (third ed. 1967), pp. 14-15.

¹⁹St. John's Chapel of Ease, Morriston, was built by Sir John Morris in 1802.

²⁰For an account of this see Rev. David Walker, *op. cit.*, pp. 19-25.

MERIONETH POLITICS IN
MID-NINETEENTH CENTURY

¹See below pp. 165-92.

²National Library of Wales MS. 10864 C (Frondirion 51). A lecture (?) on T. E. Ellis.

³M. D. Jones to E. W. Evans, dated from Bala, 10 August, 1889. N.L.W., MSS. 10852 (Frondirion 39).

⁴' Plentyn y bryniau, mab y deffroad,
  Calon Meirionydd a llygad ei wlad '.
Quoted in *Cymru*, XXXVI (January 1909), p. 99.

⁵For the political history of the county consult W. R. Williams, *The Parliamentary History of the Principality of Wales* 1541—1895 (Brecknock, 1895), pp. 114-119. See also Peter D. G. Thomas, ' The Parliamentary Representation of Merioneth during the Eighteenth Century ', *JMHS*, III, (1957-60), pp. 129-136.

⁶For Richard Richards, see *DWB*, *sub* Richards family, of Coed, p. 850.

⁷For an analysis of the election, see below pp. 298-300.

⁸For David Williams, see *DWB*, *sub* Williams family, of Bron Eryri, p. 1023-4, and *Traethawd ar Enwogion Swydd Feirion* gan Edward Davies (Caernarfon, 1870), tt. 48-50.

⁹*C. & D. H.*, 14 May, 1859.

¹⁰For the Wynnes, father and son, see *DWB*, *sub*, Wynne family, of Peniarth, pp. 103-4.

¹¹For R. W. Price, *ibid.*, *sub* Price family, of Rhiwlas, pp. 781-3.

¹²For Sir Watkin Williams Wynn, *ibid.*, *sub* Wynn family, of Wynnstay, p. 1100.

¹³For Thomas Edward Ellis, consult *Thomas Edward Ellis. Cofiant. Cyfrol I.* (1859-1886) gan T. I. Ellis (Liverpool), 1944). The quotation is taken from his evidence before the Royal Commission on Land in Wales and Monmouthshire, *Minutes of Evidence*, vol. I. Q. 16,910 *et seq.*, p. 785. See also, ' Notes on the Evidence Tendered to the Royal Commission ' in *Speeches and Addresses by the late Thomas E. Ellis*, M.P. (Wrexham, 1912), pp. 256-7.

[14]Parliamentary Papers, 1875 (1097), Vol. 2, *sub* Merioneth, p. 5. See F. M. L. Thompson, *English Landed Society in the Nineteenth Century* (1963), pp. 27 ff, for a discussion of the value of this as a source. Also, Brian Ll. James, ' The "Great Landowners" of Wales ', *J.N.L.W.*, XIV, No. 3 (1966), pp. 301-20. It will be seen that my analysis proceeds on different lines from the above.

[15]The following is based upon an analysis of the Tithe Apportionments (National Library of Wales) which, in Merioneth, were completed at various dates between 1838 and 1847. For a discussion of the Tithe Apportionments as a source consult H. C. Prince, ' The Tithe Surveys of the Mid-Nineteenth Century ', *Agricultural History Review*, Vol. III (1959), and more particularly, Colin Thomas, ' Merioneth Estates, 1790-1858 ; A Study of Agrarian Geography ', *J.M.H.S.*, Vol. V, No. iii (1967).

[16]John Bateman, *The Acre-ocracy of England* (1876). See also Brian Ll. James, *art. cit.*, p. 319.

[17]N.L.W. Wynnstay (uncatalogued) Rentals for 1859 give the extent of the Merioneth estates as 19,286 acres with an income of £7,359.9.1½. The Caerynwch estate in the parish of Dolgellau produced a rental varying from £1099 to £1408 between 1862 and 1869 : Merioneth Record Office, Caerynwch Rentals DA/III /II.

[18]On the slate industry in general consult the bibliography and references to contemporary works in D. E. Davies, *A Treatise on Slate and Slate Quarrying* (1878).

[19]See *Aur Sir Feirionydd, yn cynnwys Hanes y gwahanol wythanau eu cyswr presenol a'u gobeithion dyfodol*. Gan John Parry, Ieu. Vigra & Clogau Mine. (Dolgellau, 1862).

[20]The tithes of the Wynn estate having been merged, they do not appear in the Survey. They were valued at £94 per annum.

[21]The Vivian estate, comprising 16 properties of a total acreage of 554 acres appears to have been added to the Glan-llyn estate in 1854/5, N.L.W., Wynnstay Rentals.

[22]The term ' township ', as applied to rural Wales in the Census materials, does not carry its English connotations of a community nucleated, like a village, about the manor house, church, etc. It was a purely arbitrary division of the ancient parish drawn for administrative convenience particularly in relation to the taking of the Census.

[23]The following is based upon the Enumerators' Returns, Census of 1861, PRO H.O. 107/2510.

[24]The Tithe Award gives 339 acres.

[25]There is a wealth of evidence too diverse to quote. The best individual sources are P. P. 1870 (C.70), *Third Report* on the Employment of Children, Young Persons, and Women, in Agriculture (1867), which is by J. H. Tremenheere and devoted entirely to Wales and Monmouthshire, and cited above.

[26]J. H. Tremenheere, *Report, op. cit.*

[27]Of the total of males and females over 15 years (excluding widowed persons), vizt. 31,119, 45.2 *per cent*, or 14,076 were unmarried. For purposes of comparison 39.9 *per cent* of the same group in Glamorgan were unmarried.

[28]One gets the impression, on the basis of small surveys, that farmers tended to marry later in life than agricultural labourers. A great deal of research needs to be carried out into this basic aspect of rural family life.

[29]See Appendix, p. 164, below. Also V. Challenor Davies, ' The Decline of Rural Population in Wales with special reference to Merionethshire ', *JMHS*, II (1953-6), pp. 58, ff. Also, D. Friedlander and R. J. Roshier, ' A Study of Internal Migration in England and Wales : Part I ', *Population Studies*, XIX, No. (3 March 1966), pp. 239-179, especially the maps on pp. 252 and 253.

[30]Peter R. Roberts, ' The Gentry and the Land in Eighteenth Century Merioneth ', *JMHS* (1964) and ' The Merioneth Gentry and Local Government *circa* 1650-1838 ', *ibid.*, (1965).

[31]For the people of Llanuwchllyn the first Sunday in August was known as ' Sul Syr Watkin ' (Sir Watkin's Sunday) ' pryd y byddant yn cyrchu i'r eglwys i dalu

teyrnged ddyledus i arglwydd Wynnstay ' (when they flocked to the Church to pay their dutiful respects to the lord of Wynnstay). *Baner*, 24 October, 1866.

[32]WLCR *Report*, pp. 231 ff.

[33]There were reports of these meetings in all the North Wales newspapers. *The North Wales Chronicle* carries the fullest reports.

[34]Thus, Ruabon collected £100 and spent it on an elaborately bound Bible. *Chronicle*, 27 November, 1858. The same issue reports the funeral of Robert Owen at Newtown without comment.

[35]*Ibid.*, 27 March, 1858.

[36]*Ibid.*, 22 May, 1858. The deputation was headed by Richard Davies, Esq., later to be elected M.P. for Anglesey of which county he was High Sheriff in 1858. In his introductory speech John Foulkes, Esq., M.P. Montgomery, stated that the Calvinistic Methodist possessed nearly 1000 places of worship with a membership totalling nearly 70,000, and that 125,000 Sunday scholars were given Bible instruction. ' An organization of this magnitude, Sir Watkin, might, under other influences, become a formidable instrument for evil, but in the present case there is nothing to fear, inasmuch as it is purely religious, and not political, in its constitution, and thoroughly Protestant in its views and organisation.' In his reply, Sir Watkin declared that, ' he believed that if it had not been for the labours of Dissenters in Wales, the great mass of the people would be without religion '.

[37]*Ibid.*, 27 March, 1858.

[38]*Ibid.*, 5 March, 1859. Rhiwlas charities were distributed in Llanuwchllyn by a Calvinistic Methodist elder, and in Llanfor and Fron-goch by Ellis Roberts who was an elder at Glanrafon. Price was regarded as a handsome supporter of Dissent. He subscribed liberally to Lewis Edwards's Club at Bala.

[39]' I do not believe there is a single child in Bala that cannot read, in Welsh at least.' Evidence of Rev. John Lloyd, Rector of Llanycil, quoted in *Reports upon Certain Boroughs* by J. T. Hogg, P.P., 1837-8, XXXV, 223.

[40]See Ieuan Gwynedd Jones, ' The Anti-Corn Law Letters of Walter Griffith ', *BBCS*, XXVIII, Part I, (Nov. 1978), especially pp. 115-6.

[41]*Herald*, 28 May, 1859.

[42]The following is based on *Census of Great Britain*, 1851 : *Religious Worship—England and Wales*, P. P. 1852-3, LXXXIX. See also, Ieuan Gwynedd Jones (ed) *The Religious Census of 1851*, Vol. 2, North Wales (1981) pp. 229-81.

[43]Between 1840 and 1876 a total of 12 churches had been built or restored at a total cost of £22,010. Five of these churches were in Penllyn, vizt. Llanfor (£2,000 for restoration, by subscription), Fron-goch (a new church built at a cost of £1300). Llanuwchllyn (restored at a cost of £1760), Bala (restored at a cost of £2100) and Llandderfel (restored at a cost of £1200). Sir W. W. Wynn gave one half of the cost of restoration of the three last-named churches. P.P., 1876, LVIII (125 and 125 I), ' Returns showing the number of churches in every diocese which have been built or restored at a cost exceeding £500 since 1840 '.

[44]*Reports upon Certain Boroughs*, *op. cit.*

[45]For an account of these, see J. H. Lloyd (Peryddon) ' Hen Argraffdai a Hen Argraffwyr y Bala ', *JMHS*.

[46]This is discussed below, pp. 112 ff.

[47]Cf. Edward Parry, *Llawlyfr ar Hanes y Diwygiadau Crefyddol yn Nghymru* (Corwen, 1898), p. 101: ' . . . gwelir cryn lawer o bobl yn dyfod o'r nentydd cylchynol . . . nid am fod gan neb ohonynt fawr o olwg ar y pregethwr, nac yn disgwyl fawr oddiwrtho, ond manteisient ar y cyfle i gyfarfod a gweled eu gilydd, a chael ychydig o ddigrifwch. Arferid hyn yn fawr mewn lleoedd gwledig yn y dyddiau hyny '. (' Many people would be seen coming from the adjacent valleys, not because many of them had much acmiration for the preacher or expected much from him, but they took the opportunity to meet and see each other, and have a little fun. This was much resorted to in the country places in years gone by ').

[48]For Michael D. Jones, see in general Evan Pan Jones, *Oes a gwaith Michael D. Jones* (Bala, 1903), and Alun Davies, ' Michael D. Jones a'r Wladfa ', *T.H.S.C.*, 1966, Part I, pp. 73 ff.

[49]For Samuel Roberts, Llanbryn-mair, see in general, *idem, Cofiant y tri brawd,* (Bala, 1892), Glanmor Williams, *Samuel Roberts, Llanbrynmair* (1950), I. C. Peate (ed.), *Cilhaul ac Ysgrifau eraill* (1951). On Llanbryn-mair chapel see, I. C. Peate, *Hen Gapel Llanbrynmair,* 1739-1939 (1939). and on some aspects of the political influence of S. R. (which Dr. Peate probably exaggerates), see I. G. Jones, *art cit.*

[50]See reports of speeches in *North Wales Chronicle,* 22 May, 1858.

[51]On Lewis Edwards, see Trebor Lloyd Evans, *Lewis Edwards : ei fywyd a'i waith* (1967). For his views on the probable fate of the Welsh language see the report of his speech at the opening of the new College buildings at Bala 1867, in *Athrofa y Bala ; ei sylfaeniad a'i hagoriad,* (Bala, 1868) tt.29.

[52]Cf. the following judgement by a man not accustomed to denigrating the achievements of Welsh nonconformity : ' One formidable obstacle in the way of this (i.e. of ' the politics of intelligent conviction ') was the difference of language, which cut the people off from the political literature of England. At first, their political literature was . . . almost exclusively religious. I remember when I was a boy that all the politics of the magazine received in my father's house were compressed into about half a page of most insipid summary at the end. It is scarcely more than twenty years since the Welsh began to have anything alike a political literature '. Henry Richards, *Letters and Essays on Wales* (edn. of 1884), p. 93. The letter from which the above is taken was published in 1866. Note that Henry Richard speaks of ' the magazine ' (in the singular) taken by his father, the eminent Calvinistic Methodist divine.

[53]On these towns, see, in general, H. J. Owen, *Echoes of Old Merioneth* (1946), G. J. Williams, *Hanes Plwyf Ffestiniog* (n.d., ? 1882), R. Prys Morris, *Cantref Meirionydd* (1890), T. P. Ellis, *The Story of two Parishes : Dolgellau and Llanelltyd* (1928), G. Roberts (Gwrtheyrn), *Pum' Plwy' Penllyn* (n.d., ? 1897), Robert James (Trebor), *Dolgellau yn Hanesyddol* (1907). For the industrial background consult A. H. Dodd, *The Industrial Revolution in North Wales* (2nd ed. 1951.)

[54]*Slater's Directory* for 1850 and 1868, for example.

[55]The history of the College is to be found in Trebor Lloyd Evans *op. cit.,* chap. IV, and in G. A. Edwards, *Athrofa'r Bala,* 1838-1937 (1937).

[56]For John Parry, see *DWB,* pp. 736-7.

[57]The history of the Independent College (also called ' Athronfa'r Bala ')see R. Peris Williams, *Hanes Athrofa Bala-Bangor* (1914), and Geraint Dyfnallt Owen, *Ysgolion a Cholegau yr Annibynwyr* (1939). See also the interesting comments in T. Ll. Evans, *op. cit.,* pp. 122 ff.

[58]*DWB,* p. 495.

[59]For Michael Daniel Jones, see *ibid.,* pp. 495-6, and Pan Jones, *Oes a Gwaith . . . M. D. Jones* (1903). The best account of the work of M. D. Jones and his father in Llanuwchllyn is in R. T. Jenkins, *Hanes Cynulleidfa Hen Gapel Llanuwchllyn* (1937).

[60]For John Peter (Ioan Pedr), see *DWB,* p. 751.

[61]The course of the revival of 1859 in Merioneth can be charted in J. J. Morgan, *Hanes Dafydd Morgan Ysbytty a Diwygiad,* 59, pp. 280-348. Eifion Evans, *When He is Come : an Account of the 1858-60 Revival in Wales* (1959) contains an excellent bibliography.

[62]*Reports upon Certain Boroughs, op. cit.,* sub Bala. For the early history of the borough, see E. A. Lewis, *The Medieval Boroughs of Snowdonia, passim.,* and, more generally, Hugh J. Owen, *Echoes of Old Merioneth* (1946).

[63]The Methodist referred to was John Davies, Fronheulog, a man who was to take an active part in the political life of the county as described in this paper. On the episode, commented upon by Hogg, see Peter H. Roberts, *The Merioneth Gentry and Local Government, JMHS* (1965), pp. 36-7, and the references therein.

[64]*Chronicle,* 22 January, 1859, and Hugh J. Owen, *op. cit.,* pp. 5-6.

[65]See, for an example, *Herald,* 23 April, 1860, which prints a letter by M. D. Jones on the question of whether or not to apply the Local Government Act. See also PRO HO 13/11 for the petition (and counter-petition) of the inhabitant rate

payers, and correspondence relating thereto, for the adoption of the Local Government Act of 1858. The petition (HO 13/11/374/59) received by the Local Government Office, 25 February 1859, was signed by 51 inhabitant ratepayers ; the counter-petition, received on the same date was signed by one person only, namely, Mr. Richard Watkin Price of Rhiwlas.

66For George Price Lloyd, see *DWB*, *sub* Lloyd family, of Rhiwaedog, p. 574. Lloyd had served as High Sheriff in 1840-41 : Edward Breese, *Calendars of Gwynedd* (1873), p.84. According to the Tithe Apportionments, he owned 65 acres in the parish of Llanycil.

67*Slater's Directory*, *sub* Bala.

68See Pan Jones, *op. cit.*, pp. 68 *et passim*, and Bangor MS, 10635.

69Hugh J. Owen, *op. cit.*, pp. 5-6. See also the account in the delightful *Atgofion Andronicus* (i.e. John Williams) (1894), pp. 54-5.

70Speech by C. W. Wynn, 9 August, 1831, *Hansard*, 3rd. series, V, 1098-9. See also UNCW, Mostyn Ms. 8419, for a letter from Athelstan Corbet to E. M. Lloyd Mostyn requesting his support for a petition to parliament.

71For Sir Robert Williams Vaughan, see *DWB*, *sub* Nanney (Nannau) family, p. 680.

72*Shrewsbury Chronicle*, 13 May, 1836, *C & DH*, 14 May, 1836.

73D. G. P. Thomas, *art. cit.*

74*Hansard*, 3rd Series, V, 916.

75See, for example, Edward Davies, *Traethawd ar Enwogion Swydd Feirion* (1870).

76The Wynn (afterwards Nanney) family of Maesyneuadd is noted in *DWB*, p. 1098-9. See also J. E. Griffiths, *Pedigrees*, p. 283, from which it will be seen that for some reason Sir William did not assume the name Nanney when his father inherited by marriage the Nanney estates.

77Obituary in *The Gentleman's Magazine* (February 1856), p. 211.

78UCNW, Bangor, Maesyneuadd Deeds and Documents, Letters 33-99 are from (Sir) William Wynn to his brother Rev. John Nanney to whom the estate passed on the death of their eldest brother, Robert. From these it seems that William, at that time a lieutenant in the King's Dragoon Guards, who became engaged to Miss Long in 1801, relied upon this dowry to raise him out of his straightened circumstances.

79This was stated by Sir Richard Richards at the hustings, but I have been unable to find evidence as to its truth.

80According to *A Dictionary of Eminent Welshmen*, p. 608 (quoting *Old Wales*, I, p. 247) he had a seat at Hendregwenllian.

81*C & DH*, 21 May, 1836.

82Dated Dolgellau, 11 June, 1836, *ibid.*, 18 June, 1836.

83*Ibid.*, 4 June, 1836.

84The Protest refers to 12 freeholders having signed the requisition.

85For Richard Richards, see *DWB*, *sub*, Richards family of Coed, p. 850.

86*C & DH*, 25 June, 1836.

87Tithe Apportionment : 125 acres in Tywyn and 733 in Llanfrothen.

88*PP*, 1836, XLII (240).

89The result of the poll was as follows : from *Caernarvon and Denbigh Herald*, 25 June, 1836.

Polling Place	For Richards	For Wynn
Harlech	108	65
Dolgellau	97	7
Bala	137	5
Tywyn	58	70
Corwen	101	3
TOTALS	501	105

[90]*Journals of the House of Commons*, Vol. XCL, pp. 645-6.

[91]The petition against the return of Richards was presented in the name of Mr. Edward Scott, 14 Gower Street.

[92]This is discussed below, pp. 154-9. The Liberals appear to have sought the aid of the Reform Association. See Mostyn Ms. 8420 (UCNW, Bangor), Letter of James Coppock to the Hon. Lloyd Mostyn, dated from London 5 October, 1836, promising £30 to aid them in the registration.

[93]For William Watkin Edward Wynn, see *DWB*, *sub* Wynne family of Peniarth, p. 1103-4, and G. Tibbott, in *JMHS*, I (19), pp. 69-76.

[94]*C & DH*, 17 July, 1852.

[95]*Ibid.*, 17 July, 1852.

[96]For Wynne's Address see *ibid.*, 9 April, 1859, and Williams's Address, *ibid.*, 30 April, 1859.

[97]*Baner*, 11 May, 1859, and *C&DH*, 7 May, 1859.

[98]The result of the Poll was as follows : (from *ibid.*, 14 May, 1859).

Polling Place	For Williams	%	For Wynne	%
Harlech	172	68.8	78	31.8
Dolgellau	31	27.6	81	72.4
Bala	63	53.7	54	46.3
Tywyn	34	23.6	110	76.4
Corwen	51	43.5	66	56.5
TOTALS	351	47.4	389	52.6

[99]*Baner*, 11 May, 1859.

[100]The nature of the franchise is discussed in detail, below pp. 153 f.

[101]Gydros . . Acording to the Tithe Apportionment, was a farm of 588 acres in Llanfor owned by Thomas Fitzhugh, Esq. David Jones appears in the 1841 Register of Electors as the occupier of land over £50. He was Vice-Chairman of the Bala Union Guardians in 1840, acted as Chairman in 1842, Chairman from 1843 to 1846, and from 1852 to 1858. See G. Roberts, *Pum' Plwy' Penllyn*, pp. 105-6.

[102]*Baner*, 30 April, 1859.

[103]*Ibid.*, 7 May, 1859.

[104]A full list is printed in *ibid.*, 27 July, 1859.

[105]See above, p. 86.

[106]*NLW, MS.* 787, Minute Book of the Merioneth Reform Association.

[107]*Ibid.*, f. 3.

[108]*Baner*, 4 May, *Herald*, 30 April, 1859.

[109]In a letter to Mrs. Davies, Treborth, dated 20 July, 1865, quoted in T. C. Edwards, *Bywyd a Llythyrau y diweddar Barch. Lewis Edwards* (1901), p.443.

[110]*Minutes*, 2 May, f. 7.

[111]I have relied, so far as possible, on the Enumerators' Returns for 1851 and 1861 in my attempts to identify the persons named.

[112]On 5 May, *Minutes*, f. 14.

[113]*Ibid.*, f. 12.

[114]*Baner*, 27 July, 1859, and *WLCR*, Minutes of Evidence, Q. 6832.

[115]*Baner*, 27 July, 1859.

[116]*Ibid.*, 20 July, 1859.

[117]*Minutes*, f. 17.

[118]*Ibid.*, f. 18.

[119]*Ibid.*, ff. 18-19.

[120]*Ibid.*, f. 20.

[121]For John Pughe, see *DWB*, pp. 814-5.

[122]*Minutes*, 31 May, f. 23.

[123]E.g., *Minutes*, 21 June, f. 37, and 5 July, f. 47, when the nomination rule was waived.

124*Minutes,* 7 May (*sic.* i.e. June), f. 29-30.

125*Ibid.,* 7 May, ff. 33-4.

126*Ibid.,* 29 June, ff. 42-46. The letter, known as 'the Remonstrance', was printed in *Baner,* 20 July, 1859, as also the Chairman's covering letter.

127Printed in *Baner,* 20 July, 1859.

128*Minutes,* ff. 41 and 46, and *Baner,* 20 July, 1859. The correspondence was sent to *The Morning Star, Telegraph, Times, Daily News, Advertiser, Law,* and *Globe,* according to *Minutes,* 28 June, f. 41.

129The following is based mainly on an analysis of the Enumerators Returns for the Censuses of 1851 and 1861.

1301841 Voting List for parish of Llanfor. Robert Edwards was one of the Overseers to sign the Register. He was still in possession in 1851 (HO. 2510). See Letter in *Herald,* 27 August, 1859 for other details quoted.

131Tŷ-cerrig had been in the occupation of the same family for at least three generations, Thomas Ellis following his father, Edward Ellis, who had likewise followed his father Ellis Cadwaladr. See *Adgofion Andronicus* (i.e. John Williams), pp. 116-7. Thomas Ellis of Cynlas Fawr also abstained in 1859, but was not penalized. His brother, Edward Ellis, of Tŷ-cerrig (on the Glan-llyn estate) was evicted. See *WLCR,* Minutes of Evidence, Q. 6832.

132This was alleged in a letter in *Herald,* 3 September, 1859. Rhiwaedog was in the possession of Ellis Jones in 1841, according to the Voting Lists. The tenant in 1851 is given as Owen Roberts, though the farm was then stated to be of 180 acres. The Tithe Apportionment gives 410 acres.

133This information is based on the Tithe Apportionment, the Llanfor Voting List, the 1851 Census Returns, and a Letter in *Herald,* 3 September, 1859.

134Tithe Apportionment, and Census Returns 1861.

135Tithe Apportionments.

136*Baner,* 27 July, 1859. See also, the Statement of John Jones, Nant-hir, recorded in *Minutes,* 17 November, f. 78.

137Tithe Apportionment, and 1851 Census Returns which shows the farms to be occupied by Ellen Roberts, widow, aged 66 years, with a son John, aged 32, and another, Robert, aged 30.

138As stated in a letter in *Baner,* 3 August, 1859.

139For details, see *WLCR,* Minutes of Evidence, Q. 6832.

140For example, *Baner,* 20 July, 1859. All these statements, at the time and subsequently seem to agree, or to assume without question, that Fron-goch Church was built at the expense of R. W. Price. This is not at all clear. From the official correspondence between the local committee for the building of the Church and the Bishop of St. Asaph, it appears that Price gave the site at Fron-goch and £200, with a promise that he would give another £100 should there be a deficiency. In November 1856, subscriptions amounted to £653 8s. 0d. towards the architect's estimated cost of £920. The Church was eventually built at a cost of £1300 paid for by the subscription, no mention being made of any paricular benefactor, which would have been the case if one person or family had made very substantial gifts. The income of the new church consisted of the rectorial tithes, Rent Charges arising within the district of Fron-goch which amounted to £96 9s. 0d. See correspondence respecting the proposed new Church in NLW Church in Wales, MSS, SA/Lets/462, 463, 474, 607, 710, 636, and 800. Also, *PP,* 1876, LVIII (C. 125 & 125 I), 'Returns showing number of churches . . . built or restored . . . since . . . 1840', p. 62 (Deanery of Penllyn Edeirnion).

141*WLCR, op. cit.,* evidence of Mr. Ivan T. Davies, Q. 6829.

142*Baner,* 24 August, 1859.

143*Minutes,* 17 November, f. 78.

144*Baner,* 20 July, 1859.

145The following is based on the Tithe Apportionments and the Census material for 1851 and 1861 cited above. *Andronicus, op. cit.,* p. 113, writes about Ellis Roberts and others as belonging to the 'upper ten' of Penllyn's religious community.

[146]For lists of Guardians see G. Roberts (Gwrtheyrn), *op. cit.*

[147]*Minutes*, 12 July, f. 49, and *passim.*

[148]*Herald*, 28 May, 1859. Letter signed ' Gutyn Ebrill, Brithdir.'

[149]On the slate industry in general, see A. H. Dodd, *The Industrial Revolution in North Wales* (2nd edn. 1951), pp. 203 ff., and in particular G. J. Williams, *Hanes Plwyf Ffestiniog* (? 1882), *passim.*

[150]The following statistics are taken from G. J. Williams, *op. cit.*, p. 107.

Exports of Slates from Ffestiniog :

1825—11,396 tons	1855— 43,279 tons
1835—18,113 "	1865— 89,293 "
1845—43,848 "	1875—140,017 "

[151]The population of, and numbers of inhabited houses in, the parish of Ffestiniog 1801-71 were as follows :

Year	Inhabited houses	Population
1801		732
1811		961
1821		1168
1831		1648
1841	559	3138
1851	671	3460
1861	885	4553
1871	1648	8055

Sources : Census Returns.

[152]A. H. Dodd, *op. cit.*, p. 220.

[153]This can be traced in the histories of the various undertakings given in G. J. Williams, *op. cit.*

[154]G. J. Williams, *op. cit.*, gives the names of agents and managers.

[155]This point is well made by A. H. Dodd, *op cit.*, and can be documented from G. J. Williams and denominational histories.

[156]For the growth in the facilities provided by the Church of England, see G. J. Williams, *op. cit.*, pp. 000 and

[157]On the Liberation Society, see below, pp. 236. The statistics on which this section is based are taken from the annual *Reports* of the Society.

[158]*Ibid.*, pp. 219 ff.

[159]An account of these conferences is to be found in *Welsh Nonconformisty and the Welsh Representation.* Papers and Speeches read and delivered at the Conferences held September and October 1866 (n.d.). Fuller accounts of some of the proceedings and speeches are to be found in some of the local newspapers.

[160]Full reports appeared in *Baner*, 3 October, 1866.

[161]*Welsh Nonconformity and Welsh Representation*, pp. 28-33.

[162]This was the Secretary of the Reform Society.

[163]*Baner*, 3 October, 1866.

[164]This section is based on the following *PP*, 1836, XLIII (240); 1837-8, XLIV (329), 1844, XXXVIII (329); 1846, XXXIII (284); 1847, XLVI (751); 1852, XLII(8), 1857 (2nd Sess.), XXXIV, (4), 1866, LVII (3736), and 1868-9, L, (418).

[165]They are preserved in the Merioneth County Record Office, Dolgellau.

[166]*Baner*, 30 September, 1868.

[167]*Ibid.*, 14 October, 1868, and *CDH*, 10 October, 1868.

[168]This election can be studied in the files of *The Merioneth Standard*, C & DH, *Herald*, and *Baner*. W.R.M. Wynne's Address is to be found in the *Merionethshire Herald*, 17 June, 1865, and that of David Williams in, e.g. *Baner*, 28 June, 1865. They are dated 7 June from Peniarth and Castell Deudraeth respectively.

[169]There are stray references to the recent introduction of game on the Rhiwlas estates in speeches and newspapers articles.

[170]*Baner*, 19 July, 1865 prints the lists of names.

171Reports of this appeared in, e.g. *Ibid.*, 19 July, 1865.

172In his evidence before the Hartington Committee. *PP*, 1870, VI (115), Q. 6584.

173In an Address to the Electors, dated 26 July, printed in *Baner*, 2 August, 1865.

174The votes were cast as follows :

Voting Place	For Williams	For Wynne
Harlech	248	129
Tywyn	84	172
Dolgellau	77	98
Bala	78	177
Corwen	88	99
TOTAL	575	615

Baner, 26 July, 1865.

175The course of the election can be studied in the *C&DH* and *Baner*, etc.

176*Baner*, 14 October, 1868.

177This was obviously the import of a sermon preached by him in 1865, *Baner*, 28 June, 1865.

178The question of the cost of the election was probably a major consideration also. The previous election had cost him £3,065 5s. 8d. as against Williams's cost of £1.070 4s. 3d. See *PP*, 1866, LVI (160). As it was, he was faced with a bill for £2,083 6s. 11d.—and the knowledge that David Williams was being supported without cost to himself. See *ibid.*, 1868/9, L, (424) for the election expenses.

179Quoted in *Cymru, art. cit.* (' Deudraeth Castle stands secure, And Peniarth is in ruins ').

CARDIGANSHIRE POLITICS IN MID-NINETEENTH CENTURY

1' Etholiadau Ceredigion a Meirionydd, gan Awdur "Adgofion am Ysgol Neuaddlwyd",' *Y Traethodydd*, 3rd Series, Vol. IV (1865), pp. 488-512.

For another example of his polemical style see *Kilsby Jones's Deliverance on Toryism versus Liberalism. An Address delivered at Dolgelley, on Friday, July 21st, 1865 to the Electors of Merionethshire* (Aberystwyth, 1865).

2Both John Matthews and John Jones are noticed in *DWB* (1959), the former *sub. nom.* John Matthews (1773-1848), his father.

3See the letter of John Matthews to E. L. Pryse, Esq., dated 28 August 1856, in Letters of John Matthews, NLW MS. 8321.

4The letters of Kilsby to John Jones are preserved in NLW MS. 3291.

5*The Welshman*, 12 August, 1864. The election is best studied in this weekly newspaper and in the files of *Baner*.

6Details of the poll are as follows, based on *The Welshman*, 21 July, 1865 ;

Polling District	Votes Cast	For Lloyd	For Davies	% Lloyd	% Davies
Cardigan ..	425	360	65	84.7	15.3
Aberaeron ..	514	299	215	58.1	41.9
Lampeter ..	220	94	126	42.7	57.3
Tregaron ..	386	96	290	24.9	75.1
Llandysul ..	263	200	63	76.1	23.9
Aberystwyth ..	851	461	390	54.1	45.9
	2659	1510	1149	56.7	43.3

[7]For Davies's Address see *Baner*, 2 August 1865 ; it is also printed in full in Kilsby's article cited above. See also the article ' Etholiad Aberteifi ' in *Baner*, 26 July, 1865. Henry Richard's Address, dated from London, 14 July, 1865, can be read in *ibid.*, 19 July, 1865, or in *Y Byd Cymreig*, 13 July, 1865. For typical comment see the review of Kilsby's *Traethodydd* article in *Y Cronicl*, Vol. XXIII (November 1865), p. 303.

[8]On this see an interesting correspondence in *The Welshman*, 1 September, 1865. Davies estimated that the construction of the railway from Lampeter to Aber- aeron would cost £110,000 (including rolling stock). Of this sum, £30,000 could be borrowed, leaving £80,000 to be raised locally—a quarter of what the whole of Wales had subscribed during the past seven years towards the cost of construcing 700 miles of railways. Obviously, Davies himself would not invest in the venture.

[9]The edition of 1883 was used in the preparation of this paper.

[10]*PP*, 1874, LXXII (1097).

[11]J. M. Howells, in his paper ' The Crosswood Estate, 1547-1947, ' *Ceredigion*, (1956), shows that the estate, though heavily encumbered, was still intact. Income from rents in 1870 totalled £10,590, and lead royalties averaged £3,725 *per annum* between 1860 and 1868 (ibid., pp. 15-16).

[12]The holdings of the major landed proprietors were as follows :

Lisburne	42,890 acres	
Pryse	26,684	
Powell	21,933	91,507
Harford	5,782	
Gwynne	3,794	9,576
		101,083

Total acreage of county	398,657
Total waste in county	6,971
Total cultivated acreage	391,686

[13]Details are as follows :

7 families owned a total of	27,752	acres
20 families owned a total of	58,256	"
18 families owned a total of	32,370	"
	118,378	acres

[14]E. Walford, *The County Families of the United Kingdom* (1860), lists 25 Cardigan- shire families. The 1864 edition of Burke's *County Families* lists 46.

[15]For John Lloyd Davies see *Dictionary of Welsh Biography* and Benjamin Williams (Gwynionydd), *Enwogion Ceredigion* (1869), pp. 35-6.

[16]Aspects of the social life of Aberystwyth in the early part of the century have been described by W. J. Lewis, *Ceredigion* 1959 and 1960. For more recent work, especially on the social structure and political life of Aberystwyth, see Ieuan Gwynedd Jones (ed.), *Aberystwyth 1277-1977* (1977).

[17]Thus, at Aberystwyth, Bridge Street was regarded as the centre of the working- class district. See *Aberystwyth Observer*, 5 January, 1867.

[18]Population Returns, PRO, HO 107, RG9/4198.

[19]It would be tedious to multiply examples of these attitudes ; students of the periodical literature of those years will be familiar with them ; almost any issue, for example, of the *Baner* in election years will furnish examples.

20*Yr Athraw.* Cylchgrawn Misol dan olygiaeth y Parch. William Thomas, MA., September, 1865, prints an article on ' Bugeiliaid Sir Aberteifi '. Beneath the romantic, lyrical view of the writer (presumably the editor) are the realities of a hard, cruel life for the children of the small farmers, of poverty too great to admit the effective exploitation of the elementary means of education provided by the chapels.

21*Aberystwyth Observer,* 29 June, 1867. This judgement should be compared with the section on Aberystwyth in the Municipal Corporations Report of 1835.

22The most revealing and reliable account is to be found in a letter of John Matthews, referred to above, to his son John Matthews, of Amlwch, dated 22 July, 1865, in NLW MS. 8321. This should be compared with Richard's own account in *Baner,* 19 July, 1865. For the rôle of the Liberation Society in these affairs see, in general, below, pp. 236 f, and the Minute Book of the Parliamentary Sub-Committee under 29 June, 3, 4, 6, and 8 July, 1865. The report of this committee to the Executive Committee on 21 July makes it clear that Richard's decision to retire was made on the advice of people present at the Aberaeron meeting (*see* Liberation Society Minute Books, IV, L.C.C., A/Lib/3, Minute 563). The Minute Book of the Parliamentary SubCommittee is L.C.C., A/Lib/13.

23Mr. Matthews was embarrassed because Henry Richard's agents were at that moment in the front parlour discussing Richard's prospects. The unexpected new-comers were shown into the back parlour, and so the two rival parties were kept separate. See letter cited above in NLW MS. 8321.

24It would be interesting to know how many of these were Cardiganshire men and how many Irish.

25David Williams, ' The Census of Religious Worship of 1851 in Cardiganshire,' *Ceredigion,* IV, Number 2 (1961). See also I. G. Jones, ' The Elections of 1865 and 1868,' *T. H. S. C.,* (1964 Pt 1.), pp. 45-9 and 67-8.

26The Independents appear to have believed that the northern part of the county had been lost to their denomination by the activities of Mr. Thomas Gray, the successor to the famous Philip Pugh, whose Methodistical tendencies and con-nections had been such as to discourage the subsequent attempts early in the century of Azariah Shadrach to re-establish the churches in the region of Llwyn-piod, Blaenpennal, and Lledrod. ' Yr ydym,' wrote the historians of the Inde-pendent churches, ' yn teimlo fod yn bur annaturiol fod yr hen enwad a gymerodd y meddiant cyntaf o'r wlad hono wedi ei gau allan yn llwyr o honi . . . trwy anffyddlondeb un a aeth yno i'w wasanaethu '. T. Rees and J. Thomas, *Hanes Eglwysi Annibynol Cymru,* IV (1875), p. 210.

27One correspondent made much of the fact that Davies engaged the Reverend T. C. Edwards, son of Dr. Lewis Edwards of Bala, to preach to his workmen— ' *y navvies* beiddgar ac anystyriol sydd wrth y cannoedd yn ei wasanaethu '— presumably in vacation time. *Baner,* 12 July, 1865.

28For a survey of this see below, pp. 236.

29This information is based on the Secretary's Cash Book for the years 1844-6 (L.C.C. A/Lib/89), and thereafter on the published annual *Reports.*

30*Baner,* 19 July, 1865.

31The quotation is taken from the letters of John Matthews, *op. cit.* On Capel-y-Drindod see Evan Davies, *Hanes Plwyf Llangunllo* (Llandysul, 1905), pp. 85-6.

32For Bwlch-y-Groes Chapel see Rees and Thomas, *op. cit.,* IV, p. 206.

33Referring to the visit of Richard's agents on the business of the election, John Matthews wrote, ' I did not know what to do, as the Methodists at Aberystwyth were placed in a very awkward predicament. Our old chapel the Tabernacle is erected on Lease on the Col's land ; this lease is now approaching its termination and we have been in correspondence with the Col. for a renewal of the lease intending immediately on obtaining that renewal to commence renovating the old Tab. and spending some thousand pounds or more in so doing. The Col. has promised us the renewal of the lease ; but owing to some difficulties arising from the settlement of the Nanteos property the thing had not been completed. Under the circumstances I was crippled. I could not promise to take any active part in the business without consulting the friends lest I whould compromise the matter and bring myself into trouble with the brethren.' John Matthews to his son, 22 July, 1865, NLW MS. 8321.

34' From time immemorial there has been one (i.e., a church rate) in that parish, proposed almost always by the Churchwarden, who has acted in that capacity for nearly forty years. He is an "Independent" in religion, and the principal persons who have attended the vestry (for the purpose of making a rate) belong to the same denomination, and when I asked them if they really wished for it their reply was they did not desire to alter the *"hen gwstwm"*. However, within the last two years some murmurs have arisen against the rate, and I this year wrote to the vestry recommending its abandonment.' Copy of a letter of Sir Thomas Lloyd (in Kilby's hand), in Ivon Letters, NLW MS. 3291, Folder 21.

35*Baner*, 19 July 1865.

36Davies's Address to the Cardiganshire electors, *Baner*, 2 August, 1865.

37For Cobden's letters to Richard, 1849-65, see Cobden Papers, Vols. XI-XIII, BM Add. MSS. 43657-9.

38Kilsby to John Jones, 21 November 1865, Ivon Letters, NLW MS. 3291. *Baner*, 14 June, 1865, prints the pre-election manifesto of the South Wales Committee of the Liberation Society, meeting at Aberdare the previous May.

39For some of Davies's gifts, see the letter of John Matthews to his son already cited.

40*Ibid.*

41*Aberystwyth Observer*, 24 August, 1865. For a review of Morley's gifts to Welsh causes, see the interesting paper by Henry Richard in Edwin Hodder, *The Life of Samuel Morley* (1887), pp. 294-301.

42See Liberation Society Minute Books, L.C.C. A/Lib/3, Minute 598 (27 October, 1865), *et seq*, and *ibid.*, Minute 774, where he is paid £7.15.6 expenses for carrying out the registration (19 October, 1866).

43Kilsby to John Jones, 21 November, 1865, Ivon Letters, *op. cit.* There is an interesting reference to the National Freehold Land Society in a letter of Cobden to Henry Richard, 20 August, 1852, in the Cobden Papers cited above, which suggests that Richard, as secretary of the Peace Society, was interested in this method of political organization. Richard was one of the Londoners whom Kilsby consulted.

44I have seen only one reference to this, in *Baner*, 26 July, 1865.

45Based on the Ivon Letters, *op. cit.*

46See Thomas Nicholas, *Middle and High Class Schools, and University Education for Wales* (1853), and *The Welshman*, among other newspapers, 2 September, 1864, for reports of the discussion on Nicholas's paper on the same subject before the Social Science section of the National Eisteddfod at Llandudno.

47The newspaper scheme can be studied in the Ivon Letters, *op. cit.*

48*Aberystwyth Observer*, 22 August, 1865. See also *Baner*, 26 July, 1865.

49Colonel Lewes, of Llanllŷr, Inglis Jones, of Derry Ormond, A. Saunders Davies, of Pentre, J. B. Harford, of Falcondale, were all mentioned, as was Howell Gwyn, of Neath, from outside the country. *The Welshman*, 12 August, 1864 *passim*. It is clear from correspondence in the same newspaper in June 1865 that Trawscoed was not responding to demands that the Lisburnes should give a lead.

50Ibid., 8 December, 1865.

51Both voted against Gladstone's amendment on borough franchises. Both abstained from voting on Gladstone's amendment concerning the borough franchise, 12 April, 1867. In a letter to the *Aberystwyth Observer*, 27 April, 1867, Lloyd explained that he had done so because he was convinced that the government's proposal was more liberal than Gladstone's, and pointing out that Liberals like Dillwyn had carried their objections to the point of voting against their party.

52These developments can be traced in the files of *The Welshman*, *Aberystwyth Observer*, and *Baner*.

⁵³*PP*, 1868-9, L (424). The 1865 election cost Sir Thomas Lloyd £3,300.19.8, and David Davies £2,969.17.9. Ibid., 1866, LVI (160).

⁵⁴See, for example, Slater's *Directory* for 1868. *The Cambrian*, 11 September, 1868, reprints an article from *The Mining Journal* on the crucial rôle Richards was expected to play, as an industrialist, in the economic development of Cardiganshire. The county's future prosperity, it pointed out, ' is bound up wholly and solely with the prosperity of their mines—if their mineral interests languish, every other department of their trade and commerce suffers, and there can be no general expansion of industrial pursuits '.

⁵⁵These movements can be traced in the letters of John Matthews, *op. cit.*, especially E. M. Richards to Matthews, 17 August, 1868, David Davies to same, 1 August, 1868, and Evan Davies to same, 17 August, 1868. See also, for example, Richard's speech in *Aberystwyth Observer*, 22 August, 1868.

⁵⁶*The Welshman*, 23 October, 1868.

⁵⁷Examples of these attitudes can be found in the speeches made at the nomination meeting for the borough seat at Aberystwyth, *The Welshman*, 31 July, 1868, and in letters in the correspondence columns of the newspapers, e.g., ibid., 9 November, 1868.

⁵⁸*Aberystwyth Observer*, 22 August, 1868.

⁵⁹For Vaughan's two Addresses see *Aberystwyth Observer*, 11 July and 5 September, 1868.

⁶⁰For Thomas Harries's evidence before the Hartington Commission, see Report from the Select Committee on Parliamentary and Municipal Elections, *PP*, 1868-9, VIII (352), and 1870, VI (115).

⁶¹For details of the poll see *T.H.S.C.*, (1964), p. 65, note 57.

THE ELECTION OF 1868
IN MERTHYR TYDFIL

¹Richard polled 11,683, Fothergill 7,139, and Bruce 5,776 votes. The official returns are given in *PP*, 1868-69, Vol. L (424).

²See Grant Duff, "Henry Austin Bruce, first Baron Aberdare" (after 1873), *DNB*, Supplement 1, p. 322.

³W. R. Williams, *The Parliamentary History of . . . Wales* (Brecknock 1895), p. 111.

⁴*Daily News*, November 17, 1868.

⁵*PP*, 1874, LXXII (1097) "Return of owners of land, 1872-73", *sub*. Lord Aberdare, Glamorganshire.

⁶*Morning Star*, December 4, 1868, analyzed the significance of the swing to liberalism in Wales and attributed it to the strength of nonconformity. The *Daily News*, November 18, 1868, stated that, next to the defeat of John Stuart Mill at Westminster, that of Bruce was the most to be deplored. See also *Manchester Guardian*, November 18, 1868.

⁷See the evidence of G. T. Clark in *PP*, 1867-68, XXIX (*Reports from commissioners*) [3980-81], "Royal commissioners on trade unions, fifth report," pp. 82-93 ; the Dowlais papers in the Glamorgan County Record Office, Cardiff ; A. Dalziel, *The Colliers' Strike in South Wales* (Cardiff, 1872), p. 18.

⁸*PP*. 1831-32, Vol. XLII, (141), "Reports from commissioners on proposed divisions of counties and boundaries of boroughs," Parts VII and VIII ; *PP*, 1867-68, Vol. XX (3972), "Boundaries Commission report."

⁹*PP*, 1866, LVII (3626), "Electors returns, 1865-66."

¹⁰*PP*, 1866, Vol. XVII (170).

¹¹*PP*, 1868-69, Vol. L (419).

¹²N. Gash, *Politics in the Age of Peel* (London, 1953), pp. 199-200.

[13]C. Seymour, *Electoral Reform in England and Wales* (New Haven, 1915), chap. iii.

[14]See *Aberdare Times*, June 29 and July 9, 1867.

[15]*Aberdare Times*, June 29, 1867. See also *Seren Cymru*, December 13, 1867.

[16]Robert Crawshay to Thomas Stephens, November 5, 1868, *NLW*, Cyfarthfa Papers, "Letter book, 1865-70." See also Crawshay's eve-of-the-poll statement reported in *Merthyr Star*, April 9, 1867 ; *Dowlais and Aberdare Gazette*, April 17, 1867 ; *Merthyr Express*, November 21, 1868.

[17]DWB, *sub* Thomas Price, and Ieuan Gwynedd Jones, "Dr. Thomas Price and the Election of 1868 ', *WHR*, 2, No. 2 (1964), pp. 147-172 and No. 3 (1965), pp. 251-270.

[18]*Cambrian*, September 26, 1862 ; *Nonconformist*, XX (1862), 727-832.

[19]James was to represent Merthyr in parliament, 1880-88, see W. R. Williams, *op. cit.*, p. 111.

[20]*Aberdare Times*, July 27 and 31, 1867 ; *Cardiff Times*, July 13 and September 3, 1867 ; *Baner* July 31, 1867.

[21]See *Aberdare Times*, October 5, 1867, and above, pp. 165-92.

[22]*Daily Post*, September 14, 1867. For Richard's close association with the philanthropist Samuel Morley see Edwin Hodder, *Life of Samuel Morley* (London 1887), pp. 293-301, and Charles S. Miall, *Henry Richard, M.P. : a biography* (London, 1889) p. 155.

[23]For Cobden's letters to Richard, 1849-65, see Cobden papers, Vols. XI-XIII, *BM* Add. MSS 43657-59.

[24]Richard became a member of the executive committee of the Liberation Society in June, 1862, when the Welsh campaign was being organized. See Liberation Society "Minute book," Vol. IV, minute 79 (June 13, 1862) *LCC*, MS A/LIB /3. See below, p. 260.

[25]See Henry Richard, *Letters and Essays on Wales* (London, 1884), pp. 80-89.

[26]*Aberdare Times*, October 26, 1867.

[27]In this connection it is interesting to note that of the thirty-nine chapels in Aberdare twenty-eight belonged to the three oldest dissenting denominations (i.e., the Independents, Baptists, and Unitarians), and in Merthyr twenty-seven out of a total of forty-two. Of the four Unitarian ministers in the constituency, three held executive posts on the Nonconformists Representation Committee. See Jones and Williams, *The Religious Census of* 1851, op. cit., pp. 163-190.

[28]*Baner*, September 25, 1867 ; *Merthyr Telegraph*, September 21, 1867. The work by Ernest Jones discussed at this meeting was evidently the lecture on labour and capital later published as a pamphlet. Extracts from this are printed in John Saville, *Ernest Jones, Chartist* (London, 1952), pp. 80, 227-30.

[29]E.g., see *Aberdare Times*, July 13, 1867 ; *Seren Cymru*, December 13, 1867. For Bruce's sanguine views on his prospects see Bruce to Lord de Grey, October 2 and 30, 1868, Ripon Papers, Vol. XLIV, *BM*, Add. MSS 43,534.

[30]The movement of coal prices and wages during this period can be studied conveniently in Dalziel ; the course of the strike itself in the *Cardiff and Merthyr Guardian*, *Merthyr Telegraph*, and *Y Gwron*, November 1857 to February 1858. For Bruce's telegram to the home office requesting the removal of the troops see H. A. Bruce to Home Office, December 5, 1857, Public Record Office, H.O. 45/7239t.

[31]The situation, from the point of view of the ironmasters, was analyzed in a memorandum by W. Menelaus dated July 1866 (Dowlais papers, D/Dg, section 3, box 5).

[32]Dafydd Morgannwg, *Hanes Morgannwg* (Aberdare, 1874), pp. 63-64, gives a list (incomplete) of these explosions.

[33]Nixon expounded his views in a letter published in the London and South Wales newspapers, See, e.g., *Aberdare Times*, November 23, 1867. He also issued a pamphlet, *The single shift system the cause of double the loss of life* (Cardiff, 1867). For the reactions of the colliers see *Y Gwladgarwr*, November 23, 1867, and *Seren Cymru*, January 3, 1868.

[34]*Gwladgarwr*, December 14 and 21, 1867.

35*Ibid.*, February 1, 1868 ; and *Cardiff and Merthyr Guardians*, February 1, 1868. For the decision to petition parliament see *Seren Cymru*, Febuary 28, 1868.

36See *Gwladgarwr*, January-March, 1868. *Seren Cymru*, March **27**, 1868, reviewed the first edition of the pamphlet (issued in Welsh and in English), *Double and single shift working compared* (Aberdare, 1868).

37*Aberdare Times*, January 18, 1868. Cf. the reports of the lectures given by Samuel Roberts upon his return from America in *Cronicl*, March, April, and May 1868. See David Rees's articles in *Diwygiwr* May 1868 ; and Thomas Gee's editorials in *Baner*, March-May, especially that of April 15, 1868, on the state of representation.

38*Aberdare Times*, May 9, 1868. The petition was reported to be sixty-five feet long.

39The activities of the Liberation Society in Wales after 1862 are most conveniently studied in the files of the *Nonconformist*, see below pp. 000.

40*Aberdare Times*, February 15 and 22, March 7, and April 4, 1868. See also Bruce's speech on the second reading of the Education of the Poor Bill, July 10, 1867, Great Britain, 3 *Hansard*, CLXXXVIII (1867), 1317-42. The speech was later published as a pamphlet.

41For these efforts see Henry Richard to Thomas Gee, August 25, 1868 (supporting these attacks) ; and Thomas Stephens to Thomas Gee, Sept. 12, 1868 (protesting against the attacks), *NLW*, Thomas Gee correspondence, MSS 8305. For Gee's participation in these attacks on Bruce see *Baner*, February 12, 1867, and June 12 and 24, July 8, and August 12 and 19, 1868 ; T. Gwynn Jones, *Cofiant Thomas Gee* (Denbigh, 1913), pp. 174-89. See also Bruce's "Second address" in *Aberdare Times*, October 10, 1868 ; and his speeches in *Merthyr Telegraph*, October 4, 1868, and in *Baner*, September 9, 1868.

42E.g. Bruce's pamphlet, *Merthyr Tydfil in 1852* (Merthyr, 1852). See also the ecturers reprinted in *Lecturers and addresses by . . . Henry Austin Bruce* (London n.d.).

43*Merthyr Star*, April 17, 1867.

44For the activities of these societies see the files of the *Merthyr Star* and *Gwladgarwr*.

45*Merthyr Star*, June 5, 1867 ; *Merthyr Telegraph*, October 10, 1868.

46Great Britain, 3 *Hansard*, CXCII (June 12, 1868) 1498-1503 ; *Times*, June 5, 13, and 15, 1868.

473 *Hansard*, CXCII (June 12, 1863), 1503.

48*Times*, June 13, 1868.

49*Ibid.*, June 15, 1868.

50The Bruce family held the royalties from most of the coal being worked in the Mountain Ash district. In March 1868 Bruce had written to his father J. Bruce-Pryce, to the effect that the double-shift system would be greatly to the advantage of the landlord (*Letters of Lord Aberdare* [Oxford, 1902], I, 253-54).

51Printed in *Gwladgarwr*, October 16, 1868.

52"Address to the working men electors of Merthyr Tydfil, Aberdare and Vaynor," *Aberdare Times*, October 10, 1868.

53The Guest letter is printed in the *Cardiff and Merthyr Guardian*, October 17, 1868.

54*Merthyr Epxress*, November 21, 1868.

55For the reaction of the electorate see *Aberdare Times*, October 24, 1868 ; *Seren Cymru*, October 30, 1868.

56One paper reported that Bruce told a meeting : "You may hold up your dirty hands against me, but tomorrow I'll be Member for Merthyr in spite of you" (*Aberdare Times*, October 17, 1868).

57The meeting was called at the invitation of Bruce (*Merthyr Telegraph*, October 24, 1868). For accounts of the meeting see the *Aberdare Times*, November 7, 1868 ; *Baner*, November 4, 1868.

58The Dowlais papers in the Glamorgan Record Office throw considerable light on these differences.

[59]*Aberdare Times*, October 2, 1868 ; *Merthyr Telegraph*, October 17 and 24, 1868.
[60]*Aberdare Times*, August 29, and November 14, 1868.
[61]See the *Times*, November 23, 1868 ; *Manchester Guardian*, November 18, 1868 ; *Saturday Review*, XXVI (1868), 667-68 ; and W. N. Molesworth, *The history of England, 1830-1874* (2nd ed. ; London, 1874), III, 353-56.
[62]*Manchester Guardian*, December 9, 1868. Bruce seems not to have realized the significance of what had happened. Shortly after the election, he told a friend that Richard represented the chapel *eisteddfod* and Fothergill the low, selfish political morality of the majority (Bruce to Lord de Grey, November 18 and December 5, 1868, Ripon papers, Vol. XLIV, British Museum, Add. MSS 43,534). Years later, Bruce was still interpreting the events of the election in personal terms (*Letters of Lord Aberdare*, II, 169).

RELIGION AND SOCIETY

[1]Horace Mann, ' On the Statistical Position of Religious Bodies in England and Wales ', *Journal of the Royal Statistical Society*, XVIII (1855), p. 155.
[2]*Census of Great Britain* 1851 : *Religious Worship* : *England and Wales* (1953), pp. xc-xciii.
[3]' I dare say, that upon closer examination, certain peculiarities, of social condition or otherwise, would be discovered as distinguishing the counties in which dissent is powerful, from those in which the Church predominates ', *art. cit.*, p. 156.
[4]See, for example, W. S. F. Pickering, ' The 1851 religious census—a useless experiment ? ', *British Journal of Sociology*, XVIII, No. 4 (December, 1967), pp. 382 ff., R. M. Goodridge, ' The Religious Condition of the West Country in 1851 ', *Social Compass* : *International Review of Socio-Religious Studies*, XIV, No. 4 (1697), p. 285 ff., John D. Gay, *The Geography of Religion in England* (1971) and David Martin, *A Sociology of English Religion* (1967). Full references are to be found in Gay. For Wales, see above pp. 18 f., and *The Religious Census of* 1851, op. cit., pp. xi-xxxv.
[5]K. S. Inglis, *Churches and the Working Classes in Victorian England* (1963).
[6]The following is based on the *Report*.
[7]*Ibid.*, p. cliii.
[8]Edward Miall, *The British Churches in relation to the British People* (1849).
[9]Census Report of 1851.
[10]Census Report of 1861.
[11]C. Booth, *Life and Labour of the People in London*, Vol. 7, *Religious Influences* (1920-3). See also Andrew Mearns, *The Bitter Cry of Outcast London* (1883) ed. with other selections by Anthony S. Wohn (1970).
[12]See, for example, Asa Briggs, *Victorian Cities* (1964). Also J. D. Marshall, ' Colonisation as a Factor in the Planting of Towns in North-West England ' in H. J. Dyos(ed.), *The Study of Urban History* (1968), which also contains a full detailed bibliography.
[13]Harold Carter, *The Towns of Wales* (1966) and his paper, ' Phases of Town Growth in Wales ' in Dyos, *op. cit.*
[14]N.L.W., MS. 4943.
[15]See I. G. Jones, ' The South Wales Collier in Mid-nineteenth Century ', *Victorian South Wales—Architecture, Industry and Society* (Victorian Society 1971).
[16]See, for example, T. W. Rammell, *Report . . . on a Preliminary Inquiry into . . . the Sanitary Condition of the Town of Merthyr Tydfil* (1850), and ' Labour and the Poor. The Mining and Manufacturing Towns of South Wales ', *Morning Chronicel*, March to April 1850.
[17]F. Engels, ' The Condition of the Working Class in England in 1844 ' in Karl Marx and Frederick Engels, *On Britain* (Moscow, 1953), pp. 158-9.
[18]E. Miall, *op. cit.*

19H. Mann, *op. cit.*, pp. clviii ff.
20H. J. Dyos, *Victorian Suburb* (1961).
21*Report*, pp. viii-ix, and the note on p. viii.
22For a discussion of the difference between ' pre-Millenialism ' and ' post-Millenialism ' see J. F. C. Harrison, *Robert Owen and the Owenties in Great Britain and America. The Quest for a New Moral World* (1969), pp. 92 ff., and the same author's article in *Bulletin of the Society of Labour History*, 22 (1971).
23See R. Currie, *Methodism Divided* (1968).

THE LIBERATION SOCIETY
AND WELSH POLITICS

1In *Studies in Stuart Wales* (1952), p. 215.
2See, for example, Rev. John Roberts in *Y Cronicl*, April 1862, and Rev. David Rees in *Y Diwygiwr*, February 1861.
3For a history of the Deputies see B. L. Manning, *The Protestant Dissenting Deputies*, edited by O. Greenwood (1952).
4*A Sketch of the History and Proceedings of the Deputies appointed to protect the Civil Rights of the Protestant Dissenters* (1813), p. 4.
5After describing the efforts of the Deputies on behalf of Rev. Lewis Rees of Llanbrynmair (the father of Dr. Abraham Rees), the authors of the *Sketch* comment thus : ' The knowledge that a body existed in the metropolis for obtaining the protection of the law in favour of Dissenting Ministers served, in a considerable degree, to restrain the violence of their persecutors.' *Ibid.*, p. 24.
6Manning, *op. cit.*, pp. 289-90.
7The *Sketch* contains a classified list of cases in which the Deputies interfered. Details of these are to be found in the *Minutes of the Dissenting Deputies, Guildhall* MSS. 3083/1-10.
8For the activities of the Protestant Society see James Bennett, *History of Dissenters during the last thirty years from 1808 to 1838* (1839) ; B. Brook, *A History of Religious Liberty . . . to the death of George III* (1820), *II*, 438 *et seq.* ; H. S. Skeats, *A History of the Free Churches of England, 1688-1851* (1868), pp. 558 *et seq.* ; and Raymond G. Cowherd, *The Politics of English Dissent* (1959), p. 20.
9' Bond of Indemnity ', dated 17 November 1857, winding up the Society, and transferring its assets to the Dissenting Deputies. Manuscripts in the Dr. Williams's Library.
10*Ibid.*, f. 1.
11The Protestant Society : Treasurer's Book. Manuscript in the Dr. Williams's Library.
12The Protestant Society : Minute Book, f. 10. Manuscript in the Dr. Williams's Library.
13See *Report of the Fisrt Triennial Conference, May* 1847 (1847).
14The Protestant Society : Minute Book, ff. 11-12.
15*Minutes of the Dissenting Deputies, Guildhall* MS. 3083/7.
16Ibid., Guildhall MS 3083/8, ff. 33 *et seq.*
17Ibid., Guildhall MS. 3083/8, f. 19.
18' Brief Statement of the Case of Protestant Dissenters ', in *Minutes of the United Committee appointed to consider the Grievances under which Dissenters now labour with a view to their Redress*, Guildhall MSS. 3086/1, ff. 127-33. Also published as a pamphlet and printed in the newspapers (e.g. *Patriot*, 8 January 1834) and magazines.
19Robert Winter resigned mainly because he was convinced that the new policy being pursued was ' incompatible with Christian Obligation ', would ' engender religious strife and . . . bring down Protestant Dissenters from the higher Ground of Christian Independence . . . to the much lower grade of political party '. Minutes of the Dissenting Deputies, Guildhall MS. 3083/8, f. 252.
20Skeats, op. cit., p. 598.

[21]A. Miall, *The Life of Edward Miall* (1884), pp. 38 *et seq.* See also J. Waddington, IV, 551-3, for extracts from articles in the early numbers of the *Nonconformist*, in which Miall expounds his views.

[22]H. S. Skeats, op. cit., p. 606.

[23]R. G. Cowherd, op. cit., p. 111.

[24]For details of the Leicester Conference, 7 December, 1843, and subsequent arrangements for the London Conference, see the files of the *Nonconformist*, and the paper of Dr. A. F. Cox read at the London Conference, 30 April 1844, ' History of the circumstances which have led to the conference, and justifications of the movement ', in *Proceedings of the First Anti-State Church Conference* (1844).

[25]*Seren Gomer*, March and April 1844, and *Diwygiwr*, May 1844, the former acknowledging a letter from Dr. Cox on methods of appointing delegates to the proposed Conference, the latter reporting a meeting of the West Glamorgan Independent Association at Swansea which appointed such delegates.

[26]*Diwygiwr*, July 1844, *passim*.

[27]See *Minutes of the Third General Meeting of the Congregational Union of England and Wales* (1833), Resolution XI, p. 41. The Articles are to be found in the *Congregational Year Book*, and are printed in J. Waddington, op. cit., pp. 652-6. For the relevance of Article IX referred to, see H. S. Skeats, op. cit., p. 591.

[28]Anti-State-Church Association, ' Secretary's Cash Book ', L.C.C. Record Office, MS. A/LIB/89.

[29]The analysis which follows is based on statistics abstracted from the annual reports of the Association.

[30]Delegates to conferences were not required to be subscribing members : all that was required was ' an implied concurrence in the Society's objects and in the propriety of organized efforts to obtain for them legislative sanction '. Liberation Society Minute Books, L.C.C. MS. A/LIB/S, M.867 (29 October, 1858). See also A/LIB/3, M.115 (19 September, 1862).

[31]See N. McCord, *The Anti-Corn Law League* (1958), pp. 103-7, for an account of the 1841 Manchester Conference of Ministers, and references therein, especially to J. Waddington, op. cit., IV, 556-64. For the attitude of the Association to the League, see *Report of the First Triennial Conference* (1847): ' They abstained, during the continuance of the Anti-Corn Law League, from visiting the centre of the manufacturing districts, in which that powerful and successful organization held its head-quarters ' (p. 7). Also, *Address*, dated 1 July, 1852, in which the Association claims to be the successor of the League in destroying religious monopolies. A/LIB /1 M.824-6.

[32]*Report of the First Triennial Conference* (1847), pp. 7-8.

[33]William Sharman Crawford, member for Rochdale, 1841-51, when he retired and was followed by Edward Miall, see *Proceedings . . . 1844* (1844). Crawford and Miall had been associated in the leadership of the Complete Suffrage Union, for which see A. Miall, *Life of Edward Miall* (1884), p. 85. The fullest account of the activities of the CSU in Wales is to be found in Ryland Wallace, ' Political Reform Societies in Wales, 1840-86 ', unpublished Ph.D thesis, (Wales 1978).

[34]For detailed reports see *Y Diwygiwr*, September 1844.

[35]*Ibid.*, pp. 350.

[36]S.R. was one of the conveners of the Machynlleth Conference and one of its joint secretaries. He also sat on the publications translation committee. In this context it is interesting to note that S.R. had translated into Welsh *The Faith, Church Order, and Discipline of the Congregational Dissenters* (1834) on behalf of the Congregational Union, 5,000 copies of which were printed. See *Fourth* Annual Report of the Congregational Union (1834), pp. 4-5.

[37]Not until 1848 was a local committee appointed at Merthyr Tydfil. A committee had been set up earlier at Cardiff.

[38]Editors of Welsh magazines were constantly drawing attention to this deficiency : e.g., *Y Diwygiwr*, July 1847. Miall regularly opened the columns of the Nonconformist to Welsh Dissenting affairs. Writing in 1850, Miall thought the

English newspapers in Wales scarcely worthy of notice—though he excepted the *Principality* from this judgement.

39Statistics are abstracted from the annual reports.
40*Minutes of Meetings of Council, May* 1848(1848).
41*DNB, sub. nom.* John Carvell Williams.
42*Minutes of . . . Council,* 1848.
43*Report of the Third Triennial Conference, November* 1853 (1853).
44*Report of the Second Triennial Conference,* April 1850 (1850), p. 8.
45Liberation Society Minute Books, Vol. 2, M.429 (27 March, 1851), M. 763 (15 April, 1852).
46A/LIB/S M.287 (31 October, 1850).
47*Ibid.,* M.885 (14 October, 1852) and M.929 (28, October, 1852).
48*Report of . . .* 1853 (1853).
49*Ibid.,* pp. 6-7. On the question whether these m.p.s. would work together as a party the *Report* was cautious, but it was emphasized that ' in the present balanced state of parties even so small a force as that at the disposal of Anti-State-Churchmen may be able, at times, to exert a decisive influence '.
50*Ibid.,* Resolution IX, moved by Edward Baines.
51Edward Miall's paper ' The Prospects and Duties of the Society in relation to the House of Commons, and to its constituent bodies ', in *ibid.,* pp. 29-41.
52*Ibid.,* p. 40.
53*Y Diwygiwr,* December 1853, p. 381.
54An editor was appointed for the first time in October 1851.
55The circulation of this periodical during the first six months of its existence (June to December 1855) was a little under 1,600 copies. Of these, 1,440 were distributed gratiously (to £1 subscribers, m.p.s. editors, colleges, etc.). The total cost to the Society was a little over £66. A/LIB/2 M.470 (14 December, 1855). Later, in May 1856, the *Liberator* was sent gratiously to 5s. subscribers ; ibid., M.374.
56S/LIB/2 M.1187 (21 June, 1861) : Hansard, 3rd series, CLXIII, col. 1322, 19 June, 1861.
57*Eighteenth Annual Report,* 2 *May* 1863 (1863) and A/LIB/3 M.286 (23 October, 1863). (Liberation Society Minute Book III, A/LIB/2 M.1206 (27 September, 1861).
58Liberation Society Minute Book III, A/LIB/2 M.789 (19 February, 1858).
59*Report of the Fifth Triennial Conference, June* 1859 (1859). ' An issue which has involved a loss to the popular party in Parliament must necessarily affect unfavourably the parliamentary position of Voluntaries.' Cf. also Liberation Society Minute Book III, A/LIB/2 M.946 (27 April, 1859).
60*Ibid.,* A/LIB/2 M.1207 (27 September, 1861).
61*Ibid.*
62*Ibid.,* Vol. IV, A/LIB/3 M.23 (14 January, 1862).
63*Ibid.,* M. 79 (13 June) and *ibid.,* M.112 (3 September, 1862).
64*Ibid.,* M.104 (1 August) and *ibid.,* M.142 (14 November, 1862).
65The *Cambrian,* 26 September, 1862, gives lists of delegates and a full report of proceedings. Later, the Liberation Society produced a report of proceedings in English, and a Welsh translation.
66*Ibid.*
67Minute Book IV, A/LIB/3 M.119 (3 October, 1862) and *ibid.,* M.120, for the appointment of the Rev. John Rees of Swansea. In December 1865, on the recommendation of the South Wales Committee, the terms of his appointment were changed to include the whole of Wales. He resigned in May 1866 and was replaced by the Rev. Watkin Williams of Pen-coed. *Ibid.,* M.711 (25 May, 1866) and M.764 (5 October, 1866).
68The appointment of Mr. Thomas Harris of Llechryd, Cardiganshire, was recommended by the South Wales Committee in October 1866. *Ibid.,* M.598 (October 1865). At the general election of 1865 in Cardiganshire, Henry Richard,

despite unexpectedly large support, had withdrawn from the contest on the eve of the poll so as to avoid splitting the Liberal vote. For the Society's views of this election, see *ibid.*, M.560 (21 July, 1865). See above pp.

[69]Richard became a member of the Executive Committee in June 1865 : Minute Book IV. A/LIB/3 M.79 (13 June, 1862). Thereafter, no decision of importance respecting Wales was taken without first consulting him and Miall. Thus, all recommendations of the South Wales Committee were referred to him : e.g., the decision, in May 1866, to hold conferences in north Wales, *Ibid.*, M.711-13 (25 May, 1866).

[70]E.g., in October 1862 the executive accepted the views on strategy of a sub-committee that in future emphasis should be placed on the anomalies of the Established Church in Wales, Scotland, and Ireland ' with a view to preparing the public mind for parliamentary action when it shall be deemed advisable '. *Ibid.*, M.114 (5 September) and M.115 and 117 (19 September) and M.127 (17 October, 1862).

[71]*Ibid.*, M.113 (5 September, 1862).

[72]*Ibid.*, M.253 (26 June) and M.266 (7 August, 1862).

[73]*Ibid.*, M.711 (25 May, 1862). See also the introduction to *Welsh Nonconformity and the Welsh Representation, papers and speeches read and delivered at the conferrnces held September and October* 1866, published by the Society.

[74]Liberation Society Minute Book IV, A/LIB/3 M.726 (22 June, 1866). See also *Twenty-first Annual Report*, 2 *May*, 1866 (1866).

[75]Liberation Society Minute Book IV, A/LIB/3 M.748 (20 July) and M.757 (7 September, 1866).

[76]*Welsh Nonconformity and the Welsh Representation*, introduction, and *Twenty-second Annual Report*, 1 May, 1867 (1867).

[77]*Welsh Nonconformity and Welsh Representation*.

[78]Liberation Society Minute Book IV, A/LIB/3 M.766 (5 October, 1866).

[79]*Ibid.*, M.772 (19 October, 1866).

[80]*Ibid.*, M.521 (2 August) and M.535s (30 August, 1866).

[81]See above, pp 148 f.

[82]*Ibid.*, M.495 (7 June), M.503 (21 June), M.509 (5 July) and M.520 (2 August 1867). Mr. Samuel Morley was reported to have consented to contribute £500 towards the first year expenses, and the Society agreed to contribute £200. For the impact of this on Welsh Nonconformist Liberals see the speech of Dr. Thomas Price in May 1867 in *Aberdare Times*, 11 May, 1867.

[83]Liberation Society Minute Book V, A/LIB/4 M.131 (26 June, 1868). £50 was voted to this Association—and the same amount to the Reform League (M.132).

[84]*Twenty-second Annual Report*, op. cit.

[85]Hansard, 3rd series, CLXXXI. See also *Twenty first Annual Report, May* 1869 (1866), col. 1691, 7 March, 1866.

[86]E.g. in Merthyr Tydfil.

[87]E. M. Richards at Cardiganshire. See his ' Address ' in *Aberystwyth Observer*, 22 August, 1868.

[88]See above, pp. 267.

BIBLIOGRAPHY

WORKS CITED

1. MANUSCRIPTS

British Library
   Cobden Papers, vols. XI-XIII
   Ripon Papers

City of London, Guildhall Library
   Minutes of the Dissenting Deputies
   Minutes of the United Committee

Dr. Williams's Library
   Minute Books etc. of the Protestant Society

Glamorgan Record Office
   Dowlais Iron Company Papers

London County Council Record Office
   Liberation Society Minute Books
   Minutes of Anti-State-Church Association

Merioneth Record Office
   Caerynwch Rentals

National Library of Wales
   Wynnstay (uncatalogued)
   Minute Book of the Merioneth Reform Association
   Church in Wales Records
   Matthews MSS.
   Ivon Letters
   Tithe Apportionments
   Cyfarthfa Papers
   Thomas Gee MSS.

Public Record Office
   HO 127 Census of 1851. Population Returns
   HO 129 Census of 1851. Ecclesiastical Returns
   HO 13 General Board of Health and Local Government
      Office
   HO 45 Disturbances: Reports and Correspondence

University College of North Wales
   Bangor MS. 10635
   Maesyneuadd Deeds and Documents
   Mostyn MSS.

2. OFFICIAL PAPERS

Census of Great Britain, 1851
   Religious Worship—England and Wales: Report and Tables,
      P.P. 1852-3. LXXXIV
Election Expenses
   P.P. 1866. LVI (160)
   P.P. 1868-9. L (424)
Electoral Returns
   P.P. 1836. XLIII (240)
   P.P. 1837-8. XLIV (329)
   P.P. 1844. XXXVIII (329)
   P.P. 1847. XLVI (751 i-iii)
   P.P. 1852. XLII (8)
   P.P. 1866. LVII (3736)
   P.P. 1868-9. L (418)
Hansard's Parliamentary Debates. Third Series
Journals of the House of Commons
Reports upon Certain Boroughs, by J. T. Hogg
   P.P. 1837-8. XXXV (223)
Return of Owners of Land, 1872-3
   P.P. 1874. LXXII
Return of Select Committee on Parliamentary and Municipal
   Elections (Hartington Committee)
   P.P. 1870. VI (115)
Returns showing the number of churches which have been built
   or restored in every diocese . . . since 1840
   P.P. 1876. LVIII (125 and 125 I)
Report of the Commissioners of Inquiry into the Ecclesiastical
   Revenues of England and Wales, 1835.
   P.P. 1835. XXII
Royal Commission on the employment of children, young
   persons, and women in agriculture. Third Report (1867).
   P.P. 1870. XIII
Royal Commission on Land in Wales and Monmouthshire.
   Report and Minutes of Evidence. 5 vols.
   P.P. 1894. XXXVI, XXXVII
      1895. XL, XLI
      1896. XXXIII, XXXIV, XXXV
Royal Commission on proposed division of counties and bound-
   aries of boroughs (Boundary Commission Report)
   P.P. 1867-8. XX (3972)
Royal Commission on Trade Unions. Fifth Report.
   P.P. 1867-8. XXIX

3. WORKS OF REFERENCE

Breese, Edward, *Calendars of Gwynedd* (Caernarvon, 1873)
Burke, *County Families* (1864)
Dafydd Morganwg, *Hanes Morgannwg* (Aberdâr, 1874)
Dictionary of National Biography
Dictionary of Welsh Biography down to 1940
Jones, Ieuan Gwynedd, *The Religious Census of* 1851. *A Calendar
  of the Returns relating to Wales. Vol.* 2. *North Wales* (1981)
Jones, Ieuan Gwynedd and Williams, David, *The Religious
  Census of* 1851. *A Calendar of the Returns relating to Wales. Vol.* 1.
  South Wales (1976)
Lewis, Samuel, *Topographical Dictionary of Wales* (1849 edn.)
Roberts, T. R. (Asaph), *Eminent Welshmen*. I (Cardiff, 1908)
Slater's Directory for 1850
Slater's Directory for 1868
Walford, E., *The County Families of the United Kingdom* (1860)
Williams, W. R., *The Parliamentary History of the Principality of
  Wales* 1541-1895 (Brecknock, 1895)

4. NEWSPAPERS AND MAGAZINES

Aberdare Times
Aberystwyth Observer
Yr Athraw
Baner ac Amserau Cymru
Y Byd Cymreig
The Cambrian
Cardiff and Merthyr Guardian
Cardiff Times
Carnarvon and Denbigh Herald
Y Cronicl
The Daily News
Daily Post
Y Diwygiwr
Dowlais and Aberdare Gazette
Gentleman's Magazine
Y Gwladgarwr
Y Gwron
Yr Herald Gymreig
Manchester Guardian
Merioneth Herald
Merthyr Express
Merthyr Star
The Mining Journal

Morning Chronicle
Morning Star
Nonconformist
The North Wales Chronicle
Saturday Review
Seren Cymru
Seren Gomer
Shrewsbury Chronicle
The Times
The Welshman

5. CONTEMPORARY WORKS

Anon., *Double and Single Shift Working Compared* (Aberdare, 1868)
Bateman, John, *The Acre-ocracy of England* (London, 1876)
Bennett, J., *History of Dissenters . . . from 1808 to 1838* (1839)
Brook, B., *A History of Religious Liberty . . . to the Death of George III*, 2 vols. (1820)
Bruce, H.A., *Merthyr Tydfil in 1852* (Merthyr Tydfil, 1852)
Bruce, H.A., *Lecturers and Addresses* (n.d.)
Congregational Union of England and Wales: Minutes of Third General Meeting (1833)
Dalziel, A., *The Colliers' Strike in South Wales* (Cardiff, 1872)
Davies, D. E., *A Treatise on Slate and Slate Quarrying* (1878)
Davies, Edward, *Traethawd ar Enwogion Swydd Feirionydd* (Caernarfon, 1870)
Edwards, T.C., *Bywyd a Llythyrau y diweddar Barch. Lewis Edwards* (Liverpool, 1901)
Engels, F., *The Condition of the Working Class in England in 1844* in Karl Marx and Frederic Engels, *On Britain* (Moscow, 1853)
Esquiros, Alphonse, *Religious Life in England* (1867)
' Etholiadau Ceredigion a Meirionydd, gan Awdur "Adgofion am Ysgol Neuaddlwyd" ', *Y Traethodydd*, 3ydd cyfres, IV (1865)
Hodder, Edwin, *The Life of Samuel Morley* (1887)
Jones, Rev. John (Kilsby), *Deliverance on Toryism versus Liberalism. An Address delivered at Dolgelley, on Friday, July 21st 1865, to the Electors of Merionethshire* (Aberystwyth, 1865)
Labour and the Poor. The Mining and Manufacturing Towns of South Wales, *Morning Chronicle*, March to April 1850
Letters to Lord Aberdare (Oxford, 1902)
Liberation Society. Annual Reports 1844-74
Mann, Horace, ' On the statistical position of Religious Bodies in England and Wales ', *J. Royal Statistical Society* XVIII (1855)
Mearns, Andrew, *Thr Bitter Cry of Outcast London* (1883)

Miall, Charles S., *Henry Richard, M.P., a biography* (1889)

Miall, Edward, *The British Churches in Relation to the British People* (1849)

Miall, Edward, *Views of the Voluntary Principle* (2nd edn., 1850)

Molesworth, W. N., *The History of England, 1830-74* (2nd edn., London, 1874)

Nicholas, Thomas, *Middle and High Class Schools, and University Education for Wales* (1853)

Nixon, John, *The Single Shift System, the cause of double the loss of life* (Cardiff, 1867)

Parry, John, *Aur Sir Feirionnydd, yn cynnwys hanes y gwahanol wythanau . . .* (Dolgellau, 1862)

Proceedings of the First Anti-State Church Conference (1844)

Rammell, T. W., *Report on a Preliminary Inquiry into the Sanitary Condition of the Town of Merthyr Tydfil* (1850)

Rees, Thomas, *History of Protestant Nonconformity in Wales* (1861)

Rees, Thomas, *Papers and Subjects relating to Wales* (1867)

Rees, Thomas, *Miscellaneous Papers relating to Wales* (1866)

Rees, T. and Thomas, J., *Hanes Eglwysi Annibynol Cymru*, 5 vols. (1-4, Liverpool, 1871-5) and 5, (Dolgellau, 1891)

Richard, Henry, *Letters and Essays on Wales* (2nd edn., 1884)

Roberts, Samuel, *Cofiant y tri brawd* (Bala, 1892)

Skeats, H. S., *A History of the Free Churches of England, 1688-1851* (1868)

A Sketch of the History and Proceedings of the Deputies . . . (1813)

Waddington, J., *Congregational History*, vols. IV and V

Welsh Nonconformity and the Welsh Representation (London, 1866)

6. SECONDARY WORKS

Best, G. F. A., *Temporal Pillars: Queen Anne's Bounty, the Ecclesiastical Commissioners and the Church of England* (1964)

Booth, C., *Life and Labour of the People in London. Vol. 7. Religious Influences* (1920-3)

Briggs, Asa, *Victorian Cities* (1964)

Brose, Olive, J., *Church and Parliament: the Re-shaping of the Church of England, 1828-1860* (1959)

Carter, Harold, *The Towns of Wales* (1966)

Cowherd, Raymond, *The Politics of English Dissent* (1959)

Currie, Robert, *Methodism Divided. A Study in the Development of Ecumenicalism* (1968)

Davies, E. T., *Religion in the Industrial Revolution in South Wales* (1959)

Davies, Evan, *Hanes Plwyf Llangunllo* (Llandysul, 1905)

Dodd, A. H., *The Industrial Revolution in North Wales* (2nd edn., Cardiff, 1951)

Dodd, A. H., *Studies in Stuart Wales* (Cardiff, 1952)

Dyos, H. J. (ed.), *The Study of Urban History* (1968)

Edwards, G. A., *Athrofa'r Bala 1838-1937* (1937)

Ellis, Annie J. (ed.), *Speeches and Addresses by the late Thomas E. Ellis, M.P.* (Wrexham, 1912)

Ellis, T. I., *Thomas Edward Ellis. Cofiant. I* (1859-1886) (1944)

Ellis, T. P., *The Story of two Parishes: Dolgellau and Llanelltyd* (1928)

Evans, Trebor Lloyd, *Lewis Edwards: ei fywyd a'i waith* (Abertawe 1967)

Gash, N., *Politics in the Age of Peel* (1953)

Griffiths, J. E., *Pedigrees*

Harrison, J. F. C., *Robert Owen and the Owenites in Great Britain and America. The Quest for a New Moral World* (1969)

James, Robert (Trebor), *Dolgellau yn Hanesyddol* (1907)

Jenkins, R. T., *Hanes Cynulleidfa Hen Gapel Llanuwchllyn* (1937)

Jones, Evan Pan, *Oes a gwaith Michael D. Jones* (Bala, 1903)

Jones, T. Gwynn, *Cofiant Thomas Gee* (Denbigh, 1913)

Inglis, K. S., *Churches and the Working Classes in Victorian England* (1963)

Lewis, E. A., *The Medieval Boroughs of Snowdonia*

McCord, N., *The Anti-Corn Law League* (1958)

Morgan, J. J., *Hanes Dafydd Morgan Yspytty a Diwygiad '59* (Yr Wyddgrug, 1906)

Morgan, Kenneth O., *Wales in British Politics 1868-1922* (2nd edn., Cardiff, 197)

Morris, R. Prys, *Cantref Meirionydd* (1890)

Owen, Geraint Dyfnallt, *Ysgolion a Cholegau yr Annibynwyr* (Abertawe, 1939)

Owen, H. J., *Echoes of Old Merioneth* (1946)

Parry, Edward, *Llawlyfr ar Hanes y Diwygiadau Crefyddol yng Nghymru* (Corwen, 1898)

Peate, I. C., *Hen Gapel Llanbrynmair 1739-1939* (1939)

Peate, I. C. (ed.), *Cilhaul ac Ysgrifau eraill* (1951)

Roberts, G. (Gwrtheyrn), *Pum' Plwy' Penllyn* (n.d.)

Saville, John, *Ernest Jones, Chartist* (1952)

Seymour, C., *Electoral Reform in England and Wales* (New Haven, 1915: reprint 1970)

Thompson, F. M. L., *English Landed Society in the Nineteenth Century* (London, 1963)

Walker, David, *A Short History of the Parish Church of Swansea* (1967)

Williams, Glanmor, *Samuel Roberts, Llanbrynmair* (Caerdydd, 1950)

Williams, G. J., *Hanes Plwyf Ffestiniog* (n.d.)

Williams, R. Peris, *Hanes Athrofa Bala-Bangor* (1914)

7. ARTICLES

Carter, Harold, 'The phases of town growth in Wales', in H. J. Dyos (ed.), *The Study of Urban History* (1968)

Davies, Alan, 'Michael D. Jones a'r Wladfa', *T.H.S.C.* (1966), Part 1

Davies, V. Challenor, 'The Decline of Rural Population in Wales, with special reference to Merionethshire', *J.M.H.S.* 11 (1953-6)

Friedlander, D. and Roshier, R. J., 'A Study of internal migration in England and Wales', Part I, *Population Studies* XIX, iii (1966)

Glock, Charles E., 'The Religious Revival in America' in Birbaum and G. Lenzer, *Sociology and Religion* (New Jersey, 1969)

Goodridge, R. M., 'The Religious Condition of the West Country in 1851', *Social Compass: International Review of Socio-Religious Studies* XIV, No. 4 (1967)

Howells, J. M., 'The Crosswood Estate, 1547-1947', *Ceredigion* (1956)

James, Brian Ll., 'The "Great Landowners" of Wales', *J.N.L.W.* XIV, No. 3 (1966)

Jones, Ieuan Gwynedd, 'The South Wales collier in Mid-nineteenth century', *Victorian South Wales—Architecture, Industry and Society* (Victorian Society, 1971)

Jones, Ieuan Gwynedd, 'The Election of 1865 and 1868 in Wales, with special reference to Cardiganshire and Merthyr Tydfil', *T.H.S.C.*, Part I (1964)

Jones, Ieuan Gwynedd, 'The Anti-Corn Law Letters of Walter Griffith', *B.B.C.S.* XXVIII, Part I (1978)

Lewis, J. Parry, 'The anglicization of Glamorgan', *Morgannwg* IV (1960)

Lloyd, J. H. (Peryddon), 'Hen argraffwyr y Bala', *J.M.H.S.*

Marshall, J. D., 'Colonisation as a factor in the planning of towns in northwest England', in H. J. Dyos (ed.), *The Study of Urban History* (1968)

Pickering, W. S. F., 'The 1851 Religious Census—a useless experiment?', *Brit. J. of Sociology* XVIII (1967)

Prince, H. C., 'The Tithe Surveys of the Mid-Nineteenth Century', *Agricultural History Review* III (1959)

Roberts, Peter R., 'The Gentry and the Land in Eighteenth Century Merioneth', *J.M.H.S.* (1964)

Roberts, Peter R., 'The Merioneth Gentry and Local Government *circa* 1650-1838', *J.M.H.S.* (1965)

Roberts, R. O., 'The development and decline of copper and other non-ferrous industries in South Wales', *T.H.S.C.* (1965)

Thomas, Colin, 'Merioneth Estates, 1790-1858: a study of agrarian geography ', *J.M.H.S.* V, No. iii (1967)

Thomas, P.D.G., 'The Parliamentary representation of Merioneth during the eighteenth century ', *J.M.H.S.* iii (1957-60)

Ward, W. R., 'The Tithe Question ', *J. Eccl. Hist.* XVI (1965)

Williams, David, 'The Census of Religious Worship of 1851 in Cardiganshire ', *Ceredigion* IV (1961)

Williams, D. Trevor, 'The Economic Development of Swansea and of the Swansea District to 1921 ', (1940)

Williams, D. Trevor, 'Gower: a study in linguistic movements and historical geography ', *Arch. Camb.* (1934)

Additional Reading

The following lists a selection of secondary works of more recent date. Some of the books contain bibliographies but the reader should consult H. J. Hanham (ed.), *Bibliography of British History 1851-1814* (1976) and for Wales *A Bibliography of the History of Wales* (2nd edn., 1962) and its supplements in *B.B.C.S.* XX, XXII, XXIII and XXIV (1963-72). The *Welsh History Review* publishes an annual list of articles on Welsh history, and unpublished dissertations are listed in Alun Eirug Davies (ed.), *Welsh Language and Welsh Dissertations 1887-1971* (1973).

Bassett, T. M., *The Welsh Baptists* (Swansea, 1977)

Best, Geoffrey, *Mid-Victorian Britain 1851-1871* (1971)

Binfield, Clyde, *So Down to Prayers. Studies in English Nonconformity 1780-1920* (1977)

Burn, W. L., *The Age of Equipoise. A study of the Mid-Victorian Generation* (1964)

Cawardine, R., 'The Welsh Evangelical Community and "Finney's Revival" ', *J. Ecc. Hist.* 29 (1978)

Coleman, B.I., *The Church of England in the Mid-Nineteenth Century* (Hist. Assoc. Pamphlet 98, 1980)

Edwards, Hywel Teifi, 'Gwyl Gwalia '. *Yr Eisteddfod Genedlaethol yn Oes Aur Victoria 1858-1868* (Llandysul, 1980)

Ellis, T. L., The University College of Wales, Aberystwyth, 1872-1972 (Cardiff 1972)

Foster, J., *Class Struggle and the Industrial Revolution* (1974)

Fraser, Derek, *Urban Politics in Victorian England* (1977)

Gilbert, A. D., *Religion and Society in Industrial England. Church, Chapel and Social Change 1740-1914* (1976)

Hanham, H. J., *Elections and Party Management: Politics in the Time of Disraeli and Gladstone* (1959)

Hanham, H. J., *The Reformed Electoral System in Great Britain* 1831-1914 (Hist. Assoc. Pamphlet G. 69, 1968)

Harrison, J. F. C., *The Early Victorians* 1832-51 (1971)

Hennock, E. P., *Fit and Proper Persons: Ideal and Reality in Nineteenth Century Urban Government* (1973)

Hilling, John B., *Cardiff and the Valleys* (1973)

Hollis, Patricia (ed.), *Pressure from Without in Early Victorian England* (1974)

Howell, David, *Land and People in Nineteenth-Century Wales* (1977)

John, Angela, ' The Chartist Endurance ', *Morgannwg* XV (1971)

Jones, Ieuan Gwynedd, ' Dr. Thomas Price and the Election of 1868 in Merthyr Tydfil: a study in Nonconformist Politics ', Part 1, *W.H.R.* 2, No. 2 (1964), Part 2, *W.H.R.* 2, No. 3 (1965)

Jones, Ieuan Gwynedd, ' Religious Condition of the Counties of Brecon and Radnor as revealed in the Census of Religious Worship in 1851 ' in Jones and Walker (eds.), *Links with the Past* (1974)

Jones, Ieuan Gwynedd, *Health, Wealth and Politics in Victorian Wales* (Swansea U.C., 1979)

Jones, Ieuan Gwynedd (ed.), *Aberystwyth* 1277-1977 (1977)

Jones, Iorwerth, *David Rees y Cynhyrfiwr* (Abertawe, 1971)

Jones, R. Tudur, ' Origins of the Nonconformist Disestablishment Campaign ', *J. Hist. Soc. of the Church in Wales* XX (1970)

Jones, R. Tudur, *Hanes Annibynwyr Cymru* (Abertawe, 1966)

Jones, R. Tudur, *Yr Undeb. Hanes Undeb yr Annibynwyr Cymraeg* 1872-1972 (Abertawe, 1975)

Lambert, W. R., ' Some working class attitudes towards organized religion in nineteenth century Wales ', *Llafur* vol. 2, No. 1 (1976)

Lewis T. H., *Y Mormoniaid yng Nghymru* (1956)

Machin, G. I. T., *Politics and the Churches in Great Britain* 1832-68 (1977)

McLeod, H., ' Class, Community and Religion: the Religious Geography of Nineteenth Century England ', *Sociological Yearbook of Religion in Britain* 6, ed. M. Hill (1973)

Millward, E. G., ' Canu byd i'w le ', *Y Traethodydd* (Ionawr, 1981)

Minchinton, W. E. (ed.), *Industrial South Wales* 1750-1914. *Essays in Welsh Economic History* (1969)

Mitchison, Rosalind (ed.), *The Roots of Nationalism* (1980)

Moore, R., *Pit-Men, Preachers and Politics: the Effects of Methodism in a Durham Mining Community* (C.U.P., 1974)

Morgan, Jane, ' Denbigh's *Annus Mirabilis*: the Borough and County Elections of 1868 ', *W.H.R.* 7, No. 2 (December 1974)

Morgan, Walter T., ' The Diocese of St. Davids in the nineteenth century ', *J. Hist. Soc. of the Church in Wales*, Part I, No. 26 (1971), Part II, No. 27 (1972), Part III, No. 28 (1973)

Nossiter, T. J., *Influence, Opinion and Political Idioms in Reformed England. Case Studies from the North-East* 1832-74 (1975)

O'Leary, Cornelius, *The Elimination of Corrupt Practices in British Elections* (1962)

Prest, John, *Politics in the Age of Cobden* (1977)

Pretty, David A., ' Richard Davies and Nonconformist Radicalism in Anglesey, 1837-68: a study of sectarian and middle class politics ', *W.H.R.* 9, No. 4 (1979)

Pryce, W. T. R., ' Industrialism, Urbanization, and the Maintenance of Culture Areas: North-east Wales in the Mid-Nineteenth Century ', *W.H.R.* 7, No. 3 (June 1975)

Rees, R.D., ' South Wales and Monmouthshire Newspapers under the Stamp Acts ', *W.H.R.* 1, No. 3 (1962)

Robson, R. (ed.), *Ideas and Institutions of Victorian Britain*: *Essays in Honour of George Kitson-Clark* (1967)

Royle, E., *Victorian Infidels* (Manchester, 1974)

Smith, David (ed.), *A People and a Proletariat. Essays in the History of Wales*, 1780-1880 (1980)

Smith, F. B., *The Making of the Second Reform Act* (1966)

Vincent, J. R., *Pollbooks: How Victorians Voted* (1977)

Walker, David (ed.), *A History of the Church in Wales* (1976)

Williams, A. H., *Cymru Oes Victoria* (1975)

Williams, David, *A History of Modern Wales* (2nd edn., 1977)

Williams, David, *The Rebecca Riots. A study in agrarian discontent* (Cardiff, 2nd edn., 1967)

Williams, Glanmor (ed.), *Merthyr Politics: the Making of a Working-Class Tradition* (Cardiff, 1966)

Williams, Glanmor, *Religion, Language and Nationality in Wales* (Cardiff, 1979)

Wills, Wilton D., ' The Established Church in the Diocese of Llandaff 1850-70: a study of the evangelical movement in the South Wales Coalfield ', *W.H.R.* 4, No. 3 (June 1969)

INDEX

A

Aberaeron 168, 264
Aberafan 281, 283
Aberdare 194-5
  collieries 205-6
  press in 295
  strike of 1857-8, 205
Aberdare, Lord. See Bruce, H.A.
Aberdaron 24, 25, 38
Abererch 26
Abergavenny 284
Aberystwyth 168-9
Aberystwyth Observer newspaper 183
Accommodation Ratio 63-4, 65-6
Agriculture
  Agents 101
  Grievances 100-1
Anti-Catholicism 111
Anti-Corn Law League 183, 246, 252, 257
Anti-State-Church Association. See Liberation Society.
Anwyl, T. P. 90
Ardudwy 88, 89, 92, 122
Athrofa'r Bala 107-8, 112
Attendance Ratio 30

B

Bala 22, 23, 98, 102, 106, 111-7, 118, 127, 129, 132, 141, 148, 157, 161, 231, 264
Ballot 118, 197, 203
Ballot Act 86
Baner ac Amserau Cymru newspaper 105, 129, 137, 140, 143, 180, 294
Bangor 23, 25, 30-1, 38, 41
Bangor District 40-1
Banks, William John 90
Baptists 27, 28, 29, 39-40, 63, 67, 198, 247
  General 28
Batchelor, John 261
Beaumaris 280
Beehive, The newspaper 295
Bethesda 29, 37, 284
Betws Garmon 24, 41
Betws-y-coed 24
Biddulph, Col. 134

Bird, John 89
Bishopston 60
Booth, Charles 222-3
Botwnog 24
Boulcott, John Ellercat 90, 121-2
Brecon 22
Brecon Borough 118, 280
Breese, John 117
Bridgend District 59, 65
Bright, John 117, 118, 160, 193
Bruce, Henry Austin 190, 193ff., 197, 202
  and strike of 1857-8 204
  and radical nonconformity 207, 208
  relations with colliers 208-9
  and Select Committee on Mines 209-10
  and working-class radicalism 202-3
Builth 22
Bunting, Jabez 28, 231

C

Caernarfon 23, 25, 30, 38
  Voters in 277, 281, 295
  District 40, 41
  County 126
  Bank Quay 29
Capel y Drindod 180
Cardiff 24
  Election of 1852
  Trades Council 296
  District 59, 65
Cardigan 22, 168
Cardiganshire Estates :
  Abermâd 171
  Allt-lwyd 171
  Allt-yr-odyn 171
  Betws Bledrws 171
  Bronwydd 171, 177, 181
  Falcondale 170
  Glan-Rheidol 171
  Gogerddan 169, 170, 173, 176-7
  Hafod 171
  Highmead 171
  Llanaeron 171
  Llanana 171
  Llanfair 171
  Llidiart 171
  Mabws 171

331